FUNDAMENTALS OF TELEMEDICINE AND TELEHEALTH

FUNDAMENTALS OF TELEMEDICINE AND TELEHEALTH

Edited by

SHASHI GOGIA

Sub Editors

MAGDALA NOVAES & ARINDAM BASU

Copy Editors

KRITI GOGIA & SPRIHA GOGIA

Library of Congress Cataloging-in-Publication Data
A catalog record for this book is available from the Library of Congress

British Library Cataloguing-in-Publication Data
A catalogue record for this book is available from the British Library

ISBN: 978-0-12-814309-4

For information on all Academic Press publications
visit our website at https://www.elsevier.com/books-and-journals

Publisher: Stacy Masucci
Acquisition Editor: Rafael Teixeira
Editorial Project Manager: Megan Ashdown
Production Project Manager: Debasish Ghosh
Cover Designer: Matthew Limbert

Typeset by SPi Global, India

Working together
to grow libraries in
developing countries

www.elsevier.com • www.bookaid.org

Contents

List of Contributors   ix
Acknowledgments   xi

Section I
Telecare basics

1. Overview
Shashi Gogia

2. Rationale, history, and basics of telehealth
Shashi Gogia, Gunnar Hartvigsen

Definitions   11
History of telemedicine and telehealth   12
Situations where telehealth has a role   17
Telehealth services are reshaping healthcare   30

3. Management of patient healthcare information
Pramod David Jacob, Shashi Gogia, Spriha Gogia, Filipe Santana da Silva, Kleber Soares de Araujo

Introduction   35
Definitions of EMR and EHR   36
Application of EHRs in telehealth   40
Data entry   41
Acquiring and utilizing nontextual data—images, sound, and more   42
Alerts and triggers   50
Healthcare data analytics   51
Analytics approaches   55

4. Technology considerations
Gunnar Hartvigsen, Shashi Gogia, Maurizio Mattoli

Overview: Infrastructure requirement   59
How to ensure effective communication   69
Video conferencing (VC)   74
Example of video-conference system for emergency care   78
Standards and certification   81

Section II
Working together for health

5. Platforms for collaborative process
Arindam Basu, Shashi Gogia, Magdala de Araújo Novaes

Introduction: Patients as partners in care	93
Telehealth platforms	103
Computer assisted care	107

6. Patient-centered care
Marcia Ito

Introduction	115
eHealth in patient engagement	117
Patient portal	121

7. Maintaining and sustaining a telehealth-based ecosystem
Oommen John, Shashi Gogia, Filipe Santana da Silva

What is a telehealth-based ecosystem?	127
Role of telehealth in health system strengthening	128
Roles and responsibilities in a telehealth system	128
Planning a project	133
Analytics	139

8. Tele-education
Luiz Roberto de Oliveira, Gustavo Silveira Dantas, Shashi Gogia,
Manoj Kumar Singh, Sunita Maheshwari

Introduction	145
Distance education in the context of professional work in health	146
Digital health workforce: de novo skill set	149
Use and utility of virtual teaching in education	153
A case study of e-teaching in cardiology from India	156

Section III
Telemedicine

9. Telesupport for the primary care practitioner
Shashi Gogia, BipinKumar Rathod, Carlos Aita, Charles Umeh, Devashish Saini, G.S. Jaiya

Introduction	161
Telemedicine in primary healthcare	163

Why are doctors reluctant to adopt telehealth 168
Telemedicine for community healthcare workers 172
Tele support for nurse practitioners 175
Tele support for wounds, ulcers, and lymphedema 178

10. Telecare within different specialties

Magdala de Araújo Novaes, Gunnar Hartvigsen, Ana Estela Haddad, Arjun Kalyanpur, Danielle Santos Alves, Ganesh A. Joshi, Keila Taciane Martins de Melo Oliveira, Kriti Gogia, Shashi Gogia, Manoj Rai Mehta, Mariana Boulitreaux Siqueira Campos Barros, Sunita Maheshwari, Praveen K., Feroz Latif, Sejal Shah, Shivani Ghoshal, Rohit Raghav Gupta, Arindam Basu, Sanjay Bedi, Denise Garrido Silva, Magaly Bushatsky, Rodrigo da Silva Dias, Ana Emília Figueiredo de Oliveira

Introduction 185
Teleradiology 187
Telepathology 195
Teleophthalmology 199
Teledermatology 203
Telecardiology 206
Teleobstetrics/prenatal telemedicine service 212
Telecare in geriatrics 215
Teleoncology 217
Teleneurology 221
Telediabetes 223
Telepsychiatry and telemental health 226
Telesurgery 230
Teleotorhinolaryngology 235
Teledentistry 237
Teleemergency service 239
Tele-ICU 242
Teledialysis 244
Telerehabilitation 248

11. Telecare during travel and for special situations

Gunnar Hartvigsen, Shashi Gogia, Suzanne Bakken, Anthony Pho, Andre Henriksen, Anandhi Ramachandran, U.S. Mohalanobish

Introduction 255
Maritime telemedicine 257
Telemedicine in commercial aviation 259
Arctic telemedicine 263
Telemedicine for prison populations 265
Medical tourism 267
Telehealth in disasters 272

12. Mobile health (mHealth)

Sriram Iyengar, Meghan Corin Bradway, Eirk Årsand, Shashi Gogia, Pramod David Jacob

Introduction 277
mHealth in supporting health workers 281
Developing apps for mobile devices 284

Persuasive technology and mHealth   290

mHealth evaluation   293

Section IV

Issues and future of telehealth

13. Medicolegal, ethical, and regulatory guidelines pertaining to telehealth

Maurice Mars

Telemedicine law   298

Medical ethics and telemedicine   298

14. Disruptive technologies: Present and future

Magdala de Araújo Novaes, Arindam Basu, Abhishek Gattani, Amadeu Campos de Nutes, Shashi Gogia, Fernando Sales

Introduction   305

Telehomecare   306

Tele-robotics in healthcare including in surgery   309

Artificial intelligence and IoT in healthcare   314

Virtual reality in health   321

Blockchain   325

Big data   328

15. Worldwide initiatives

Christopher Pearce, Ed Brown, Shashi Gogia, Charles Noble, Magdala de Araújo Novaes

Australian experience   331

Telehealth in Brazil   334

Telemedicine/telehealth in Canada   337

India case study   339

Telemedicine in Africa   340

Summary of learnings   341

A final word   342

Glossary   **343**

References   **347**

Index   **375**

List of Contributors

Abhishek **Gattani**	0000-0001-9269-7965
Amadeu Sá **de Campos Filho**	0000-0002-8660-854X
Ana Emilia **Oliveira**	0000-0003-4371-4815
Ana Estela **Haddad**	0000-0002-0693-9014
Anandhi **Ramachandran**	0000-0003-2234-6830
Andre **Henriksen**	0000-0002-0918-7444
Anthony **Pho**	0000-0002-9959-3541
Arindam **Basu**	0000-0003-2326-2292
Arjun **Kalyanpur**	0000-0003-2761-7273
Bipin Kumar **Rathod**	0000-0001-5071-5854
Carlos André Aita **Schmitz**	0000-0002-9003-9704
Charles **Umeh**	0000-0001-6478-9466
Christopher **Pearce**	0000-0001-5371-8196
Danielle Santos **Alves**	0000-0003-0034-5255
Denise Garrido **Silva**	0000-0002-3953-008X
Devashish **Saini**	0000-0002-9869-1705
Edward **Brown**	0000-0003-2114-4479
Eirik **Årsand**	0000-0002-9520-1408
Fernando José Ribeiro **Sales**	0000-0002-7827-9289
Filipe Santana **da Silva**	0000-0002-6803-1407
Ganesh Arun **Joshi**	0000-0002-5750-0255
Gunnar **Hartvigsen**	0000-0001-8771-9867
Guriqbal **Jaiya**	0000-0002-7557-3570
Gustavo Silveira **Dantas**	0000-0002-9657-8936
Karen **Waite**	0000-0003-4669-168X
Keilla Taciane Martins **de Melo Oliveira**	0000-0003-2330-4210
Kleber Soares **de Araujo**	0000-0001-8818-6177

Kriti **Gogia**	0000-0002-4123-5151
Luiz Roberto **de Oliveira**	0000-0002-9368-0927
Magdala **de Araujo Novaes**	0000-0002-5494-319X
Manoj Kumar **Singh**	0000-0002-8699-7205
Manoj Rai **Mehta**	0000-0002-8165-3200
Marcia **Ito**	0000-0003-4799-2433
Mariana **Boulitreaux**	0000-0002-3576-2369
Maurice **Mars**	0000-0001-8784-780X
Maurizio **Mattoli**	0000-0001-8302-0311
Meghan Corin **Bradway**	0000-0003-4540-225X
Oommen **John**	0000-0002-9008-1726
Otávio Pereira **D'Ávila**	0000-0003-1852-7858
Pramod David **Jacob**	0000-0001-6478-9457
Praveen **Kumar**	0000-0001-7112-7023
Rodrigo **Dias**	0000-0002-1315-7205
Rohit **Gupta**	0000-0002-6415-8427
Sanjay **Bedi**	0000-0002-6478-6095
Sejal **Shah**	0000-0002-8158-0371
Shashi **Gogia**	0000-0003-2682-1520
Shivani **Ghoshal**	0000-0002-8283-197X
Spriha **Gogia**	0000-0002-6347-038X
Sriram **Iyengar**	0000-0002-7292-430X
Sunita **Maheshwari**	0000-0002-3850-3477
Suzanne **Bakken**	0000-0001-6202-6001
U.S. **Mohalanobish**	0000-0002-9587-4178

Acknowledgments

I start with thanking all my teachers especially those at AIIMS, New Delhi who inculcated in me not only the spirit of inquiry but also the nobility and empathy required to practice medicine and surgery. The encouragement continued even after leaving AIIMS as some of them particularly Professors Sneh Bhargava and Anand Malaviya are still appreciative and full of advice for the role that Health Informatics in general and Telehealth in particular has to play in transforming modern heatlhcare.

This book would not have been possible without the work done through our own Society for Administration of Telemedicine and Healthcare Informatics (SATHI) and its members. Working with SATHI gave us the confidence that telehealth can bridge some of the existing health disparities between the haves and have-nots besides promising to become one of the essential components in healthcare delivery for the future. One direct outcome was my becoming a part of the International Medical Informatics Association (IMIA) telehealth working group (WG) with the assignment of a leadership role.

The IMIA Telehealth WG was revived in 2010 through the efforts of then Vice President (VP) for Working Groups – Dr. Hyeoun-Ae Park of South Korea with her handing over charge of the WG activities to me and Anthony Maeder. She, as well as the succeeding VPs of WGs – namely, Ms. Tze Yun Leong (Singapore) and Ms. Helen Ying Wu (China) continued with their encouragement and support of our activities. They, as well as the entire IMIA community need to be thanked as they helped the WG get the relevant exposure, which led Rafael Teixeira, the acquisitions editor of Elsevier, to contact us. Thank you, Rafael, for understanding the need and relevance of this book.

Besides the above, there is a long list of supporters and friends within IMIA whom we wish to thank though it would be pertinent to state that it is not possible to name all. The IMIA CEO Elaine Huesing (Canada) and Brenda Faye (South Africa) who runs the IMIA virtual office deserve special mention in this regard. We start with the presidents during the term of existence of this WG - Reinhold Haux; Antoine Geissbuhler; Lincoln de Assis Moura; Hyeoun-Ae Park; Christoph Lehmann; and Sabine Koch. Other names, which come to mind are Casimir Kulikowski; Craig Kuziemsky; Khalid Moidu; Klaus Veil; Kyunghi Cho; Lyn Hammer, Michio Kimura; Mowafa Househ; Peter Murray; Brigitte Seroussi; Ted Shortliffe; Vimla Patel; and Vajira Dissanayake.

Regarding the book, in August 2016, Rafael met and encouraged some WG members to undertake the writing of what was hoped to be a textbook for undergraduates. Over the next three years – up to the launch in end August 2019, almost all our members – close to 60 as of date - have been active participants and contributors to this effort. The members are spread across the globe; they took time off work, stayed awake at unearthly hours to discuss and plan the content, and also patiently listened to me urging them to complete their chapter contents on time.

A special thanks to the two coeditors - Magdala de Araújo Novaes from Brazil and Arindam Basu from New Zealand. They constantly guided me and agreed to take up additional tasks. My daughters-Spriha Gogia and Kriti Gogia assisted in copy editing the content.

Thanks to the chapter editors Arindam Basu; Christopher Pearce; Gunnar Hartvigsen; Luiz Roberto de Oliveira; Magdala de Araújo Novaes; Marcia Ito; Maurice Mars; Oommen John; Pramod David Jacob and Sriram Iyengar for picking up the task and also finishing well within the deadlines. Thanks to the authors Abhishek Gattani; Amadeu Sá de Campos Filho; Ana Estela Haddad; Anandhi Ramachandran; Andre Henriksen; Arjun Kalyanpur; Bipin Kumar Rathod; Carlos André Aita Schmitz; Charles Umeh; Danielle Santos Alves; Devashish Saini; Edward Brown; Eirik Årsand; Fernando José Ribeiro Sales; Filipe Santana da Silva; Ganesh Arun Joshi; Guriqbal Singh Jaiya; Gustavo Silveira Dantas; Karen Waite; Keilla Taciane Martins de Melo Oliveira; Kleber Soares de Araujo; Kriti Gogia; Manoj Kumar Singh; Manoj Rai Mehta; Mariana Boulitreau Siqueira Campos Barros; Maurizio Mattoli; Meghan Corin Bradway; Otávio Pereira D'Ávila; Parveen K; Rodrigo da Silva Dias; Rohit Raghav Gupta; Sanjay Bedi; Shivani Ghoshal; Spriha Gogia; Sejal Shah; Sunita Maheshwari; Suzanne Bakken; and U S Mohalanobish. Thanks to all their coauthors as well.

A thank you to the reviewers, the initial two remain anonymous, but gave us adequate hints on what needed to be told. After compilation, Anthony Maeder and Christopher Pearce read the drafts and gave us further suggestions for a course correction.

Thanks to my wife, Arun Rekha, who was always there to support me in this task.

I also express my sincere gratitude to the editorial team of Elsevier, in particular to Ms. Megan Ashdown; Ms. Narmatha Mohan; and Mr. Debasish Ghosh for their efficiency and professionalism. Without them, this book would still be in progress. I thank the publisher Stacy Masucci, cover designer Mathew Limbert besides the other unnamed professionals who have worked, and are still doing so behind the scenes, for the professional layout and proof-reading.

Telecare basics

Overview

Shashi Gogia

Society for Administration of Telemedicine and Healthcare Informatics, New Delhi, India

While trekking in the Himalayas, one early morning, I had to stop to allow four persons to pass. They were carrying a wooden cot and strapped to the cot was a 50 years old man with a plaster splint and dressing window suggestive of a compound fracture. He was clearly being carried to the hospital. The procession had already travelled a few kilometers, but still, it would take another kilometer to reach the road and vehicle. Transit time from home to the hospital would be 2–3 h on a minimum and around the same for return. A simple wound dressing, which would ordinarily take 10 min, had now cost five man-days and 50 times the original price. That was a motivating moment for me to look for a solution to cut down such unnecessary cost of healthcare provision. Many of the authors in this book have had similar experiences.

Costs of healthcare delivery are not always the same as costs incurred to achieve good health. The cost of travel to a health facility and back, though rarely considered, is a major impediment for those located in remote locations. Lack of care providers locally, along with other poor health infrastructure, often exacerbates health disparities. While expectedly a major problem in the developing world, which suffers from infrastructure weakness, especially poor transport networks, remote and underserved areas exist in almost every country. This specially includes the United States, Canada, and Australia, which have large swathes of rural areas.

A 2015 Indian movie, *Manjhi*, described the true story of a man who single handedly cut a road across a mountain in remorse after his wife died; he had been unable to get her to the hospital in time. He did not want others to suffer the same fate.[1] In today's time, a simple mobile device could have provided this much needed support through telehealth, which can literally help one to cross mountains with minimal effort.

Telehealth, literally means "healing at a distance." It is increasingly viewed as a mechanism to deliver more efficient and patient-centered healthcare services to individuals who face physical and financial barriers to access quality healthcare support. Advances in Information and Communication Technology (ICT) coupled with demand for novel approaches to care has enabled GPs, nurses, and other health workers in the community to collaborate and address health disparities through deployment of telehealth technology. Even while initially, the objective was to save costs and time spent on physical travel by patients or health providers, sometimes both; today, information processing and Internet have widened the scope to a range of solutions, some of which were never even imagined in the past. Like the TV remote, it is increasingly more than just a convenience. Many patients are already hooked on, but the healthcare fraternity needs to understand how it works.

Telehealth is only one of the many areas where ICT is supporting healthcare, though admittedly one of the most promising ones. To fully utilize the benefits, a better understanding of ICT itself is first required. ICT has two components. The first is Information Technology (IT), which is actually information processing, and the other component is Communication (C), which means transmission of information, but also involves technology.

Information processing follows four discrete steps known with the acronym DIKW (Fig. 1). The very basic is **data**, a jargon of bits and bytes initially created through input devices, stored in the form of memory at various places and transmitted or communicated. Humanly understandable data is **information**. The Internet, for example, is a constant flow

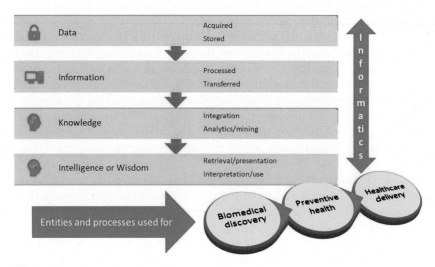

FIG. 1   Data flow in health IT systems.

of information across billions of devices. Useful information becomes **knowledge**, and finally, garnering benefits of knowledge is what can be called intelligence or **wisdom**, which can translate to appropriate action, meaning better healthcare delivery in the current context.

Healthcare has been among the last to fully utilize the benefits of the ICT revolution, which has resulted in a sea change in other sectors. Take the aviation sector as an example. The 2014 figure of 100,000 flights every day is rising.[2] Airlines spend 17% of their budget on ICT. This budget seems justified as it allows seamless ticket bookings, enables millions of pieces of luggage to reach their destination in tandem with the passenger, and ensures flights take off and land on time and, most importantly, with complete safety. Similarly, weather prediction, which used to be a joke, advanced far in accuracy with the introduction of super computers and high-level calculations.

Although, the body's processes are far more complex than the weather, similar or even greater advances in healthcare are possible by using similar technologies. Processing skills of today's PCs and smartphones are no less than super computers. Telehealth is only one of the many benefits of such injection of technology as described in the case of the Aravind Eye Hospitals[3] (Box 1).

We first briefly describe what telemedicine and telehealth mean—exact definitions are in the next chapter. **Telemedicine** is a provision of clinical care remotely, using clinical processes such as teleconsultation, telediagnosis, etc. **Telehealth** not only incorporates telemedicine but also goes beyond, with additional indirect benefits. These include understanding health indices, providing preventive health support and medical education—remotely delivered for professionals as well as public—and

---

BOX 1

Aravind eye-care system

The Aravind group of eye hospitals from South India introduced assembly line techniques to eye surgery, managing to notch up over 300,000 cases per year at extremely and unparalleled low costs.

Patients are remotely identified, investigated, and then brought to the hospital in groups for the actual procedure—say a cataract. Then, they are sent back the same day for later remote stitch removal and glasses. The fees charged include transportation. Complication rates are lower than anywhere in the world. Telehealth processes, some of them developed in-house, assist this rapid and efficient turnover. They were the pioneers of teleophthalmology in India.

correcting a shortage of essential supplies etc. Electronic health (eHealth) is a term used for whenever any form of electronics is involved for health provision, support, or management.[4] (WHO is now trying to gather a consensus to use the term Digital Health instead.) eHealth also incorporates CDSS, analytics, and many other tools, which go towards creating a broad-based personal and public health strategy. Telemedicine and telehealth, even while having variations, are used as interconvertible terms. At many places, we use the term **telecare,** which, though self-explanatory, as yet does not have a published reference.

Another term is mobile health (**mHealth**), which is similar, but is restricted to the process, that is, electronic healthcare delivery through mobile devices. Mobile usage has outnumbered computers. Besides being mobile and handy, features like location identification and sharing, messaging service, gyroscope, movement sensors and built-in camera have expanded the scope to special health apps like fitness trackers and wellness support enabling patient-centered care and sometimes, obviate the need of a health provider. mHealth has expanded the scope beyond traditional telehealth, justifying a separate name and an exclusive chapter in this book.

The world's over seven billion and rising population incorporates anthropological, societal, and cultural differences besides the variation in the environment, economic capability, institutional support for health, etc. There are, hence, a relatively unlimited number of health problems with as many treatment processes. Chronic diseases and increasing life span mean even greater challenges for the patient and the provider. Care provision is rising in complexity. Insurance rarely compensates for the lack of easy access to the provider, though that may be changing.

Till lately, healthcare delivery used to remain concentrated in the hands of health professionals. However, a persons' health is rarely personal; it does affect others around him. Hence, many well-wishers and family try to step in to provide solutions. Going to the doctor is expensive and involves time and effort. Many who are not trained in healthcare, especially ICT professionals, have found it a lucrative market and try to provide solutions. Only a few of these can be recommended and identifying the better ones is another rationale behind this book.

Most clinicians have not been very supportive of telehealth. Catering to it requires additional learning, there is a higher expenditure on time and effort due to frequent interruptions, and despite everything, information remains incomplete. There are also legal hurdles related to open data sharing and patient privacy. The public is more enthusiastic; 76% of US citizens, for example, prefer telecare over a physician.[5] They use trusted search engines and social networking tools for information and communicate through e-mail, WhatsApp, and Skype. All may be called a special category of telehealth, but these are frowned upon by clinicians for the lack of security and privacy. Such solutions may even be harmful when there are issues related to accuracy and validity of the gathered knowledge. Clinicians find patients who gather information from the Internet and other sources a problem (Fig. 2).

Some support for telehealth is creeping in, such as day to day care for the aged as well as in chronic diseases where a daily trip to the doctor would make the costs prohibitive. As also, during emergencies.

ICT systems can help reduce the rising complexity of healthcare delivery through knowledge systems and checkbacks. And since telehealth requires working with an ICT system, incorporating knowledge systems, checkbacks, and other such can be seamless. However, knowledge about ICT-based healthcare support then becomes important. In 2006, there were 26,000 EMRs in the United States. Using one needed an understanding of its processes and workflows. As of 2017, there are around 325,000 apps.[6] These also keep on changing with variations, issues, and bugs offering complexity in adoption and implementation. Patients are going to use them and ask the provider on their benefits and issues.

Overall, 75% of ICT projects do not reach the desired level of success; in healthcare the failure rate is even higher. Fortunately, success rate is improving.[7] Rapid advances have lowered costs of ICT implementation, made it easier to use, and widened reach but still the initial investors who lost out are wary.

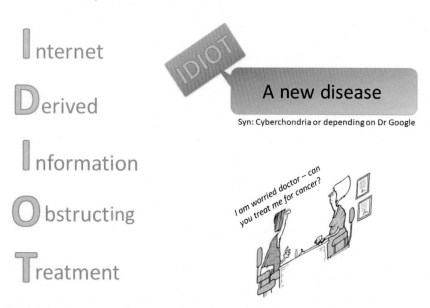

Internet

Derived

Information

Obstructing

Treatment

A new disease

Syn: Cyberchondria or depending on Dr Google

I am worried doctor – can you treat me for cancer?

FIG. 2 Poster at a GP's clinic reflecting a certain tiredness with Internet-derived knowledge. Courtesy Dr. T.P. Singh, New Delhi, India.

The few successful telehealth projects have been those wherein ICT was used to supplement, rather than replace the care provider, a small cog in the larger picture as seen in the exemplified case of Aravind Hospitals.[3]

One reason for the lack of general success of ICT in healthcare has been hype related to the technology. ICT has many unpredicted side effects. A change management approach helps make ICT incorporation easy (Fig. 3). The most important component is people; they have to be orientated, motivated, and trained. This sometimes needs additional incentives, as such training is over and above what is routinely taught during medical school.

Fortunately, the perception that the older generation is less accommodative to change can now be challenged after seeing the widespread usage of smart mobiles. Better and easy to use software systems, read technology as shown in Fig. 3, do help ease adoption. If the change is gradual, for example, extending the use of familiar day-to-day applications like WhatsApp, e-mail, or video conferencing, success is assured. Additional incremental use, like extended use of familiar applications as mentioned earlier, is what can be called an evolutionary change. A project mode, on the other hand, is revolutionary. Revolutions tend to force change, which leads to resistance. This book is an effort towards an evolutionary change.

This book has four main sections, broken into 15 chapters with 101 subsections written by 40 main authors, as well as a few additional coauthors. The authors came from across the globe, many from places where English is a foreign language. During editing, there was a fear of losing in translation, the essence of what the original author wanted to convey. Retaining consistency of the terms deployed was also challenging, besides a need to remove areas of duplicity between various submissions, for example, definitions. Some of these duplications persist because there were chances of interrupting a seamless flow of information. The attempt has focused toward an easier read, and better understanding.

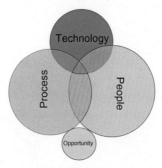

FIG. 3   Success of any new **technology** project, specially using ICT, depends on a complex interplay of **processes,** which need to be added or changed, and the **people** working with it. Luck or opportunity also plays a role. *(Size of the circles approximately reflects the relative role that each component plays.)*

The first section is **basics** wherein after the current overview; Chapter 2 defines telehealth, its build-up though history and some of its learnings, and the overall importance of telecare in the existing health systems. It ends with what the future beholds. Chapter 3 details the creation of health-related data, its storage in the form of EHRs, and how to utilize it further. Chapter 4 talks about the other components of technology behind telehealth, its implementation, and related protocols and standards.

The second section, **working together,** talks about how patients, clinicians, and other care providers can work together for efficient health delivery. Chapter 5 covers the creation of a healthcare team without the consideration of physical barriers; Chapter 6 looks at this from the individual patient's perspective—what can be called patient-centered care; Chapter 7 looks at telehealth projects, either standalone or what is rather a preferable incorporation of remote support in any organization or care support system; and finally, Chapter 8 is about how tele itself has all the tools for advanced training and creation of tele-enabled workforce. Distance education is now possible and has been found useful for all grades of health professionals, starting from the village-level worker to the high-end specialist.

The third section is about **telemedicine** in its classic sense. Chapter 9 is dealing with solutions at the primary care level; Chapter 10 covers special solutions and components required among individual specialities; and Chapter 11 caters to individual situations wherein telecare is maybe the only or at least the ideal solution. Examples are problems like disasters and less accessible places likes prisons, ships, and aviation. Chapter 12 is about mHealth, its nuances and how mobiles are and can be used for health support.

The last section deals with **issues and the future**. Chapter 13 incorporates legal and ethical issues; Chapter 14 discusses advances with an eye to the future like telehomecare, blockchain, robotics, AI, IoT, and AR/VR. The book ends with specific case studies and their learnings from the developing and the developed world.

There is a combined glossary of acronyms and common terms, which are used across multiple chapters. References are also placed at the end to avoid duplication. Since this is designed as a textbook, we avoid too many detailed references.

Technology is changing very rapidly. It is almost like a race for new ideas and innovations. For a book like this, to keep up with the latest changes is challenging as we all know that some of them may not even see the light of the day. The only way to compensate is to try to do revisions earlier rather than later, which we hope to do. Interestingly, this chapter was deliberately written last, and even while we were doing the final revision, WHO announced that the term digital health will be preferred to eHealth.

In conclusion

The author recently received a call routed through a web search engine. "Can your telemedicine solution cure my cold?" It was a difficult question to answer, as medical care by itself is yet to deliver for a cold. However, telehealth does offer innovative and holistic solutions for a multitude of diseases humanity is faced with, without the constraints of time and distance.

Rationale, history, and basics of telehealth

Shashi Gogia

Society for Administration of Telemedicine and Healthcare Informatics (SATHI), New Delhi, India

Definitions

Tele ~ *distance* medicine *or* health is the use of information and communication technologies (ICTs) to deliver health services where there is physical separation between care providers and/or the recipients over both long and short distances. It is about *transmitting* voice, data, images, and information *rather than moving* care recipients, health professionals, or educators. It encompasses preventive as well as curative aspects of healthcare services for recipients. The interactions can be between care recipient(s), care providers or educators, and lately also computerized devices—standalone, as well as working though a mobile.

Telemedicine describes remote clinical services in the form of patient and clinician contact. It includes diagnosis, monitoring, advice, reminders, education, intervention, and remote admissions. Variations include clinicians discussing a case over video conference; telementoring, which means overseeing a procedure being done by a less trained person; digital monitoring with live feed or application combinations; and forwarding of test reports for interpretation by a specialist. Other examples are home monitoring of the aged or infirm through continuous feeding of patient health data, client to practitioner online conference, videophone interpretation during a consult, and also robotic surgery. In emergent situations, such support can save vital seconds and, in chronic care, cut down frequent travel, saving travel cost and time.

In **telehealth** the scope expands beyond telemedicine to administrative meetings and other nonclinical services too, like inclusion of preventative

11

and promotive components. Also included is tele-education, for patients or care providers, through distance learning, meetings, supervision, and presentations.

Besides saving in physical transportation, which could be by the care recipient, the provider, or both, all variants support achievement of quality aims, addressing barriers to care through innovative means and leveraging the proliferation of technology in an increasingly mobile-friendly and technology-centric population.

The information collected can be further processed and analyzed to plan a long-term health strategy of an increasing aged population, many living alone in diverse locations, with a rising number of chronic conditions.

eHealth, (currently Digital Health is the term preferred by WHO) an even broader term, has over 51 definitions[4] including "The use of information and communication technologies (ICT) in support of health and health-related field, including health care services, health surveillance and health education, knowledge and research."

Another one is "eHealth is the use, in the health sector, of digital data - transmitted, stored and retrieved electronically- in support of health care, both at the local site and at a distance." And yet another *eHealth is an emerging field in the intersection of medical informatics, public health, and business, referring to health services and information delivered or enhanced through the Internet and related technologies. In a broader sense the term characterizes not only a technical development but also a state of mind, a way of thinking, an attitude, and a commitment for networked, global thinking, to improve healthcare locally, regionally, and worldwide by using information and communication technology.*

Examples include treating patients, conducting research, educating the health workforce, tracking diseases, and monitoring public health. Another term **mHealth** is further discussed in the succeeding text.

Any of the previous terms can be used interchangeably, but the term *telecare* will mostly be used in this book. This term has no written definition but however would be best understood as encompassing any kind of healthcare where remote support is incorporated. Artificial intelligence (AI), CDSS, and a multitude of direct patient or physician support methods are beyond the scope of this book.

History of telemedicine and telehealth

Efforts for communication beyond the hearing range, that is, smoke signals, drums, and pigeon carriers, have been part of human civilization since its inception. They were also used to access healthcare. The inequality in the availability of good healthcare between the higher and lower classes existed even then, with both the highest quality care and ready access to the same, restricted to kings and such. The elderly and infirm often sent representatives and/or used messages to convey information on symptoms and bring home a diagnosis and treatment options.

Telecommunication, as we know it today, followed the discovery of electricity in the 19th century. As technology developed and wired communication became increasingly commonplace, the ideas surrounding telehealth began to emerge. During the American civil war, telegraphs were used to deliver mortality lists and medical care to soldiers.

The telephone was easier to use than the telegraph; thus access to public began to emerge as well. The earliest telehealth encounter can be traced to its inventor Alexander Graham Bell, in 1876. He had called for help from his assistant Mr. Watson after spilling an acid on his trousers.[8] *The Lancet* in 1879 described a doctor's successful diagnosis of a child over the telephone in the middle of the night and subsequently discussed the potential of remote patient care in order to avoid unnecessary house visits.[9]

The concept of telemedicine evolved in 1905 thanks to a Dutch physiologist who utilized the telephone for transmission and monitoring of cardiac sounds and rhythms. Bicycle-powered radios were used to request for medical help from Australia's flying doctors' services almost as soon as it started.

Formal recognition of the term telemedicine started in the 1920s when two-way television and audio signals were used to communicate. In the 1940s, in Pennsylvania state, transmission of radiography was done through telephone circuits between cities 20 miles apart. The first uses of telemedicine to transmit video, images, and complex medical data occurred in the late 1950s and early 1960s. In 1959 the University of Nebraska used interactive television (IATV) to transmit neurological examinations, widely considered as the first case of a real-time video telemedicine consultation. Telepsychiatry, through remote counseling, followed.

When the National Aeronautics and Space Administration (NASA) began plans to send astronauts into space, the need for telemedicine became all too clear. For monitoring purposes, telemedicine capabilities were built into the spacecraft as well as the first spacesuits. In the 1960s, NASA, Lockheed Corporation, and the U.S. Indian Health Service joined together to work on Space Technology Applied to Rural Papago Advanced Health Care (STARPAHC) project to provide telemedicine access to an American Indian reservation via telecommunication links similar to the one used for space stations. Different projects were funded across North America and Canada in order to realize the exciting potential of this new innovation.

Other programs followed, focusing on the transmission of medical data such as fluoroscopy images, X-rays, heart and chest sounds from a stethoscope, and electrocardiograms (ECGs). The main motivations of these early projects were as follows:

- Providing access to healthcare in rural areas
- Medical emergencies

Radiology was the first medical specialty to fully embrace telemedicine in the 1980s. This was a natural advance from PACS, that is, enterprise level digitization of medical images. PACS was conceived as a cost and space-saving advantage wherein X-ray images were stored in a digital format. This allowed instant access to current and prior images using computer monitors at different locations in the radiology department as well as within wards. Allowing remote access was the next step, which was enabled first for the hospital's own radiologists, so that they could report from home. Now, they report from anywhere across the globe (refer the "Teleradiology" section in Chapter 10).

One of the oldest known telecardiology systems for tele-transmissions of ECGs was established in Gwalior, India, in 1975.[10] This system enabled wireless transmission of ECG from the moving ICU van or the patients' home to the central station in the ICU of the department of medicine. Transmission through frequency modulation helped eliminate background noise. This system was also used to monitor patients with pacemakers in remote areas. The central control unit at the ICU was able to correctly interpret arrhythmia.

Internet use, though widespread by the turn of the century, impacted telehealth much later as the initial systems required higher bandwidth than what was initially available. Among the earliest to benefit were specialities dependent on the interpretation of audio or images, either still or moving (video). Examples of the former were patient conversations, heart sounds, and speech therapy, while the latter included dermatology, cardiology (ECG, echo, and angiograms), ophthalmology, and pathology; a third group was if care could be administered through video conference (psychiatry). Special tools to enable transfer emerged, for example, tele-stethoscope and tele-ECG, and for telepathology, specialized microscopes exist wherein the movement of the slide viewer could be remotely controlled, as well as zoomed in on a real-time basis.

India has been an early leader in telecare among the developing countries. The need was emphasized by a large rural population, between 60% and 70% of the total, where even the few officially posted doctors would rarely be present on duty. Efforts were spearheaded by Indian Space Research Organization (ISRO) along with a special school for telemedicine which was established in the city of Lucknow. In 2001, this center provided consults to pilgrims gathered in the city of Allahabad to take a dip in the Ganges for the Kumbh festival.[11] Emergency remote support provided to high altitude trekkers in the Himalayas after an avalanche made it extremely popular and well known. CPCs and medical seminars with an audience from across the country are being held almost since inception. Telemedicine linkages exist to clinics in remote areas, like Ladakh and Andaman Islands, and also to many hospitals in African countries.[12] ISRO provided opportunities to neighboring countries, for example, Nepal and Bhutan, to use Indian satellites for their own programs. China has similarly assisted Mongolia, Argentina, and Iran.

Almost all early deployments of telemedicine were large undertakings as there was a requirement of special staff and organizational changes. Large projects were created—mostly for government or defense. They were clunky and expensive, hence unsustainable. Customized hardware and software had been created for a specific use, like telepsychiatry. Maintenance was frequently required and not available locally. The inability of various software to talk to each other lead to initiatives toward standardization. Even the few projects that survived the initial phases soon became outmoded due to rapid advances and changes in technology.

The available connectivity option was the key decider for projects, which initially were phone lines (dialup Internet), GPRS, or satellite. ISDN was a cheaper option than satellite and less erratic than others but held sway only for a few years, soon overtaken by broadband Internet and now 3G, 4G, 5G, etc. through mobiles.

There have been other advances:

- memory and storage (databases, object-store for large files such as images and video) and easy availability—through backup servers, which can dynamically increase as per demand load
- standardization (MP4, PNG, etc.)
- security (encryption, password protection, access levels, etc.)
- application development—new programming languages (Java, JavaScript, dotnet, etc.), frameworks, and open-source software (Apache)
- the cloud and virtual servers such as Amazon Web Services (AWS)
- methods to digitize information (digital cameras, scanners, etc.)

Usage of existing computing devices—belonging to patient or physician—helped bring down costs, besides being easy to use, as little further special training was required.

Telemedicine 2.0 was a relatively late beneficiary of this information explosion. Internet protocols allowed support for practically all information and traffic needed for telemedicine, including the following:

- patient education (text, images, and video)
- medical images such as X-rays and scans (DICOM image standards)
- real-time audio and video consultation
- vital signs and other body measurements (ECG, temperature, etc.)

However, there have been objections to provide telecare by clinicians. Some feel that an inability to touch the patient means the interaction is less than ideal and the consult is slow, incomplete, and not to the requisite quality, making them more liable. Reimbursement policies are not very clear; the patient sitting outside their chamber is more paying and less demanding on time.

The current situation

Despite the challenges, many countries like Norway,[13] Canada, Australia, and others within the EU have well-established telehealth programs. A rising number of the aged, many living alone and unable to travel frequently, along with the presence of citizens in an area where access is regularly hampered by distance and climate, offer justification for such projects. A single unified EHR for all citizens makes it easier to implement,[14] but this is as yet exists only in the smaller countries where the need for telehealth is also less. In the United States, efforts to create EHRs for all its citizens through incentives and penalties have given a major push toward eHealth.

Smartphones have had a major impact on public health. There are now an over 325,000 health apps,[6] which remind patients to take their medicine, transmit their health information, and even act as daily fitness trackers. Functions like GPS and cameras allow for improved collection of health data. Software, hardware, and attachments are available to make the mobile work as an e-stethoscope, slit lamp, and microscope using a clip-on lens. A probe for ultrasound, pulse oximeter, and monitor can be added to a special device created, which means that information is not only obtained, but also transmitted seamlessly.

EMR vendors employ the Internet with access to medical information for medical providers and patients. Alongside, patient portals have come up allowing patients to look up their lab results, refill prescriptions, or send a secure message to their physician. Infant monitors allow parents to work. Portable monitors diagnose and send a message to the clinician about cardiac arrhythmias and falls. Drones are enabling emergency care by their capacity of delivering blood samples, medicines as well as medical support to a remote location. An ambulance transferring a patient from a trauma site directly to the operating suite with a surgeon in readiness is considered routine today.

The public is accessing telecare in preference to a physician visit.[15] This is done through search engines; use of social media; and sometimes communicating through e-mail, WhatsApp, Skype, or even desktop sharing over and above-specialized applications. Many of the former have privacy concerns and generally frowned upon by academics and experts.

The situation in developing countries is a little depressing. While a near parity exists on the availability of latest software and hardware between developed and developing world—absence of this parity is an invitation to software piracy, poor connectivity remains an issue. Even where ICT infrastructure is available, more basic health concerns like water and sanitation, even food sometimes, which telehealth will never correct, take precedence. There are notable exceptions that are mentioned in individual chapters.

In conclusion, telehealth has become routine in many fields, and the future is bright, though not to the desired extent considering that the initial goal was for improving health access and better care for remote and rural populations. There is better focus and agreement on its use for care of the aged and infirm.

Situations where telehealth has a role

Let us look at the situations that require remote support. There could be an immobility of the patient, for example, someone bed ridden, sick, having a fracture or paralysis and in need of urgent help. Immobility or lack of immediate availability could also be of the provider, in the form of not enough specialists, day off work, or on leave. Another set is an unsurmountable physical barrier disallowing access to the care giver, like for astronauts in space, passengers in a ship or airplane, prisoners, patients who have been quarantined, and those visiting or staying at remote islands and mountain peaks.

Less commented about, but far more frequent candidates for telecare are those with chronic diseases. Here, cost cutting becomes important as there is need for frequent visits even while suffering from a less serious problem. Need for funds for travel, days off work, etc. can be decreased. Recurrent physician visits interfere with day-to-day work. Simple filing and review of test reports, which mostly can be possible remotely, may be the only interaction required. Examples are blood sugar and HbA1C for diabetics, blood pressure in hypertensives, and renal parameters for those with kidney disease, etc.

Some more examples are provided hereby with many more specific instances in the later chapters. In many infectious diseases, physician-patient contact has to be minimized due to fear of transmission of infection. Travel of a high-level public figure, politician, or even a criminal has many issues for security and other reasons like avoidance of a preying media.

Telemedicine largely provides remote assessment, and diagnosis, 90% of which, in older times, was dependent on simple history and examination, most of which, can be digitized but requires effort. Digitization of investigations is easier. And its rising contribution has created a better rationale for telecare. For example, gallstones found on ultrasound are an indication for surgery, and once the preoperative evaluation is complete, patient needs to travel only once for the procedure. Preliminary evaluation, including other tests as well as follow-up stitch removal, can be done locally.

But many clinicians have been averse to deliver remote care as many components, such as patient examination may be insufficient. A frequent complaint is "I do not feel satisfied till I have touched the patient, neither is the patient satisfied." However, surveys of patients have shown the latter to be a myth. All that the patient wants is complete attention and a serious listening to their problems, which a face-to-face online contact can and does provide. On the other hand, talking on a mobile, glancing at your watch or even outside for the next patient, even while your hand is examining a patient, is much more off-putting.

Other reasons for resistance of clinicians to telehealth include fears of litigation, lack of confidence in understanding the full spectrum of the patients' problem online, as well as of staff and related capability across long distances, legal safety beyond borders, and lack of reimbursement. But the role of telecare is well recognized. With the rising dependence of investigations for diagnosis, not touching the patient is possibly considered normal. There are also guidelines about the need for self-protection, if there is a suspected contagious disease.

In summary, telecare may provide incomplete care, but nevertheless, does provide some care. Whether any telesupport will be worthwhile depends on the alternatives. An important aspect is ensuring that the telesupport has quality in some ways to the level as a physical visit or at least covers up for or compensates some gap in care provision.

Types of telecare

Let us begin by classifying the various methods of administering remote care. The first two are traditional; the latter ones came up with advancing technology. Currently a hybrid of almost all types is used:

1. **Real time** or **synchronous**—here, information or data is transferred live. Video conferencing between a patient and the healthcare provider is the prime example. Others include live viewing of ultrasounds or angiograms as they are taking place, streaming of procedures from the OR, or of heart sounds using a tele-stethoscope. This is a convenient and easy form of telemedicine but requires high bandwidth, constant connectivity, and investment in related hardware.
2. **Store and forward (S&F)** or **asynchronous**—information is recorded and transferred. It can be stored locally or in a server depending on when connectivity becomes available. Viewing, comments, and even incorporation of the data into a different server can occur at the convenience of the other participants of the telehealth stream. It is less dependent on constant connectivity but more complicated to administer. Choice of software and interconnectivity standards has a greater role—as interpretations may differ.
3. **Telemonitoring or remote monitoring**—medical devices record and process personal information and transmit continuously (*real time*) or in a processed summary form (*asynchronously*) to the clinician. Examples are home care devices for old age and infirm as well as tele-ICU.
4. Mobile health or **mHealth**[a] is a special form of Digital Health. Smart mobiles have computing power and connectivity access better than

[a]Chapter 12 explains this in detail.

specialized telemedicine systems of the past. They are inexpensive, have inbuilt audio and video, are flexible to allow both real time, and store and forward transmission as well as viewing from almost anywhere. Telemonitoring through inbuilt or even add-on sensors allows a single device to be a complete telehealth solution for a range of different problems. Many specialized applications or apps can directly inform the patient about their health status.

Real time telecare is relatively easy to do but has a high dependence on technology and connectivity. Since it is visual and also easy to understand with a certain wow factor, that made it the major form to be advertised, as well as sold. However, getting outcomes remains a challenge, with pitfalls in the form of the need of constant connectivity, an inability to garner the entire information in one go, call drops, and a high dependence on training to get the best value. Most failures, as mentioned in the history section were because this type of telecare was oversold. However, real time remains to be the most popular type aided by cheaper connectivity and hardware. It is a major component of mHealth. Most cameras, standalone as well as within microscopes and endoscopes, X-rays, MRIs, etc. use digital formats; hence, sharing or transmitting on a real-time basis is easy.

S&F essentially depends on gathering patient information and sharing the same after processing. While sharing photos, there is need to create a relevant case of whose photo? and why an opinion is required. This required typing not only by the referring person, but also by the expert who may have some further questions or is providing the opinion in the form of a written prescription or advice. Sending scanned copies or photographs of prescriptions and reports is also extremely time-consuming besides being inefficient as the specialist might be just wanting to know the ESR and CRP, but will have to one by scroll through the entire set of 9 or 10 pages of the sent reports. The doctors' scrawl is famous for unreadability, photographs of such handwritten text, one can imagine would be even more difficult to interpret. Simple typing of the relevant information is also inefficient, slow and a reason for mistakes which may get accentuated, if anything, by autocorrect. This has been another reason for failure of telemedicine systems of the past. We now describe a better way.

Any student starting clinical courses undergoes a grilling about the value of medical documentation. Documentation helps to create the diagnosis through compilation and assessment of various components like history, examination, and test reports. Following the diagnosis, some advice, medication, or procedure, and maybe a combination of all three, is done.

Documentation of almost all components of care can be digitized (see Fig. 1), which was previously done on paper but is now largely done

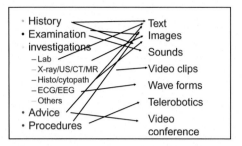

FIG. 1 Digitalization of a patients' medical record breaks the components into text, sound, or images. ECGs/EEGs constitute wave forms. Video conference allows face-to-face interaction.

electronically, that is, an EHR. An EHR on sharing enables a virtual physician-patient interaction and is in a way, the easiest form of telehealth.[b]

Images and sound require usage of simple devices like camera and microphone. However, newer advanced devices can extend the scope of telecare as they can read and process information far beyond what the human body is capable of. Examples include GPS; implantable sensors; swallowable miniature cameras, which can see inside the body; and, not to forget, artificial intelligence, which does the information processing at electronic speeds.

Such methods are changing health diagnosis and care delivery and side by side enabling telecare. Once an entry is made, information can travel anywhere within nanoseconds, even before the patient comes back, say from the operating room (OR) or radiology department. Whether the patient is present in the next room or across the globe becomes irrelevant.

Following the prescription, there is a period of follow-up; reassessment; and change of plan as per need, with further advice/procedure. In chronic diseases, such processes continue on a long-term basis. Data availability through the EHR allows remote care to become as good as physical care.

We need to remember, however, that virtual interaction is slightly deficient when compared with the physical one, as procedures and more importantly, somewhat essential components of a physical examination like palpation and smell cannot be done remotely. These limitations are getting obviated through newer sensors and robotics.

The consultant's time is the most expensive element of a physician-patient interaction. To save time, many practices ask residents or sometimes patients themselves, to fill forms. This can be done remotely and also the direct questioning. Such forms can be provided beforehand for a type of store and forward interaction. On-screen forms are not only faster to work with, but with incorporation in an EMR, searchability is

---

[b]More details of the components of EHR are in Chapter 3.

immediate and better. Templates, drop-down lists, CDSS, and other forms of automation, like highlighting relevant answers or reports, are standard components of an EHR.

Telecare is easier for revisits and follow-up, hence highly recommended. Imagine going on a daily basis for reporting on your urine output or blood sugar when all it may need is a small or maybe no change in medication. Secondary uses of information entered are easy to incorporate in a telehealth-enabled environment. These include analytics, public health strategy, and also remote medical education through video conference and web streaming.

EHRs have made a team approach easier but have made healthcare more complicated.[16] The best storage for an EHR is cloud[c] based, but here, constant connectivity is essential. There are reasons beyond telehealth for the rationale behind EHRs and meaningful use. Examples include the clarity of printed reports (see Box 1), CDSS, AI[c], prevention of drug

---

BOX 1

Computerized prescriptions

The concluding section any of visit to the health provider is the advice which can be hand written or printed text. Advice generally constitutes a drug prescription, or suggestion for a procedure, but also may be an order for further investigations. There are many arguments favoring a printed prescription as against the famous doctors' scrawl. Previously the printing was through a typewriter, but now the same is done digitally. And digitization makes remote care easy. The same links can allow for the printing to be done remotely. They also allow for patient evaluation and follow up notes. Besides that, a digitally authenticated signature can also be stamped on it. In many countries, prescription are being directly sent to the pharmacy. It is also possible to provide summary guidelines or handouts, for example, a diet chart that the patient can view online or take a print. Advantages over physical handouts include the following:

A. The number of choices is relatively unlimited, so it can be individualized to very specific needs.

B. Further on the spot editing widens the choices even further.

C. There can be built-in error checking for drug-drug interactions as well as of glaringly incorrect advice, which are known components of ePrescriptions.

---

[c] Abbreviations used throughout this book are explained fully in the Glossary.

interactions, avoidance of repetitive investigations, and facilitation of a team approach, and this is what constitutes **eHealth**.

Common other examples of store and forward include patients asking for help through e-mail or WhatsApp, which are, however, frowned upon by telehealth experts, mainly for security and privacy concerns.

Another method of classifying telehealth is by defining the partners and the direction of the flow of information. These **Telehealth Streams** are hereby listed as follows:

- **Between patient and provider.** Phone calls, emails along with text, or multimedia messaging services are used to explain the problem at hand and request for an appointment at the first instance and later to review investigation reports, assess progress, and provide online prescriptions. Social media and commercial tools like Skype as well as a range of ready-to-use apps have made this stream very diverse.
- **Between providers of different levels**. If patients are considered as tier 0, healthcare delivery is classified under primary care (GP, tier 1), secondary (specialist, tier 2), or tertiary (super specialist, tier 3) with costs escalating with each rise in level. Tier 1 may even be provided at the subprimary level, meaning the nurse practitioner. In this stream, interactions take place between tiers for assistance in diagnosis and for management of emergencies. Information flow is more focused and better directed as compared with the previous stream. A complete history may be provided, and also a more detailed examination conducted by the remote practitioners. While procedures and advanced care is done at higher centers, follow-up like stitch removal, dressings, or prescriptions for pain is again relegated to the remote caregivers. This is the most important form of telehealth. Boxes 2 and 3 are two representative examples.

BOX 2

Telemental health after the tsunami in India

Village-level counselling was provided from Chennai for patients with PTSD following the 2004 tsunami in India.[429] Village-level volunteers were trained to identify symptoms of PTSD; such patients were collected and asked to remotely consult the psychiatrist sitting in their hospital at an appointed time. Two suicides had been prevented from just one location, where the evaluation took place. *Read more on this in the subchapters on telepsychiatry (Chapter 10) as well as telemedicine in disasters (Chapter 11).*

BOX 3

Teleophthalmology example

In Mizoram, India, a hilly state, with poor roads, eye problems especially cataracts are common. Eye surgeons are found only in towns which are at a 6–12 h driving distance, the latter meaning an overnight halt generally with a relative accompanying. A cataract surgery would mean an average of five such trips, some for preoperative assessment. Reasons for wasted trips included "this is not cataract," "surgery not recommended at this stage," "diabetes control required," "the list is full for the next 2 days," and "doctor has gone on leave." In the teleophthalmology project run by SATHI,[147] trained ophthalmic assistants did preoperative workup, fixed appointments so that there is only one visit required for the day of surgery, and also performed postop care like stitch removal and glasses. Instead of five average trips for, say, a cataract, only one was required—that is, for the actual surgery, saving 80% of travel costs.

- **Between providers of the same level.** Formal tele-education is through online CMEs, meetings and webinars. Medical schools with less than ideal number of faculty can benefit from classes held elsewhere.[17] Most conferences these days have a remote speaker and remote delegate component. Many a time, one may be confronted with an atypical case or need help for a complication from a more experienced colleague. Online discussion forums like plastic_surgery@yahogroups.com and bulletin boards are a more informal set. There has been a recent flood of groups operating on WhatsApp, Telegram, and other mobile platforms.
- **Within an enterprise.** An example is cardiac hospital chains, wherein angiograms are done in a set of peripheral franchises, and then patients are referred for surgery to the higher center. Follow-up care is again local with unified billing and care administration.
- **For public health purposes.** Data collection and analytics; discussions within the team for health administration; online meetings; healthcare system integration; assessment of need for support in emergencies; inventory management to ensure the flow of essential supplies; etc.
- **Home healthcare**. The patient stays at home mostly with ICT-based monitoring with or without involvement of medical personnel. Home Healthcare is being used extensively in developed countries for care of the aged and infirm.[d]

---

[d]There is a section on this in the last chapter.

Telehealth allows multiple, different disciplines to merge and deliver a much more uniform level of care using the efficiency and accessibility of everyday technology. Increasing usage of telehealth challenges the notions of traditional healthcare delivery, and different populations are starting to experience better quality, access, and personalized care in their lives.

Classification based on connectivity. It is mentioned only in passing. During the early days the connectivity option used to be a major decider of projects, for example, the data sent by phone, SMS, or satellite link. Omnipresence of the broadband Internet as well as 4G and 5G has overcome these barriers. Such issues still predominate in some areas of the developing world.

Classification based on specialty. While there is a complete chapter devoted to it, it would be easy to understand that those specialities that use images as an important component were among the earlier ones to adapt to telecare. An abbreviated list of the top departments or services, which have benefited from telehealth, is provided in Table 1.

The rationale behind telehealth (why)

Telehealth systems and processes provide benefits for a range of stakeholders, although many may not be aware of it. There are issues also, that constitute a *Why not.*

For the patient. Faster, efficient, and cheaper care delivery without the constraints of time and distance. Travel costs are decreased. One must remember that this is required both for the patient and the accompanying relatives, who not only have to take the day off from work but also pay for the stay in hotels. Much of such stay before the procedure can be wasteful, for example, delay in appointment for a particular test or simple issues like *specialist is on leave* or *you have to come fasting*. Since the workup is done jointly over time with the help of the referring doctor, there is less chance of preprocedure tests being missed. Postprocedure care is also done locally. Outcomes improve—no wonder 76% of U.S. citizens elect telecare over a physical visit.[5]

For nurse practitioners and GPs. Medical knowledge today is not humanly manageable. Being a GP is one of the most difficult jobs as one never knows what the next patient will have. ICT not only provides access to written knowledge but also creates instant referral to a particular specialist. Hence, GPs and nurse practitioners can cater to a wider range of problems and better satisfy health needs within their local community leading to an expansion of clientele, who are more confident about the GPs capability. Results improve as one learns, even while the patients are jointly managed.

Specialists. One neurologist for around 200,000 population in the United Kingdom[18] is considered less than ideal. However, many

TABLE 1 Departments which can benefit from telecare.

Service	Important components	Role
Wound care	Unless very serious, wounds should be managed at the subprimary level. Requires transfer of images mostly. Sometimes telementoring and VC	Very high
Radiology	Images and video. Preexisting digitization and PACS make it easy. DICOM a specific standard	Very high
Dermatology	Images. Most problems are chronic, so decrease in frequency of visits is important	Very high
Cardiology	Tele-ECG, telestethoscope, and emergency support for MI	High
Ophthalmology	Images, which used to be taken through a slit lamp, an ophthalmoscope, and a fundoscope, can now be replaced by smart mobiles with special attachments	High
Psychiatry	Video conference and face-to-face contact for counseling	High
Pathology	Images and opinion. Special microscopes allow remote manipulation of the slide	Moderately high
Intensive care	Monitoring devices and emergency support	Moderately high
Emergency care	Allows care to begin as soon as a 911 call is made	Moderately high
Rehabilitation	Immobility of patients is a constant concern	Moderately low
Pediatrics	Emergency support and telemonitoring home-based care. A comfortable environment and access to parents is helpful for child development	Moderately low
Orthopedics	X-ray films. Home monitoring of splints and dressings. Emergency support	Low
Neurology	Tele-ICUs with robotic assistants and home care	Low
Plastic surgery	For preop assessment, planning, and also follow-up care (See example in Box 4)	Low

specialists do not manage to find adequate work because patients are unable to reach them because of time or distance. Many specialists cover different hospitals on different days with much time wasted in traveling. Referrals done through the ePlatform are faster and easier with a high patient satisfaction rate. Cardiologists and neurologists can cover a range of hospital CCUs and ICUs and control administration

---

BOX 4
———————

Example of Telecare in Plastic Surgery

For a felt need, a patient can consult a plastic surgeon directly online or through his GP.

Photographs are sent, and a complete preoperative assessment is done beforehand. A face-to-face meeting through VC is done to discuss the finer counselling points like what surgery is to be done, costs, postop care, and expected outcomes.

Travel is hence restricted to only for the date of the procedure, unless some further tests or evaluation is required. After surgery—generally done as a daycare—the patient comes back, and the GP does the stitch removal and minor dressings. Emergency management is done jointly with the plastic surgeon.

With such processes, cleft lip and palate surgery is being done by the thousands in Varanasi, India. A short documentary of this clinic (*Smile Pinki*) was awarded an Oscar in 2008.[575]

---

of streptokinase for MI and stroke,[19] respectively, even while staying at home. Patients do go window shopping for specialists, but they are more likely to freeze the decision after contact is established in any way. Specialists also need to refer their patients to other specialists, for example, a diabetic person with a stroke would need an endocrinologist and many a times an eye surgeon, a nephrologist, a vascular surgeon for diabetic foot, etc.

Telemedicine can be further classified according to the **care process**—whether it is for consultation/monitoring/appointment provision or simple data collection.

In summary, the advantages of telehealth can be listed as per the U.S. Government Accountability Office, 2017:

- increases access to specialized and timely urgent care,
- increases the capacity and efficiency of specialists,
- reduces wait times for appointments and follow-up visits,
- reduces emergency department visits and the time patients spend in hospitals,
- reduces the discomfort and anxiety associated with patients traveling to receive services,
- reduces the costs and carbon emissions associated with patient travel,
- connects care teams to provide greater continuity of care,

- connects remote family members with long-stay patients,
- connects healthcare professionals for knowledge sharing,
- integrates with conventional care delivery models,
- keeps patients in their homes and communities longer.

Some issues

Clinicians remain relatively averse to telecare as compared with patients. These issues are discussed in Table 2, as well in Chapter 9.

The process (how)

While processes employed for telecare are detailed in the rest of the book, a sample flow chart is provided in Fig. 2 on how a telecare provider can do the coordination. The telecare administrator can be the health-care provider himself, an outsourced agency, or directly operated by the government or insurance provider.

Another example of utilizing S&F is a simple creation of an EHR as described previously:

- All medical records stored in the form of an EHR. This would include the basic demography in the form of *name, age, gender, social and economic factors, and geography* along with summary of complaints, history, diagnosis and progress, and relevant reports sorted according importance.
- On need for opinion, patients' record with all images and reports is transmitted. A tentative diagnosis and reason for referral needs to be provided in addition to the preceding text. It is important that relevant reports be highlighted, with, if possible, markings of the area of concern in an X-ray. A small note on the immediate problem for which

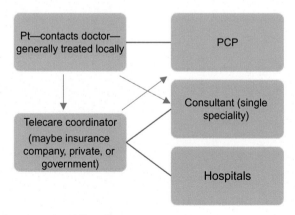

FIG. 2 A simple onine referral flow chart.

TABLE 2 Issues linked with Telecare.

	Type	Problem	Explanation	Possible solution	Serious?
1	Clinical	Care provision with less than ideal information or misinformation	Examination and procedures not possible	Knowing the limits and stating them upfront. Clinical decision support using adaptive learning methods; ICT should not override the clinicians	Yes
2	Administrative	Cross-border care (multijurisdictional)	Licensing rules may restrict care provision across borders of various countries and, sometimes, states	Governance and cooperation	No
3	Administrative	Care provision by relatively less or untrained persons	It is always difficult to know whether the supposed care provider is a fraud or hack Sometimes, family members are asked to answer a query	Ensuring guidelines ("Map of Med" for telehealth)	Yes
4	Technical	Lack of emergency support and retrieval care	Inadequate connectivity or broken links to the requisite support team	High bandwidth connectivity; systems interoperability	Yes
5	Administrative	Diversion of funding from more deserving immediate problems (and lack of funding through conventional mechanisms)	Telehealth systems have been promoted as a technology answer to each and every problem (a major reason for failures)	Health economics and cost-benefit analyses; public-private funding models	No
6	Administrative/ technical	Bias toward "best-connected" demographic (including developing world)	Telehealth was supposed to decrease the rich-poor gap allowing developing countries to leap frog. It has not happened	Scalable solutions; platform independence of services; better penetration of connectivity	Maybe
7	Clinical	Unusability of patient remote monitoring information (including adverse events) especially on software upgrade	High-end systems do fail. A system for local maintenance and availability of trained persons is a constant need	Automated customized personal surveillance systems; enthusiasts and promoters; help and support on version change	Yes

8	Technical	Noninteroperability of monitoring devices/sensors	As above	Standards and open systems	No
9	Technical	User acceptability of new telehealth technology (games, avatars, and immersion). Intrusive—asking for too many passwords	The best of systems fail because of human factors. An unused technology or system is literally useless	Participatory design; interventions targeting youth; training; proper reimbursements	No
10	Clinical	Services established outside ordinary protocols; weak links to EHRs	Occurs whenever change management principles are ignored	Include the service into the traditional healthcare system and EHRs (if available)	No
11	Personnel	Loss of interpersonal relationships due to wrong words and misinterpretation	Miscommunication and misinformation are common, for example, autotyping leading to wrong words	Rechecks; a general slowdown; Guidelines	Yes
12	Personnel	Loss of respect for timelines	Calls for help on a 24/7 basis—sometimes the care seeker is in a different time zone	Strict appointment system; guidelines	Yes
13	General	No clear method of reimbursement. Care access through unconventional means competing with regular channels	Insurance companies do not reimburse the travel and time cost. In India, telehealth has had higher success rate as healthcare expenses are out of pocket	Creation of telehealth-related care and reimbursement protocols; engagement of insurance companies	Yes

Adapted from Gogia SB, Maeder A, Mars M, Hartvigsen G, Basu A, Abbott P. Unintended consequences of tele health, and their possible solutions. Contribution of the IMIA Working Group on telehealth. Yearb Med Inform. 2016;(1):41–46. doi:10.15265/IY-2016-012.

I. Telecare basics

the opinion was sort will ensure satisfaction and shorter visit time—consultants' time being the most expensive component of any consult. If a cloud-based EHR is being utilized access to the patients record to the specialist may be the only step required.

- Specialist reviews the data either before or on appointed time.
- History and clinical examination done online, which could be in the form of direct questioning or whatever, are examinations possible online, for example, finger movements for suspected tendon injury. Alternatively the PCP or coordinator is asked to do some tests like BP, pulse, and pinch sensation. Further tests are in the form of repeat or additional investigations, pictures or X-rays.
- The last step by the online consultant could be in the form of
  - provision of an online prescription,
  - referring doctor informed on what to do,
  - patient asked to come for procedure,
  - patient given next appointment, which could be physical or online,
  - explain next steps, anticipated problems as well as means of transfer.

The clinician may initiate steps in anticipation like the OR made ready for urgent procedure even before the patient arrives.

Telehealth services are reshaping healthcare

Gunnar Hartvigsen

According to the American medical doctor Eric Topol,[21] we are facing a transformation from today's medicine, which he describes as old and dumbed down to a new, personalized medicine that is facilitated by digitizing humans. What we see, he explains, is a super convergence of wireless sensors, genomics, medical imaging, information systems, mobile connectivity, Internet, social networking, and computational power. Through a creative deconstruction of "old medicine," a new form of medicine will be established.

One of the areas this transformation is happening is telehealth. For several decades, telehealth has become important but still remains a small-scale health service and technology. This is about to change with the use of all kinds of telehealth services that are "coming to your home." New technologies are reintroducing a digital version of the house calls where people are taken care of at their bedside. We are in the middle of a telehealth revolution in which ICT, medical devices, sensor systems, and new telehealth services are reshaping parts of healthcare. According to Bruce Judson (2017), this development is driven by several factors[22]:

1. Health authorities' approval of remote diagnostic tools, in particular the U.S. FDA.

2. The advancement of different telehealth platforms for managing chronic conditions and achieving specific patient outcomes.
3. The development of different telehealth services offered by private and public healthcare organizations and systems.
4. Innovative direct-to-consumer initiatives by Samsung, Apple, American Well, and others.
5. Do-it-yourself (DIY) initiatives that force healthcare institutions and industry to change their business models and open up their devises and systems.
6. Social media and cloud-based solutions have moved healthcare initiatives from healthcare professionals to patients and relatives.
7. Standardization enables exchange of health data between all stakeholders in healthcare.

Health authorities' approval of remote diagnostic tools has been very important for the advancement of telehealth services.[22] In many countries, healthcare organizations and services are not allowed to use nonapproved diagnostic tools. Healthcare Information and Management Systems Societies (HIMSS) reported that 36 connected health apps and devices had received clearance from the U.S. Food and Drug Administration in 2016.[23] This number will rise to 51 next year.[24] Examples of the approved devices include VivaLnk's Fever Scout, which is a peel-and-stick continuous thermometer for children; Shenzhen Kingyield's Bluetooth-connected wrist-worn blood pressure monitor that sends data to a smartphone for archiving or evaluation; and CareTaker's extended wrist-worn (including a finger cuff) continuously connected blood pressure and heart rate sensor. The data is sent to an Android phone or tablet or directly to a hospital via cellular networks. An interesting functionality is the device's ability to operate as a wearable hub for recording and displaying. In this way, data from other devices like weight scales, glucometers, thermometers, and spirometers can be displayed on the tablet.

The advancement of different telehealth platforms for managing chronic conditions and achieving specific patient outcomes are important for the advancement of telehealth.[22] An example of a telehealth platform is TytoCare's ecosystem of connected tools for remote medical examinations. TytoCare provides complete virtual visit, including physical exam. TytoCare Home includes otoscope (ears), stethoscope (heart, lung, and abdomen), basal thermometer, and digital camera (skin and throat). According to the company, TytoCare enables doctors to remotely diagnose conditions such as ear infections, flu, upper respiratory infections, sinus infections, pink eye, rashes, bug bites, wounds, sore throat, and pneumonia more accurately.[25] With TytoCare and similar devices, people with chronic conditions can monitor their health status from their own homes.

Side to side, working at the clinicians' end are Web-based programs like IBM's Watson and UpToDate by Wolters Kluwer, which have CDSS as well as inbuilt search engines to help make a diagnosis, be it for a patient they are seeing or remotely.

There are many different telehealth service systems on offer by private and public healthcare organizations.[22] One example is doctor on demand. It offers a mobile app providing access to doctors, psychologists, and other healthcare providers. The company was cofounded by Phillip McGraw and allows patients to video chat with doctors instead of physically visiting them. High in the complexity scale, we find Mercy Health Virtual Care Center in St. Louis, Montana, which is the world's first large hospital without any patients. Mercy Virtual Care Center hosts 330 specialized medical professionals and zero patients. Through the use of high-resolution two-way cameras, online-enabled instruments, and real-time monitoring of vital signs, Mercy's medical professionals can visit their patients regardless of being in one of Mercy's traditional hospitals or a physician office or even in the patient's home. Mercy's telehealth programs includes **Mercy SafeWatch** (doctors and nurses monitor patients' vital signs and provide a second set of eyes to bedside caregivers in 30 ICUs across five states), **Telestroke** (patients with symptoms of a stroke who come to one of the 30 emergency departments [EDs] without a neurologist present can be seen immediately by a neurologist via a two-way audio and video connection), **Virtual Hospitalists** (a team of doctors is dedicated to seeing patients within the hospital 24/7 using virtual care technology), and **Home Monitoring** (Mercy provides continuous monitoring for more than 3800 patients, intervening quickly when needed). On the other end of the complexity scale, we find telehealth services based on technology like text-based SMS and standard smartphone photo and video services, presented, for example, by the WHO.[26]

Another factor for the development of telehealth services is the innovative direct-to-consumer initiatives by Samsung, Apple, American Well, and others.[22] Together with American Well, Samsung's Ask an Expert (AAE) offers users to connect, via video, to contact of the 1200 board-certified licensed physicians. American Well presents their service as a connected healthcare ecosystem. In addition to the telehealth features, both Android- and iOS-based smartphones offer a lot of health, fitness, lifestyle, and food/nutrition services. American Well provides complete telehealth service to connect patients and doctors via video-based applications. The company was, in 2015, the first to be accredited by the American Telemedicine Association for online patient consultations.

The fifth contributor to the telehealth revolution is the do-it-yourself (DIY) initiatives that force healthcare institutions and industry to change their business models and open up their devises and systems. One of the initiatives is the Nightscout project, which "is an open source, *DIY* project that allows real time access to a CGM [continuous glucose monitoring] data via personal website, smartwatch viewers, or apps and widgets available for smartphones."[27] Many of the diabetes DIY projects use the hashtag #WeAreNotWaiting to present what they are discussing or developing, including platforms, apps and cloud-based solutions. Some of the groups have reverse engineered existing products to get access to proprietary data formats. In this way, they have been able to develop new solutions for the users, for example, to make blood glucose data from CGMs available for everyone and not only for the CGM user.

The next contributor is social media and cloud-based solutions, which have moved healthcare initiatives from healthcare professionals to patients and relatives. One of the most known services is PatientsLikeMe.[28] With more than 600,000 members, living with more than 2800 conditions, people with chronic health conditions can get together and share their experiences living with their disease. The company was founded in 2004. In its new initiative, DigitalMe, a "virtual you" for each patient is created by combining multiple sources of health data, including biological, experimental, medical, and environmental data. The company states that: "There's a small chance that what you contribute may help you directly, but we will continue to learn from each other along the way. The goal is to advance what is known about disease, health and aging, and continue building a health learning system that can give people a better quality of life for longer." In 2017 the U.S. business magazine Fast Company appointed PatientsLikeMe as one of the top 10 most innovative companies in biotech. In the other end of the complexity scale are different patient organizations and interest groups' use of Facebook to connect with their users.

A crucial factor for the realization of telehealth is the use of standards—standardization enables exchange of health data between all stakeholders in healthcare. When Norway, for example, in the beginning of the 1990s developed teleradiology in its northern areas, the first obstacle was to convince vendors involved in the service to implement a larger portion of the DICOM standard for medical images.[13] The problem with standards is that there are a lot of them. In some areas, however, we see a convergence of standards. In the exchange of health data, Health Level 7 (HL7) has become the dominant standard for the exchange of health data. Health Level 7 (HL7) International is "a not-for-profit, ANSI-accredited standards developing organization dedicated to providing a comprehensive framework and related standards for the exchange, integration, sharing, and retrieval of electronic health information that supports clinical practice and the management, delivery and evaluation of health services."[29]

The list of factors for the development of telehealth services is not complete, but the factors earlier are among the most important factors.

What is undoubtedly important for this development is that technology is playing a vital role in healthcare disruptions in general. One example is the alliance between Amazon, Berkshire Hathaway, and JPMorgan who are looking for new ways of organizing healthcare for the employees. One of the ideas they are discussing is to make an online healthcare dashboard that based on the condition they chose from a drop-down menu will connect their employees with the best doctor in that particular field.[13]

Management of patient healthcare information
Healthcare-related information flow, access, and availability

Pramod David Jacob
dWise Healthcare IT Solutions, Bangalore, India

Introduction

Treating a patient, especially one who has a chronic condition like hypertension, requires multiple consults. During each consult, it is important to have constant availability of the relevant healthcare information regarding the patient's condition, past results, past interventions, and treatment(s) undertaken.[30] If this information, termed as a longitudinal health record (LHR) of the patient, is made available, the continuity of care and records of effective and some ineffective interventions will contribute to better outcomes, compared with treating the patient on basis of information gleaned from the current single or a few visits to the same provider. To ensure availability of such relevant information during the consult, harnessing of Healthcare Information Technology (HIT) is essential, as compilation and access to the patient's longitudinal health record cannot be effectively achieved with paper medical records. This becomes even more challenging when the patient moves from one health facility to another. This is equally applicable for face-to-face consults as to telehealth-based remote consults.

Furthermore, if multiple clinicians from different geographical locations are required to simultaneously discuss, evaluate, and plan the care of the patient, all of them will ideally need access to this patient's record, which again would be possible only if the information is digital.

Seamless continuity of care is important also in chronic diseases,[31] like hypertension and diabetes wherein the provider himself may need to be changed or become temporarily unavailable due to leave, illness, retirement, and so on. Easy availability of information is even more challenging during remote consults, and the remote provider is unlikely to be a constant care provider for any patient.

To enable such transitions an ecosystem needs to be present, which allows transfer of patient-centric healthcare information to the new provider. Depending on patients to carry paper medical records, test results, images, prescriptions and other healthcare documents, is cumbersome not only to carry, but also for viewing by the new provider. The patient might consider bills to be important, but going through them is painful for the clinician. An ecosystem of maintaining a long-term health record can only be provided using HIT and electronic health records (EHR). Here the design is such that information irrelevant for the clinician like bills is easy to ignore.

The most effective and efficient healthcare programs are believed to be in the developed world especially Scandinavia, the United Kingdom, and Canada. The underlying paradigm of success in these countries is the effective deployment of primary care being the gateway of healthcare for their citizens. Patients' first point of contact and principal healthcare provider is their primary care provider or PCP. Most healthcare problems are handled at the PCP level including controlling chronic conditions such as hypertension and diabetes. Only patients beyond the control of the PCP are referred further to secondary and tertiary care. Hence the major flow of healthcare information about a given patient, such as a summary statement, patient's longitudinal health record, and referrals, flows from the primary to the secondary to the tertiary levels (Fig. 1). Of course, there is some reverse flow that is from tertiary to secondary and directly to primary care. Examples include discharge summaries and responses/recommendations to referrals. Here again, having a digital pathway for flow of information is more effective than paper. Having this digital pathway is the reason why the aforementioned countries have a very effective primary care HIT/EHR system, and this system is used by most of their primary care providers. Examples are GPICT in the United Kingdom and the Canada Health Infoway systems.[32]

Definitions of EMR and EHR

Electronic medical record (EMR): An electronic record of healthcare information of an individual that is created, gathered, managed, and consulted by authorized clinicians and staff within one healthcare organization.

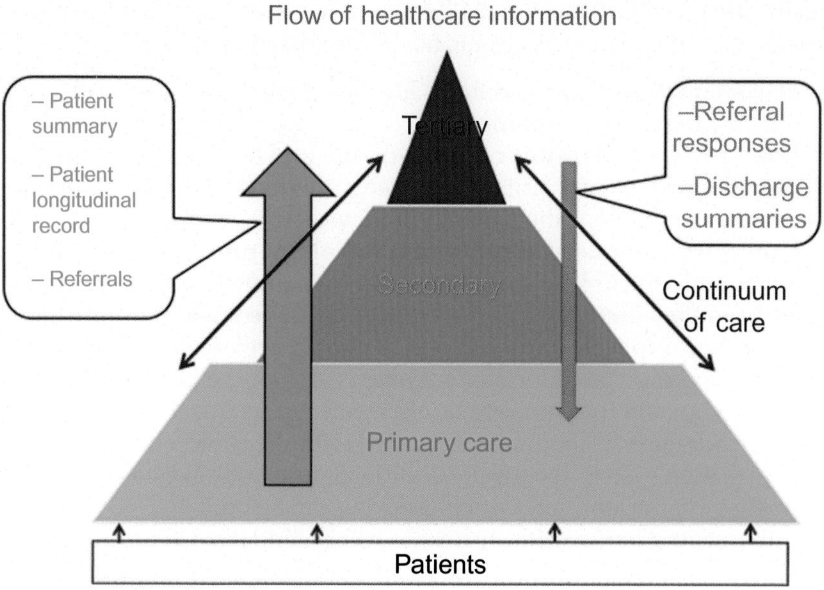

Flow of healthcare information

FIG. 1   Flow of healthcare information for continuity of care.

Electronic health record (EHR): An electronic record of healthcare information of an individual that conforms to recommended interoperability standards for HIT and that are created, managed, and consulted by authorized clinicians and staff across multiple healthcare organizations. It represents the concept of a longitudinal health record of the individual.

Basically an EHR collates multiple EMRs across multiple healthcare organizations into a single comprehensive longitudinal or lifetime record for an individual patient. For this to materialize, multiple EMRs need to be capable of exchanging data with each other, a term called *interoperability*. Interoperability is obtained through following certain standardized coding. Examples include ICD-10 for diagnosis, LOINC for lab results, and HL7 for messaging. These are detailed in a subsequent chapter.

Features and functionalities of the EHR

Ambulatory or outpatient EHR

When we say an OPD clinic is paperless, besides replacing paper medical records, the EHR also replaces hand-filled lab forms and prescriptions. The functions of ordering tests and medication are also done electronically. Therefore, from the perspective of the doctors, nurses, and healthcare providers, the OP EHR needs to have the following features to function as an effective electronic healthcare delivery system:

- **Documentation of clinical notes** like history and exam generally done by the doctor/provider.
- **Chart review and results review**—this feature lets the doctor or care provider review past visits by a patient, previous results of lab tests, and the medications the patient is and was on.
- **Orders for laboratory, medications, radiology, procedures,** etc. These are put into the EHR and electronically transmitted to the respective areas where billing and the service will be carried out. The software checks for duplicate orders. The EHR should preferably be interfaced with the clinic's lab information system (LIS) for the lab orders to go through and the results to be electronically sent back against the order. Similarly, it should be interfaced with the clinic's pharmacy information system too, where additional functions like correct drug dosage, timing, and interaction checking can be built in.
- **A messaging or emailing system** to receive and send messages like abnormal test results and referrals and to communicate via email with other members of the provider team to follow up on a patient's care.
- The EHR should be well integrated with the clinic **administration** system to automate many back-office processes, for example, triggering of a charge for a clinic visit in the billing system, after the doctor closes an encounter in the EHR.
- Basic information about the patient, which starts with **demography**, and features of history and examination, investigations and diagnosis, procedures planned and executed, prescriptions, progress reports, and a possibility of **automatic creation of summary** overall review of the presenting problem and current status at all times.
- **Setting up of clinical protocols and templates,** for example, the protocol for pneumonia. This helps in standardizing interventions and treatments using evidence-based medicine (EBM) for best practice.
- **Alerts and clinical decision support** (CDS) features can be set up that helps in checking for errors and improving patient safety, for example, do penicillin sensitivity test before prescribing penicillin injections.

Inpatient EHR

In a very broad sense, an inpatient visit starts from admission, goes through treatment and procedures, and ends with discharge. This sequence is termed as an "inpatient episode."

Important features of an Inpatient EHR

1. **Chart and results** review—as described earlier.

2. **Clinical documentation**—for clinical notes like progress notes and nursing notes. It is more complex and comprehensive than the OP EHR, with features like data input flow sheets into which data like pulse rate, BP, and temperature can be put in at specified intervals. There is significantly more nursing and ancillary staff documentation in the inpatient environment.

3. **Computerized provider order entry (CPOE)**—for putting in orders for labs, medications, procedures, etc. For inpatient care, it has to be more real time and robust than in the OPD. There is a need to handle many more types of orders like IV drips with rate of administration, dietary orders, physiotherapy orders, with details of repeat orders and their results.

4. **Electronic medication administration record (eMAR)**—This is a function that logs the administration of medications electronically (usually using bar code technology) or manually. It helps in reconciliation of administration of medication vis-a-vis the medication orders given for a patient in the CPOE system.

5. **Care plan**—nursing care plans function for planning of patient care, communicating patient care needs among the nursing and support teams, and documenting the changes in the patient's condition and the patient's response to all aspects of the treatment.

6. **Worklists**—this is a list generated for the nursing and support staff, informing them of the patients under their care and what is to be done as tasks and interventions for each of their patients, for example, prepare patient X in bed number Y for surgery at 9 a.m.

7. Messaging/email system—as described earlier.

8. Order sets, clinical protocols, and templates—setting up templates and order sets for standardized clinical protocols in the inpatient arena, for example, protocol for chest pain. This facilitates implementing of standard evidence-based guidelines for best practice across the healthcare organization.

9. Alerts and clinical decision support (CDS) can be set up that help in checking for errors and making correct clinical decisions, like dose adjustments for renal insufficiency. These features are very important for the inpatient EHR as they lead to significant reduction in medication and other errors and improve patient safety.

It is advisable to implement the various features of the inpatient EHR in stages, rather than trying to switch on all features in one go, like starting with clinical documentation and then progressing onto order entry (CPOE), then to care plan, and so on.

Application of EHRs in telehealth

Whether a healthcare provider is providing intervention to a patient in person or remotely, the same principles apply regarding the availability of the patient's past healthcare information, decision support features, and continuity of care with use of an electronic system being better. It is best if the telehealth system is integrated with an EHR system to provide the above. A sharable source of information that is constantly upgraded—exactly what constitutes an EHR—allows seamless telesupport.

The main modes of telecare were mentioned in the previous chapter. We exemplify further.

1. **Store and forward**—a classic scenario would be to chart out the process as is done in teleradiology. As an example, some hospitals in rural and semirural parts of the United States do not have an availability of radiologists to interpret images such as CT scans and MRIs especially during nonoffice hours. So, they have tie-ups with teleradiology companies like Teleradiology Solutions,[a] who have a panel of board certified radiologists on call in their offices in Bangalore, India (due to time difference between the United States and India—when it is night or nonoffice hours in the United States, it is daytime and office hours in India). Using the store and forward mode, these images are sent across to India via secure networks, where they are downloaded and studied; inferences drawn and the impression reported is sent back to the US hospital. This can be done within matter of minutes—depending on the priority and urgency. The inference sent back is then incorporated as part of the patient's record in the US hospital's EHR system.
2. **Real time**—during a remote consult, it is best if the healthcare provider providing the remote healthcare service is on an EHR system for the same reasons as mentioned for face-to-face consults. There are two approaches in providing EHR access of the concerned patient's record to the remote provider.
   a. **As a separate application** from the telehealth application. Here the provider must sign into the telehealth platform and separately into the EHR system for accessing the patient's record. This requires the provider having to toggle between two applications, not very efficient or in alignment to the clinical workflow of the provider.
   b. The preferred approach is to have the EHR system **integrated** within the telehealth platform. EHR integration with the telehealth system makes a better alignment of workflows and ensures continuity of care for the patient.

[a] See the section on teleradiology in Chapter 8.

An integrated telehealth-EHR system lets the healthcare provider consult solely within the telehealth platform. After signing into the integrated platform, the provider can see inbound or scheduled patient requests and patients in the "virtual waiting room." The provider first reviews the patient's medical record that has been pulled into the telehealth platform from the EHR system, to understand the patient's medical history and reason for the remote consult, then goes onto the video consult with the patient. During the remote consult the provider's notes are directly entered into the telehealth platform. Once the remote consult is complete and the provider has done the needed documentation and necessary recommendations, a visit summary is sent from the telehealth platform to the EHR system and incorporated into the patient's record in the EHR. Both systems communicate with one another through bidirectional integration, and the provider only needs to work within the telehealth platform, instead of toggling between the telehealth platform and the EHR system.

Data entry

Shashi Gogia

If we understand the DIKW,[b] we can understand that information or knowledge is based on data. In telehealth, data is transmitted and would have to have a certain origin from some source, either prior or immediate. Data has to come from somewhere, which means an initial interaction through an input device—though later it could be from a particular storage point (memory) which could be another computer, device, or the Internet. This would be a camera for images, a microphone for sound, and the monitor or related sensor for telemonitoring, but the most important input device of all remains to be the keyboard or keypad (on mobile) for text. Text is also the greatest unifier of all the data as the various images, sounds, or even sensor-generated information has to be contextual and easily searchable, which, at least as of now, is only through text.

Even while computer systems and connectivity are constantly following Moore's law,[c] the slowest link in the chain remains to be textual data entry. It slows down the day-to-day work and already has affected EHR adoption in the United States.[33] Typing is not easy. Clinicians are used to writing by hand or simply dictating through the Dictaphones, with secretaries typing out their letters. Spoken words are not a routine part of medical documentation. Even if they were, they would be a reason for further slowing down care processes. For those who do not understand this, they just need to time themselves in completing the reading of this page as against getting text-to-speech software to verbalize it.

[b] Explained in Chapter 1 and Glossary and the section on analytics.

[c] This is explained fully in Chapter 5.

It was expected that conversion of spoken words to text would have worked. It has not, though initially an entire new service industry was created called medical transcription. It still exists in the form of medical documentation for patients in the United States wherein data entry operators in various places within India and the Philippines convert the dictated words to written text so that it can be loaded into the HIS or used for insurance claims.

HIPAA and related higher security requirements affected telecare.[34] Medical transcription has somewhat been, but not completely, replaced by penetration of EHRs wherein data entry has to be immediate and concurrent, that is, most entries made directly by the clinician himself. Voice recognition software exists but is still not perfect, as medical terms are not so common. There are many methods added on hence, for faster entry of text. These are typeahead, auto correction, etc. but are equally likely to create mistakes.[d] Misinterpretation of what is written can lead to issues, and hence, there is a great need for standards.

Acquiring and utilizing nontextual data—images, sound, and more

Relevance and need for storing information beyond text as part of the medical record have increased over the years. Their role in making telecare easy has already been discussed. Paper-based medical records generally do have clip-ons of ECGs and X-rays that could be individual films or kept with the reports in an envelope. Sometimes, photos are also included. Storing them and maintaining the clarity over the years were a challenge. Even sound recordings like an audiogram were done through visual means.

As described previously, digitized information constitutes text, images, and sounds. These need to be stored as part of the EHR or care document. Capturing text is as simple as typing, though better done through a structured approach (see section on standards); we now explain how images and multimedia can be acquired and incorporated for efficient diagnosis.

Images

A picture is known to be worth a thousand words. But it is also possible to create a wrong picture, which in a literal sense would mean wrong words leading to misinformation and hence remain incomplete or become misleading. What can be incorrect?

A. **The picture itself**—that is, shooting the wrong lesion or from the wrong angle, poor focus, and lack of zoom. In a physical world or even during real-time transmission, there are chances to correct this. These are decreased once the image is stored into memory or seen asynchronously.

[d]These are discussed more in Chapter 4.

B. **Problems in storage and later searches**—pictures and any multimedia files can only be searched through text-based descriptive tags. If they are part of an EMR, then indexing gets automated by creation of linkages to the UHID. Linkage is done in two forms: (i) A link is provided to the server, that is, the filepath is stored, *or* (ii) the picture is stored directly in the database.

In option (i) a separate web-based media server is used to allow access at all times once anyone clicks on the link. The ability to read that particular file should be available at the remote end (see Table 1). Option (ii) obviates this problem as storage is in the same server but this makes the database more data heavy and affects speed of access of even unrelated text. Hence, (i) is preferred. The server privilege settings ensure the privacy—it can even ensure that the access is restricted to those who click on the link provided within the EHR that has been displayed—which is turn is encrypted, so that just copying

TABLE 1   Various imaging formats.

Type	Description	Explanation and remarks
JPEG (.jpg, .jpeg, and .jpe)	From Joint Photographic Experts Group	The most popular format of storage, web, or printing. Images are compressed and lossy to result in a relatively small-size file. JPEG 2000 is relatively lossless and has better image quality than DICOM. JPEG is not recommended for drawings, which are better done as TIFF (if layered), PNG, or bmp
RAW	Proprietary depending on camera	Most cameras record the image along with metadata like white balance, exposure setting, time, and date. Size increases in proportion to the number of pixels—hence terms like 16 Mpx. Converted to TIFF for editing or to JPG for storage and transfer. DNG is a nonproprietary generic form of RAW
TIFF (.tif)	Tagged Image File Format	Uncompressed and thus contain a lot of detailed image data with exactness, which can be edited like through Adobe Photoshop. TIFFs are also extremely flexible in terms of color and content (layers and image tags). Not suitable for web or transfer
GIF (.gif)	Graphics Interchange Format	Compresses images by limiting the color range but is lossless. Suitable for the web and/or for animations that are essentially many images with minor changes replacing each other in quick succession. Suitable for teaching but not teleconsults or prints
PNG (.png)	Portable Network Graphics	A replacement for GIF as that used to be proprietary but allows more color flexibility and equally recognized by all browsers hence used for the net. Can be extremely large sized. Not as editable as compared with TIFF but allows transparencies

the link and pasting to the browser will not allow access. Hence, only those who get access to a particular patients' record can view the same.

C. **Problems in transmission**—videos and some higher resolution images need high bandwidth. Hence, slow or absent connectivity, or a link to an incorrect source as well as mismatched standards will lead to error or loss of clarity. Correctable by ensuring connectivity standards.

But first, let us understand how image digitization occurs.

The eye recognizes an image through signal generation by the rods and cones in the retina caused by bouncing photons. Exact color identification is through calibrating the mixture of three basic colors—red, green, and blue (RGB). A photograph is similarly represented by a series of dots of various colors. Digital recording of an image is a two-dimensional (2D) placement of these dots, also called pixels. Image clarity depends on how fine the pixel is, that is, the higher the number of dots per square centimeter, the better the image quality. Each pixel is stored as a bit, and hence an image is also a bitmap. The color range of each pixel can vary from 0 (no color) to the requested finesse or classification of the color range—generally up to 255. Black, hence, carries a value of (0,0,0), that is, zero for all colors, and white would be (255,255,255). The exact color depends on the right mix; hence, (255,0,0) is all red. Grey would have the same value for all RGB colors, for example, (127,127,127). Additional data is required in black and white for brightness and contrast. While RGB works for HTML and in monitors, for printing, a separate combination called cyan, magenta, yellow, and black (CMYK) is preferred as these printing inks combine better, resulting in brighter output.

The TV monitor reads signals by popping of the electrons (pixels or dots) on a phosphor screen. The image quality simply depends on the total number of pixels created; hence, standard VGA (640×480) means exactly that, which is, 640 lines in a horizontal plane and 480 in the vertical plane = 307,200 pixels.

If we put the same number of pixels in a larger screen, individual dots become visible as squares—also called the pixelating of the image (Picture 1). Flat screen monitors use diodes with each diode behaving as a pixel. A high-definition TV (HDTV) would be 1920×1080, also called 1080p describing the number of vertical lines This number of lines need to rise further as the image size is increased. Currently, 4K (3820) and 8K, called ultrahigh definition (UHD), are normal, and even 16K is coming up.

Obviously the file size increases with the number of pixels, and hence, compression is used in transmission. Compression techniques use a combination of methods.

1. Decrease the size hence the number of pixels but that would mean to loss of clarity if and when the image needs to be enlarged again.

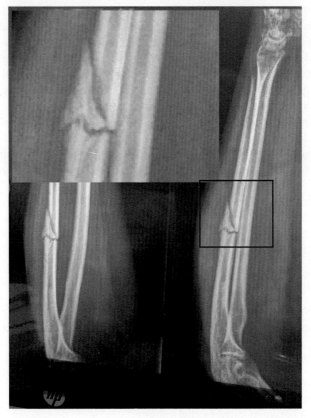

PICTURE 1   DICOM image and a small square enlarged to show how pixelation occurs.

2. Identify a single RGB value for areas with similar or flat composition like all black and map their X- and Y-values.
3. Tone down the color variation. For example, GIF images use a lower color range.
   Compression can be *lossy*, that is, there is some loss of clarity or *lossless*.
D. **Inability to interpret** correctly at the other end underlying a need for semantic standards. That is not much of a concern as there are many common and free to use standards like JPEG, PNG, and MP4.

DICOM is the standard format used to share radiology images and videos. It is necessarily lossless but fortunately is mostly black and white. Even the colors used, for example, in a Doppler scan, are very basic. Most digital X-ray machines, including CT and MR, have inbuilt DICOM software, which allows seamless information transfer of the image to any other location. A DICOM image will include many textual details, for example, name, gender age, image position, and many other characteristics in the image itself. Many of previous forms of DICOM used to be proprietary—that is, compression technique followed by one that could not be decompressed unless one had the original DICOM reader. Thus a clinician would be helpless to second advice the patient who brought a CD (compact disc) of his angiogram along. However now, open-source cross platform DICOM readers are available.

For transferring other images the form of compression used varies. Technical knowledge of file formats is important to understand how to save storage space and more importantly ensuring relatively lossless transfer, considering the available connectivity. Table 1 explains various formats.

In summary, quality is best maintained in RAW or TIFF, transfer by JPG (small size) or PNG, and finally net viewing by JPG, PNG, or GIF. If the other end does not have a proper viewer of the file, there will be an inability to view or interpret.

Recording images

Photographs help the initial diagnosis and management far more than the human eye as they can be stored lifelong and have different views, close-ups, etc. For correct interpretation, however, some basic standards are required. These include uniformity of the following:

- Position of the patient including background.
- Position and exposure settings of the camera.
- Distance between camera and subject.
- Ambient lighting (daylight gives the best photographs, but conditions vary between time of day and seasons).
- Other settings (e.g., direct flash not recommended for close-ups).
- Text within the frame—this helps in identifying the patient—name, UHID, date, etc.
- For quality, images are best transmitted as PNG or JPG.
- More details as necessary—for example, an ulcer can have a ruler or graph to measure size.[35,36] Special software which can measure size automatically as well as monitor progress is available.

Digitization of X-rays

Most modern radiology centers would have equipment wherein the image is created de novo in a digital format. That option may not exist in remote areas, or there may be times when the patient brings along an X-ray that needs to be transmitted. In such a case, this analog image has to be digitized. Unlike photographs or paper documents, X-rays cannot be scanned by a simple scanner not only because they are thick and may be

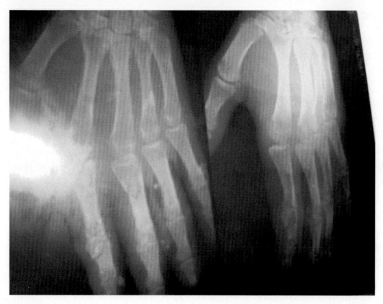

PICTURE 2   Photo taken against a standard viewbox causes a glare of the tubelight.

larger than the scanner but also because the images are transparent, which means they cannot be viewed using reflected light, only by being held up against a light.

Special X-ray scanners are expensive. A much simpler method is to simply place the film on a flat screen monitor, which is set to an all-white background (a modern X-ray viewer works exactly the same way) and click with a digital camera or even a smart mobile. A stand will ensure lack of movement blur. Remember that taking such a photograph using older tubelight-based viewers screens would cause a glare (Picture 2).

- Searching for stored photos, videos, and other multimedia is a difficult preposition. There has to be a method for linking an image to a patient. Storage within an EMR means direct linking, but just storing the filepath keeps the database size small. In the absence of an EMR, a special image software to index and correlate the images like ADS is recommended. Apps are available for usage in mobiles like Dicompass DICOM Camera http://www.dicompass. cz and DICOM-Shot for iOS. One must remember that sharing data that can identify the patient across the Internet is not allowed without adequate security or privileged access as per HIPAA rules. Special care needs to be exercised not to include the face within the photograph.

Sound

A stethoscope around the neck maybe the quintessential image of a doctor, but its actual usage is when it communicates sounds to the ear. These heart and breath sounds remain fleeting memories to be noted as text in the case sheet to help reach a diagnosis. Telehealth enables sound transfer as is, so that the clinician gets to use his own judgment in defining the normal and abnormal.

The telephone was the first telecare modality. It converted sound waves to electrical signals and back as and when required. Gramophone records and tapes were analog storage forms. Digitization converts the waveforms into sampling bits, that is, frequency and amplitudes are converted to a series of numbers against time. Raw digitization, used in CDs and DVDs (digital versatile disc), is called pulse code modulation (PCM) that is lossless but heavy, consuming roughly about 34 MB per minute for 24-bit 96 kHz stereo.

For transmission purposes, compression is the norm, and a wide variety of compressed audio file formats exist. Almost all decrease the file size but rarely affect quality, so it cannot be called lossy. As described for images earlier, all that the user needs to know is whether an appropriate file or signal reader exists at the other end. The older ones like WAV for Windows and AIFF for Mac are OS specific. These had little compression. The most commonly used today is Moving Pictures Expert Group version 3 (MPEG-3)—MP4 is for audio-video—see in the succeeding text. Another one is OGG that is not a format per se but allows seamless conversion in between, not only for audio but also for all forms of multimedia.

For proper interpretation, standardization of the recording process is important.

- The source (e.g., mouth of the person speaking) should be close to and also at a consistent distance from the microphone.
  - A collar mike ensures that head movements do not cause variation.
  - The hand piece like of a standard telephone ensures consistent distance, not so a flat-surfaced mobile.
  - Smart mobiles especially have a chance that your finger is inadvertently closing off the mike. Since the same is on one side, it is better held in the appropriate hand (see Fig. 2).

- The amount of background noise makes a difference. So, record in a closed room.
- For live transmission, if two-way sound is being used through the PC, like in a video conference, there are chances of the sound from the other end being retransmitted as an echo. Headphones avoid this. If they are not available, keep your side microphone muted till you wish to speak. (Noise canceling headphones only cancel noise reaching the ears, not the mike!) If the speaker is facing the mike, a shrieking noise (called feedback) erupts, which is essentially an endless cycle of the

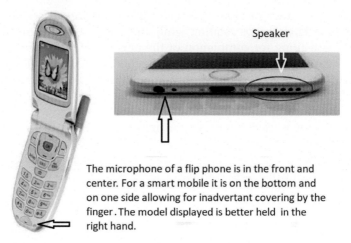

Speaker

The microphone of a flip phone is in the front and center. For a smart mobile it is on the bottom and on one side allowing for inadvertant covering by the finger. The model displayed is better held in the right hand.

FIG. 2 Flip phones have a microphone in the front, while that of a smart mobile is below—the latter can be inadvertently covered by the finger by mistake. Also since the microphone is on one side, holding the phone where the mouth is closer is important.

sound from the speaker reentering the mike and getting amplified. Mute the mike or local speaker immediately. A unidirectional mike helps but may cut off the sound on head turning.

EMRs allow for the preservation of sound recordings in a similar way to images, that is, as part of the database or linked files.

Video is multiple images or frames changing at a constant rate to give an impression of movement. Minimum is 7.5 Hz or frames per second. **Multimedia** is essentially a combination of sound and video. Video conferencing (VC) is two-way real-time multimedia. While the chapter on VC discusses more details of how to maintain VC quality, we discuss here the various formats and methods for recorded multimedia, which can be stored or linked to the EMR.

Sharing multimedia content is important for remote diagnosis. For example, functional status of the hand, gait, and eye movements are used for understanding a problem and planning surgery. Similarly, a plastic surgeon can assess the results of a dynamic muscle transfer and provide appropriate instructions to the therapist. Multimedia is also important for video-based learning. It is routinely used during presentations.

Live TV means the signals of each frame with accompanying audio signals are received, displayed, and destroyed. If the signal is lost or weak, a wavy pattern appears. Net-based transmission, for example, YouTube, uses a different method called streaming. Here the data comes in packets, which can be slower or faster than the required pixelization (read frame construction) rate. A set number of frames are stored in a temporary memory in the user device before display.

During the times of slow Internet, one can notice phases when the hourglass or circle keeps rotating while the image itself remains frozen. The app is waiting for completion of the next set of frames before it restarts. The wavy pattern is never seen. Another choice (called Torrent) is a complete download of the entire multimedia file and then viewing. It requires time before start but ensures uninterrupted viewing once and only when the download is completed.

Compression is used, but in general, multimedia files use lower quality than a standard image for each frame. Codecs (*coding-decoding*) are various digital audio-video compression and decompression formats used in transmission. The one most commonly used is H264.

Recording formats compress the individual frames in various ways and also have to ensure that the sound is in sync. The most well-known are MP4 and *Audio/Video Interface* (AVI). Software to transfer one file format to another exists. Remember that normal camera recordings are in raw format. These will never upload on the net. Video sharing apps like YouTube or conferencing ones like Livestream, Citrix, Webex, and Zoom do the conversion at their own end, and as long as one is working within the same app, viewing is without issue. For sharing your own videos, one has to ensure that the same is viewable by all browsers. The format should preferably be mentioned. The best format for web viewing is small web format (swf) also called Shockwave Flash by Adobe—special viewers compatible for all browsers and devices are easily downloadable.

Alerts and triggers

Kleber Soares de Araujo

Alerts and triggers in electronic health records are about providing the right information at the right time of decision-making. Why use an alert? Why use a reminder in an electronic medical record? These questions should be answered thoroughly before implementing any changes to your electronic health record and clinical decision support system. What are your objectives? Raising attention when there is a drug to drug interaction?[10, 11] Disease to drug interaction? An increase in the early warning score of a patient in the medical floor? A risk of a systemic inflammatory response from a patient with a urinary tract infection in the emergency room?

Keep in mind that introducing new reminders and alerts into your electronic health record should be part of a broader strategy to provide safer care, improve clinical outcomes, and/or enhance cost-effectiveness.[13]

So, first, check whether there is a real need for the inclusion of a new alert and identify which indicators or metrics might be impacted with its inclusion.[14] After assuring the need, look for the right timing. This is a critical step, and an experienced clinician might help you in identifying the exact moment a particular decision is made by the healthcare professional when assessing the patient. That is the proper time to offer help as an alert.

So how is this done? If you need to remind that there is a risk to the patient's health, one message in bold or in red might be enough. If you intend to induce her/him to record more details about a particular situation before he/she makes the decision, perhaps an alert with an electronic form might be the way. Remember that describing the source of the content and who was in charge during the order of the publication in the electronic health record tends to raise credibility from the clinical staff.

Patient S visits his primary care provider for his annual visit. After the provider welcomes the patient, he notices an alert on his screen. His patient is due for a colonoscopy. The provider clicks the alert for more information during the visit and finds that the alert was triggered due to the patients' age and family history. The provider discusses this with the patient and refers him for a colonoscopy.

Alerts are not created to curtail the freedom of the health professionals, but to promote an opportunity of learning and scientific updating in an issue that is a priority for the institution and that adherence to this good practice can positively impact the indicators being monitored by the area of interest.

A great challenge is the risk of alert fatigue,[15] that is, when the professional no longer pays attention to the alert. If alerts are showing obvious information out of the context, content or there are an excessive number of messages, professionals might override it. Setting up an alert committee with regular interactions can help monitor the results and continuously adapt the alert strategy. Put together the alert metrics, how many times it has been fired, how many times it has been complied versus refused, and what is the relationship between the expected action and actions other than expected.[16]

If necessary, adjust your alert, check whether the criteria for triggering them are correct, review, and update them.[17] Alerts can be a very effective way of communicating with your clinical staff but can also be a burden to their workload. Use it with caution.

Healthcare data analytics

Spriha Gogia

Medical knowledge has expanded greatly. Currently, information required for day-to-day care is more than what the human brain can store or process. In the United States a typical visit with a provider is 15 min long.[37] Within that time, they are expected to hear the patient's story, distill medically relevant information, complete the needed screens in the EHR, render potential diagnoses taking into account past medical history, and then discuss next steps or a treatment plan, all the while showing a human face to the patient. A GP has to manage a wider range of problems and see many more patients a day than any specialist. A specialist, defined as one *who knows more and more about less and less*, may get more time but that is still not enough considering the amount of extra counseling required. A televisit, even if not shorter, is more complicated as there are periods of data loss and inability to examine the patient fully.

Documentation is an essential component for care delivery in this day and age. They also make telecare simple and easy. But documentation is supposedly taking more and more time from patient care leading to resistance for widespread adoption of EHRs,[38] the very heart and soul of store and forward. However, there is a sound rationale behind usage of EHRs. Technology more than compensates for the extra effort. This chapter is devoted to a discussion on these benefits.

As discussed elsewhere, ICT systems have four progressive stages, namely, *Data → Information → Knowledge → Wisdom*. Telehealth primarily involves *sharing* health information. Data analytics involves knowledge and wisdom. Thus using data created for telehealth for public health purposes is an excellent value addition.

Patient K is HIV positive and has been on antiretroviral therapy for a few years. She has been complaining of bleeding for several months, but the cause for the bleeding has been hard to detect. After 3 months of fruitless investigations, her provider decides to run her case through a new software tool that analyzes all clinical notes in the EHR. The tool returns that the patient first complained of bleeding 6 months ago, which coincides with the time her ART medication was changed. The provider changes her medication again, and the patients' bleeding resolves.

Data creation and storage are maximum with EHRs—the most ideal telehealth system. If used appropriately, EHRs serve as repositories of large volumes of structured medical information.[39] Analytics helps make full use of this big data.[40] The examples of patients S and K in the accompanying boxes are stories of real patients whose treatment benefitted vastly from the use of analytics.

Some uses of data analytics are mentioned in the succeeding text.

Population and public health

Data analytics is an important tool in trying to understand the health needs of the patient population. A provider sees patients every day, yet it is hard for him to know how many of his panel have a specific condition or need. Analytics can serve to arrive at this information at the provider, hospital, city, county, or any other level as needed.

Analytics has an important role to play prior to the implementation of any new public health program.

What disease should be the focus? In which clinics/hospitals/locations? Which patients should be enrolled? What are the social needs of this population?

These are examples of questions that need answers when a new program is being considered.

A well-designed analytic project can answer such questions. Moreover, analytics of EHR data can also be used to track the progress of the program (program evaluation) and to assess its final impact.

At a higher level, health departments can benefit vastly from a well-connected EHR network. It helps identify disease outbreaks and other emergent health needs. The role of telehealth is especially important in this scenario as remote locations are often ignored in any such analysis, largely related to poor data collection and access to the same from these locations. On the other hand, telehealth reaches out to these very remote locations. The fact that data is entered for telesupport purposes means analytics provides value addition with no extra cost.

Data-driven decision-making

Analytics is the backbone of data-driven decision-making. For instance, analytics can be used to identify volumes and types of patients to identify the needs of the patient population so that resources can be allocated accordingly. Analyzing the visit times of patients would identify the busiest times of the day. Shifts of staff can then be adjusted to meet this demand. In a larger healthcare system, staff can be deployed to different locations on different days/times based on this analysis. This would serve the dual purpose of making care more patient centric as it would reduce wait times. In the case of telehealth, this can be even more useful as the same physician could serve areas that are geographically far apart.

Clinical decision support system

EHRs should be used to arrive at the patient's diagnosis and treatment plan. However, often, the chart of a patient with multiple conditions is so detailed that healthcare provider does not even have the time to review it in its entirety. This problem is further compounded when the patient has visited several providers for his care. A simple EHR will store all information; an intelligent one will highlight and show the important portions.

However, a warning is required here. What may be deemed as important for one user may be the reverse for another. A well-functioning clinical decision support system takes into account the patients' information and indicates the best course of action based on current guidelines. Thus analytics can serve to reduce the time needed by the provider to arrive at the treatment plan. However, for this to work, it is essential that the algorithms that run behind the CDSSs run as per current clinical judgment and guidelines. The reason why a certain course is recommended should be transparent (and NOT a black box). Furthermore, these need to be updated as guidelines and opinions change. These sticky points are often the reason behind mistrust in CDSS among physicians.

Data analytics in the context of telehealth

Analytics can be done most efficiently when data is available in a structured form. In telehealth, data is created and shared across vast distances. A properly implemented telehealth solution requires good documentation within the EHR.

Let us consider the case of specialized clinics using telehealth spread across a particular district, county, or state. We would like to know the number of patients being treated at these clinics and the specific problems that they are presenting for. Analytics would help provide an insight into disease prevalence and incidence. Specific measures can be initiated for prevention. The number and types of physicians, nurses and other workers, medical labs, and equipment can be allocated as per need. One example of a good use of analytics would be to create geomaps, that is, overlay geographic regions with the number of patients presenting and the kinds of conditions they are presenting for. This sort of analysis is especially important in resource-constrained areas where telehealth is an attempt to solve the problem of the lack of resources and medical facilities.

Example case

Merging analytics in a telehealth program

The SATHI project in Mizoram[147] was awarded for two reasons—(A) reducing costs of eye care for rural populations and (B) providing data on the prevalence of eye problems in these communities. Interestingly the primary reason the project got funds was (A) but had to face many roadblocks due to poor connectivity; hence, outcomes took time. However, (B) facilitated by sending data regularly by whatever connectivity that could be obtained—including a physical delivery of the USBs by courier had appreciable outcomes much earlier.

The importance of standardization[e]

Any analytic project is only as good as the data that is used. Standardization is extremely important in the context of analytics and has impacts on the quality of an analysis.[40] For instance, the results of an analysis using information entered by providers in the same hospital system who have access to two different screens with disparate drop-down lists would be poor. Healthcare professionals are often unaware or oblivious to the uses of the information entered by them in the EHR. As healthcare analytics becomes mainstream, this needs to change. While interconnectivity standards are important to allow data collection and a very basic need for telehealth, semantic standards like ICD and SNOMED have great role in analytics. Analytics also requires that data should be present and of good quality, that is, complete with accurate information. Targeted training of the staff for understanding the relevance and process of data entry in appropriate screens (as well as cross training for review and backup) is hence of considerable importance. Additional measures include the following:

- Regular training of staff—even when it is hard to achieve due to time constraints.
- Engagement and incentivize staff during lunch hours and recognition of superusers to encourage healthy competition.
- Request and incorporate feedback wherever possible.
- Cross training of staff to allow for sick and vacation time.
- Quick review should be built in to the workflow and results of analysis/report shared—with due acknowledgment of the staff entering data.

Analytics approaches

Filipe Santana da Silva and Spriha Gogia

The process of BI and analytics for healthcare is based on four tasks[131] (Fig. 3).

For analytics purposes, there are several approaches. Some that can be applied for the telehealth domain are

- Statistical modeling[579]
- Textual analytics[580]
- Predictive analytics[581]

[e]Standards are discussed in the next chapter.

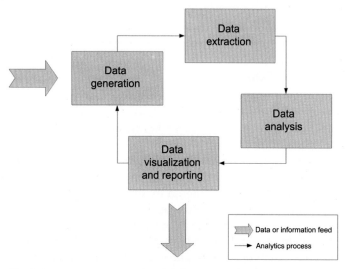

FIG. 3   The four main components of analytics are interrelated.

Even while these have been described earlier in this chapter, the last one needs a more detailed note. Predictive analytics are a set of methods that includes statistical models and empirical methods in order to create empirical predictions. It is important to note that predictive analytics contrasts with predictive theory, with the latter being dependent on a causal hypothesis.

For information systems, predictive analytics for information systems enables the generation of new theories, developing new measures, comparing competing theories, improving theories, assessing the relevance of theories, and assessing predictability of a given empirical phenomena.[581]

A practical example of predictive analytics would be the evaluation of the likelihood of a given user to request telehealth services. For instance, whether a user who had in the past requested a teleconsulting session is going to request the service again; or, whether the one who attended a tele-education webinar is going to participate again.

For creating predictive analysis, one needs to define a predictive model. Shmueli and Koppius[581] have described eight steps in order to create a predictive model, which are:

1. **Goal definition**, i.e., the accurate and careful definition on what needs to be predicted;
2. **Data collection and study design**, i.e., from where did the data come from and how is it going to be analyzed. In this phase, it is important to distinguish if the prediction will be made with observational or experimental data, and what instruments for data collection will be used (the preference should be of raw data). Other components

include sample definition, data dimension (all necessary variables taken into account, and hierarchical design with the consideration that having bigger groups are better than more analysis groups);

3. **Data preparation**, i.e., organization (remove null or missing values, for example) and identification of possible data subsets used for specific tasks, such as a training set, to evaluate performance or model selection;

4. **Exploratory data analysis (EDA)**, i.e., summarizing data to reduce their dimension. This can be performed in two ways, numerically or with the support of visualizations (such as graphs or tables);

5. **Choice of variables**, i.e., the user may choose the variables according to some possible constraints, such as data availability (if there are enough data to support prediction), predictive goal (if it is directly related to what is being measured) and measurement precision (if the indicator used is supposed to be extremely precise);

6. **Choice of potential methods**, i.e., strategies to be employed and ensure a reliable prediction outcome. There are data-driven algorithms (neural networks, classification trees, or the k-nearest neighbor), shrinkage methods (reducing variance, increasing prediction accuracy), or ensembles (several different models, reducing sample variance, to achieve the better possible prediction);

7. **Evaluation, validation, and model selection**, i.e., generating predictions with evaluation datasets, comparing training and evaluation sets indicators, and to find the balance between bias and variance (respectively); and,

8. **Model use and reporting**, i.e., whether the model is accurate and what do the results mean. Graphs and summaries are often used to report the outcome of predictive model as useful.

The applicability of predictive analytics for telehealth and telemedicine projects can be regarded as an important asset. Considering most data produced in telehealth projects is gathered with the support of diverse information systems, the available methods that seem suitable for the task are:

- Movement analytics[582]
- Pair analytics[583]

User-web analytics

Examples of predictive analytics are available in literature and can be extended in order to support telehealth services and projects. For instance, structured and unstructured data from EHR together with artificial intelligence approaches can be applied in order to identify disease outbreaks in disease-frequent communities.[584] Approaches of this type can be used in order to support identifying population vulnerabilities and address these in a timely manner.

Technology considerations

Gunnar Hartvigsen

University of Tromsø—The Arctic University of Norway, Tromso, Norway

Overview: Infrastructure requirement

Gunnar Hartvigsen

Patient's care requires healthcare professionals sharing information and interacting with each other in a coordinated way, such to provide an appropriate continuity of care, as decisions are made based on available information and knowledge. Indeed, healthcare is a communication industry,[41] and ICT is changing the way information and knowledge are retrieved, recorded, created, and managed, posing not only new opportunities but also new challenges.

Communication links are the key to creation of telesystems, but telehealth requires extra considerations. Here, medical data is obtained through a variety of sources. It has to be collected with ease, processed into information and knowledge, stored (if S&F), and then transferred as required to the right location. The target personnel have to have privileged access, and information should not wander into prying eyes. It is going to be used by clinicians, public health personnel, and patients for direct or indirect health support with each having their own sociocultural milieu and related preferences, choices, and comfort levels. Input could be manual or from body-mounted (wearables), stationary sensors and other devices that detect activity and state of residence. For such systems to succeed, there is a need for integration of patient data from these different sources. Following that, data and information has to be interpreted properly—a process called interoperability—and further discussed under the section on standards.

The following restrictions on deployment of telehealth may apply:

- **Ease of use**: The equipment/solutions must be simple to use.
- **Reliability**: The system must be stable and safe, run without interruptions, and provide reliable measured values.
- **Security**: Data security has to be safeguarded.
- **Availability**: There needs to be a responsive system at all times of need.

Hardware used for telecare is not much different from other computer systems, except that access to others through networking is mandatory. An add-on to the hardware could be additional devices, that is, probes and sensors that connect directly with patients or input seamless health-related data. Whenever present, these can add much to the cost not only for the probe but also for the requisite training. The exact value preposition they offer depends on how much these will be used. Tailoring will be required obviously, depending on local availability, not only of the initial cost of hardware, but also of maintenance, repair, and service. A good system will ensure backup methods and needs to allow a variety of choices especially of the nonfixed components like software and connectivity.

Connectivity just means communication or how various devices and systems talk to each other. Many forms exist, wired or wireless, and as stated earlier there is little or no difference between telehealth systems as compared to other computer systems. Most telehealth systems, though not all, do require high bandwidth. However, with rising data speed consequent to wider penetration of 3G/4G/5G and fiberoptic as well as wired broadband, lately, this has become less of a constraint.

Video conferencing may possibly be considered as a relatively essential component of any telecare platform, unless only indirect benefits are being sought.

Bringing it altogether is challenging

Telecare can and does take place without special equipment. For example, requirements for telecommunication-based supervision within a private home include diseases that do not require the permanent presence of health or life-critical monitoring equipment. Mostly, only a phone call, WhatsApp, or email is used. More savvy patients can sometimes use a video link using Skype and, increasingly, Facetime, other video callers, etc. These need a certain familiarity with not only the technology behind it but also the related security issues. Hence these are frowned up by clinicians and experts, who recommend specialized apps or equipment.

The specialized and high-end tools need deeper discussion. It is important that the communication, technical, and power infrastructure meets the necessary medical and security requirements. There is also the consideration that even if we can do monitoring for possible life-threatening problems, the same without an ability to correct the issue immediately will be a reason for frustration. More so if one remembers that there is an added cost of retaining such a system. An example would be the vital sign monitor previously considered an essential component of a comprehensive telemedicine system in India.[a] However, there was no possibility of anyone being able to start an intravenous drip for a precipitous drop in the blood pressure!

Telehealth-enabled diseases include chronic diseases that are "under control," such as COPD/asthma, heart disease/cardiopathy, diabetes, high blood pressure/hypertension, rheumatologic disorders, ulcers, and lymphedema. These are suitable for home care enabling requests for remote care and support from the patient end. There are more wherein the patients benefit indirectly. Here the personnel engaged are health providers of various capabilities like remote counselling, mentoring, and helping in emergencies and disasters, ICU care, etc.

Because of structural changes in the healthcare sector in the last decade(s), our understanding of healthcare has been challenged (see Table 1). The treatment has changed, or is about to change, from episodic care to continuous care and from individual providers to a team of healthcare workers.[42] Instead of focusing on the caregiver, the focus is shifting toward the well-informed patient (patient empowerment). The healthcare workers (will) have access to shared distributed electronic health records, in accordance with his/her level of authorization. In addition to "advanced telemedicine," we now see the emergence of "super advanced telemedicine," which includes outsourced hospital services and virtual care centers like Mercy Health Virtual Care Center in St. Louis, MO, which can be described as the world's first hospital without any patients: "We have the medical team here, but with technology like highly-sensitive cameras and real-time vital signs, our providers can 'see' patients where they are.

TABLE 1 Simple and advanced telehealth.[44]

	Simple telehealth		Advanced telehealth
	Telemedicine	**Telehomecare**	**Telemedicine**
Where	Ward ↔ hospital	Patient's home ↔ Homecare central/general practitioner	Ward ↔ Hospital Patient's home ↔ Homecare central/ general practitioner
How	Broadband (optical, IP, 4G/5G)	Broadband (optical, IP, 4G/5G)	Broadband (optical, IP, 5G)
Who	Clinician ↔ Clinician	Patient ↔ Nurse/ doctor	Clinician ↔ Clinician Patient ↔ Nurse /Clinician

[a]It used to be, but not any longer—see budgeting section in Chapter 7.

That may be in one of Mercy's traditional hospitals, a physician office or in some cases, the patient's home."[43]

Healthcare service is characterized by the following new advances[42]:

- The welfare state will not be able to meet upcoming increases in healthcare based on today's solutions, when it comes to both financing and personnel—we must rethink our healthcare service.
- Healthcare personnel have, or are about to have, a complete overview of patients' treatment workflow in most developed countries.
- Patients have access to their health data.
- Patients have, more and more control of their own health. This requires that the patients have more knowledge of their own health—diseases, treatment, alternatives, etc.
- Healthcare has somewhat become a global merchandise.
- Technology is the driving force in the development of healthcare services (Table 2)[42].

Part of this development is visible today. A revolution is brewing of sorts. Doctors and other healthcare personnel are returning to people's homes through telemedicine solutions. A Fortune article from 2017 argues as follows[45]:

> At the turn of the 20th century, getting a checkup in America frequently meant your doctor came to you. Armed with a modest black bag of tools and old-fashioned medical know-how, physicians of yore would often take care of you, right at your bedside. As quaint as that image may seem today, it is in some ways, a vision of the future. New technologies are bringing back the house call—or a digital version of it, anyway.

TABLE 2   Current and expected structural changes in healthcare mostly related with changes in technology.

Yesterday/today	Today/tomorrow
Episodic care	Continuing care
Focus in service provider	Focus on the well-informed patient
Individual approach	Team-based approach
Disease treatment	Health promotion—how to stay healthy
Institutionalized care	Community-oriented care
Each healthcare worker has his/her own journal system	Shared distributed electronic health record
Department/hospital focus	Enterprise focus—health as merchandise

Source: Yellowlees P. Telemedicine Enabled Homecare. Phoenix, AZ: American Telemedicine Association 2000: Pragmatic Approaches & Emerging Applications; May 22, 2000.

There are changing roles for patients/clients/consumers leading to the previously mentioned as follows:

- Longer life span with a rising number of aged people
- Concomitant increase in chronic diseases
- Most people want to spend their old age in their own homes
- Dissolution of extended families
- Development of intelligent/smart houses
- Service providers must find new ways to spend less time with the patients

In summary, most patients are at home and being taken care of by self or other people in their homes. With that, we get the following:

- access to care from different groups (caring personnel, family, and friends)
- increased cost-effectiveness (in those cases that transport is eliminated and compared with the cost of a caring home)
- shorter time for access to treatment
- increased contact with health personnel (including through electronic media)
- increased safety through frequent monitoring of vital body functions
- early detection of health problems

The most important argument favoring telehomecare for the elderly is increased safety and sense of comfort for the patient and their relatives. This can be implemented through smart home devices like timers on the kitchen stove and coffee machine, or there can be more advanced solutions like fall sensors and advanced safety sensors. Such intelligent systems may be standalone, or used in combination with telehomecare systems. For people with dementia, we can use alarms that alert when they leave their house. In this way, smart house technology will function as a sort of invisible servant that looks after the resident(s) on a 24/7 basis.

The organizational problems will be central in the development of smart house solutions. Appropriate modes of communication between the smart house and the traditional care service, however, need to be found or created, for example, an alarm has no value in the absence of existing mechanisms to take actions based on the alarm. There is also the issue of false alarms, which are likely to occur. Through the integration of smart house technology with the rest of the healthcare service, the foundation for many new and existing services can be made. Examples are remote supervision of the medical condition for patients with chronic diseases and those with special needs like infants (see Case study 1). It may also be possible to find new ways of communication between patients and the care service—in particular if the user interface is adapted to the user's need and level of interaction.

CASE STUDY 1

Your baby's safety is your responsibility...

 'call me picky, but is'nt keeping babies safe is what parents were designed for'..that comes from a Mom who was destined to monitor her baby's heart rate and oxygen levels from early infancy...that was how she came to use the 'Owlet', a sensor built into a baby bootie. The problems of procurement and import were solved with persistence but the larger issue however was how would she use the data on her baby's heart rate & oxygen levels to keep her safe..not to talk about the false alarms which the Owlet gave and which quite often than not panicked her..inspite of all this that any alarm from the gizmo-false or otherwise, would atleast make her to check on her baby and make her responsible for its safety..though how often with all those alarms she would call up her doc is a moot point.

Courtsey Dr AJ, a pediatrician. His daughter was the child's mother who required long-term monitoring for possible recurrence of a viral cardiomyopathy. The baby is now 4 years and without monitor.

The experience from the former Norwegian Centre for Telemedicine has shown that progress from pilot systems and stand-alone experiments with telemedicine systems to the final implementation in the health service may be long-winded. The equipment must be certified, operational routines must be made, the infrastructure must be in place, the market/receiver must be prepared, the health authorities must be convinced that the system will work, cost-benefit must be studied, etc. This is a cumbersome process, which again requires that the complete, or at least the relevant, part of the infrastructure must be in place.

It might be important to have an active and open relationship to the possible ethical problems such systems imply. In these kinds of systems, it is important that the users and/or their relatives decide by themselves to what extent they want to use these new possibilities.

A prerequisite for the use of telemedicine equipment and telemedicine-based monitoring is that there is a communication infrastructure both in the home and from the home and to the respective departments as well as to the healthcare workers that need to be kept informed about the patient's condition. Intelligent systems in the home may reduce the need for personnel. Such systems generally focus on increased security, safety, and comfort.

Some solutions and devices

More and more companies are providing healthcare services to people's homes. We provide some current examples in the United States, where companies like American Well and Doctor on Demand are providing people for staying in remote locations.

An important driver behind this development is national health authorities' approval of telemedicine devices. Many of these are managed through peoples' smartphones. The devices are classified into two groups: those serving ordinary people and those for people with chronic conditions. We present a few, more or less randomly chosen examples of devices and application representing these two groups.

For people with cardiac problems, the company InfoBionic has developed a remote patient monitoring system, MoMe Kardia, to discover cardiac arrhythmias in patients by sensing ECG, respiration, and motion. The lightweight monitoring device can be carried as a necklace or an attachment to the belt. MoMe communicates data via a person's smartphone to a cloud-based platform where the data is evaluated. According to InfoBionic, the device works as a Holter, Event, and Mobile Cardiac Telemetry (MCT) monitor. This means, if a physician gets to feel that the patient's cardiac symptoms require another type of monitoring technology, he/she can change the device remotely to any one of three main monitoring modes.

A physician can access the patient's data via the web or through iOS and Android apps. His dashboard will provide views of patient monitoring progress and generates automated reporting in multiple parameters and data displays.

For people with diabetes, there are many alternatives. One system is Medtronic's Guardian Connect mobile continuous glucose monitor (CGM) and app. Medtronic also deliver a CGM called MiniMed Connect for users of both a Medtronic CGM and the company's insulin pump. Both systems show diabetes data on the mobile app. MiniMed Connect system is used by people who are on Medtronic's insulin pumps integrated with CGM, while the Guardian Connect system is a standalone CGM system used by people on insulin injections. The Guardian Connect system lets people record diabetes-related activities, like meals, exercise, and insulin intakes. They can also have the device to send text message alerts about high or low blood glucose to a care partner or upload the data into Medtronic's CareLink diabetes therapy management platform.

For people with asthma and other respiratory conditions, such as COPD and cystic fibrosis, Sparo Labs app-connected spirometer Wing helps them to track their lung function and manage their condition. Wing works by connecting the sensor to a smartphone and then measuring the fastest speed (forced exhalation) and maximum volume (peak flow volume) a person can exhale in one second. The scores are presented on the smartphone display with a "stoplight zone" system (green, yellow, or red) and a description of how the lungs are currently doing. The idea behind it is to allow the patient to learn how to anticipate an attack and adjust medication(s) and/or avoid particular triggers. By using metadata, for example, geographical location, the patient might get warnings about the different weather conditions like heat, cold air, and humidity. Patients are the primary Wing target audience for the next few months, as Sparo currently has no formal partnerships with healthcare providers or pharmaceutical companies.

One major player in telemedicine is American Well. According to their web site, the company "offers software, services, and access to clinical services – everything you need to offer a complete telehealth service – whether you are a health plan, an employer, or a delivery network. Our mobile and web service connects doctors with patients for live, on-demand video visits over the internet and handles all the administration, security, and record keeping that modern healthcare requires."[46]

American Well's mission is to connect patients with doctors, using a secure video system. The company offers patients immediate urgent care web visits in most of the US states. Their telehealth service runs on computers and Android- and iOS-based smartphones, which lets "a doctor or nurse to tap into a pool of on-call specialists and connect for an immediate video consult in any setting, from the office to the patient's bedside to the ER. Equip any point of care with specialists, without the cost of full-time onsite staff or travel."

American Well offers a lot of different services and functionalities, both for patients and clinicians (see Box 1). American Well is a good representative for a growing number of companies and health institutions—the doctors are returning to people's homes, although not physically but virtually.

Twine Health represents, in many ways, the new type of healthcare services in which the clinicians and patients plan the treatment together. The company was founded by the former physician John Moore, who felt that the lack of contact with his patients outside his office hours was problematic: "I was very frustrated and embarrassed with my inability to provide care outside of the office. I made many diagnoses, yet there was no way to support my patients after they left my office."

In Twine Health, which has now been taken over by Fitbit, patients worked with their doctors to create action plans with goals that mattered to them, then use devices and apps to track their progress, and to build self-efficacy and create new behaviors. In this way, patients and doctors got to mutually agree on how to proceed with their treatment. For example, if the goal was to lower the patient's blood pressure, the plan helped ensure it is reached. A combination of exercise, diet, and medicine was offered, with appropriate support through tightly integrated communication tools. After the mandatory first interview, patients communicate with the care team through a tablet application that displays their daily schedules, like intake of medication, measurement of blood pressure using a smart blood pressure cuff, and dissemination of information to patients regarding necessary certain actions as required. Simple measurements like pulse, blood pressure, and glucose are

BOX 1

American Well product features
(from americanwell.com)

American Well offerings for patients:

- Live video visits on web and mobile
- Telephone visits via the concierge service
- Co-pay management
- Apple Health integration
- Patient PHR/visit record
- Ability to review provider profiles
- Real-time insurance eligibility
- Ability to choose the provider you already see
- Image sharing
- Google Maps pharmacy selection
- Access to practices and service lines like medical, behavioral health, and diet/nutrition
- All-new web experience
- Enhanced medical history intake
- Self-scheduling—by preferred date or doctor
- Invite caregivers and family to a visit with multiway video
- Previsit chat in the app
- Share your visit summary with your PCP

For clinicians, the company offers the following:

- Live video visits on mobile and web
- EMR integration
- eRX and medication history through Surescripts
- Real-time patient data
- iPhone provider mobile app
- Secure messaging
- Provider-initiated visits
- Enhanced availability modes—AskMe mode makes doctors potentially available without committing to an appointment
- Accept/decline visits on mobile
- Mobile previsit review and postvisit wrap-up
- Mobile secure messaging
- Enhanced scheduling tools—on demand or scheduled
- Telephone visits via the concierge service
- Guidelines to treat entire populations through Insight API
- Invite additional participants to a visit with multiway video
- Sidekick app to snap photos and send to consulting providers

communicated to the physician's office. The tablet allows patients to discuss with a health coach and get appreciation for keeping up with the treatment plan. Hence, patients get to take charge of their own treatment.

Another good representative of the development is TytoCare (Boxes 2 and 3). The company argues that it "provides *The Missing Link in Telehealth* – a complete virtual visit, including physical exam, designed to replicate a visit to the doctor's office. With TytoCare, doctors can diagnose more conditions more accurately, making the promise of telehealth a reality."[25]

The foundation of the company was inspired by one of the cofounders' experience with his own children who needed frequent visits to the

---

BOX 2

TytoPro features
(from www.tytopro.com)

TytoPro features

- TytoPro device with high resolution camera, no-touch infrared basal thermometer, digital stethoscope (with volume, bell, and diaphragm filters), digital otoscope and tongue depressor adaptors
- TytoVisit platform with Clinician Dashboard for conducting "exam and forward" and "live video telehealth exams," plus EHR integration
- TytoApp
- Earbuds

TytoPro can be used in different ways

- Extend specialist services to remote locations when needed such as schools, nursing and home care facilities, clinics, employee work sites, urgent care and EMTs
- Get a quick and easy specialist consult
- Examine, capture and share images with patients to explain diagnosis and motivate treatment
- Send exam data to EHR for continuity of care

Benefits of using TytoPro include:

- Extend the reach of your specialists
- Reduce readmission rates
- Recover patient visits and revenue lost to ER or urgent care
- Improve continuity of care
- Motivate treatment
- Improve patient satisfaction

BOX 3

T y t o H o m e f e a t u r e s
(f r o m w w w . t y t o p r o . c o m)

TytoHome features include

- a device for examining the ears (otoscope), throat (camera), heart (stethoscope), lungs (stethoscope), abdomen(stethoscope), skin (camera), and capturing heart rate and temperature data (basal thermometer)
- TytoApp for live video telehealth exams with the patient's physician or "exam and forward" for later diagnosis

TytoHome allows

- Enabling the doctor to remotely diagnose conditions such as ear infections, flu, upper respiratory infections, sinus infections, pink eye, rashes, bug bites, wounds, sore throat, and pneumonia
- Monitoring chronic conditions without leaving home
- Use from everywhere as long as there is a network connection. It could be at home, in the office, and even on vacation.

---

pediatrician. TytoCare's main product is a portable device for parents to inspect their own children and then consult a clinician to analyze the results. TytoCare essentially lets the ordinary user, who maybe without a medical background or training, to be in charge of the technical basics of a pediatrician's visit at home. The user then makes the images and recordings available for a clinician who takes care of the diagnostics via video chat.

There are many other companies offering different specific devices like Nokia Technologies Withings Thermo—a WiFi-enabled thermometer that measures temperature from the temporal artery on the user's forehead. Readings are displayed on the device's side. In addition, the measurement is automatically sent to a companion smartphone app, where users can allocate the number to a particular user and, if desired, make a note.

How to ensure effective communication
Shashi Gogia

Introduction

Effective telehealth requires a persons' absence physically to be replaced by an effective form of tele to allow the healthcare interaction to proceed smoothly. Human-to-human communication depends on voice along with gestures of the hand, face, and to a lesser extent even other parts of the body like shrugging of shoulders or rolling up of eyes. A final message is received in consideration of all the previously mentioned.

Tele is electronic communication beyond visible or hearing range. Telecommunication has constraints, which go beyond the technology, that is, a message may not be created, be incomplete, may not have been sent, not have been received, may have inadequate compliance to standards, and so on. The crux lies in proper transmission after the creation of an effectively readable message, though we may have failures even if the previously mentioned are perfectly in order. This subsection talks about the technology behind video-conferencing and software communication but also goes beyond the same on how to ensure that the right message goes across every time and not create communication gaps.

All forms of electronic communication, whether or not concerning telehealth, depend on a certain level of basics like input and output. Proper input is the first step of data creation. The same can be transmitted only if relevant data exist, else the adage *garbage in garbage out* or GIGO[47] applies. GIGO, in its strictest sense, applies to software systems wherein processes are in place to ensure that data entry and flow follow a certain standard methodology. But getting the right software with included ease-of-use features in the healthcare domain is a challenge. Such systems necessarily have to be designed and developed by ICT professionals, but their understanding of how healthcare operates is somewhat limited.

The most important at all times is the correct contextual information as to which patient is being sent by whom and to which doctor. Here a proper identification processes, for each, patient as well as the care provider(s) have to be made and with linkages to national level IDs like the Social Security Number in the United States and the Aadhar card in India for patients, medical license number for providers, and so on. However, these are restricted by national choices as well as related privacy and data security issues.

Ensuring accuracy also means that the data creation is easy and unambiguous. Some more examples:

Gender—A patient could be *male* (M) or *female* (F), with a third type—*transgender* (T) being officially recognized in most countries. Some systems will allow a fourth type—*not known* but can also be *not mentioned*. A good software will allow the possibility of all these four choices through processes called as data format, which means only these four choices exist. The storage or transfer could be of the full text or preferably only the first character.

When the entry is less restrictive, that is, not from a preexisting choice but a person physically typing the same, another rule to ensure correctness of entry is called upon. This is *data validation* wherein an inappropriate entry may be refused or there is a related message. This would happen if the person making the entry does not know the term transgender but instead prefers the term intersex or even hermaphrodite.

Dates—In the United States, which also happens to be the place where most software majors are based, the date format is month, date, year also known as *mm/dd/yyyy*—the year can be 4 digits (read 2018) or 2 digits when 18 will suffice. However, the format followed in most other countries is date, month, and then year or *dd/mm/yy*. A system following the latter will reject the entry 06/22/15, as no 22nd month exists. The system may not understand that these data originated in the United States or may just have been handled by an operating system made in the United States, which means almost all, that is, Windows, Mac, IoS, Android, etc. Standardized systems ensure that dates are transferred and processed only in the format of year → month → date (yyyy-mm-dd) whatever may be the entry format.

Displaying the date during output may occur differently. This is known as display format that can make a readable date as per the viewers' choice. For the date earlier (i.e., 06/22/15), it could be read as June 22, 2015 if date format is *mmm/dd/yyyy*, or it could be Sunday 22nd June 2015 (*dddd/mmmm/yyyy*). You will note that the actual date has not changed.

Display formats have little to do with how the entry is made or validation checks. They are only concerned with readability. In the gender example (earlier), an entry of F will be having a display format of female. That is only required at the client's end, that is, the person viewing the data. The control on entry is called Edit Format, and it ensures correctness at the time of data entry. For example, for the month of June, an entry of 31 as the day will generate an error—converting the sixth month to 00. With the US date format (*mm/dd/yy*), we enter the month first, so that makes it easier to work with. The standardized format of *yyyy-mm-dd* will even adjust the maximum dates for February to be 28 or 29 depending on whether it is a leap year.

Two-digit years (*yy*) used to be the norm during olden times—when computer memory used to be a constraint. Hence 19 automatically became 2019, while 45 would mean 1945. Now that people do survive beyond 100 years, there is a need for insisting on *yyyy* at least in the *date of birth* field.

Edit formats exist for numbers, including variants like whole numbers (integer) and those with decimal values (numeric, float, real, etc.), dates and datetimes, as well as certain types of text entries.

Blood pressure—Edit Format would be XXX/YYY wherein the number before "/" (XXX) is the systolic value in mmHg and the latter (YYY) would be diastolic. A validation check would ensure that there is always an entry of "/".

Email is text with numbers allowed, but the entire sequence has to have an "@" value followed by with one or more dots subsequently. This check can only be through data validation, and no Edit Format is possible.

Validation checks do slow down data entry and may even stall the system. Repeated messages appear asking the user to correct an error, but the location of the error may be confusing, as checks take place on exiting the relevant field where the incorrect entry had been made previously. But most probably, by now, the user is concentrating on the next input item!

Further, in many apps, validation checking is performed in bulk for an entire set of fields, during the save command (or what is called updating) which could be many inputs later.

Validation-related slowdowns are more for cloud-based servers. The reason for this is that it takes precious seconds for the information to reach the server—sometimes literally travelling across the globe—the user may be entering in Australia, but the server may be located (currently most are) in California. For a form with many fields, updates are best done en masse, rather than one by one as a refresh takes time. But this also means simultaneous but individual validation checks of each of the multitude of entries. Simultaneous validation checks for many fields together would also mean that there has to be a method of marking the incorrect entry; otherwise, there is much confusion. For example, you might find a red-colored note next to it "The entered email address is invalid." Sometimes an asterisk (*) is placed next to the field as a check for possible incorrect entries before initiating an update.

Understanding data formats and related validation issues means users have to be trained on how to tackle them. This is a slow learning curve. Clinicians are busy persons and do not have time for such training. They also face a paucity of time for making any entry, especially ones with complicated or less understood formats.

Data entry does interfere with patient time and is reflected in slow and poor usage of EHRs[48] in general, despite incentives being offered, in the United States for example. Some systems are more open-ended and allow free text, which would resemble writing the clinicians' notes. Even here, the time taken for typing is a challenge especially for those from the older generation. This can be shortened by many tools—being mentioned only in brief here:

- **Dropdown and Multiselect lists** (one can select more than one choice). For example, occupation may be driver, teacher, student, agricultural worker, etc.
- **Type ahead**. That is, when the entered data is matched to an expected value. Typing the URL in your browser or search engine is a typical example. Within a form—especially when using a smart mobile— the full and anticipated correct spelling(s) of a word occurs, but this means a high chance of mistyping.
- **Default entries**. That is, automation of most likely choice—<History of smoking>—is "None." If that hopeful instance is incorrect, that is a "Yes" choice, another field appears where the user can enter the number of cigarettes per day, duration, etc.—and even these may have default values. Date of first visit is normally defaulted to the current date, that is, when entry is being made.
- **Assumed data based on previous entries**. *Correspondence address is generally the permanent address* but can be changed—sometimes a checkbox is provided to confirm.

- **Conversion of audio notes to text is done through software**. Current technology promises around 90% accuracy, which means 10% inaccuracy—making it unsuitable for a health software as there are literally, life and death issues.
- Many persons like to type fast, and any smart mobile user would recognize the problems with the tools that correct misspelt text and type ahead. These are a reason many a time for incorrect entries and consequent misinformation. (A common one faced by the authors of this book was conversion of EHR to HER!) Remember that drug brand names (as also persons names), are among the more common ones to be (mis)corrected. Besides words in the local language which are used in day to day conversations - remembering that the spellchecker maybe in a different variant of English or may even not be English, which could replace correct words with jargon.

Despite all the earlier forms of assistance (exact provision depends on the software application being used), data input or entry time is a major challenge—it is literally the slowest component of ICT usage, a human handiwork and executed at human speeds. Data processing and transfer, on the other hand, occur at electronic speeds. Transfer however also depends on the distance to the server. In a cloud-based system, it means the information travels once to the server and then back even if both locations for input and output are exactly the same. Cloud-based servers also have issues regarding the time allowed for a person to make the entry. This problem, called session expiry, is done to ensure security but is a reason for extreme frustration.

Besides the controls and challenges in the data entry and output, there are also other issues. Most need to be solved by the software developer but obviously need discussion with the user (generally the clinician). First is whether the entry should be open-ended, for example, history taking or subclassified like examination findings that could have fields for pulse, blood pressure, etc., with specific formats. Even history may be broken up into complaints (with/without duration of each), past and present and family history—some even have specifics for brother, sister, mother, father, etc.

Another is whether to allow the null (i.e., a blank field) or make it essential. For example, there cannot be a history without a single complaint! Higher number of essential fields will mean more checks, which are going to slow the entry time—remember a validation check will be invoked whenever an essential field has not been entered at all. There will be variations of what is essential and what is not, for specific situations and specialties. But telehealth is necessarily team based and cross specialty. Hence the developer maybe faced with a Hobson's choice. S&F data exchange has further issues of incomplete or incorrect interpretation at the other end that is better covered by the section on standards.

Real-time information fortunately is more automated as the entry, and output is more dependent on the system. That we discuss next.

Video conferencing (VC)

Shashi Gogia

A video conference is a two-point or multipoint communication tool where face-to-face live communication takes place using multimedia. It utilizes audio and video inputs that are uploaded and downloaded at the requisite ends in a seamless manner. Older telemedicine systems used a camera with an inbuilt communication methodology. Sophisticated systems exist, like the camera focusing, and turn itself toward the speaker, automatic mixing into multipoint screens. However, such systems like by Polycom™ are expensive for day-to-day telehealth purposes. They also necessitate use of multiple screens. The VC screen would be separated from the EMR, and there was less chance of merging both, though one would argue that there is little need (of merging), as each and every point of the discussion—introductions of personnel, a welcome hello, etc.—would be irrelevant for the care provision. Also, such stored multimedia content generally consumes gigabytes of space with little or no possibility of analytics and becomes relatively useless later.

However, the simplicity and instant start with little user effort has resulted in VC, being described as the high point (and for some the only form) of telemedicine. Older VC methods used a direct connection either through satellite, VPN or ISDN, since the required bandwidth was not sufficient for two-way video streaming.

Proper telehealth should be a mixture of both real-time and S&F. VC allows the feel and satisfaction of the doctors' presence, while S&F is time saving, allowing relevant documentation like the patients' history, radiology, investigation reports, etc. for deeper analysis both immediate and in the long term.

Lately the scene has changed to allow cheaper home-based systems, with VC managed through personal computers; laptops; and mobiles, which is now the most common. Such development had its roots in systems that allowed text messaging via the Internet wherein voice was later added called Voice over Internet Protocol (VoIP). Later, sharing of live video became enabled over VoIP as a form of a multimedia message. Current tools allow additional inputs to be shared in the form of a white board, live chat, or messaging, sharing files and common viewing of the EMR.

There are many solutions that provide VC along with online meeting support; Skype is the oldest and best known. Originally point to point, it allows multipoint support and screen sharing. Other examples like Google plus, Yahoo! messenger, and AOL messenger are extensions of their email applications. Facebook also allows live chat, but security is a concern—highlighted by the election of US President Trump. One must remember that there are strict guidelines against sharing health data. One has also to understand that VC is data intensive, and many systems have failed because the provided connectivity was not enough. However, better systems currently adjust to lower clarity (of video) based on the amount of available connectivity.

Dedicated online meeting programs that require a license make for better security. Examples are Webex™, GotoMeeting (Citrix)™, Zoom™, Teamviewer™, and of late even Skype. All also allow mobile-based conferencing. These also provide an option of remote desktop control and sharing, which in turn allows online support and help for problems faced while working with any software—important since EHRs and telehealth apps need much learning. Such comprehensive solutions purely as a part of a telehealth solution are coming up but, not as yet commonplace.

Use of such meeting solutions in mobile phones, however, is challenging due to the small screen, and there are multiple components. The advantage however is that the phone number by itself is necessarily unique and allows easy passage through relevant security protocols. Pure VC on mobile includes Facetime (Apple) wherein iMessage is a separate application. WhatsApp, WeChat, Telegram, Slack, etc. allow both to run as part of the same application.

One has to remember that constant connectivity speed needs to be maintained right from (1) the starting point, then (2) to the local switch (i.e., network provider), and then (3) to the server and from there on (4,5,6,...) (traversing a similar path) to the other locations, which could be more than one. Mixing and displays depend on the application and can be at the server level (similar display at all ends) or at the client end—generally the latter, as that adjusts better to the local needs.

A totally VC-based teleconsult has many challenges, the biggest being the time of the doctor, aside from low connectivity speed. Teleconsultations may allow face-to-face meeting, but when one has to examine or view the leg or an X-ray or reports, a screen display makes for a difficult read—a moving frame necessary means that the pixel size is smaller to maintain the appropriate screen refresh rate.

The above-mentioned systems require voice and multimedia inputs through codecs and related standards, many of which have been described previously,[b] Codec H264 is the standard protocol for videos. In VC, a lossy image is allowed as constant communication is more important, while some reduction in clarity can be adjusted to. Compression is mostly the norm through reduction of frame size, that is, an image of dimensions 192×144 is one-fourth the size of a frame of 384×288, and hence it would require one-fourth of the bandwidth too for transfer. In case one is working with still images, for example, a document photo, screenshot (here the pixel rate of the remote screen may matter), or X-rays, the frame refresh rate can decreased. This allow for better clarity even if data speed is slow. A frame refresh only once every minute—adequate

[b]See Chapter 3—Acquiring Sound, Images, and Video.

for an X-ray—would allow an image 450 times the number of pixels in the same data speed of a routine VC—remembering that normal refresh should be 7.5 MHz (= frames per second) for the eye to discern movement.

VC can be on a one-to-one basis, that is point to point (P2P), wherein two people are talking to each other or as part of a multipoint conference wherein multiple persons participate. In the latter, most systems would allow for the video of each person to be visible in a side bar, while the main person speaking would be visible in an enlarged mode. The main screen could also be a presentation, originating from the speaker. Each participant has to set his individual sound and video upload settings beforehand. The sound can be though a normal phone call or through an accompanying VoIP. All the incoming calls, videos, etc. are finally laid out as a single multimedia stream by the provider company, and then the same is transmitted through appropriate connectivity to the participant's screen.

However, successful VC requires much effort. The general principles, with a focus on multipoint conferencing, are as follows:

1. At the hospital, a separate room should be set aside for the equipment, as it takes up a certain amount of space, and this also makes it available to more users. The setting should be "uncluttered," that is, with walls and curtains in soft and solid colors. Strong patterns in the background or the participants' clothing may be a distracting factor. It is wise to speak calmly and at an even rate. Sudden movement can create a disturbance and interference in the picture.[49]
2. For patients, single rooms are desirable so that they can talk to the doctor alone, or together with local healthcare staff. The optimal frequency for VC should be assessed (may not be needed every day). To ensure continuity, the same doctor should be responsible for contact with the satellite centers over a continuous period (e.g., 1 month).[49]
3. Make sure the appointment is at a time that is comfortable and convenient for all participants. This becomes a bigger challenge when there are going to be participants from across the global—meetings of authors and editors for this very book raised such challenges.
4. A dress code is similarly required including combing your hair (shoes maybe optional!). When one is sitting at home, one conveniently forgets that they are very visible to other participants (So forget about doing VC from your bedroom!)
5. Older systems allowed a separate camera that could be mounted at a particular place where they could ensure only what was required to be revealed of their home and office would be revealed. This is not possible any longer as current laptops and even desktops have a camera at the top of the screen that *does not move* to face the speaker. Mobile-based VC is simpler, better done with the mobile placed on a stand, but not without challenges (see Chapter 12).

6. It is important to have a round of introductions—the system normally allows for the name to be displayed while speaking.

7. Microphone and ear plugs are better than speakers for sound quality, but do not obviate the need for a soundproof closed room. The main convenience is in stopping an echo effect caused by 2-3-s delay of audio reaching across and coming back through the listeners' device as a fresh audio note. Any participant who does not have head mikes should remain muted at any time he/she is not speaking. Feedback (the loud crescendo-type tinny sound when the mike faces the speaker) is another problem best avoided thus. Also remember that noise cancelling headphones may not cut external noise for the audience at the other end!

8. Speaking out of turn is another frequent cause for confusion. Hence the conference organizer needs to have a moderator. Most systems allow a form of digital hand raising, but even better is that comments or questions be entered into the accompanying chat box.

9. Hybrid meetings are wherein there is a physical presence in a room but some of the members are connected online. If this room has multiple speakers, a tabletop multidirectional mike would be preferred.

10. Similarly, for the hybrid meeting, more sophisticated cameras with turning to face the speaker would be important.

11. The final speed and clarity depend on a calculated average bandwidth wherein some persons may lose the voice or video. During an ongoing conversation, it is even recommended that users switch off their video input to allow for better clarity all around.

12. When making a presentation or on-screen discussions, it is important to remember that only one screen is normally allowed for sharing with others. The choice could be the entire desktop or just a particular opened presentation or document—even a running EHR screen.

13. Special problems, mostly of noise and no sound, emanate when switching from external mike to internal sounds of the system (e.g., when one wants to run an onscreen explanatory video) during a conference call. Solving these tests the skills of even professional broadcasters.

14. A possibility of remote control of the screen being viewed may be allowed for annotations. However again not more than one remote entity should do that.

Now, we discuss some recommendations for VC as part of health support. We assume that the target is a possible teleconsultation, and the same is being done through a telemedicine app:

1. While the caller (a patient or preferably the local care provider) may use a mobile or desktop, for the clinician, a desktop will be better as he should be comfortable and not moving around.

2. Patient-related data—history, investigation reports, etc.—should be available through S&F for viewing in the same screen or sometimes a parallel side screen. The same depends on the system being used.
3. An ambient light source, preferably daylight from a window, should be behind the camera even if a desktop-mounted camera, that is, the speaker, faces the light. Many systems allow for a light to be switched on when the video is active, but such lighting is rarely adequate and if so may cause a glare or redeye of the speaker.
4. Provide an appointment roster; for example, *Dr A shall be ready and awaiting calls from 1600 to 1700 hours.*
5. A background screen or display board behind the caller and more importantly the clinician should reveal the identification and location of the consulting parties.
6. The display screens should allow all the desired components with large enough fonts to avoid discomfort and specially, squinting, which one must understand will be seen immediately on the other end, to allow and sometimes may be glaringly enlarged on two screens.
7. Special telemedicine apps include all the previously mentioned in an all-to-all inclusive system. They also support creation of ePrescriptions, which are made by the clinicians but can be printed remotely with digital signatures, etc.
8. Even though many now do all work through a mobile phone, the small screen is however a hindrance; hence tablet computers should be considered a minimum.
9. Most important is try to ensure eye-to-eye contact with the patient (you just need to keep viewing your own video box to see if that is what it appears) as that shows empathy and concern.

Example of video-conference system for emergency care

Gunnar Hartvigsen

Telemedicine is a vital part of emergency care in Northern Norway. Emergency care is difficult in the high mountains and off shore, particularly during winter time. To make emergency medical knowledge available in emergency situations on the island of Spitsbergen (almost at 80 degrees north), the former Norwegian Centre for Telemedicine (NST), together with the Acute Unit at University Hospital of North Norway (UNN) and Longyearbyen hospital, developed a telemedicine system called videoconferencing acute medical conference (VAKe). VAKe connects the emergency treatment room at Longyearbyen Hospital to the Emergency Medical Communications Center (AMK)[50] at UNN, which in turn provides access to a wide range of medical specialists.

Clinicians at Longyearbyen hospital get in contact with UNN by pressing the button on the VAKe display named "Call AMK UNN." The design idea is that in emergency situations, the device should be very simple to use. The acute ward at Svalbard hospital was, in addition to a camera on the wall, equipped with a ceiling mounted camera. This camera has motion and zoom functions that can be controlled from the UNN so that the medical specialists can study the desired areas of the injured patient. All vital signs measurements from the patient such as ECG, pulse, oxygen saturation, and temperature are sent to UNN so that both sites have access to the same patient information. It has also been emphasized that good, sensible placed microphones are needed to provide good conditions for dialogue between the two locations regardless of where they are positioned in the room.[13] VAKe has proved that access to images has improved understanding of the situation, resulted in correct advice, and thus had positive therapeutic consequences.

For the specialists at UNN, who obviously have to evaluate the patient's condition from remote, their ability to "recreate the patient" is crucial for the evaluation: What kind of data do you as a specialist need to give appropriate advice and/or make decision(s) about optimal treatment when you do not have the patient in front of you? A good approach is to establish good routines based on adequate data: audio, images, visual data, written data, and trained healthcare personnel remotely who the specialist can instruct to do what he/she obviously cannot do with the patient.

The typical setting with participants at Longyearbyen hospital and UNN in Tromsø includesthe following (Tables 3–5):

The VAKe system became immediately a success story after it was installed at Longyearbyen hospital. It very quickly turned out to be very useful to avoid unnecessary transportation by plane to the mainland or give support for stabilizing a patient. After the system became known among healthcare workers, other healthcare organizations on the mainland asked for the same service.

According to the project leader of VAKe, Oddvar Hagen, positive experiences with the VAKe system included the following[13]:

- The technology worked well.
- Better support and workflow.
- "Closer" teamwork.

TABLE 3   Details of staff working at the Telemedicine facility.

Longyearbyen hospital	UNN
• GP/surgeon	• AMK-doctor
• Anesthesia nurse	• AMK-nurse
• Surgical nurse	• Surgeon
	• Anesthesia specialist
	• Neurosurgeon

TABLE 4   List of equipment at UNN Emergency unit (AMK).

Equipment	Manufacturer	Model	Number
Codex	Tandberg	6000 MXP	1
Ceiling mic	Tandberg	Audio Science	1
Headphones	AKG	HSD 200 SR/OC	2
Audio/video control unit	Crestron	Professional media processor MP2E	1
Touch panel	Crestron	Wired 5.7-inch tabletop touch panel CT-1550	2
Mixer	Behringer	Eurorack UB802 1	1
Distribution amplifier	Extron	P/2 DA 2PLUS	1
TV	ATEC	LCD 37″ HD ready	2
Camera	Sony	EVI D70 "robot camera"	1
TV	Hitachi	37PD5200	2

TABLE 5   List of equipment at Longyearbyen hospital.

Equipment	Manufacturer	Model	Number
Codex	Tandberg	990 MXP	1
Ceiling mic	Tandberg	Audio Science	1
Headphones	AKG	HSD 200 SR/OC	2
Audio/video control unit	Crestron	Professional Media Processor MP2E	1
Touch panel	Crestron	Wired 5.7-inch tabletop touch panel CT 1550	1
Camera	Sony	EVI D70 "robot camera"	1
TV (LCD 23″)	Hyundai	HLT2310	1
Sound mixer	Behringer	Eurorack UB802	1
Transformer	Noratel	IMED 300	1

- It saves time, tasks solved in parallel.
- The nurses felt safer in situations with severely injured patients.
- Reduced stress, especially after the first use.
- Specialists at the University Hospital had a better understanding of the condition of the remotely located patient.
- Positive impact on patient care.
- Improved team function.

Negative experiences included the following[13]:

- Monitoring and cooperation: If "they" help "us" or "see us in the cards"?
- Sensitive initial phase, vulnerable to interference
- Disruptive communications.
- "Keen" specialists.
- The communication was not well structured.
- No clear operational procedures.
- The need for the work routines and "rules."
- Need for more exercise.

The medical specialists at UNN argued that visual information gives a better platform for decision-making. They were more confident by giving advice base on visual information. Also, eye contact made it easier to get acceptance for the suggested treatment procedures.[13] Hence, the introduction of the VAKe system resulted in important organizational changes for the routines at UNN. Now, multidisciplinary medical teams sit together for both emergency teleconference and general emergency cases. Previous participation was mostly through a phone call from the different hospital departments.

Standards and certification

Maurizio Mattoli

As per International Standards Organization (ISO), "A **standard** is a document that provides requirements, specifications, guidelines or characteristics that can be used consistently to ensure that materials, products, processes and services are fit for their purpose."

The ability to exchange information safely and securely about the patient at a distance is the ultimate enabling factor in telehealth, and this applies to all forms: real-time, store and forward, remote monitoring, and more. Whenever we attempt to do telecare, we need to adopt the relevant and proper protocols and standards to enable the information exchange (transmission) through different systems and physical media.

We must also establish, as in any system, the distant participating parties' identity, privileges, and authorization. Alongside, there is a need to ensure the availability, integrity, and confidentiality of the information and ensure the exchange and transfer is secure, especially when this takes place through a third-party or public infrastructure. That's why interoperability and information security standards are even more critical in this case of care provision, as they contribute to reliability and safety. They form the prerequisites of any medical act, especially if carried out at a distance, since here the chances are higher.

But there is yet another—less obvious—safety issue related to it. We must also make sure we can preserve the meaning of information as it flows across different systems and different caregivers get access to it. In fact, as pointed out by Coiera,[51] besides others working on communication and information theory applied to healthcare, in practice, individuals do not know the same things, and the resulting issue is that the receiver's knowledge may alter the effectiveness of a message. So, let's say we succeed in making information about a patient reach the next patient's point of care (either physical or virtual) because we were able to manage what we call functional or syntactical interoperability.[c] Will this info still be clear enough to let the next care provider understand, interpret, and use it correctly? Someone who has different knowledge and in a different context and time from the one that generated the information. Will she/he still correctly understand, interpret, and make proper use of such information?

The following example may help understand this issue. This example may hold true for either a physical patient referral or a virtual patient referral to a specialist. Let's say the medical history summary of the patient comes with "MS" as one of the previous diagnoses for the patient. "MS" is an acronym that could either refer to the following:

- multiple sclerosis
- mitral stenosis

How should the specialist interpret that piece of information? He or she might need to remove this ambiguity somehow. In the case of an S&F teleconsultation, it could be even harder to clarify, as neither the patient nor other caregivers are immediately available to help as solving the puzzle would imply a need for further interactions and lead onto further latencies. Or—another example—let's say the medical history summary of the patient says "diabetes" only. "Diabetes" alone is ambiguous, as it does not specify what type of diabetes the patient is suffering. And so on, many other examples can be made where the use of acronyms, abbreviations,[52] and eponyms[53] may put at risk the meaning and interpretation of different kinds of clinical information about the patient.

So here comes the challenge we call semantic interoperability,[d] defined as the *"ability to exchange information* between different systems **and** to use the information transferred, i.e., *preserving the meaning of information."*

[c]Syntactic interoperability refers to the packaging and transmission mechanisms for data. It enables the information exchange, yet alone does not ensure data will be also always understood.

[d]Semantic interoperability is the ability of computer systems to exchange data with unambiguous, shared meaning. Semantic interoperability is a requirement to enable machine computable logic, inferencing, knowledge discovery, and data federation between information systems (definition from Wikipedia, accessed February 2018, https://en.wikipedia.org/wiki/Semantic_interoperability).

The latter is usually addressed by "coding" information versus what we call "controlled vocabularies" or standard terminologies, to ensure nonambiguous meaning, but this comes with a coding effort that may be low or high depending on several implementation aspects.

Note: To enable knowledge-based CDSS attached to an EHR, EHR information must be coded (i.e., made not ambiguous). Otherwise, CDSS "if-then" rules will not work correctly. For instance, a rule may say something like, "IF **drug_1** is taken AND **drug_2** is being prescribed/taken THEN send a warning to the user," that will not work safely and correctly if input drug information is ambiguous (i.e., not coded).

In this section, we will review several technology standards addressing interoperability in healthcare, both syntactical and semantic. We will briefly mention the challenges and the benefits that may arise from their adoption, their primary purpose, features of the most relevant ones, and some of the new and most promising ones. Still, in doing this, we should keep in mind that interoperability itself, in its broader definition, is still a challenge in most of the world.

Messaging and data exchange standards

These standards define the structure and data content of electronic messages enabling information sharing. A message is a portion or unit of information sent from one system to another. For instance, a message from a laboratory information system (LIS) sending a patient's lab tests results to a clinical information system (CIS) or an EHR.

Examples of messaging and data exchange standards used in healthcare systems:

HL7 v2.x and v3: messaging standard to exchange clinical, administrative, and financial information in the context of healthcare. v2 is one of the most common and worldwide used standards in healthcare systems. It is used to exchange messages triggered by events between many different hospital systems within a healthcare provider. For instance, messages/events about patient admission, transfer and discharge, scheduling, laboratory orders/results, patient information updates, and many more; "x" stands for several of the subversions of the v2 standard (e.g., v2.7, v2.7.1, and v2.8). On the other hand, v3 represents a new approach to clinical information exchange based on a model-driven methodology (see HL7's Reference Information Model, http://www.hl7.org/implement/standards/rim.cfm). It has a higher information representation power and several benefits compared with the previous version. However, that comes at price in the form of higher complexity and implementation costs. There is also no backward compatibility with the previous version. So far, v3 has not seen broad adoption, despite the fact that countries like Canada and Australia officially embraced it. The standard is developed and maintained by Health

Level Seven (HL7). See www.hl7.org. To some extent, the newer and interestingly, open-source FHIR (see later) makes it likely that the same will never be used.

Digital Imaging and Communications in Medicine (DICOM): is an international standard to transmit, store, retrieve, print, process, and display medical imaging information. This is almost the most universally used standard in the context of medical imaging, for example, radiology information systems (RIS), picture archive and communications systems (PACS), and medical imaging viewers. Developed by National Electronics Manufacturers Association (NEMA). See www.nema.org and www.dicomstandard.org/. There used to be many proprietory versions, in the past disallowing information exchange; now, this is less of an issue. Open-source versions allow easy adoption by any one.

Clinical Data Interchange Standards Consortium (CDISC) standards suite: data structure format for reporting data collected in clinical research studies; it evolved into a broader suite of data standards, enhancing the quality, efficiency, and cost-effectiveness of clinical research processes. Developed and maintained by CISC. See www.cdisc.org/.

National Council for Prescription Drug Programs (NCPDP): data interchange standards for the pharmacy domain (prescriptions transfers, billing, and more). See http://www.ncpdp.org/.

Accredited Standards Committee (ASC) X12: electronic messaging standards for transactions, eligibility, and payments. Developed and maintained by X12, chartered by the American National Standards Institute (ANSI). See www.x12.org/x12org/index.cfm.

Institute of Electrical and Electronics Engineers Standard 1073 (IEEE 1073): messaging standard for communication between medical devices. Developed and maintained by IEEE. See http://ieeexplore.ieee.org/document/713466/.

Terminology standards

Terminology or vocabulary standards are directly related to the meaning (semantics) of the information exchanged. By assigning unique codes to the information, they allow the receiver to relate it to the corresponding concepts managed within the controlled vocabularies (in the form of either classifications or ontologies) where the meaning is defined by the standard vocabulary itself, which means that the information is understood the same way by all participating parties. This aspect is key not only in the context of information exchange but also whenever you want to harness the benefits from knowledge-based clinical decision support systems or CDSS (as already mentioned, they direly need nonambiguous information). Standards enhance research and knowledge discovery capabilities in healthcare. Ensuring precise meaning of any "input" information improves many of related processes and allows information reuse. It allows the principle "capture once, use many times."

Examples of messaging and data exchange standards used in healthcare systems:

WHO ICD-9, ICD-10, ICD-O, and ICD-11*: International Classification of Diseases (ICD) is the standard diagnostic classifications for epidemiology, health management, quality, and clinical purposes. Translated into 43 languages and used by 117 countries to monitor incidence and prevalence of diseases. Also used to monitor outcomes and allocate resources in healthcare. Developed and maintained by the World Health Organization (WHO).[e] (http://www.who.int/classifications/icd/en).

Logical Observation Identifiers, Names, and Codes (LOINC): a universal code system standard for the electronic exchange and gathering of clinical results (e.g., laboratory tests, clinical observations, outcomes management, and research). Often implemented into laboratory information systems (LIS) interfaces and related software. Developed and maintained by the Regenstrief Institute. See http://www.regenstrief.org/resources/loinc/.

Systematized Nomenclature in Medicine—Clinical Terms (SNOMED CT): a controlled coded clinical terminology for use in electronic health records (EHRs). SNOMED CT represents clinical information meaningfully with adequate detail for clinical recording (e.g., clinical findings, procedures, body structures, organisms, specimens, substances, and pharmaceutical), facilitating EHR guidelines implementation, decision support systems integration, and clinical research among several benefits. It is one of the most comprehensive reference terminology standards for semantic interoperability together with LOINC. SNOMED CT has several mappings toward ICD10 (WHO), and ICD 11 has been made in close coordination. But it is much more as it can represent clinical ideas in more detail than any other standard classifications. SNOMED CT is used by more than 5000 affiliate licensees worldwide, maintained and distributed by SNOMED International (a trade name of the International Health Terminology Standards Development Organization, IHTSDO), a not-for-profit organization having currently 30 member countries. See https://www.snomed.org.

RxNorm provides normalized names for clinical drugs, linking its names to several drug vocabularies commonly used in pharmacy management and drug interaction software (see CDSS). It has two main components: a normalized naming system for generic and branded drugs and a tool for supporting semantic interoperability between drug terminologies and pharmacy knowledge base systems. Developed by the US National Library of Medicine (NLM). See https://www.nlm.nih.gov/research/umls/rxnorm/.

ICD-10 Procedure Coding System (ICD-10-PCS): it is a procedure classification for classifying procedures performed in hospital inpatient healthcare settings in the United States that is intended for use by

---

[e] ICD-11 was released in June 2018, but adoption will take time.

healthcare professionals, healthcare organizations, and insurance programs. Developed by 3M Health Information Sys. for the Centers for Medicare and Medicaid Services (CMS), the latter is the US government agency responsible for overseeing all changes and modifications to the ICD-10-PCS. See https://www.cms.gov.

Unified Medical Language System (UMLS): it is a set of files and software tools that bring together many health and biomedical vocabularies and standards to enable interoperability between computer systems. It has a metathesaurus, containing terms and codes from many vocabularies (including CPT, ICD-10-CM, LOINC, MeSH, RxNorm, and SNOMED CT). A semantic network made of broad categories (semantic types) and their relationships (semantic relations) and a set of natural language processing tools called SPECIALIST Lexicon and Lexical Tools. Developed by the US National Library of Medicine (NLM). See https://www.nlm.nih.gov/research/umls/.

Document standards

Continuity of Care Record (CCR): it is a patient health summary record specification containing the most timely and relevant core health information about a patient that can be sent (electronically) from one caregiver to another, also aimed at creating a standard of health information needed when a patient is transferred or referred or seen by another healthcare professional or caregiver, expressed in the standard data interchange language extensible markup language (XML). Developed and maintained by ASTM Subcommittee E31.25 and other organizations. See https://www.astm.org/COMMIT/SUBCOMMIT/E3125.htm.

Clinical Document Architecture (CDA): is a document markup standard that specifies the structure and semantics of clinical documents for exchange between healthcare providers and patients. It ensures the following characteristics within a clinical document: persistence, stewardship, potential for authentication, context, wholeness, and human readability. A CDA can contain any clinical content; for instance, a CDA document could be a discharge summary, imaging report, admission and physical, pathology report, and more.

Continuity of Care Document (CCD): combines the benefits of ASTM Continuity of Care Record (CCR) and the HL7 Clinical Document Architecture (CDA) to specify the encoding, structure, and semantics of a patient summary clinical document for exchange. It defines a set of templates representing the typical sections of a summary record and expresses these templates as constraints on CDA.

Coordination, harmonization, and convergence of standards

We just had a review of many standards related to interoperability in healthcare. Let's see a practical example of how some of those standards we mentioned may "work together" into some implementation.

For instance, we might want to further send an ECG report already received from a remote ECG system to the corresponding patient's record in the GP's local EHR system. We could use a *messaging standard* like HL7 v2.x to provide the transport and message specification format. Then, "inside" the v2 message itself, we could pack, as part of its payload, the clinical document we want to send, the ECG report in this case. The document structure and semantics of the "embedded" ECG report could make use of a *document standard* like the CDA, which would define the document structure and also establish a *terminology standard*, like SNOMED CT, for instance, which might have been used to code the ECG finding information that comes within such ECG report. This way we get transportation, structure, and coding of information. So, this could be an example of how three different types of standards cooperate to make information transport possible and to ensure univocal information meaning. The following diagram (Fig. 1) will try to represent this example in a simplified view.

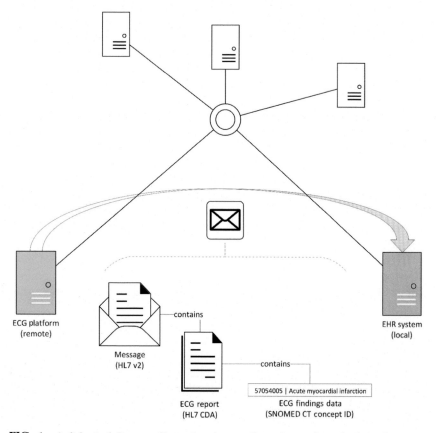

FIG. 1 A didactical diagram illustrating the coordinated use of standards in document exchange.

The previous is just a very rough example since many other additional aspects need to be addressed. For instance, how should we establish correct and consistent patient and physician identification included in the ECG report document? Is there some common "source of truth" that would be consistent both for sending and receiving systems, even in the case of exchange between different organizations caring for the same patient? These and many other aspects must be "agreed upon" to achieve interoperability in a broader sense. In the next subsections, we are going to mention some of the more relevant initiatives aiming at establishing a coordinate use of standards to achieve interoperability in healthcare.

Integrating the healthcare enterprise—IHE

As shown in the previous example, to accomplish some goals related to an information exchange context, we had to choose some of the many different available standards related to interoperability (both syntactical and semantical). It means that every time we want to address some information exchange involving different systems developed, managed, or maintained by different parties, we have to agree with all participating parties on what standards should be used (or find some way to translate them to make exchange possible between different systems).

The organization called Integrating the Healthcare Enterprise (IHE) has been established precisely to address such coordination needs. As IHE itself states, "IHE is an initiative by healthcare professionals and industry to improve the way computer systems in healthcare share information. IHE promotes the coordinated use of established standards such as DICOM and HL7 to address specific clinical needs in support of optimal patient care. Systems developed in accordance with IHE communicate with one another better, are easier to implement, and enable care providers to use information more effectively."[54]

IHE collects case requirements, identifies available standards, and develops technical guidelines which manufacturers can implement. The main result of this process is a set of "integration profiles" that describe specific solutions to integration challenge within different domains (e.g., radiology, cardiology, eye care). An integration profile establishes standards used by each system's actors, allowing cooperation to address specified needs. So, for instance, the "scheduled workflow" within the radiology domain establishes the flow of information that supports efficient patient care workflow in a typical imaging encounter. It specifies transactions that keep the consistency of patient information from registration through ordering, scheduling, imaging acquisition, storage, and viewing. The specification also establishes the underlying standards to be used in such transactions (DICOM and HL7 in this case).

IHE also organizes what are called Connectathon(s). These are interoperability testing events gathering hundreds of industry developers and vendors to collaborate and test implementations through test scenarios, which are called IHE profiles—the ECG example is one of them. In this, disparate vendors gather in separate cubicles, a clinical scenario—like the ECG and report as earlier is provided to one who in turn sends to another vendor's system. The receipt accuracy is checked. And if successful, developers and vendors are issued "IHE Integration Statements" related to their products. This helps prospective purchasers to gain confidence of product integration capabilities. More recent, IHE integration profiles also make use of other promising and emerging standards like openEHR and FHIR (see next section). For more information, see https://www.ihe.net/.

Emerging interoperability standards

HL7 Fast Healthcare Interoperability Resources—FHIR

A standard specifying data formats and elements called "resources" (e.g., patient, practitioner, encounter, CarePlan), together with an application programming interface (API) for exchanging the resources using modern web-based technology and standards (e.g., XML, JSON, HTTP, and OAuth). It defines a simple framework for extending and adapting the existing resources. All systems can read these extensions, and their definitions can be retrieved using the same framework. So, it is both flexible and easy to implement, particularly suitable for mobile devices. FHIR is very promising, it has reached version 4 (i.e., first Normative Content + Trial Use Developments) as of December 2018 and was incorporated into several IHE integration profiles related to mobile access and more. The specification is free to use. See https://www.hl7.org/fhir/.

Standard development organizations

Technical standard development is a systematic process requiring coordinating, producing, releasing, revising, amending, and reissuing those standards among other activities. Those organizations primarily engaging in such activities are called standard development organizations (SDO). Usually, most standards are voluntary, while some of them may become mandatory if regulators define them as a legal requirement. Here is a list of some of the most relevant SDOs related to interoperability for health information systems.

International Standards Organisation (ISO)/TC 215 health informatics

ISO is an international standard development and accreditation organization, established as a worldwide federation of national standard bodies. The ISO Technical Committee (TC) 215 Health Informatics covers health information and communication technology (ICT) to promote interoperability and compatibility between systems. ISO TC 215 has several working groups. Many of the already mentioned above standards have also been incorporated as ISO standards. ISO/TC 215 has direct responsibility on more than 180 published ISO standards, ranging from medical devices to personal and electronic healthcare record standards. See https://www.iso.org/committee/54960.html.

Health Level Seven (HL7) International: it is a not-for-profit standard development organization (SDO) accredited by the American National Standards Institute (ANSI) for developing healthcare-related standards. It has responsibility for a broad suite of standards larger than those we already mentioned (v2, v3, or CDA). Among others, HL7 also manages the Arden Syntax and HL7 EHR Functional Model (FM). It is probably the most well-known SDO related to health information systems. See http://www.hl7.org/. FHIR is an open-source project supported by HL7.

openEHR Foundation: a not-for-profit company of University College London, the United Kingdom. Owner of openEHR trademark and standard, licensing and making available openEHR artifacts at no cost, openEHR is also a virtual community working to enable semantic interoperability, mainly focused on clinical information systems and electronic healthcare records. So far, openEHR is not regarded as a formal (*de jure*) SDO. See https://www.openehr.org

International Health Terminology Standards Development Organisation (IHTSDO) or SNOMED International: See section under SNOMED.

WHO: it has developed the entire range of ICD.

Working together for health

5

Platforms for collaborative process

Arindam Basu

School of Health Sciences, University of Canterbury, Christchurch, New Zealand

Introduction: Patients as partners in care

Arindam Basu

L is a 50-year-old nonsmoker male with the history of hypertension controlled with ACE inhibitors. He is otherwise healthy and works as a manager of a private company. In December, he was spending an end-of-the-year weekend with his family at a resort located 60 km south of Kolkata, the nearest large city. The resort management employed a newly qualified medical doctor as their medical officer. On Sunday at midnight, L suddenly started bleeding from his nose ("epistaxis"). The doctor on the house attended him but found it difficult to control the bleeding; he wanted to pack sterile gauze inside L's nasal cavity to control the bleeding but was not sure how to do so. The doctor accessed an online medical group that he subscribed to, and with the help of an ENT surgeon in the group, he managed to insert a nasal pack and discussed subsequent management. The ENT surgeon who was available online helped the local doctor to control L's epistaxis successfully and detailed to him the subsequent management. The next morning, L left the resort and attended an ENT outpatient clinic in Kolkata for further assessment.

Worldwide, an estimated 17 per 10,000 people attend emergency rooms or primary care doctors with nosebleed.[55] The case earlier describes a situation where a medical doctor delivers face-to-face care for a patient' but uses elements of distance-based care: the patient ("L"), the primary care doctor, and the ENT specialist ("remote specialist") who advised the primary care doctor ("local doctor") were geographically separated, but the care was delivered on time. This was possible because the local doctor collaborated with a remote specialist to deliver care. Thus part of the care was distance based and was Internet mediated. Such delivery of care is an example where providers, patients, and payers come together either just in time and collaborate or forge "participatory health care."

Doctors working in remote locations are likely to need further help to be able to respond to emergency situations. They can be helped through tools of participatory care and collaboration. In this chapter, we will describe principles and processes of collaborative and participatory health care in distance care settings.

Principles and practice of medicine and health sciences have been described from the perspective of information science.[56] Health-care data and information flow through "interactants," that is, patients, providers, and others such as payers and insurers who interact with each other to keep the system running. Patients, providers, and payers play different roles and have different expectations of each other in the delivery of health services and in ensuring quality of care.[57]

Tucker (2001) has argued that the quality of health-care delivery improves when patients and providers are viewed as equal partners in care.[58] As a step in that direction, Haidet and Paterniti (2010) have argued a need for narrative-based history taking. In narrative-based history taking, the physician incorporates principles of biomedical knowledge that he or she knows best, but the style of taking the history is so conversational that the patients too can participate, rather than simple passive watching or only providing information that the doctor needs. They argue that while doctors are familiar with complex biomedical knowledge and use such terms at the bedside, the patient is less likely to understand such technical complexity, preferring a more conversational style that includes nonverbal communication. Traditionally, doctors are not trained to tap that kind of information.[59] Anne Townsend et al. (2015) conducted a focus group interview of 32 doctors and patients in Canada and identified three themes in such interactions in times where doctors and patients are connected and how they deal with each other—(1) changing roles of doctors, where she identified subthemes of "being prepared" and "responsibilities" for the providers; (2) partnerships, with a subtheme of trust between providers and patients; and (3) tensions and burdens of the providers with their patients.[60] Such interactions are possible in inpatient and outpatient settings where patients and providers can meet in person with each other. But what happens when the providers and patients are separated from each other? This is where distance-based technology and collaborative and participatory nature of engagements between patients and providers enable effective and efficient care processes.

Penetration of the Internet is increasing across the world, and the roster of Internet users is growing, making online access through either desktop computers or mobile devices nearly ubiquitous for people across the world. China has over 700 million Internet users (52% population), and

India has over 450 million Internet users (38% of the population); Internet access is increasing in all the developing countries.[a]

Access to the Internet enables single or multiple patients in remote locations and single or multiple providers who are distantly located to participate in consultations and arrive at clinical decisions. In such settings, patients and providers "meet" online, through the use of social networking apps (e.g., WeChat or WhatsApp) or through email listservs and discussion groups. This may be considered an informal mode for telehealth; it is possible for more formal platforms to incorporate and facilitate such interactions.

In 1965 Gordon Moore predicted that in foreseeable time, manufacturers will continue to double the density of components in integrated circuits.[61] This has turned out in the form of a self-fulfilling prophecy that sets the pace of modern computing, referred to as Moore's law.[62] Three developments have converged in this space: Access to the Internet is increasing for most people worldwide; exponential growth in computational speed and capacity has occurred; computers and handheld devices have become affordable. In turn, these have resulted in pervasiveness of computers in our daily lives. In medical care the use of virtual reality systems, computer-assisted care, and social networking systems continue to connect providers and patients. On this basis, Jackie Boucher (2010) has argued that using personal health records (PHRs) in addition to electronic health records (EHRs) can bring about a shift in the relationship between health-care providers and patients.[63]

Telehealth and the access to always-on Internet for health information have challenged the notion that for care to take place, the provider and the patient must be in the same place and time. Further, Internet and telehealth applications have disrupted the traditional power relationships that used to exist between a provider and a patient based on the assumption that the provider was the sole source of knowledge and therefore vested with higher authority; now, information sourcing is more open and can be accessed freely both by the patients and providers. Such ubiquity of information has opened up a new opportunity driven by a need: that of fostering collaborations between providers and patients and patients themselves. Collaborative telehealth enables a network where patients, providers, and payers of care can work together to coordinate a process of care.

Emergent models of care: From paternalistic models and transaction to participatory care

The patient walks into the clinic and registers to meet with the doctor. This registration can be done over the phone (a few days to a few minutes earlier as well); the patient then waits to see the doctor; and finally, she is

[a]See http://www.internetlivestats.com/internet-users-by-country/.

ushered into the clinic. The patient enters the clinic room, and the doctor and patient engage in learning from each other. At this point the doctor learns the symptoms from the patient, observes the signs, physically examines the patient, and orders radiological and biochemical investigations. Based on the discussion with the patient, clinical examination, and investigation of the radiological and biochemical findings, the doctor, in consultation with the patient, charts a management plan. This occurs in the context of conventional, real-time, face-to-face interaction between doctors and patients.

Nicola Bragazzi (2013) would describe the earlier description of patient-physician interaction as *P Zero* (P0) process of care where the doctor mainly controls the information and the patient remains a passive recipient of information. This model is also referred to as paternalistic care.[64] Such care delivery is agnostic of a 21st century reality: patients can get connected to the Internet and identify the symptoms of their diseases, connect to repositories like **WebMD** that provides them with information on their symptoms and diseases, or access the many sites such as **Pubmed**. They can also access histories of other patients using social networking sites such as **patientslikeme.com**; many patients share their genetic data or provide samples to companies that can analyze their genomes and provide feedback on the patients' risk factors. Numerous wearable devices provide information on their states of health (**Google Fit** and **Apple Health,** e.g., are two software included in android- and IoS-based devices, respectively, that enable tracking one's state of health). The integration of genomic information, capability of big data analysis, availability of digital data storage and transmission of results (as in telemedicine/telehealth), and the use of systems medicine that study networks at genomic, molecular, and social network levels is referred to as "personalized, predictive, preventive, and participatory" health. Leroy Hood (2006) has described this approach to medical care as "P4 medicine."[65]

Besides patient-patient linkages, there exist doctor-doctor linkages. Primary care doctors work in villages where clinical resources are scarce. These doctors look after a wide age range of patients, from children to the elderly patients, and frequently need second opinions of more experienced professionals or experts to confirm a diagnosis or to properly define the therapeutic plan. The distance of reference centers or even the lack of specialists in the city is a scenario for them to seek support for clinical case discussion through telehealth resources. The interprofessional collaboration in this case has no patient participation, but involves clinicians' inputs. A wide range of tools can be used to facilitate such exchange of information between professionals. These include synchronous (real-time) or asynchronous (store-and-forward) communication, from open platforms such as WhatsApp, Skype, or telehealth platforms that ensure the confidentiality of the shared data and auditing. In Brazil, for example, the country with the largest public health telehealth program in the world,[66] the use of telehealth platforms with restricted access to identified professionals is widely used, connecting professionals at all levels of health care, primary care, middle and high complexity for second opinion, or telediagnosis (remote tests report).

Another challenge is that of intercultural understanding on the part of caregivers. As the scope of telehealth and remote delivery of care increases and as international travel and flow of immigrants and refugees become commonplace, in addition to meeting patients from their own countries and cultural contexts, doctors need to be mindful about "seeing" patients from other parts of the world as well. Such intercultural understanding is integral to the delivery of care. Anne Fadiman (1997) has described such a cross-cultural narrative in her book *The Spirit Catches You and You Fall Down*. This narrative is around a Hmong family who are immigrants to the United States, and the family has several encounters with the US health-care system where the daughter of the family has epilepsy and presents to US physicians. There are initial misunderstandings between the caregiving team about the daughter's epilepsy and the doctors' approach toward treating the daughter, but with deeper understanding by the US doctors of the patient's cultural situation, they were able to decide on a workable care plan for the patient.[67] Anecdotal evidence, such as this, suggests the importance of patient stories as part of the care process, and unless a collaborative process is forged between the patient perspective and the physicians, the effectiveness of the care process will suffer.

Easy availability of the Internet and electronic connectivity has enabled patients to develop their own networks and seek professional consultation from such networks. An illustrative case is that of Salvatore Iaconesi, an Italian designer. Iaconesi was diagnosed with brain tumor and decided to open up his medical history to the Internet to find solutions from users all over the world; he referred this as "open sourcing" his illness.[64,68]

As we have discussed in this section, better connectivity and ubiquitous nature of the Internet have enabled providers and patients to organize themselves and form associations where they can search and share information. Next, we will discuss and describe the tools and argue how can these collaborations be forged in the context of telehealth, where the patients and providers are all over the world. To start with, what are some of the tools that patients and physicians can use who will need to manage distance-based care?

Emails and discussion forums

The Internet is a network of computers that are given an address each (this is referred to as IP address or Internet protocol address). Using this specific address, it is possible to identify the geographical location of a computer from where a message is passed onto the global network. The Internet was founded on the basis of ARPANET, a US Department of Defense project led by Vint Cerf in the 1960s.

The history of emails is older than the history of the Internet. In the early days, email was passed as messages, and the senders would stick these messages in the folder of the intended recipients. In 1972 Ray Tomlinson suggested the use of the "@" character as addresses to intended recipients to specific machines. A protocol referred to as the simple mail transport protocol was used to send and deliver messages, and later on, post office protocol (POP) was developed.

Email applications present an always-on, Internet-based communication tool where a patient can provide either a snapshot of history along with attached multimedia files to the provider and the provider not only receives a record but also can report back and provide advice that is relevant and timely. Email can be between one provider and one patient or more than one provider and one patient; in situations where group consultation can be useful, email can be used for many-to-many conversations. Here, groups of providers and groups of patients can be included in the conversation.

Although emails have become the de facto communication and collaboration tool, they have limitations attributed to how email is used. Emails must be manually typed; this opens up inherent risks of spelling errors—autocorrection can distort the patient or the provider's original meaning and intention to communicate. Grammatical errors or a simple miss of a comma may be misinterpreted. Correcting and rechecking slows down processes, leading to user resistance. Compare this with a face-to-face interaction, here the patient, who has a set of complaints, will approach the clinician or care provider and accompany the words with gestures of the face or hand or both. This means that an incorrect word will be mapped against facial features and gestures. But even online face-to-face meetings may be a cause for miscommunication to a lesser extent. Just turning away, an ill-focused camera or the wrong amount of light may make facing each other or gesture recognition difficult. Online communication both by text or real time requires training.[69] Emails also pose several security-related challenges that can leak personal information to unintended participants in the process. It is not possible to identify or encrypt who originally wrote the email, that is, whether it is the tentative patient, and on the other hand, it is difficult for the sender to definitely know whether the email was at all opened by the intended recipient. It is difficult to integrate emails into clinic operations in a day-to-day basis as emails cannot be automatically routed to the recipients or merge the transactions into medical records. Despite the popularity and simplicity of emails, Katz and Moyer (2004) have stated that email is "not the answer" for an efficient communication between patients and doctors.[70]

Jarkko Oikarinen developed the Internet Relay Chat (IRC) in the summer of 1988 at the University of Oulu in Finland. IRC allows individuals to communicate and post messages to each other in real time and has very small footprint (not much resources are required). It requires availability of the Internet for communication. IRCs are more versatile than emails in the sense that they allow real-time communication for a patient with a doctor; like emails, they require that a client be installed on the machine from where the patient or the doctor has initiated conversation and these access IRC servers. IRCs are meant for group conversations, and as a result, they share similar disadvantages with respect to patient privacy and risks of information leakage to unintended recipients as emails. Modern versions of IRCs like WhatsApp and WeChat are more advanced, and the sharing and conversations can include direct calls and voice too, besides inclusion of a range of multimedia and documents. They also have encryption so that privacy is less of a concern.

Randale Sechrest, in 2010, described how patients use the Internet from an orthopedic surgeon's perspective.[71] He had argued that in contrast to other disciplines, health-care providers are slow to take up the Internet in applying to their field; in particular, there was evidence that surgeons had at that time, disconnected themselves from Internet-based information while communicating with patients. They emphasized that providers need to distinguish between direct physical component of the care provision like surgeries and other specialized procedures by medical colleagues and the "information component" of the work they did. In other words, create a distinction between what the patient needs to know between other relevant information that needs to be exchanged between the patient and clinician.

Over time, almost all information has shifted to the Internet. Self-advertising portals have given way to a more organized "chaos" of information in microblogs and other sources. It is therefore time to organize web-based dissemination of information more efficiently toward health-care delivery. Sechrest has suggested that there should be information access for patients and a need for the same to be disseminated in an easy-to-follow multimedia content. Like all web-based information, accessing it should be easy. Many forget that Google is a brand, not a generic term. However, it does convey the meaning like no other words can. This needs suitable metadata and other ways to organize the information. While emails, discussions, and web-based sharing and parking of information are useful for patients, microblogs and social networking have added another dimension to the patient-provider collaboration that we discuss now. We provide a sample set of resources in Table 1.

TABLE 1 Description of resources.

Site	URL	Description
OpenNotes	https://www.opennotes.org/	Collaborative visit notes for patients and health-care providers
Sermo	http://www.sermo.com/	A social networking site for physicians and patients
Doximity	https://www.doximity.com/	Social networking site for physicians and patients
DailyRounds	https://www.dailyrounds.org/	Social networking app targeted toward doctors
DailyRounds blog	https://medium.com/doctors-of-the-world/	Anyone can participate, a blog from the developers of the daily rounds
QuantiaMD	https://secure.quantiamd.com/home/tour	An educational site, mainly for physicians, not so much for patients
Among doctors	https://amongdoctors.com/	Social networking site for physicians
GomerBlog	https://amongdoctors.com/	A website for the physician community
Google Plus Medical Community	https://plus.google.com/communities/103008363755731074852	Using Google plus to seek answers and guidance, for both doctors and patients
G-med	http://g-med.com/login?ReturnUrl=%2f	Global physician network, directed at physicians, not patients
Facmedicine	https://forum.facmedicine.com/	Discussion forum for medical doctors and medical students
allnurses	http://allnurses.com/	Discussion forum for nurses
Medical Geeks	http://www.medicalgeek.com/	A forum dedicated to the discussion of medical topics and anyone can contribute
MedHelp	http://www.medhelp.org/	An online community aimed at patients who can seek answers for their health issues

Rxreddit	https://www.reddit.com/r/medicine/	A reddit subreddit aimed at medical professionals
Medical conditions and diseases (Quora)	https://www.quora.com/topic/Medical-Conditions-and-Diseases	A quora question and answer site where anyone can post questions and answers on medical topics and advices
GHD online	https://www.ghdonline.org/	Global online network of professionals cutting across clinical disciplines, and patients too can join
Patientslikeme	https://www.patientslikeme.com	Patients like me are a portal where patients can organize and ask questions. Providers can join as guests
User-driven health care	A Facebook group for patients and physicians alike	A Facebook group where patients, caregivers, and doctors communicate
Communities of Participatory Medicine (e-patients)	https://connect.participatorymedicine.org/home	Engaged patient or e-patient portal
WebMD	https://www.webmd.com/	A portal where physicians and patients can find information and share information and expertise
HealthUnlocked	https://healthunlocked.com/	Patient information portal
Health Stackexchange	https://health.stackexchange.com/	Exchange of information between physicians, health caregivers, and patients
OpenClinical iPath	http://www.openclinical.org/os_iPath.html	Open-source pathology discussion and learning system, open to anyone
OpenHIE	https://ohie.org/	Open-source information sharing system
Health Information for All	http://www.hifa.org (many variants, in language, e.g., French, Spanish, Portuguese, and some country specific ones)	Email discussion forum(s) that promotes easy availability of health information—especially in Africa and the developing world

For a comprehensive list of studies on open notes and collaboration between patients and caregivers, see https://www.opennotes.org/about/research/.

Social media and networking for distance-based care

In 2006 Jack Dorsey (twitter handle: @jack) founded Twitter (URL: http://www.twitter.com); in the beginning, he used short messaging system for communication in Twitter. As the number of characters were limited in SMS that was used in cell phones then, a twitter user was restricted to use 140 characters to express ideas and opinions in much the same way one would use a weblog (referred to as "blog"). This application and class of applications were referred to as microblog. Over time, Ev Williams and Biz Stone (twitter handle: @Biz) joined the group, and Twitter matured into a communication platform where users would create a username and password and would share 140 character messages to the world and to selected group of "friends" and "followers" (for a history of Twitter, see https://www.lifewire.com/history-of-twitter-3288854). For specific topics, you can add "hashtags" (represented with symbol "#"), and this would indicate specific keywords that the users would generate to indicate topic-based discussions. As a user, you can create groups and organize discussions and share images and sound bites. At present (as of 2018) a user on Twitter can use 280 characters to express ideas and share opinions.

The team of Chris Hughes, Eduardo Saverin, Andrew McCollum, Dustin Moskovitz, and Mark Zuckerberg established Facebook in 2004 based on the name taken from similar named documents distributed to students and staff at Harvard University (see https://www.theguardian.com/technology/2007/jul/25/media.newmedia). Over time, Facebook evolved to connect users in a network where the users were "known" to each other or connected in some way ("small networks"). Like Twitter, Facebook relies on hashtags and threaded discussions of topics.

The use of social media and networking is useful for the training of providers and can be useful for patient care. Mesquita et al. (2017) have conducted an integrative review where they accessed scholarly publications on the use of Facebook, Twitter, and WhatsApp for use in the training of nurses. They found that in about 20% of the situations, the educators were using these social media tools for teaching nurses; however, besides describing the finding of social media tools being beneficial in teaching nursing students, the authors also raised alerts about ethical issues around information leakage and disclosure, and they suggested that these considerations need review.[72] In a review on the use of smartphones for pain management as adjunct to other treatments, Eckard et al. (2016) found that smartphone- and Internet-based applications that employ online journals facilitate improved communication between patient and providers and allow for more personalized care and improved pain management.[73] Irena Spasic and colleagues (2015) developed a knee rehabilitation app based on Facebook platform (TRAK App, URL: http://apps.facebook.com/kneetrak/)

and conducted a feasibility study. Using standardized measurements, they found that for both patients and providers, a web-based approach allowed for communication, information dissemination, exercise progression, and self-management.[74]

The earlier findings suggest that web-based applications and social media applications can be used to build collaborations between patients and providers. But there are caveats about social networking and related collaborative practices between doctors and patients that we must be aware of. Guseh et al. (2009) have argued that while social networking sites provide scope of professional development for young doctors and foster educational opportunities, these benefits are eclipsed by the possibility that such networking sites can be misused with effects on ethics and patient-provider relationships.[75] Even while no specific instances were reported, they discussed several possibilities that the doctors can expose, or even possibly, misuse privacy of patients therefore putting patients at risk. Based on this, they recommend that physicians should avoid whatever could possibly be a dual relationship with their patients, one professional and the other personal. Also, doctors should be conservative about their online profile and use such privacy settings that disallow open disclosure about their personal lives. They advise that doctors should not invite patients into their social networks (they only discussed Facebook). They did not consider the perspective of telehealth or delivery of medical advice over a distance or a partnership model of care where patients and physicians could use social networking sites. We discuss this next.

Telehealth platforms

Magdala de Araújo Novaes

Telehealth platforms are digital environments that allow health professionals to interact with each other and with their patients to promote patient care, education, and health research and to support health-care management. Unlike open social networks (e.g., Facebook), these platforms are environments designed to meet the specific needs of telehealth services; restrict access to managers, health professionals, and patients; and must comply with quality and safety standards under current policies in each country. Therefore such platforms are secure and evidence-based networks specifically tailored for the care of individual or groups of patients.

Geographical or temporal separation between the actors involved in the health collaboration process characterizes telehealth practices. Situations where the use of these systems become important to continue patient care and, in many cases, become the only way to assist patients include the lack of specialists or physicians in the patient's hometown and hard-to-reach places. These systems go beyond conventional text-based technologies to capture vital signs, images, audios, and video feeds. Communication channels in these systems include instant messages or real-time video transmission that help to set up contexts to evaluate the patient or to share experiences and in-depth technique scientific knowledge among colleagues.

A telehealth platform can allow communication synchronously, with instant messaging and audio-video transmission in real time, or asynchronously, by exchange messages with text, images, or audio-videos already recorded. The use of such media can help remote specialists to evaluate the patients or for providing agility and usability to describe the clinical case using textual description. The different modalities of telehealth practices use the platforms as follows: teleconsulting, telediagnostic (remote diagnostic), telemonitoring, medical second opinion, telesurveillance, teleeducation, and others (see Fig. 1).

In teleconsulting for second opinions or for soliciting expert opinion, a telehealth platform is used solely for health professionals. In other situations the platforms are open to be used by both the providers and the patient. In such situations the provider is responsible for conducting the assessment, guiding the patient, analyzing data collected from connected devices, and where necessary interacting with other specialists to manage

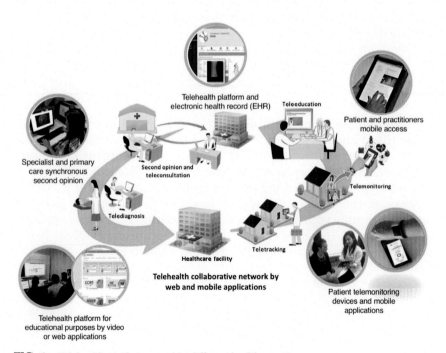

FIG. 1 Telehealth platforms used in different health practices.

the patient. In case of emergencies a telehealth platform can be used to provide professional "lifeguard" resources to enable care with specialist support by sharing data, images, video, and audio. In primary care, teleconsulting is frequently used by doctors to discuss diagnostic hypotheses, plan treatment, or triage the need for referral to another specialist in the referral network.

Teleconsultation and telemonitoring

In teleconsultation the patient interacts directly with the health professional using the telehealth platform. Any intervention of another professional with the patient in the same room is optional. In these cases, telehealth platforms allow interactions using real-time audio, video, or both. Some platforms allow to connect sensors, wearables, and other devices so that it is possible to transmit physical signs and biometric and physiological data including blood glucose, blood pressure, and heartbeats to help health professional evaluate the patient at a distance. These devices and sensors are frequently connected to telemonitoring platforms, where collection, recording, and transmission of data are done with predefined periodicity, or from monitoring an alert event. In such situations, health professionals analyze the data that they receive and act accordingly while delivering care for these patients.

As an illustrative example of a telemonitoring platform, think of an application that assists a patient to control weight. The telemonitoring platform monitors the patient's physical activity and the individual's records of meals and calories consumed in a day and transmits the data for analysis by professionals. The professionals can then act on the basis of received data to help the patient reduce weight. Here the telemonitoring platform is used with active participation of the patient. In other situations, users may have their data collected through connected devices, for example, blood glucose for diabetics or blood pressure measurements for a hypertensive patient. Such monitoring may lead to prevention or in the postdischarge planning and treatment in patients with heart attack or stroke. In yet other scenario, telemonitoring platforms can be integrated in home care equipment to enable continuous monitoring and generate emergency alerts or for elderly patients, who can be continuously monitored with sensors that transmit an alert when the patient suffers a fall at home.

Telediagnosis

Telediagnosis refers to remote diagnosis ("tele" means remote, prefixed to diagnosis). These platforms are designed to enable transmission of physical examination records and medical reports remotely or concurrently to a specialist at a different or the same geographical location. The examining specialist doctor may be located in the same geographical region at the same time of the examination, or the specialist may be remotely located: the transmission platform is designed to work identically. Telediagnostic platforms ensure that records of images and videos preserve the diagnostic quality even after being subjected to compression procedures for transmission. The use of the Digital Imaging and Communications in Medicine (DICOM) standard is a recommended requirement to allow heavy file traffic without impairing efficiency in use. A limitation might be low connection speed for data transmission or restrictions with bandwidth. Therefore, balancing image quality, efficiency in use, and available bandwidth pose significant challenges to telediagnostic platforms.

Teletracking

Teletracking uses questionnaires and protocols to study occurrences of determined behaviors, comorbid conditions, or the clinical condition of individuals. Various platforms provide one or more reference protocols for the domain knowledge, that is, the evaluation of mental health conditions. While some platforms use pre-defined questionnaires and instruments, other platforms allow the user to create self-reported instruments and questionnaires. Teletracking is used with mobile devices and smartphones or has a web interface that sends collected data to a server. Asynchronous or offline transmission of data is useful for remote surveillance, enabling managers the capacity of early detection of epidemics.

Telehealth services and software platforms

Telehealth services and software platforms provide a channel of communication among patients and doctors via video calls using multiple types of devices. Some platforms may provide inter-health-care integration services to consult and update clinical records from patients under treatment. Telehealth platforms can include workflow management (for managing the activities of the medical staff) and billing integration services. We describe three platforms: the Brazilian HealthNet, the American MDLIVE, and the Australian HealthDirect.

The HealthNet (http://www.nutes.ufpe.br/healthnet/) is a software platform that was developed and currently maintained by the Telehealth Center (NUTES)[76] of Federal University of Pernambuco (UFPE). This software platform integrates a public, government-funded telehealth service that is composed of professionals from the Brazilian government's Unified Health System (SUS). The HealthNet platform supports teleconsulting (second opinion) and telediagnostic services to health service practitioners, via web pages and phone services. In teleconsulting, health-care practitioners may submit their technical questions to a remote health-care specialist, which may address a clinical case, including patient's information and clinical records or a nonspecific patient-related question, that is, a clinical question. In telediagnostic platforms, health-care practitioners may submit clinical examination reports in the platform, also including the patient's information and the exam results by itself for obtaining a medical opinion from a remote health-care specialist.

The MDLIVE (https://www.mdlive.com/) is a private telehealth service of the American organization MDLIVE Medical Group, PA. This telehealth service supports remote medical consults for patients in the comfort of their homes or in any other location at any time, including weekends and holidays. MDLIVE is supported by a software platform that includes a website, a mobile app, and a call center for phone-only consults, with the option of performing medical consults via video calls. Patients have the option of being automatically assigned to a physician according to their condition and other personal information or to directly choose a physician, who made themselves available. The software platform has the ability of maintain the patient's health summary and in some cases to integrate with external health systems to obtain its most recent version, prior to a remote consult. MDLIVE can help patients with more than 50 routine conditions and may even send prescriptions to the patient's nearest pharmacy.

The HealthDirect (https://www.healthdirect.gov.au/) is a public and government-funded Australian telehealth service for providing online information and free helplines on health care. General public may contact HealthDirect to obtain information on health advices, health-care centers, and medicines and even perform an online symptom checker. This free telehealth service is performed via a software platform that includes online webpages, mobile apps, and a telephone hotline.

Computer assisted care

Shashi Gogia

Changes in knowledge and advances have made efficient and up-to-date management of clinical problems a clinician faces challenging and possibly, beyond the learning capability of any individual. By 2020, it is estimated that knowledge about the body, health, and health care is projected to double every 73 days. Computer-based processing allows not only information transfer (telehealth) but also the process of generation of knowledge and wisdom—referred to as artificial intelligence (AI). There are many advanced sensors that extend the traditional five senses, which help in diagnosis and treatment. These can not only assist, but also may sometimes replace the care provider.

Identification of the problem is considered the first and most important step towards solving the problem. Traditionally, medical students are taught that 90% of the diagnosis is achievable through history and examination. Investigations and radiology have made diagnosis easier and also increased the possibility of it becoming more automated.

Diagnosis is considered an art and involves deductive capability of processing various inputs from a myriad of presenting complaints, findings, investigation reports, radiology, and other inputs into a final list or sometimes, even a single one (loosely referred to as "I'm feeling lucky") final conclusion. All five senses traditionally used to be employed—for instance, tasting urine for sweetness of sugar—was conducted to diagnose diabetes in the 19th century.[77] Traditionally, clinical methods are drilled into the clinician's brain through years of training, observation, systematic studying, and experience gained through examination of patients seen in the past. Computer systems can do similar processing with some differences.

In many situations, they can score higher too. Advanced sensors can go far beyond human ones; for example, GPS is essentially satellite vision. Drones are mobile cameras and can have 360-degree vision; robotic scopes travel through the intestines. ECG and ultrasound recordings can be done from within the esophagus, vagina, intestines, or rectum. Genome sequencing literally takes sensors to a submolecular level. All these senses cannot be utilized without high-level processing. A point to consider is that most biochemical investigations, for instance, blood sugar, serum bilirubin, serum ammonia, and radiology-based investigations, are basically artificial sensors. Fitbits are wearable devices fitted with sensors that provide warnings as well.

A clinician might get tired, take leave, needs to spend time for family, needs to eat, and has to socialize. In contrast, computer systems have no such issues. Such systems can be trained to achieve very specific tasks and create targeted solutions that would otherwise require involvement of specialists—mobile apps are typical examples.

Development of software and telesystems, robotic solutions, and other tools that contain inbuilt learning or machine learning algorithms share similarity with drugs when it comes to scalability.[b] Once they have been produced, their replication is scalable, a process that is unlike the training of clinicians, each of whom has to be individually groomed. Within such tools, calculations can be incorporated relatively easily and results read off even while the examination is underway. This is relevant, for instance, in the estimation of the size of an ulcer. Pattern recognition is the norm now for ECGs and many CT/MR scans.[c] A few advantages of these systems are worth considering:

- Investigation reports already highlight abnormal values—it may be in bold fonts or in a different color.
- Holter systems even while active on a 24/7 basis wake up to record and highlight abnormal episodes.

[b]Read the last subchapter *AI and IoT In Healthcare* for more on this topic.
[c]See Chapters 9 and 14.

- These systems enable coordination and sharing data between various sensors.
- If these systems are connected to the Internet, coordination and data sharing can occur literally on a global scale.
- Memory storage and recall are faster.

Initial forays of artificial intelligence in medicine began in the 1960s with expert systems created algorithms for diagnosis. The most well known of these was MYCIN, credited to Ted Shortliffe, which suggested the ideal antibiotic for a particular disease.[78] It was found, theoretically, to be better than a clinician!

Currently available AI systems

Clinical decision support systems (CDSS), in particular diagnostic decision support systems, may be described as linkage between health observations and health knowledge to influence health choices by clinicians for improved health care. The basic components of these systems are as follows:

- a dynamic (medical) knowledge base
- an inferential mechanism (usually a set of rules derived from the experts and evidence-based medicine)
- implemented through medical logic modules (MLM) based on a language such as Arden syntax[79]

Such systems can be based on expert systems or artificial neural networks or both (connectionist expert systems).

Computerized Provider Order Entry (CPOE) has been designed to stop the harm that a wrong prescription can cause, for example, cross checking for counteracting drugs in the same prescription, like algorithms to flag possible interactions between a beta blocker and a beta agonist, under or more importantly excessive dosage, two different drugs with a similar base element. Simple targeted software can provide an algorithm or management process for a problem frequently encountered. An example is disease activity measurement in Ankylosing Spondilitis (see Fig. 2).

Examples of CDSS with incorporation of net-based search to give complete knowledge base include Uptodate from Wolters Kluwer, ClinicalKey from Elsevier (see Box 1), and Watson from IBM.

Telerobotics—discussed elsewhere—is a form of computer-assisted care wherein the devices have a certain mobility. These can be a help in diagnosis and therapeutics. While there is more on this in the other chapters, we conclude this chapter with an innovation wherein humans and computer systems collaborate seamlessly (see Box 2).

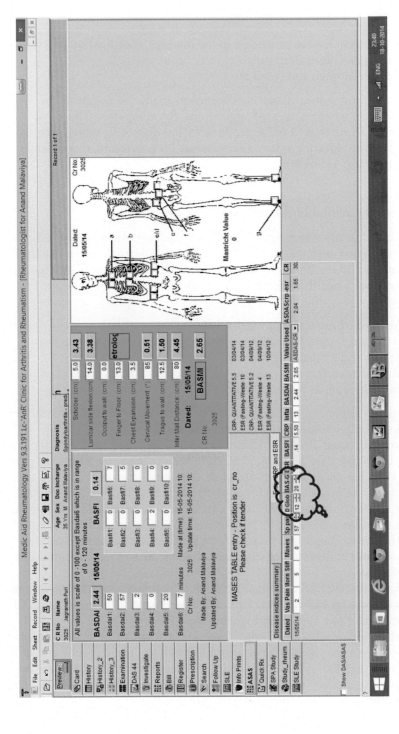

FIG. 2 Disease activity index in ankylosing spondylitis. *Source:* AMLA Mediquip.

BOX 1

Clinicalkey

ClinicalKey is a clinical search engine that supports clinical decisions by making it easier to find and apply relevant knowledge. ClinicalKey enables organizations to find clinical answers faster and make smarter point-of-care decisions. It combines in-depth medical content with Smart Search technology, making critical answers more discoverable.

Only ClinicalKey provides access to Elsevier's medical portfolio of content—the latest books, journals, multimedia, and more covering over 30 medical and surgical specialties. Moreover, it is indexed daily and continues to be updated as new resources are published, ensuring that the most current evidence is incorporated.

The Smart Search technology is based on an intuitive search engine that analyzes medical queries as they're being typed, searches related content automatically, and suggests shortcuts to finding relevant answers quickly.

ClinicalKey is accessible from any device, including tablets and mobile phones, enabling practitioners to work more efficiently and provide better quality care.

Other features such as scoped search, filters, retained search history, saved content, and presentation maker help clinicians and organizations use their time more effectively while improving the quality of care provided.

Permission from Elsevier India.

BOX 2

Electronic skin—an example of wearable electronics

Electronic skin (e-skin) mimics natural skin and can find broad applications in robotics and biomedical systems

E-skin is a flat malleable electronic circuit that convey a mechanical stimulus in a convenient way to the beneath distributed sensor arrays. These circuits acquire and preprocess sensor signals and transmit the information to the next higher level of ICT infrastructure within a system. They create an effective and reliable way to extract and process data, allowing meaningful actions like automatic reflexes, contact type recognition, and surface feature detection. There is a layer that protects the inner electronic system from damages due to interactions with the outside.[576]

continued

BOX 2   (*cont'd*)

Zhou et al. (2018) developed a dynamic covalent thermoset-based e-skin, which is connected through robust covalent bonds, rendering the resulting devices good chemical and thermal stability at service condition. Tactile, temperature, flow, and humidity sensing capabilities are realized. This e-skin can be rehealed when it is damaged and can be fully recycled at room temperature, which has rarely, if at all, been demonstrated for e-skin.[577] After rehealing or recycling the e-skin regains mechanical and electrical properties comparable with the original e-skin. In addition, malleability enables the e-skin to permanently conform to complex, curved surfaces without introducing excessive interfacial stresses. These properties of the e-skin yield an economical and eco-friendly technology that can find broad applications in robotics, prosthetics, health care, and human-computer interface, using inputs from GPS and sensors.

Conclusion

In this chapter, we provided an overview of the tools of collaboration and participatory care for patients and doctors. Participatory health, described as the process of health-care delivery where patients and physicians play equal roles in information sharing and care management, is increasingly becoming the norm of care worldwide. Telehealth provides a platform where patients and physicians and other providers can share and cocreate treatment and wellness. We discussed a set of tools and their history; we outlined the development and usage of emails, web-based tools, and augmented and virtual reality applications for developing and building collaborative nature of care planning for physicians and patients. A range of tools are available at this time to develop care planning in collaboration with patients that doctors who work in remote settings can use. In resource-limited settings, the use of emails and Internet relay chats can provide asynchronous and real-time sharing of clinical information and care planning; however, these tools are limited by the fact that they have security risks and they are not always intuitive by way of identification of patients and physicians and they are open to misuse or usage problems can lead to misinterpretation of data. Other tools such as video conferencing and the use of the graphical user interface based on web browsers are useful in overcoming limitations of email, but these tools can be technologically complex and demanding.

A range of telehealth platforms allow health professionals to interact with each other and with their patients to organize patient care, educate patients, conduct health research, and support health-care management.

Telediagnosis, teleconsultation, and teletracking services enable physicians and patients to communicate with each other in ways that are different from participatory social network platforms. Computer-assisted care combined with social networks and telehealth extend the efficiency and scope of collaborative health care even further. This chapter provided a brief overview of the key technologies and links; other chapters in this text provide more detailed information on these platforms and services.

Patient-centered care

Marcia Ito[a,b]

[a]IBM Research, Sao Paulo, Brazil, [b]Brazilian Health Informatics Association (SBIS), Sao Paulo, Brazil

Introduction

Chronic diseases are among the challenges of health and economic development in the 21st century, as they affect quality of life of the people, with ill effects on productivity and spending. It is estimated that annually, approximately 14 million people between the ages of 30 and 70 die from chronic diseases. There is an expected loss of $7 trillion in productivity and spending over the next 20 years if no action is taken.[80] Costs increase exponentially with the increase in the number of chronic conditions. In the United States, about 80% of Medicare costs are for patients having four or more chronic conditions.[81] Such patients require care through a team of different health professionals (Fig. 1) who need to understand not only his disease but all its dimensions related to the biopsychosocial perspectives of the team members. The patient may also be considered as a team member with sharing of power and responsibility. This therapeutic alliance needs mutual understanding as the doctor and other providers are also persons.[82]

For efficient care delivery, caregivers should be aware of even the minor nuances of care delivery offered by others. Each care provider, due to a multitude of patients, would be able to devote only a small percent of his time for each patient, while the patient or relatives would be able to devote much more time and effort. Even while most clinicians find it disrupting, it does raise a question whether the patient himself could be a leader of his own care efforts. This creates a new concept, "patient-centered care" or PCC.

Basically, PCC caters to the patient's psychosocial and physical needs. It is about patient's concerns and priorities for care and regards the collaboration between the patient and his/her care team including the health professionals. It motivates patients to make decisions about their own care and emphasizes the need for coordination among members of the care

Fundamentals of Telemedicine and Telehealth
https://doi.org/10.1016/B978-0-12-814309-4.00006-9

FIG. 1 Patients are in the center of care, and they are assisted by a team of different health professionals.

team, resources, and support systems.[83] It encourages patients to review their medical records, lifts the restrictions on family involvement in care, and possibly lowers the noise levels in hospital.[84] Finally, communication and coordination between all of the stakeholders are crucial to providing appropriate patient-centered care.[85]

The concept of patient health management through coordinated care teams has been explored by several authors since the late 1960s. Several definitions have been proposed, the most cited being the care coordination study, conducted by Stanford University in 2007, which describes it as: "The deliberate organization of patient care activities between two or more participants (including the patient) involved in patient's care to facilitate the appropriate delivery of health care services. Organizing care involves the marshaling of personnel and other resources needed to carry out all required patient care activities and is often managed by the exchange of information among participants responsible for different aspects of care".[86]

Care coordination aims to reduce the fragmentation of care and improve delivery of health services. Studies conducted by Medicare[87] in 2007 showed that most of the care coordination programs practiced by US healthcare institutions have not succeeded. They also found that those with success had a common characteristic that the relationship between the care coordinator and the patient went beyond the medical service. The coordinator understood the patients' needs and connected to him personally. The relationship between the coordinator and the patient was felt to be important because the treatment involved behavior change and choices that were under the control of the patient. At such an instance the coordinator acts as a counselor and, thereby, has fundamental importance for the patient's decisions. Other studies have similarly indicated that successful programs hinge on the long-term and trusting relationships built between the patient, the care team, and within the care team members.[88,89]

Care coordination is a necessary tool that supports the health professionals, patients, and caregivers. In this, ICT plays an important role, providing information about the disease and treatment besides clarifying doubts and facilitating access and exchange of information among professionals, patients, and caregivers and finally supporting communication and interaction between them.[80,90] Telehealth support systems can further help in organizing everyone's activities with alerts, information exchange, and access to health records and provide educational information.

eHealth in patient engagement

According to Ball et al.[91] patient engagement contributes towards meaningful exchange of information assisting care adherence and leads further to improved care, better experience, and lower costs, the essence of PCC. Also, WHO[92] affirms that the patient engagement until now has been ignored in most countries and healthcare institutions, despite evidence that patients thus engaged tend to use fewer healthcare resources, make better decisions, and get better outcomes. Hence, patient engagement is a good way to ensure the sustainability of health systems and maybe essential to improve population health.

Patient compliance, patient adherence, and patient engagement have different definitions. Patient compliance is the degree to which a patient adheres to a prescribed medical treatment. Adherence refers to the continuity of the medical treatment, which depends on a number of factors, for example, the cost of medications or the complexity of the treatment. Engagement refers to the patient taking an active role in protecting his health, choosing appropriate treatment methodologies for episodes of ill health, and managing chronic problems. All three complement each other. Without compliance, we do not have adherence, and without both, we do not have the engagement. Fig. 2 explains this schematically.

Based on the above, WHO[93] makes the following recommendations:

(1) Educate providers and health professionals about patient engagement.
(2) Promote patients to be involved with their health.
(3) Find additional ways to involve patients.
(4) Recognize the importance of the patients physical-social-cultural environment.
(5) Enable a favorable and supportive environment.

FIG. 2   The relationship between compliance, adherence, and engagement.

So, methods, systems, and tools that help governments, health authorities, or payers to improve engagement at the population or individual patient level are key to the success of these programs. ICT helps, and more specifically in the 21st century, eHealth seems to be a perfect way to improve the patient engagement. It provides necessary information and improves communication between various stakeholders besides imparting education to the patient about his disease and treatment. Some of this is required for the health professional too, at the very least, on how to communicate better besides other engagement approaches.

Strategies to address patient engagement as recommended by WHO[14] include improved health literacy, treatment decision-making, and self-management of chronic conditions. Here, health literacy[94] is "the ability to make sound health decisions in the context of everyday life—at home, in the community, at the workplace, the health care system, the market place and the political arena." Health information and education must be necessary to improve health literacy. Nutbeam[95] has defined three health literacy levels:

- **Functional**: basic skills in reading and writing, for basic understanding of the health context.
- **Interactive**: more advanced cognitive literacy and social skills, which permits the patient or relative to be an active participant in care delivery.
- **Critical**: ability to analyze and use the information to decide what is better for his/her health.

Health literacy constitutes the basic core of patient engagement. It helps improve shared decision-making, allowing the patient to choose the appropriate treatment and other options for a healthy life. It also assists self-monitoring and consequent self-care. Technology helps increase health literacy, for example, learning about anatomy, medications, health terms, and his disease, but should only be on a need to know basis.

Many new technologies and applications have appeared in the health domain over the past few decades. This includes access by people for information related to health.[96] Patients need to understand all components of health delivery like assessment, diagnosis interventions, education, and consultations. Information access methods can include webinars and conferences, access to patient portals or applications for specific disease or clinical conditions as pregnancy, hypertension monitoring, and so on. The role of mobile technology for patient engagement is especially important.

Another barrier would be digital literacy, related to the wide variation between patient's capabilities to fully understand technology and its utilization. A formal definition[97]—"Digital literacy is the capabilities which fit someone for living, learning, working, participating and thriving in a digital society." mHealth is an example. Application developers consider the public, local cultural, and socioeconomic contexts before promoting usage and adoption. Ease of use is important which involves the interface having a mixture of multimedia formats like, graphics, images, sound, video etc., use of native language(s) and most importantly restricting the communication to a need to know basis. However, some graphics and medical images may be difficult for the public to comprehend.

The final issue to be considered is technology acceptance. The technology acceptance model (TAM)[98] shows perceived usefulness and perceived ease of use affecting (a) attitude towards using (b) behavioral intention to use and (c) actual system use. The following limitations in the adoption of telehealth have been described[99]: (1) issues of privacy and confidentiality, (2) fear of technology breakdown and equipment failure, (3) loss of face-to-face contact with healthcare professionals, and (4) overdependence (i.e., on the telehealth service).

Notable methods and techniques to develop such applications include use of avatars or video conference when the professional perceives that the patient/caregiver may be afraid to lose the comfort of face-to-face contact. It is important to demonstrate that these services are an add-on and not a replacement of existing services and to explain antecedent benefits.

Now, we discuss the technology used to improve patient engagement and education:

- **Automated messages and text/SMS** is a quick way to keep in touch with the patient and support their self-monitoring efforts. Automated messages can be sent to remind the patient about his appointment, take medicine, drink water, do exercises, and so on. Also, some educational tips to improve knowledge about the patient's disease or treatment can be sent. Automated reminders and SMS/other messaging services have been described to be more useful than traditional in-person communication.[100] But, maybe for the elderly, less digitally literate and others uncomfortable with the use of this kind of technology, mobile phone calls including voice messaging may be better.

- **Videoconferencing** can be an ideal alternative for when one or both stakeholders cannot be physically present in the same place, which could be related to difficult-to-reach locations, paucity of time, difficulty to leave home, fear of social stigma (e.g., HIV positive, leprosy, etc.), and lack of transportation. Sometimes, videoconferencing is better than the message or writing approach because one can provide additional options, like chat, screen sharing, and recorded videos, and the entire meeting can be recorded for later recall.[a] Facial expressions give clues to both stakeholders regarding their level of understanding. Informed consent and other ethical consideration especially patients' privacy are legitimate concerns, which need to be handled professionally.

- **Online support groups** are another important vehicle of patient engagement. The patient can share his experience with others and discuss it with peers and professionals. Here, it is possible to use chatbots or conversational AI technology for support. Schumaker et al.[101] described the chatbot as a system that "seeks to mimic conversation rather than understand it." The first chatbot called ELIZA[102] was able to establish a conversation with human beings. It was based on the rephrasing of input sentences, following a set of predefined rules. There are now a growing number of voice recognition devices, for example, *Cortona* (MS Windows) *Alexa* (Amazon), *Siri* (Mac), and Google Home. Such technologies can play a role in care provision like attending to the patient, and caregiver call for help on a 24/7 basis. Hybrid technologies where both humans and chatbots interact with patients and caregivers can also exist.

- **Serious game and gamified applications**: Serious game is defined as "digital games used for purposes other than mere entertainment," and gamified applications refers to "software that incorporates elements of games." Examples of gamification elements are points, badges, leader boards, clear goals, challenges, levels, progress, feedback, rewards, stories, or themes. All these can have a role in motivating patient engagement or promote health. Gamification has been shown to be effective in increasing engagement as a part of online applications.[103]

However, effectiveness will remain weak if there is lack of trust in the healthcare professional, underlying the need for a healthy and mutual relationship between the provider and the patient. Whatever

[a] Fully discussed in Chapter 4.

the medium, the patient has to be comfortable in informing the clinicians about his/her health beliefs and worries besides other potential barriers to engagement. A fully informed clinician will be able to offer better outcomes.

Patient portal

Since the 1990s, starting with MyChart (https://www.mypatientchart.org/MyChart/) and Indivo (http://indivohealth.org/), patient portals are becoming increasingly popular. Initially, they were means to gain access by patients for their personal clinical data, with the purpose being solved by linking with the EHR. From 2006 onwards the processes started getting modified, allowing patients to enter the data themselves. In the process, they became what could be called a personal health record (PHR). Tang et al.[104] defined a PHR in Markle Foundation's *Connecting for Health Collaborative* as "an electronic application through which individuals as well as caregivers could access, manage, and share their health information, in a private, secure, and confidential environment." So, now patient could not only access their data but also communicate feelings and perceptions about their health conditions.[105]

Patient portals offer access to the patient to one or more of the following: (1) EMR data, (2) test results, (3) printing or export of the portal data, (4) medication refills, (5) appointment scheduling, (6) procure referrals, (7) access to general medical information such as guidelines, and (8) creation of secure messaging between the patient and the institution.[106] Thus it can be surmised that patient portals are tools for patient's engagement, besides allowing patient-centered care and promoting coordination between health professionals.

Current guidelines for the development of patient portals are somewhat similar to the meaningful use (MU) criteria of the CMS EHR incentive program. Most patient portals are web-based applications, but some mobile applications too have been developed. Similarly, patient diaries can be aggregated into patient portals.

Electronic patient diaries permit the patient to collect health data, like their vitals, medications, hospital visits, symptoms, and well-being experiences (capturing patient's quality of life). Data collection can be manual or through IoT devices, and the health professional can access the data on a real time remotely or through S&F during the patient appointment.

Patient diaries empower patients because they facilitate self-monitoring. With the coupling of decision support systems, feedback may be provided to the patient through notifications and alerts. Patient diaries have been found to (1) reduce unsystematic and systematic errors by a better understanding of the patient's history, (2) provide better insight into the diagnosis and treatment processes, and (3) offer fresh options to the patient.[107,108]

Thus, the patient portal can be an all-in-all tool supporting consumer health a single and common application that facilitates ease of use and patient engagement.

Lyles et al.[109] discuss about making online patient portals accessible for all. The US government considers them to be a necessary tool for patient empowerment. But guidelines are needed to ensure that the more health conscious and digitally literate are not harmed. This topic is consistent with Web Content Accessibility Guideline (WCAG) standards which state that: (1) The content on a website has to be perceivable to the full range of users, (2) users should be able to navigate and operate the same, (3) users should be able to understand the content and how to navigate (the concern in patient portals will also pertain to health literacy), and (4) the need for cross platform capability and accommodation for assistive technologies. Some further recommendations are as follows:

(1) User-friendly design.
(2) Educational content should adopt and allow access in the language(s) most commonly spoken by the system's target population (defined as 5% of the population or 1000 or more patients served). Here, simple translation is not sufficient because a variety of cultural and linguistic differences need to be catered to.
(3) A well-defined in-person and online training program needs to be in place to decrease issues related to health and digital literacy, which also encourages the patient to use the portal. Partnership with libraries and other communities based on organizations with experience in digital literacy promotion does help. Online education and self-management support material could be used as supplement but can never substitute in-person education.
(4) Promoting portal use by family and caregivers is known to influence patient behavior. Thus they also need to possess knowledge about the disease and current condition and thereafter how to deal with it. This in turn helps motivate the patient towards continuity of care.
(5) Health systems and academic institutions can support implementation through development of technologies that can help overcome communication barriers and comprehension of complex medical terminology.

Another issue is eHealth literacy, as opposed to health literacy[110]. Norman et al. define eHealth literacy as "the ability to seek, find, understand, and appraise health information from electronic sources and apply this knowledge gained to addressing or solving a health problem." This definition allows to broaden the way of studying the problem by separating the skills (general and specific) that compose the lack of understanding about health by consumer health. Identification of the problematic skills in the target public makes it possible to find the solution and thereby design a suitable portal for each type of consumer health informatics.[111]

We conclude by explaining Chronic Patient Relationship Management (CPRM) model[90] a single tool that allows care coordination programs and promotes patient engagement in a collaborative environment. The CPRM model uses customer relationship management (CRM) concepts in managing the relationship between the patient and his/her physician to improve medical care. Table 1 shows the concepts that were adapted from the CRM to the CPRM model.

The CPRM model was developed to assist the chronic patient allowing adequate control of the disease based on the best practices and the psychosocial context of the patient. Therefore, with the concepts of the model, it was possible to think in ways to improve the patient's adherence and the follow-up of these patients by health professionals (Table 2).

Thus, by adapting CRM technology architecture, an application can be created that integrates the EMR/EHR, PHR, decision support systems (DSS), and eHealth solutions to allow personalized monitoring. However, coordinating the care activities performed by caregivers is as important as increasing patient access to health services.

TABLE 1 Adapted from the comparative table between CRM and the model proposed by CPRM.[90]

CRM concepts	CPRM model
Personalized relationship	Personalized treatment
Motivate the customer's loyalty to the brand	Motivate the adherence to the treatment
Know about the customer base	Know the patient's profile and his relationship with the disease
Collection of information about the customer	Collection of information about the patient
Capacity of capturing the information, analyze quickly, and react immediately to the customer's demand	Capacity of capturing the information, analyze through a specialist system and react quickly to the patient's demand
Use of business intelligence tools to analyze the customer	Use of data science techniques to analyze the patient's behavioral and the disease's profiles and tendencies
Establish with the best clients a relationship of constant learning—determine strategic actions	Learning with "successful patients" to determine actions and strategies in the management of them

TABLE 2   Adapted from the comparative table between the concepts of the old model and CPRMs.[11]

Concept	Old model	CPRM model
Focus	Disease/illness	Patient
Strategy	Disease control in accordance with existing standards (epidemiologic studies)	Control of the health considering the person biological context and psychosocial (individual/personalized analytics)
Approach	Use of medications and guidelines "standardized"	Interactivity, confidence, awareness, credibility, shared decision making and personalized guidance
Collection of information and orientation	Information and data scattered throughout the organization or between organizations Get the information only in the medical appointment	Integrated all the information—personalized healthcare information New ways to communicate with each other in any time
Relationship	Distrust and authoritarianism	Partnership
Indicators	Results of tests and clinical assessments sporadic	Test results, frequent clinical assessments, analysis of patient satisfaction, and also their engagement

The extended architecture (Fig. 3) has (1) the operational module containing (a) the hospital information system (HIS) that stores the patient's administrative data such as the costs of the treatment performed, (b) the (EMR) that has a high reliability for subsequent analysis, and (c) the (PHR) that is information provided by the patient and therefore less reliable but nevertheless important to alert the care team; (2) the analytical module that adds the patient care coordination system to those that already existed in the GRPC model; and (3) the collaborative module that will have personal assistants for the patients (patient diary), the care team, and the care coordinator (care and coordination plans). A conversational system allows patients, care team members, and the coordinator to "talk" to the system and to each other. Such functionalities and database that implement the CPRM model is called the collaborative patient care system

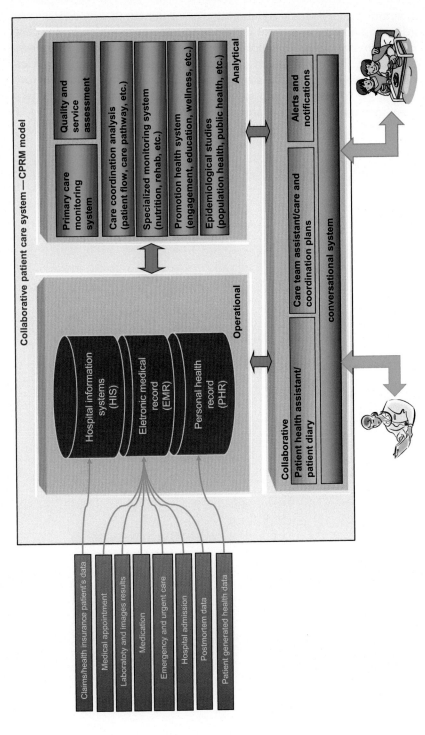

FIG. 3   Adapted from extended CPRM model architecture.[90]

In summary, CPRM is a collaborative environment that facilitates care coordination, improves patient information and visualization by the care team, improves patient flow, optimizes resources from different services, and assists in the development of criteria and metrics for health service quality and patient engagement. However, there are other solutions too, and we hope to motivate you to develop new models and frameworks that can increase consumer health experiences and engagement.

Maintaining and sustaining a telehealth-based ecosystem

Oommen John[a,b]

[a]The George Institute for Global Health India, New Delhi, India,
[b]University of New South Wales, Sydney, NSW, Australia

What is a telehealth-based ecosystem?

Each institution or organization is based on certain long-term goals or objectives—which could be in the constitution or even laws of the stated organization. For example, delivering quality healthcare to each and every citizen is a responsibility of the government. A telehealth-based ecosystem would be wherein one or more components use ICT or *tele*-based support for healthcare delivery. Such needs could be for people staying in remote islands or for astronauts in the space shuttle. Australia started a flying doctor service for its rural populations; mountaineering expeditions beyond a certain number would get approval only if a doctor accompanies; Tele[112] medicine was a possible replacement for many of these requirements, and its availability has helped improve norms. However, each situation has nuances, and these need to be addressed with specifics.

Definitions and types of telehealth, that is, *synchronous, asynchronous,* and *telemonitoring*, have been provided previously and need not be repeated here, but it needs to be remembered that a prerequisite for any type of remote care is a high-quality communication network.[112]

In high-income countries and regions with good ICT infrastructure, telehealth applications cover a broad spectrum of services that focus on diagnosis and clinical management. Point of care measuring devices, which can monitor heart rate, blood pressure, and blood glucose levels, are increasingly used to remotely monitor and manage patients with acute and chronic illnesses.[112]

127

In low-income countries and in regions with limited infrastructure, telehealth applications are primarily used to link health-care providers with specialists, referral hospitals, and tertiary care centers.[113]

Role of telehealth in health system strengthening

It is well known that during the development of telemedicine and telehealth, research focused on specific topics, such as feasibility and cost-effectiveness need to be undertaken. While the potential benefits and possible uses have been extensively described (e.g., improving quality, promoting safety, and expanding access),[114] there is also a body of literature that outlines barriers and challenges to implementation and widespread adoption of telehealth.[115]

Despite significant investments into telehealth by governments and funding agencies, examples of implementations that resulted in improved health outcomes at national levels are scarce. Integration of these innovations into health programs has been limited, as empirical evidence could not show value in terms of cost, performance, and health outcomes.[116]

Recent systematic analysis has identified many challenges that contributed to the suboptimal impact of telehealth initiatives. Even while factors thought to influence implementation processes and their outcomes could be identified, the underlying mechanisms at work could not be well characterized or explained.

The WHO health system building blocks provide an excellent framework for developing telehealth solutions that are designed to bridge the existing gaps in the health delivery ecosystem. Rather than being perceived as siloed, stand-alone solutions, telehealth strategies should be viewed as integral systems that should fit into existing health system functions and complement the health system goals of health service provision; a well-performing health workforce; a functioning health information system; cost-effective use of medical products, vaccines, and technologies; along with accountability and governance.[117]

Roles and responsibilities in a telehealth system

Introducing telehealth initiatives into the health-care system requires detailed planning, coordination and communication among health-care professionals, patients, informal caregivers, end users, and all other stakeholders. While defining the scope and objectives of the telehealth projects, identification of the roles and timely allocation of responsibilities are critical (Fig. 1).

Though technology (hardware and software) is a core component of a telehealth system, human resources are also a critical component in the

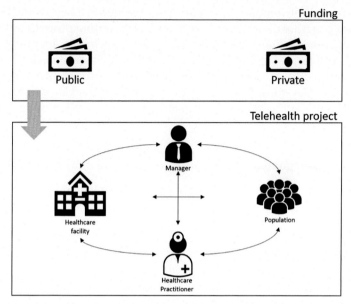

FIG. 1 Generic model from funding to the proper telehealth initiative.

development and implementation of a successful telehealth program. They are stakeholders determining success, and therefore defining their functions, roles, and responsibilities at the outset is an essential component of the design of a telehealth program. Each telehealth program will need to determine how each function will be addressed, for example, would it be existing staff delivering the telehealth services or would there be new staff required. These decisions are determined by understanding the type of service envisaged, service levels, size of the site, and available funding.

Defining the various functions helps outline roles and responsibilities. The following would be the major components of a telehealth program:

1. Project management
2. Program management
3. Site coordination
4. Clinical oversight and referrals
5. Clinical service provision
6. Technical support

Project management

The role of the project management team is to define the project; identify and engage stakeholders; as well as track and manage specific steps, timelines, and budgets using specific tools. The project manager is responsible for the overall development, undertaking the needs assessments besides outlining program descriptions, creating and executing project work plans while addressing the changing needs and requirements, identifying targeted resources, assigning individuals with related responsibilities, and managing day-to-day operational aspects of the project and a changing scope if any. Day-to-day accounting including the tracking and reporting of team hours and expenses and managing of the project budget are an additional part.

Program management

This function covers advocacy and general management activities such as increasing organizational awareness regarding the telehealth program; ongoing human resources management, policies, and procedures; coordinating with patient care departments; educating clinical departments; providing the guidance and training necessary to meet the needs of patients being served; coordinating the interaction between the practitioners; and tracking customer satisfaction, data collection on service utilization, and performance monitoring and reporting.

Site coordination

This function covers all activities related to operations and helping the end users at both the patient as well as the provider sites. The success of the remote patient site is critical to the overall success of the entire telehealth program. Embedded within the site coordination role should be a telehealth champion, who would serve as the specific point of contact, supporting all stakeholders in the smooth operations of the services.

Clinical oversight and referral

The main objective of a telehealth program is to ensure that the best quality of clinical interaction is provided to those seeking care; this can be assured through outlining the minimum standards of care that could be achieved through telehealth and what needs to be referred for an in-person clinical evaluation. The clinical oversight role should define the minimum standards for each telehealth project and review the referrals for in-person consultation.

Clinical service provision

This function covers the provision of clinical care through remote consultations, with assignment of responsibility for leading and conducting the actual patient interaction. Various methods or streams of telehealth provision exist; the two most common are (1) a practitioner directly providing remote care and (2) the practitioner only guiding the patient's primary provider. The remote care support may or may not have a real-time component with the patient. That is, only documents are exchanged for opinion whether a physical transfer of the patient is required or not. A cardiac angiogram or a cataract image may be sent regarding a need for a surgical procedure and relevant appointments given to the patient to seek a detailed evaluation in person.

Technical support

This function is toward ensuring that the equipment and network is functioning optimally, with minimum downtime and best usability, which is an important aspect of technical support. Having the technical support at the site is key to ensuring that there is ongoing technical support to the users of the telehealth services.

Key considerations in staffing a telehealth program

Implementing telehealth is a multidimensional effort, and therefore the staff need to be quick learners, adept at handling change management with a commitment to change. Identifying interested and enthusiastic individuals champions will be committed to making things work is a key quality to look for in potential candidates for the role. It is important to have key staff that have a flexible work style and a customer-service orientation with patient-centered focus.

Project management in telehealth

The development process of a telehealth platform should start with multidisciplinary project management. A multidisciplinary team of researchers, developers, and users (designers, technicians, health-care professionals, and health-care researchers) must guide the project management and conduct the planning in time and space.[118]

Value specification refers to goal setting and to defining the functional and organizational requirements to realize the potential of the telehealth initiative. It is aimed at exploring the range of possible improvements in health care and otherwise as well as the limitations to realize these expected values. The specified values have to be translated by the stakeholders into functionalities of the design and critical factors for the implementation.[119]

The overall needs for a particular project or even its components need to be first strategized. And then among the potential gaps, one can summarize if a telecomponent would lead to efficiency, lowering of costs, time savings, etc. A cost-benefit ratio has to alongside ensure that relevant infrastructure for ensuring a merging of the telecomponent exists or can be created at affordable costs. For example, if a particular location has no cardiologists, but their need is exemplified by many persons being rushed to a cardiac center following chest pain. Tele-ECG, in theory, could send every ECG to a cardiologist stationed in an ICU at a referral centre who would review the findings and respond on the clinical condition, and in case of any critical findings recommend an urgent need for intervention. The machine is provided free by the service provider, and even the rental will pay for itself once the number of ECGs crosses an X number per month. Essentially the investment in this tele-ECG service is paying for itself (see example: http://www.immilife.com/whatwedo.html).

Creating workflows and standard operating procedures (SOPs)

When planning a telehealth or telemedicine project for future development, its boundaries must be clear. For instance, like when creating a business plan, we must delimit and recognize objectively to which segment our telehealth project applies to. We have to differentiate between

1. Public-based initiative, for example, projects or services supported (promoted and funded) and developed by governmental body.
2. Private-based initiative, for example, projects or services supported by a private funding, which could be philanthropic and not for profit organizations. This is especially important as such ventures rarely make a profit in monetary terms.

In 1 the government takes the initiative toward the telehealth project development. It takes action (for instance) in the form of

- promoting population wide programs funded with public money, delivered side by side with traditional health-care services;
- promoting and/or funding projects to deliver telehealth services with research purposes.

In 2 the telehealth project development is funded (solely) by private entities. This is the case of private health-care services that implements a telehealth service to avoid the patient to come and go several times from home to the hospital to seek health-care assistance. The patient or the insurance provider could be charged directly for each or even many teleconsults over a period of time.

Intermediate and hybrid options exist. In public-private partnerships (PPP) the public sector delivering the telehealth service may subcontract or share costs with a private partner. Another example is BOOT, which means *build* by private organization, *own* and *operate* by same for a few years, and then *transfer* back to the government.

Planning a project

Shashi Gogia

A project should be built around finding the right mix of solutions working toward answering a well-described need with needs assessment as the first step. SATHI's project designed to help the victims in India suffering from the after affects of the December 2004 Tsunami is a useful example[120] (see Box 1, Fig. 2).

BOX 1

DETAILS OF THE SATHI TSUNAMI PROJECT
(WITH INCLUDED EXPLANATIONS)

Needs assessment is a prerequisite of any project wherein one evaluates a particular unaddressed health need. In the Tsunami project, this was done a month after the disaster, and a high incidence of mental effects was noted. It was also known that though 80% of survivors have immediate mental effects after a major disaster, most recover. However the symptoms persists in 4–5% problem and become cases of PTSD. Identifying these 4%–5% early is a challenge as it requires persistent follow-up and home visits preferably by trained persons within the affected community. Even while remote psychiatric care can be easily provided by a video conferencing link, the affected individuals, i.e., the one in need of counseling have to be first identified within the community by constant monitoring by trained persons. Persons felt to be at risk needed to get regular consults. Bringing such patients to the psychiatry center would be an arduous task if one realizes the number of possible victims.

The other steps followed included an evaluation of the existing health system for adequacy and possible areas of reinforcement. A personal visit to the tsunami affected area was done and with interviews of NGOs who could be potential partners—both in the periphery as well as the expert end. The range of possible support from the government was discussed so that only action that would be allowed within the public health and legal frame work was performed.

Concept marketing and orientation of the persons representing the volunteering NGO was a constant component of each discussion. The **connectivity** needs had to be identified, and steps taken to provide the same through an appropriate local Telecom vendor. After

Continued

BOX 1   *(Cont'd)*

each visit the project was redesigned. A formal order of the systems (hardware and software) was placed only after clearly understanding what needs to be done and whether the personnel were already or could be trained to handle them.

MOUs were created between the various identified partners of the project.

Installation of systems was done in the identified locations.

Training was required for identified remote personnel who were either: (1) fieldworkers in the community doing house-to-house surveys and (2) telemedicine technicians—conducting the actual remote counselling encounter. The psychiatrists at the expert end were also trained on the finer nuances of video conferencing (see Chapter 4).

Test sessions were held before a formal launch under SATHI's supervision and an engineering representative from the vendor.

– **Streamlining** of the project was required during the actual running of the systems and conducting the sessions. It included troubleshooting and fine-tuning the protocols. An important component was the setting up of a Telemedicine Consultation Session (TCS) timetable.
– **Feedback** was obtained on a regular basis with reporting mechanisms in place.
– **Outcome analysis**, done by an outside agency, was planned at the outset as this was to be a pilot.

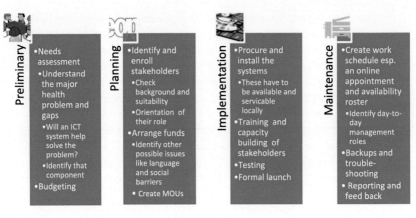

FIG. 2   Project components. From the SATHI Tsunami project.

Appointment roster

A telesystem involves stakeholders in different social, cultural, and geographical regions. Communication is an essential component, but finding a common time for meeting is a challenge. It has to be necessarily a common meeting time when there is a synchronous or real-time transfer, for example, video conferencing. This problem accentuates when there are geographical and specially time zone differences between the participants.

Such problems are less for the asynchronous mode, the sender just sends a message and hopes the recipient receives the same and replies within a short interval, however, there always will be details that need to be verified; hence, all teleconsults have a real-time component. These visits also increase the satisfaction of the patient as they are now sure of actually being seen. The clinician gains similar confidence and motivation to do what is required.

Ideally, such appointments also include the asynchronous components—wherein complaints and other important information like the patient history and important investigation reports are shared upfront before the online teleconsult. This will help decrease the online visit time—the doctor's time is arguably the most expensive component of a teleconsult.

Appointments for televisits should ideally be provided at the convenience of the clinician rather than the patient remembering that the clinician is in all probability doing it as philanthropy. He is less sure of the control on patient care and will be spending more time for a less-than-ideal outcome. Also, he cannot give preference to remote patients when the ones waiting just outside the clinic door not only are paying better but also have spent time and effort to reach him physically. In a place without medical help, patients will be happy that they have had their problems listened to with less botheration about the timing of the same.

In the SATHI Tsunami projects, afternoon clinics were run thrice a week for 2 h each in the afternoon, that is, outside regular visiting hours.

Telehealth project example (prepared for budgeting and account keeping) (taken from an anonymous state government tender)

The actual project was divided in two main parts—a and b in the succeeding texts—while the remaining are essential add-on components:

a. **Teleconsultation services**: A patient may call from any location using a phone (landline or handheld) by dialing a three-digit number to receive immediate advice on call. The doctors may be able to prescribe over-the-counter (OTC) drugs based on the symptoms detailed by the patient in accordance with the prevailing laws. The details of medicine shall be sent via SMS (to the patient), and the electronic prescription shall be sent via email to the patient and nearest public health facility. Further, some of the cases may be referred to the nearest PHC/CHC/district hospital, as per requirement of physical examination, conducting diagnostic tests and/or requiring specific medicines. In such cases of referral, the capability of sharing the information with the designated facility is essential

b. **Video consultation services and patient nodes**: Video consultation services shall be provided to the patients who are referred for video consultation services by government doctors at CHCs where patient nodes are setup. The service provider for video consultation services shall be responsible for scheduling an appointment for forwarded cases/referred patients by the doctors at the CHCs/authority for video consultation services. The video consultation service providers shall establish dedicated command center(s) anywhere in India for this project. The command center(s) shall have specialist doctors for conducting video consultation with the patients.

c. **Electronic medical record (EMR)**: For every patient, medical history and detailed records of consultations shall be maintained in the EMR system, which must capture mandatory fields and should have the ability to interact/integrate with other stakeholders/ service providers for services like teleconsultation services or call center (health helpline) for telemedicine project, diagnostic centers, medicine dispensation centers/units, and central patient portal. The integration shall be done on a real-time basis.

d. **Consolidated MIS record**: This shall have all the data gathered/saved/ recorded/updated including details of any vitals/diagnostic tests.

e. **Central patient portal**: It has to capture all patient-related information and to have a common platform for all related services.

f. **Central database and hosting server**: For all of the above, it has to be expandable to cater to future demand.

g. **Specific medical equipment** as per needs of the project.

Based on the previous text, a cost breakup can be created as follows (with cost column removed).

FOR EACH REMOTE END

CAPEX (capital expenditure)

Patient end	Description
Preliminary location visit	
General	Project management
Computer hardware	Printer with computer
	Web camera

FOR EACH REMOTE END—CONT'D

CAPEX (capital expenditure)

Patient end	Description
	Digitizer/scanner for digital transmission of X-ray/CT scan/MRI
	Audio-video facility
Telemedicine kit	*This may constitute individual components or a single combined kit*
	Digital thermometer
	Glucometer
	Pulse oximeter
	BP instrument
	Height stand
	Digital ECG
	Digital stethoscope
	Weighing scale
	Fetal heart monitor
	Pediatric weighing scale
	Dermatoscope
General equipment	Stools and chairs
	Examination bed
	Work desk

OPEX (operating expenditure)

Software	Client end
Manpower (salaries)	Staff-ANM
	Staff-technician
	Project managers/Misc
Misc running costs	Stationery and other day to day consumables
	Lab reagents
	Connectivity
	Water and electricity
	Glucometer strips
	Hardware maintenance and replacement
Administration	
Insurance	

Command center	Only one controlling entire project
Preliminary location visit	

EXPERT END (ONLY 1)

CAPEX

Furniture and fixtures	
Computer hardware	
General and Misc	Establishment cost, furniture, assets
Software	**EMR (server end)**
OPEX	
Specialists	13 in number for 4–8h per day
Connectivity	
Rent and running costs	Stationery, water, others
Other costs	
Training content	
Training camps	
Liaison with govt	
Project office	
Project team	
Team travel and other expenses	
Project administration	
Project travel	
Server/AWS service	
Database	

The OPEX component can be used as a template for daily bookkeeping and items like interest added to create consolidated monthly reports.

Backup systems

Emergencies can occur anytime. In a telecare project, these problems are likely to be accentuated because of distance and relative lack of control of local developments. Avenues for correction and redressal are far more difficult but need serious attention. The problem gets accentuated with the lack of standard operating procedures (SOPs) and trained personnel. The Internet based resources is a constant help, so training on how to use online search engines and online support systems are key to success.

Analytics

Filipe Santana da Silva

With the increasing demand from population for health-care support, health-care services and systems are seeking for alternative solutions to improve quality of care, maintaining costs at a reasonable level. Two main factors are pushing this trend, for example, the increasing number of individuals bearing chronic conditions and life expectancy.

For instance, since 1940s, life expectancy in Brazil increased from 45.5 to 75.8 years in 2016.[121] Besides social security concerns, investments, and improvements, recommendations in public and private health-care services have been described by the Brazilian Institute of Geography and Statistics (free translation from Instituto Brasileiro de Geografia e Estatística, IBGE). As described by IBGE, Brazilian population is getting older, in a process similar to what is currently happening in Europe.[122]

A similar trend is underscored in the United States of America, wherein telehealth is being used to decentralize healthcare, for example, for home-care situations.[123] For instance, elderly individuals require constant evaluation and follow-up. With the support of telehealth systems and applications, individuals can have their health status scrutinized from distance, for example, blood sugar levels, heart rate, blood pressure, weight, height, or even tracking possible emergency admissions by any problem, for example, chronic obstructive pulmonary disease.[124]

For instance, in a home-care settlement, data is gathered and stored for every situation that a given individual is exposed to. If the individual bears some type of cardiac condition, data regarding her cardiac function may be gathered and stored (continuously) for monitoring possible heart issues. Timely information regarding the heart function and behavior gives the opportunity for the health-care practitioner to take the proper action when a cardiac attack takes place. Indirectly, it may reveal certain patient behavioral patterns, which may lead to actions that avoid further health problems.

The task that involves gathering, organizing, and displaying data orderly to enable decision support is known as analytics.[125] In general the term analytics is related to the task of providing summarized data and information following statistical methods and visualization approaches. Burke[126] describes analytics for the health domain as [...] *the complete series of integrated capabilities needed to provide progressively deeper statistical insights into health-related information.*

In other words, analytics encompasses the processes behind defining, creating, and making available statistical analysis of some portion of data, for a specific purpose and with great detail. For instance, an analytics application for a health-care practitioner may show the current health status of a given inpatient, for example, blood pressure, administered drugs, weight, and biochemical parameters.

Analytics can be coded directly as part of a system or made available by dedicated analytics tools. These tools frequently require complex database tasks—such as normalizing data or integrating sources—coupled with statistical analysis and insightful data visualizations.[127]

In practice an analytics tool enables the user to see relevant indicators. However, knowing what must be displayed to enable the user to have a timely decision support is related to business intelligence (BI) and a topic handled by specific methods. Analytics is frequently associated with BI, as a deep business understanding is required to deploy a useful analytics approach.

As pointed out by Burke,[126] there is a division between business analytics (which encompasses the classics of BI) and clinical analytics. The first is related to the health-care business itself, which includes performance analysis, financial reports, and utilization. The second is related to the clinical practice itself, for example, disease management, patient adherence, and patient safety analysis.[a]

Here, we do not distinguish between the proper business and clinical analytics; we consider that to each task, there are processes embedded that should be described and performed. To each scenario (or business), there are users that play different roles, such as the manager or the health-care practitioner. As from the strict business perspective or from the telehealth project, we use the term *business* without distinction, as it is used by the information technology (IT) domain.

A BI approach to enable analytics purposes can be described by a generic architecture composed of five blocks[128]:

- Data sources, for example, where raw data is stored in the form of a SQL database, spreadsheets, text files, among others;
- Data movement streaming engines (DMSE), for example, data manipulation solutions such as extraction, transformation, and load (ETL) tools;
- Data warehouse (DW) servers, for example, servers to which data warehouses are allocated to store a collection of time-indexed data that might be used to support decisionmaking[129];
- Midtier servers, for example, an intermediate layer between the databases (i.e., DW servers) and the application itself. Midtier servers create a division from database to application, avoiding the database to be in direct contact with internet traffic;
- Front-end applications, for example, the applications (Web or mobile) to which the user interacts with.

To each type of health-care practitioner, information may be interpreted differently, and (to this end) each user might have a specific visualization. For instance, in a home-care settlement, functions that individuals present

---

[a] *Topic has already been discussed in* Chapter 3.

may be of importance only to the practitioner who is responsible for monitoring such patients. Examples are blood pressure or sugar levels. In the screen, it may be important for the physicians to see the causes of previous admissions, but not for the nursing staff.

For the home-care manager, monitoring of the practitioner's activities may be of interest, for example, the rate of recurrent admissions under the care of a specific practitioner. Knowing how to handle and deploy timely data and information in such a manner are BI tasks. These tasks require deep analytical capabilities not only from the system but also from the user.

Considering that most approaches are not specifically devoted for the telehealth and telemedicine domain, literature around such tactics is gaining strength. The introduction of analytics approaches that go beyond database reports and provide processed and ready-to-use information for the user are becoming something of a standard in the health-care sector.[126,130,131] Besides economic benefits, these also enable a better support for decisionmaking, from practitioners and managers.

In this section, we are going to address some analytics topics that are specific for telehealth and telemedicine. Specifically, we are going to discuss some subtleties regarding indicators that are frequently under consideration for a telehealth project and available strategies to deploy a feasible and practical analytics approach. From the technical perspective, we deal only with front-end applications.

Let us introduce a scenario. Imagine you are a manager and also a physician in a telehealth service. This telehealth service is deployed in several manners, from primary care to high complexity procedures and home care. As a manager, you have to take care of your telehealth network as also patients under your care.

Management tasks can be performed from a distance, supported by Information and Communication Technologies (ICT), and keep track of patients under your responsibility. The same system provides tools optimized for both management and practitioners' tasks.

Basic concepts

The use of BI and analytics (BI&A) encompass three main phases. The first phase, during the 1990s, relied on data collection, extraction, and analysis (mostly) based on database management fields. On this data, simple statistical analysis like clustering, mean, median, and sorting to regression models are done. This is the common analytics approach on which several companies and health-care services rely on.

The second phase, which began in the early 2000s, relied (mostly) on web analytics. In other words, it stretches the technologies available from the first phase to include detailed data regarding the end-user interaction with web-based platforms. In other words, together with legacy data, logs from user interactions enable a deeper understanding of customers.[127] In the telehealth and telemedicine project, this can be of extreme value since the end user may interact with the health-care practitioner much later. Knowing how it works, may drive towards better results.

The third phase, from 2010 onwards, came about with the broad availability of sensors and the increasing usage of smartphones. It is the confluence of the so-called *Internet of Things* (IoT), for example, smart devices connected through the internet that carry sensors and actuators which collect data and (sometimes) react to the users.[127] In other words, data from legacy systems together with the information from sensors as well as user behavior collected with the support of smartphones enable context-related decision making.[130]

For instance, technologies from the third phase may enable tracking blood sugar levels from a distance with the support of a noninvasive sensor that streams data for a mobile application or web-based platform. A recent study described a similar application for individuals with diabetes mellitus type 1 to which the use of a continuous glucose measurement approach enabled a change in the quality of life, decreased amount of hospital admissions, and decreased glucose measurements.[132]

Commercial tools like Microsoft Power BI,[133] SAP Analytics,[134] or Tableau[135] are examples of analytics tools that include capabilities for the aforementioned BI&A phases. To some extent, these tools include similar capabilities for analytics purposes, for example, by means of displaying data interactively and by means of graphical analysis arranged as dashboards or as punctual visualizations embedded in systems parts (e.g., in electronic health records such as admission or drug administered forms).

In general, analytics applications can be classified according to its capabilities, which can be[126]

1. **Standard reports**. These constitute simple lists of raw or aggregate data with information that must be processed and interpreted by the user. An example is a list of all patients (and their diagnosis) at admission.
2. **Ad hoc reports**. These are generated as per customization to user needs, such as patients under the care of a particular practitioner between specific dates.
3. **Query drilldown**. A query interface may require a further customization by the user within a dedicated reporting environment; identify the possible contacts of a patient with tuberculosis, to ensure whether quarantine measures were fully in place.
4. **Alerts**. These can be derived from a dedicated service to which the user is able to set up notifications (visual or sounds) for a given new

information, such as when a practitioner selects an anticoagulant medicine to be administered to a patient with thrombosis.

5. **Statistical analysis**. The user may perform (or is made available to him) statistical analysis, such as when trying to identify which practitioner has better outcomes when treating pressure wounds, derived from long length inpatient stay.
6. **Forecast**. The user is able to perform trend analysis, such as when trying to identify the most promising treatment for a given patient according to previous treatments performed in the same conditions.
7. **Predictive modeling**. The user can simulate a specific situation according to the available data and the desired user scenario, such as when trying to simulate bacterial infection due to hospitalization and the applicability of the antibacterial drug for the most effective response for the inpatient.
8. **Optimization**. When the user is able to run statistical tests to identify trends in data to which the outcome might be improved, such as identifying (according to EHRs) whether and when it is more beneficial (in the long term) for patients who require a bariatric surgery to play sports.

Several types of data can be used to support such analysis.[131] Sources can be data from EHRs, Laboratory Management Information Systems (LMIS), devices used for diagnostic or monitoring, insurance claims/bills, pharmacy, human resources, supply chain, and locating systems. Additionally, user interaction with platforms may play an important role, as previously described.

In telehealth or telemedicine projects, other epidemiological data may be of interest. Geographical–read locational information may play a significant role. For instance, identifying the areas and locations that individuals without access to health-care services may indicate opportunities for the use of telehealth, like in countryside and severe climate situations (rainfall, snow, desert, among others). Genetic data may be of interest for telehealth and telemedicine. Considering the increasing demand and trend around the personalization of medical care, being prepared for such scenario is extremely important.

In every case the strategy for defining the most relevant indicators for each situation depends on the evaluation and monitoring strategy. It is relevant to properly identify the analytics methods that may bring better results for the project.

Tele-education

Luiz Roberto de Oliveira

**Department of Surgery, Federal Ceara University School of Medicine,
Fortaleza, Brazil**

Introduction

The world is rapidly changing with new advances in technology in all walks of life. Health provision is no exception; however, coping with rapid changes is a challenge. Already the initial training in medicine and healthcare is far more demanding than for any other profession. Over and above, graduation is rarely enough. Increasing specialization and super specialization came about because of patients' demand for perfection and insistence of quality, which calls for more and more learning about less and less. Whether it has helped or not is a moot point, but this training is expensive and takes precious time off from the earning years of the health professionals' life span.

Providing training on advances, some of which may lead to creation of new specialization needs the availability of trainers. Health-care provision, however, is lucrative. Patients are willing to pay higher for any new skill, but that skill will remain new and unique only till the competition sets in. And training others means increasing your own competition! Tele-education offers a means of providing better utilization of time and availability of the few professionals who are willing to train. It is well understood that ICT is not only a contributor to advances, but also provides tools and methods to make for better training. Virtual training means mistakes are also virtual; hence, possible harm by those with less experience or even yet to be qualified, gets minimized.

Distance education in the context of professional work in health

Luiz Roberto de Oliveira and Gustavo Silveira Dantas

Introduction

Distance education is somewhat old and has always had a relation with the then existing technologies. Technological resources are used to meet two basic needs: content support and transport. It is possible to identify generations of distance education through such details.[136,137] However, with the appearance of the web and in particular web 2.0, a great growth of distance education took place, with the coinage of the term web-based distance education. This characterized the beginning of a third generation of distance education. The major contrast between the third and the previous two generations is the role of the learner,[138] who need no longer be passive as a receiver, but more active, not only consuming what is delivered but also participating, venturing out in a quest of autonomy, and contributing to its production. This separation has been much discussed with several points at odds, serving only to show that there has always been some association between distance learning and the technologies existing in each epoch of its evolution.

Learning has three distinct components: who learns, who teaches, and the content. Distance education uses technological resources to overcome the impediments of time and space to allow communication between these elements. Because of its sophisticated evolution, among other reasons, it is no longer possible to ignore the facilitation resulting from the convergence of communication solutions in the Digital Society.[139]

Moran[140] conceptualized distance education as "the process of teaching and learning mediated by technologies, where teachers and students are separated spatially and/or temporally." Even while there is great potential, apprehensions of its role persist among those with a strong and deep-rooted tradition of classroom teaching, which Sabbatini[141] affirms as "the persistence of obsolete and ineffective didactic-pedagogical methodologies, in great mismatch with current reality." The resistance seems to stem much more from ignorance about educational technologies, using information and computational means in constant evolution than due to insurmountable incompatibilities.[142] A synthesis will be presented on online education, seeking to disseminate the essential ideas and considering the main myths, advantages, and disadvantages associated with web-based education.

Myths, advantages, and disadvantages in distance education

There are three myths to be broken regarding online distance education. The first is considering its practice only as an easy way to replace the teacher. The next two relate to a belief that distance education is easier and cheaper to use. Combined with these three mistakes, is the panorama of what has been called by Azevedo[136] as the "avant-garde (technological) of backwardness (pedagogical)". In other words while the technology, for educational purposes, has become indispensable, but pedagogy—as a science interested in the methods, practice, and processes of teaching to the improvement of learning—and andragogy,[139] the methods of pedagogy used in adult education, are essential.[138] It is fundamental to understand the convergence between technology, teaching, education, and learning, in all areas, including health. Recently a key attention has been given to the learning theories endorsing e-Learning.[136]

An initial step to undo misunderstandings must begin by considering that in online distance education, one should never think about dismissing the teacher whose presence is irreplaceable. This is even while it is important to constantly develop the learner's autonomy and improve his or her metacognitive perception[140] so that he can reach the stage of heutagogy,[143] that is, able to learn more and better and on account of his/her personal efforts. In online distance education, the role of the teacher is not extinguished, only modified. During face-to-face education, knowledge comes to the learner, almost exclusively, through the teacher, but in this new modality the teacher becomes a participant in the process. Teachers remain as facilitators, with maybe different functions, either for content creation and development or as tutors. The learner's position is also somewhat displaced; it is student-centered education, no longer passive, and going beyond "mere spectators, without the necessary criticism and reflection," which demands protagonism, according to the so-called active teaching and learning methodologies.[144]

The main focus of distance education should not be towards cost reduction. An understanding that this facilitates learning and better access is essential. While that may require extra expenditure, one just has to recognize that there is commiserate value generated. Distance learning allows increase in scale, constant updates, reuse of modularized components, and a reduction in the burden of attending each course individually. The overall objective, however, remains to be learning, which requires specific metrics and assessments, for example, monitoring the evasion rate, to even minimize waste.

Among its advantages are a reduction of travel costs and related risks, a wider reach with democratization of knowledge opportunities, a possibility of flexibility in deciding the hours of study, and a higher potential of receiving on-the-job training without a need to leaving one's place of work. Some of these are very relevant for the health sector. There are potential disadvantages though: the need for specialized staff (including additional training of teachers and tutors), the existence of stable and sufficient connections, and digital competence (digital and information literacy) on the part of the students. There are special challenges regarding online discipline, which is required both from the teachers as well as the students. Many do not adapt well to online teaching, sometimes due to a tendency towards procrastination or because of other digital limitations.

Hybrid teaching

This is an attempt to combine what is best in face-to-face education with what can best be obtained through distance learning. There are several important aspects of this combination, with a requirement of well-structured pedagogical planning. Online distance education is more than simply making face-to-face work on a virtual platform, configuring mere didactic transposition of books to online texts or lectures to videos, but rather proceeding to the didactic transition that adequately combines the various intelligent media, structuring various parameters to favor meaningful learning.

In digital health practice, online distance education can be combined with existing or planned telehealth and telemedicine activities in many ways. Both can harness the same technological infrastructure. It needs to be remembered that learning about the components of telecare is a constant requirement of the personnel and other stakeholders of the project.

Teacher and student training

One of the main success factors with the use of online distance education concerns the human element involved. There are three main categories: teachers (content managers and teachers), production and support staff, and finally students. Considering the latter, three groups of items need further deliberation: (1) variations in intelligence (learning styles), (2) digital and informational limitations, and (3) what may be called intrinsic characteristics (curiosity, attention, and subject knowledge). For undergraduate courses within the health domain, the current generation of university students, the so-called generation Z, offers better possibilities due to their positive understanding and attitude towards mobile distance education.

Teachers need to understand the technology, the special nuances of web-based education, and how to escape existing pitfalls. Educational institutions, especially those providing higher education, should facilitate continuous and permanent training of their faculty and provide opportunities to improve knowledge of the various uses of virtual teaching along with its synchronous (video collaboration) and asynchronous tools (moderated chat, forums, and discussion lists). The use of virtual learning environments, blogs, podcasts (audio and video), wiki tools, portfolios, repositories, among many other facilities, can be associated with face-to-face teaching to improve learning.

The health area

Health professionals currently face problems related to an overwhelming production of fresh information and the speed of its dissemination. Constant updates are possible only through ICT. Books, conventional journals, and congresses are not in a position of keeping up with the continuous and rapid generation of new knowledge in a timely manner, though many of them in any case are converting to an electronic format, for example, remote access and webinars for conferences, privileged online access for journals, and individual access using digital reading devices, including smartphones.

In addition, almost everyone needs to acquire new skills, which depend on training to be started early, ideally, during undergraduation. It is regrettable to note that gaps remain at this level of education in the various health areas, and the faster these are corrected, the more prepared future professionals will be to enter the labor market.[a] There is a need to provide better training on digital health practices, combined with better knowledge of research methodology, and also develop ethical awareness. The last needs special emphasis as it may be considered an inseparable condition for the proper use of any technology.[76, 143]

It is indispensable to understand that the workforce necessary for the consolidation of digital health in the current age, regardless of where it is introduced, requires cooperation, convergence, close dialogue, and every effort to avoid the inconveniences of tribalism.[144] This is often responsible for the failure to adopt best practices with the use of digital informational and computer health technologies.

To conclude, tele-education needs to be incorporated in educational practices from the undergraduate level onwards. This can occur side by side to imparting knowledge about other aspects of ICT in health, like the use of the electronic patient record, health information systems, decision support systems, telehealth and telemedicine, video collaboration, and teamwork training. This will facilitate the achievement of a convergent vision in the context of the new and recent digital world.

Digital health workforce: de novo skill set

Shashi Gogia

Health-care provision is complex and needs immense amount of knowledge. Lack of knowledge is critical and can be a life-and-death matter. Relatedly the need for training and capacity building is long drawn

---

[a] This book is an attempt towards the same.

out and leaves little time to learn beyond the body's biological and pathological processes, as well as possible corrective measures.

The inability to absorb all by one individual caregiver has led to specialization and even super specialization, euphemistically described as *knowing more and more about less and less*. However, the specialist has to cater to a large population base, for example, one neurologist is supposed to serve a population of around 100,000.[145] Hence, routine problems and day-to-day care have to be relegated to local workers. This is especially important for chronic disease management that needs a *"team approach."*

While how to set up the team and constitution of team members depends on the specialization, one common feature in all is the need for efficient documentation and cross communication between the team members. Such communication narrows the difference between a physical presence and telepresence. The question remains as to who shall ensure efficient data entry and seamless communication. There is a need for a special workforce for the same, the lack of which has been one of the key impediments to the development of telehealth solutions.

Health-care provision is currently the second largest industry. It is also among the largest employers. Even while remaining among the last to adopt ICT, there is nevertheless a huge need for specialized human resources, with much scope for personnel who can bridge the complex web between health provision and its facilitation with the help of ICT.

There are 325,000 health apps.[6] Most applications for HCIT are looking at the upper end of the market, but the real need is in the low-resource areas, which exist in the advanced countries too, aside from the developing world. Within the latter, poor health resources are coupled with equally poor access to ICT systems, compounded by the lack of understanding of special nuances of ICT in health. A digitally trained workforce can solve many of these problems. They will also allow wider reach of health provision and better distribution of resources.

The reasons justifying telehealth have been well distributed in this book. Detailed descriptions concentrate more on the successful examples, but failures have been numerous, and the lack of trained personnel has been an important reason contributing to most of the failures. The Venn diagram in the introductory chapter described how change management, which is essentially capacity building, is a major contributor to project success. It would be better if such capacity existed beforehand, meaning the workforce is already trained.

Finally, one must remember that such a trained workforce would also help shore up the local economy and decrease chances of rural-urban migration and ensure the true creation of a global village.

Training requirements of a digital health assistant (see Box 1)

Learning objectives

1. To be able to operate telemedicine system located at telecenter.
2. To be able to plan and organize telemedicine consultation sessions.
3. To be able to enhance people-related skills such as communications with village people and with the consulting doctor.
4. To be able to gain basic knowledge of community health emergencies for early reporting.
5. To be able to maintain accounts related to the use of telemedicine system.

From a rural area perspective, the main requirement would be health data entry operators or *Scribes* for short. These personnel would digitize health information into an EHR, facilitate video consults, and also deliver healthcare, under online support and guidance from the clinicians. Required skills include knowledge about how IT systems work, validation checks and problems of auto correction, besides troubleshooting network errors. These would be an added resource, beyond knowledge of the disease set that they are supposed to handle and the associated health terms. Knowledge of coding, that is, entry of structured data using standards like ICD and SNOMED, would make it complete, but is not essential. Here, AI would ease adoption, but as of now, personalized care and human-to-human interaction are important components; just like in flight, a pilotless aircraft so far is not used to carry personnel.

An example would be the training program for personnel working in remote areas for projects run by SATHI.[146,147] In the same, formal classroom training was organized at the central place in small batches of 15–20 persons and followed up with continuing education, online and offline through the telemedicine system itself or through internet. The initial training, even though classroom based, had content which made it participatory, interactive, full of practical exercises and games.

Learning is eased if the trainees work within the same system and use the same software and connectivity as in the planned project. On-the-job training can and should continue. A help module has to be incorporated in the telemedicine software. This should include animated illustrations, games, and demonstration of all the key processes involved in operating the telemedicine system, organizing telemedicine consultation sessions (TCS), managing the telemedicine center, and interacting with the patients or the community at large.

Training needs to be done on actual patients or health service seekers in the remote area. In the process of consultations, they will be the "learning materials." A provision of capturing the consultation process on video and reusing the same allows greater discussions or analysis.

BOX 1

Suggested curriculum (Curtsey SATHI)

1. Introduction to telemedicine
   - What is telemedicine
   - Evolution of telemedicine
   - Advantages and disadvantages of telemedicine
   - Future of telemedicine
2. Operating telemedicine system
   - What is a telemedicine system
   - Hardware and software and accessories
   - Connectivity
   - How to operate the telemedicine system
   - Do's and don'ts
   - Troubleshooting
3. Planning and organization of telemedicine consultation session (TCS)
   - What is telemedicine session
   - Prerequisites for TCS
   - Fixed day strategy
   - Planning sessions and preparing service schedule
   - EMR
   - Individual and group session
   - Online and offline consultation
   - Facilitating telemedicine consultation session
   - Counselling patients
4. Communicating with village people and doctor
5. Community health
6. Maintenance of accounts
7. Special programs catering to the unique needs of the current project

---

However, these health workers are expected to deliver the care to persons who come to them as per the outlined scope of the project. Any gap areas for delivering the same need to be addressed. For example, in the SATHI Teleophthalmology project, the 2-week training program devoted only 2 days towards IT training, using the remaining for reinforcing existing knowledge about eye examination, Snellen charts, and administering eye drops with emphasis on the possible problems in rural areas.

While the initial training helps, telecare also offers continued training distance education or rather on-the-job training. The processes and progress of each patient overseen will be a form of participatory learning. Such health workers are known to evolve into excellent caregivers. The SATHI project had funding only for 3 years, but the workers were asked to continue at better scales, because of appreciable evidence of their skills.

Use and utility of virtual teaching in education

Manoj Kumar Singh

Over the years, increasing attenuation of available teaching resources, both material and personnel, has steadily led to a diminishing quality of medical education and a consequent shortage of trained and willing manpower for teaching, service, and research. This shortage is compounded by the ever-increasing demand for trained medical personnel. Urgent steps are needed to bridge this gap and to abort this fast-developing vicious cycle of limited resources compromising the quality of teaching and training and consequently a further shortfall of trained practitioners and teachers.

One method of bridging these gaps is to develop the concept of virtual teaching, with all its nuances and associated areas like the virtual museum and the virtual library. These will, while removing the obstacles of shortage of training material and teachers, also ensure uniform quality of teaching in these areas throughout any country or state. In view of its tremendous outreach and unlimited potential, this system shows promise of becoming the prime teaching tool of the future. The use of this virtual platform, while ensuring minimum standards of quality, will also ensure that doctors are able to interact and exchange high resolution images and information with scientists all over the world.

Methods of education and the usage of VT

It seems fairly well established by now that imparting education is eminently possible using distance learning modalities (virtual teaching) and many universities, all over the world, are exploring this. The type of program or method, however, needs to be tailor-made as per specific situational requirements.

We take the example of India. A meeting of a working group set up by the Planning Commission debated at length on the usage of the virtual platform for the various aspects of healthcare. The group discussed the implications of a pilot project of the National Knowledge Network (NKN) with the All India Institute of Medical Sciences (AIIMS) being the nodal point for creation and testing of teaching modules in various areas of medicine and the possible uses to which this could be put. This is available on the internet and low level pilots have been run successfully (see Box 2).[148]

BOX 2

The AIIMS experience in virtual teaching

At AIIMS, experimentation with virtual teaching started in 2010 on a pilot basis.

Virtual teaching modules were created and tested on students at AIIMS and other medical colleges. The transmission was using the NKN cable network.

Skill modules for basic medical skills like suturing, measuring blood pressure, and phlebotomy were made and tested with medical students in various locations.

The skill modules for measuring blood pressure and handwashing were also tested on field health workers in Tanda District of Himachal Pradesh.

The results in all these were gratifying. The feedback received indicated acceptance of this method among students and teachers. The experiments also indicated a definite future role in teaching medical and surgical skills.

A similar program called National Program for Technology Enhanced Learning (NPTEL) was being run within the engineering institutes or IITs and used for transferring knowledge between institutions.[149]

The complexity of virtual teaching in medical discipline/s is highlighted by the very name selected here, that is, teaching instead of learning (as in NPTEL). The reason is that in different areas of science, engineering, and social sciences, the component of theoretical content is significant and predominant. In contrast to this, health sciences have a significant component in acquisition of skills, which could be aesthetic or manual, and a correlation that could at times be a 3D view of manual skills with theoretical knowledge. This implies that in the health sciences in general, the component of self-learning is lower than in other branches of sciences, and there is a greater emphasis on active teaching, involving skill demonstration, skill practice, and an integration of theoretical knowledge with the skill (Table 1).

Thus, for a viable program of virtual teaching in medicine, we will need a blend of different types of teaching material, varying from a simple PowerPoint with voiceover for areas that have mainly theoretical content; to 2D and 3D animated modules in areas where difficult concepts are to be explained or a time sequence delineated; to complex modules including videos interwoven with 2D and 3D constructs, for

TABLE 1 Examples of virtual teaching include.

Type	Example
• Internet-based learning	Web surfing
• Internet-based teaching	YouTube, Wikispaces
• Videoconferencing based	NPTEL
• Webinar	Web-based conference/seminar
• Computer-based animated learning	As in many programs on the net
• Animated module based	Present project
• 3D modules	Seen in some ad campaigns
• Mobile device-based learning	Android/IOS based iSchool Initiative
• Cloud-based education	Services running on the cloud, for example, • Amazon EC2 cloud for HP computing • Educational software • Data storage • Platform • Infrastructure
• 3D reconstruction (hologram based)	The future!!

areas where manual skills are to be imparted, like suturing, dissection, physical examination, and palpation.

It would be obvious from the previous text that not all types of virtual teaching can be standardized or used as part of a training program. The restrictions of access control and related licensure will remain. Otherwise, someone might start operating based on a video-based course!

Requirements for a virtual teaching platform (VTP)

For full utilization an established VTP is required to

- translate the entire curriculum into a virtual MBBS curriculum that is adequate to the needs of the country
- create virtual teaching modules in all areas of medicine, using techniques like animation (2D and 3D), digitization, videography, and simulation
- develop methods of disseminating these through various modalities, current as well as those still developing, like webinar, web conferencing, teleconferencing, and cable transmission
- develop methods for ensuring and maintaining quality in these modules

- develop mechanisms for large-scale development of teaching material while constantly monitoring and ensuring quality parameters
- develop assessment/examination strategies pari passu with the teaching

It is hoped that, given appropriate encouragement, in a short while, the virtual teaching platform will be a viable and vibrant alternative to traditional teaching and, eventually, because of its flexibility and limitlessness, may replace traditional methods of teaching.

All this will doubtless need tremendous planning, resources, and above all, time. While this project must be launched, nurtured, and developed, it may be worthwhile to also seek and implement one or more bridging, short-term solutions to meet the immediate needs.

One possible solution for this is to use a judiciously crafted blend of distance teaching, teleconferencing, and strategically placed moderators at the user end. This can well be on the lines of NPTEL, which is being used by the IITs so effectively to teach engineering and some science subjects.[149]

A case study of e-teaching in cardiology from India

Sunita Maheshwari

Cardiovascular disease (CVD) is the world's no 1 killer with 17.5 million people dying each year from CVD, an estimated 31% of all deaths worldwide.[150] In poorer countries, the effects of CVD are even worse. For example, the Indian subcontinent is home to 20% of the world's population and one of the regions with the highest burden of cardiovascular disease in the world. The Indian rural population and urban poor are facing a "double burden" with acute CVD illness in addition to a rapid growth in incidence of chronic disease. It is not just the poor who are affected. With unhealthy lifestyles, decreasing physical activity, increasing stress levels, and increasing intake of saturated fats and tobacco, the rise of CVDs is seen in the economically privileged population as well.[151,152] Cardiac disease is an issue in the pediatric population as well. With a global incidence of 1%,[153] nearly 180,000 children are born with heart defects each year in India. Of these, nearly 60,000–90,000 suffer from critical cardiac lesions requiring early intervention. Approximately 10% of present infant mortality in India may be accounted for by congenital heart diseases alone. The burden of rheumatic fever and rheumatic heart disease (RHD) currently falls disproportionately on children and young adults living in low-income countries with an incidence of an average of 0.9/1000 and accounting for 233,000 deaths annually.[154]

There is only about 1 doctor for every 1700 people in India, and it faces more than a 60% shortfall of specialists at the community health center level. There is a shortfall of 600,000 doctors and 1,000,000 nurses to reach the WHO recommendation of 1 doctor for every 1000 people. The situation is even worse when it comes to cardiologists. India trains only about 200 new cardiologists every year, and the number is not enough, given the disease burden.[155]

One solution for the inequitable distribution of specialists is telecardiology. This encompasses tele-echocardiography, tele-ECG, teleconsultations, and e-teaching. There is an acute shortage of teaching manpower in the existing medical colleges and training programs especially in Asia and Africa, particularly at the postgraduate level. There is a similar shortage of trained pediatric cardiologists available to interpret pediatric echoes and direct care, especially in rural and remote areas. Training of pediatric cardiologists is key to improving outcomes of children with heart disease. One successful example of e-teaching in India currently is described in the succeeding text.[156]

E-teaching in pediatric cardiology: From May 2010 to March 2018, 645 simultaneous e-classes in pediatric cardiology were conducted by global, though primarily Indian, faculty (Fig. 1) for DNB postgraduates across all pediatric cardiac centers in India. This allowed all trainees in pediatric cardiology to get taught similar concepts, and it enabled high-quality training, thus improving the standard of pediatric cardiac care in India. The teleteaching program was funded by Children's Heartlink

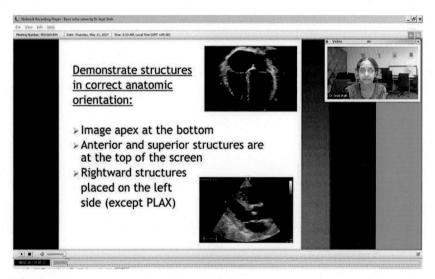

FIG. 1   Screenshot of an e-class in pediatric cardiology.

(the United States) and People4people (India) and is accredited by the National Board of Examinations, New Delhi.

There are several advantages offered by virtual live e-teaching or tele-teaching in medicine:

1. One teacher can teach multiple students in multiple geographic locations at the same time, obviating the issue of teacher shortage.
2. The same content can be disseminated to all the centers undergoing specialist training, so there is a national consensus on diagnostic and management approach among all trainees.
3. The e-classes can be recorded and replayed, so they can be viewed repeatedly by the same group or new trainees.
4. The question and answer sessions are fully interactive and similar to a normal classroom.

Conclusion

In a vast country such as India with over 1.2 billion people, the use of telecardiology and telemedicine can positively impact healthcare of patients and improve knowledge and training capabilities of medical personnel serving their needs.

Telemedicine

Telesupport for the primary care practitioner

Shashi Gogia

Society for Administration of Telemedicine and Healthcare Informatics, New Delhi, India

Introduction

Healthcare delivery is broadly classified into three types: (A) *primary* when care is provided by local practitioners or PCPs, which could be a GP if private, or in a primary or community health center (PHC/CHC), if by government agencies; (B) *secondary* wherein care is provided in a place with in-house admission and basic diagnostic facilities; and (C) *tertiary*, which means super specialized care requiring an ICU and specialized diagnostic as well as therapeutic equipment like nuclear medicine or radiotherapy. Variations of B and C exist in the form of isolated single-specialty centers like for dialysis, cardiac or eye care, and some restricted to daycare surgery.

For almost all patients, it is recommended that except for emergencies, each health-related episode should first undergo a consultation with the local PCP. If not possible to manage the same, the patient can be referred up the chain to a secondary care provider and further to the specialist. Chronic care needs more frequent visits and hence best managed by the PCP who, when faced with challenges, can and should ask for help, preferably in the form of online support. Not only does this decrease the need for travel but also provides the PCP an opportunity to learn to manage future similar episodes better. Keeping specialists in a high population area makes sense, as they have to see a certain minimum number of patients to justify their high cost of training as well as income. The United Kingdom has one neurologist per 200,000 population, somewhat half of the felt need.[145,157]

In villages or remote places, as the cost of retaining a doctor is difficult, the role of PCP is likely to be fulfilled by a nurse or CHW. They would be all the more likely to need help for anything outside routine dressings or medicine administration.

So far, this system of local care by whatever PCP is available with a need-based referral or transfer has worked well. However, rising incomes, a continuous global phenomena since the middle of the last century, have led to higher aspirations. There is also a longer life span and a higher incidence of chronic diseases, calling for a higher dependence on specialty support. This calls for a redistribution of health resources to match the demand. Costs increase as one goes up higher (see Fig. 2). Telemedicine can come in as a method to fulfill this shifting demand even while the local populace waits for actual physical redistribution of the human resources for healthcare (HRH).

Ensuring the physical presence of a doctor in each and every hamlet is challenging not simply because of monetary concerns. The reasons relate to a smaller number of patients requiring his specialized skills. Besides that, he/she shall be requiring a certain number of qualified and specially trained paramedical personnel with related equipment to ensure care quality; for example, a neurologist will need an EEG and EMG and its technician, besides the mandatory CT/MR. An important additional aspect, though less mentioned, is that qualified medical personnel do have a family of their own and keeping them in a remote place means ensuring good schools for the children, besides general social and entertainment facilities. This is problematic and adds to frustration.

From the independent practitioners' perspective, using telehealth has some additional benefits. A PCP by definition is a general practitioner (GP). He/she is the first point of contact for any health problem, be it a child, an elderly, a pregnant woman, a remote person visiting relatives, or maybe even a tourist. The initial advice has to be appropriate, even if it is further referral to the most suited specialist. The range of problems he needs to be aware about is mind boggling. Also, after the initial training in medical school, there is little chance of skill upgradation. Data about recent advances, and there have been many, are only available through the medical representatives. Continuing medical education (CME) meetings, despite fulfilling the mandated insistence in many countries for retaining the license, can never be enough. They cannot fully prepare one for what the next patient will present with. News, other media, and lately the internet are there, but then the GP should know better than the patient!

Telesupport offers something better in the form of learning on the job from a more qualified and experienced specialist. Since there is direct one-to-one contact with the patient on his/her side, it beats getting details after reading the discharge summary or notes provided after a transfer.

Telesupport is important during emergencies as chances of finding physical help are well, remote! However, similar or more justification exists for those in constant need of care, for example, the infirm; elderly; those with chronic disease, who can always get an added less understood problem; and the disabled, who cannot be transported easily.

Telemedicine in primary healthcare

Carlos Aita

The core attributes of primary healthcare centre (PHC) are to provide first-contact accessibility, relational continuity, comprehensiveness, as well as coordination of care. Among these, first-contact accessibility, by definition—the making of PHCs as the preferred care gateway for all new health problems as well as fresh episodes of an existing one (except for actual urgencies and emergencies), is considered the most important. Without first level contact, health provision cannot proceed, hence any deficiencies here, get converted to system-wide deficiencies.[158]

Healthcare delivery is evenly poised between access, quality, and cost of health provision. It is believed that any preferred choice of two, generally precludes the third. This is commonly known as Oregon's dilemma or the iron triangle of healthcare.[159] However, expanding access and improving quality in health while reducing cost is within the possibilities of telemedicine. Recent studies have shown results in this regard, both in the context of PHC and in the management of chronic conditions. Besides that, although less commonly performed, cost analyses have shown reduction in overall cost of care delivery if telehealth has been utilized.[160,161] Another essential attribute of PHC, the coordination of care—which involves referral of patients to specialist care—can also be leveraged better through telemedicine interventions.[113]

Support to primary care providers

Even in countries such as the United States, where care models are more focused on medical specialties, up to 55% of consultations occur in the primary care setting.[162] However, only 15% of family physicians surveyed by the American Academy of Family Physicians in 2014 reported current use of telemedicine, while in hospitals and specialist care, this percentage ranged from 40% to 60%.[163] Professionals working in rural areas, urgent care, emergency departments, and programs with integrated health services were more likely to use telecare; while those in practice for more than 10 years, worked in primary care, in private practice, or did not have access to an electronic medical record (EMR) were less likely to do so. Cost, training, and reimbursement issues also had a negative impact.[164]

On a daily basis, a general practice generates between 15 and 20 clinical queries, or questions for which the PCP needs to further consult the books, the Internet, or the easiest, a senior colleague.[165] Despite that, studies have revealed underutilization of telemedicine tools.[166] Even though multifactorial clinical acceptance exists, telemedicine is still largely considered a disruptive innovation (i.e., one that redefines standards, as opposed to sustaining innovation, which follows current standards). This creates barriers and is posed as a threat to traditional forms of healthcare delivery.[167] Hybrid models, which combine old technologies with new ones (e.g., telephone plus Internet), can be used to overcome this resistance. Another factor to consider is that, unlike in most developed countries, remote physician-patient interactions have been termed as illegal in many developing nations, especially in Latin America and India, limiting the scope of telemedicine.[168] After the death of a patient, the Indian Medical Association had requested its doctor members to say no to telephonic consultations.[169]

The use of telehealth tools, such as teleconsultation and electronic prescribing, increases patient access to both PHC as well as specialty care. Approximately 66% of all patients call their PCPs for reassurance, advice, or explanation of a worrying symptom.[170] Acceptance of telemedicine among patients is much higher than among providers. And, contrary to what is commonly believed, patients do not think poorly of practitioners who use the Internet for lookups during a visit, although referring to textbooks still elicits greater credibility. Patients are avid consumers of technologies such as text messaging, telephone, e-mail, personal health records, the Internet of Things, mobile apps, and decision support algorithms. However, there is a greater risk of the inverse care law applied, since patients with poorer health are less likely to use these technologies.[161] Another challenge for the clinician when following their most "connected" patients is that only 43% and 27% of health applications for iOS and Android, respectively, have any real utility.[171] On the other hand, patients are largely in favor of sharing their clinical information with providers and family members involved in their care, and nurse-led advice hotlines are well accepted. In addition, they regard virtual consultations and prescriptions as equivalent to face-to-face visits, except in situations that require physical examination. Studies have shown that, although Internet-based educational programs improve adherence to drug therapy, physical activity, and sodium control in patients with hypertension, access to health portals did not alter the frequency of PHC visits. Teleconsultation (usually by telephone) led to improvements in quality, prevented 40% of referrals for chronic conditions, and decreased absenteeism for scheduled follow-up appointments. In Brazil, since 2015, a free nationwide telephone hotline for primary care providers has helped prevent around 68% of referrals from PHC to specialist care. Similar results have been achieved by other regional-scope experiences in the country. In Belize, the use of mobile text messages (SMS) aimed at pregnant women reduced perinatal mortality by 50%. The use of SMS technology can also reduce absenteeism ("no-shows"), improve appointment scheduling, and serve for medication checks. Telephone- or Internet-based behavioral interventions have been shown to produce significant weight loss in obese adults with one or more cardiovascular risk factors, especially if combined with face-to-face visits to a general practitioner. Clinical counselling over the phone also reduced pain and optimized the use of analgesics in patients at risk of substance abuse. The adoption of a nationwide information system reduced mortality from several diseases, and the use of electronic health records reduced the number of visits, while simultaneously increasing the quality of care. In addition to gains in access and quality, there is also evidence (although from fewer published studies) that the use of telemedicine in primary care reduces costs by improving consultation time, preventing waste, improving management of patients with multimorbidity (outliers), and reducing annual expenditures per capita.[113,161]

Even taking into account the need for more rigorous studies to validate impacts on clinical outcomes, as well as the need for standardization of methods to assess costs, most authors conclude that within the current context of health systems, telemedicine has great potential to address the challenges faced by PHC. In short, both clinicians and patients have a wide range of telemedicine services at their disposal (via voice or text chat, e-mail, telephone, video conferencing, or telepresence technologies) to interact with one another, whether through sensors or decision support applications. Broad acceptance by patients and providers is increasingly making telehealth a viable core component of PHC worldwide.

Referral of patients to specialty care

Brazilian geographer Milton Santos, best known as the 1994 recipient of the Vautrin Lud Prize, once said that the geography of flows depends on fixed objects.[172] It has long been known that distance and income level determine the access to health services. This remains a current problem, and studies have sought to quantify the barrier to access posed by distance according to the increasing technological density required by health status. This is especially important in health systems that provide universal access, but do not have an organized transportation system. Physician demographics, that is, the way in which providers are distributed across in a country, affects the supply of and access to specialist health services. Population density and socioeconomic level are the main determinants when defining health workforce staffing levels and resources. Accordingly, there is major inequity between urban and rural areas and between more and less privileged regions in urban areas, with a tendency toward the worse indicators being from remote areas.[173] This occurs in both developed and developing countries. China, India, Brazil, and South

Africa account for 40% of the world's population, and all have PHC-focused health systems with universal coverage. In Brazil, PHC access is its worst-ranked attribute.[174] In addition, the concentration of physicians is only along the coast and the major cities' leading to a demographic void related to specialist care in the public health system. However, this same public health system, which serves 80% of the population employs only 5% of the country's physicians.[175]

Within the current demographic (population aging), epidemiological (increasing disease burden), and economic (increasing technological density in health) context, telemedicine interventions are able to prevent unnecessary displacement and inequality of access to the health system. They prevent the progression of patients to higher disease severity by increasing the capacity of primary care and thus increase the ability to address the most prevalent conditions. Likewise, follow-up of infrequent or even rare events may benefit from decentralization of the part of the diagnostic and therapeutic process, even if specialist care remains concentrated in major cities.

Telemedicine is an effective tool for management of chronic diseases such as heart failure, sequelae of stroke, and COPD. Studies have shown a reduction in hospitalization and emergency department attendance rates, prevention of severe episodes, reduction of mortality and costs, and increased quality as compared with usual care. Internet-based interventions produced similar results to telephone-based ones in nurse-led screening for appendicitis and guidance in cases of urinary tract infection, as well as in case management, with reductions in 30-day readmission rates. Positive effects have also been observed on several other indicators, such as reduction in no shows to specialist care appointments, improved scheduling, and identification and management of adverse drug reactions.[160]

Ongoing telediagnosis projects demonstrate that the entire statewide demand for spirometry, electrocardiography, and ophthalmological examination can be met by decentralization of specimen collection facilities/examination sites, with a reduction in costs as compared with traditional testing.[113,176] Having primary care providers themselves perform specimen collection and examination with the aid of a smartphone camera, for example, in dermatology and oral medicine, produces equivalent gains.

The adoption of technologies by health professionals, whether for clinical practice or for skill improvement, is contingent upon the perceived ease of use and gains in time, access to other professionals, and profit, which these tools may provide. This means technology interventions must be not only multifaceted but also customized if full acceptance and utilization are to be achieved.[165] In this sense, the incorporation of telemedicine into the referral and handover of care processes in health systems can increase PHC response capacity and coordination of care, improve patient adherence to treatment, reduce rehospitalization rates, and encourage the practice of quaternary prevention.[165,177] One example of this is the ECHO Program, based in New Mexico, which uses videoconferencing "telerounds" to provide expert support for the primary care management of several chronic conditions. This increases the effectiveness and productivity of the tutored groups of general practitioners. Similarly, the RegulaSUS Project in Southern Brazil managed to clear more than 100,000 patients from the waiting lists of various medical specialties; in this, two out of every three cases discussed over the phone decided to get the physical referrals cancelled!

Telemedicine for specialist care is offered in many modalities: telediagnosis (teleradiology, telepathology, and teledermatology), tele-emergency (telestroke, teletrauma, teleburns, and tele-ICU), prison medicine, and various other specialties, such as telepediatrics, telecardiology, telepulmonology, telepsychiatry, and telenursing.[178]

Some patient populations, especially the elderly, are already doing more virtual, (i.e. e-mail, telephone, and videoconference with their health providers), as opposed to face-to-face visits, with high levels of satisfaction for both the patient and the providers. Telemedicine is about to lose its disruptive nature, as it comes increasingly close to a turning point in which the pattern of use will migrate from early adopters (who are more sensitive to technological innovations) to users seeking more pragmatic applications.[179]

The way in which people access healthcare is changing. Wearable, swallowable, and injectable sensors, coupled with the evolution of mobile devices and the Internet of Things, have turned the concept of connected health into a current reality. In 2016 alone, 36 connected health apps were approved by the US FDA. Natural Cycles, an app that claims efficacy similar to that of oral contraceptives (Pearl index of 7) without medication, has been launched in Europe. Another app, Babylon, has caused heated debate by offering 24/7 artificial intelligence-based clinical screening with diagnostic accuracy and precision superior to that of physicians and nurses. Screening itself is free but can be followed by a virtual health provider visit (via chat or video conferencing) for a fee. China invested more than US$ 600 million in two medical consultation apps in 2016, and India has examples such as LiveHealth, a mobile app that allows patients to access their electronic health records and communicate with their healthcare providers.[180]

By delivering traditional healthcare services in a novel way, telemedicine is gradually being incorporated into daily practice in a hybrid, sustained manner, playing an additive or even substitutive role to conventional healthcare delivery methods in places underserved (or not served at all) by health networks, as in the case of teleconsultation and telediagnosis. On the other hand, in a manner consistent with advances in ethics and technology, it is beginning to permeate all health interventions, as a "meta"-health service of sorts. Telemedicine thus becomes an organizer of the flow of information, people, and inputs in healthcare networks, impacting the optimization of funding and increasing access to and quality of care.[181]

Why are doctors reluctant to adopt telehealth

Devashish Saini/G.S. Jaiya

Doctors are (slowly) adopting telemedicine

While established wisdom says doctors are generally averse to innovations in information technology, recent years have seen a growing, albeit somewhat reluctant, acceptance.[182] Many forms of remote consultations are already mainstream, mostly as add-ons to the primary face-to-face patient-doctor consultations.

Most outpatient practices and inpatient units provide their patients an on-call number of a doctor on the team, who can answer questions; offer clarifications; review test reports; and, in case of unexpected symptoms, help triage the patient appropriately. Sometimes, this happens through a home-visit nurse or health volunteer, and more recently, this is aided by video conference and remote monitoring tools. Many consultants also offer ways and means for patients to contact them directly after the first consultation—either through dedicated apps or social media apps. Sharing of personal phone numbers by consultants is not mainstream but quite common, and some component of follow-up care may happen over phone, SMS, or an app. In practices where teleconsultations are available, physicians are using them for routine and administrative queries, like dietary restrictions, fitness certificates or prescription refills.

Peer consultations are very common, and doctors are utilizing their formal and informal online social networks to get help on questions related to clinical care of problem cases. These networks range from alumni networks to speciality groups to learning apps bringing geographically disparate doctors together on the same platform. Some group practices and inpatient units have groups on social media apps or within the EMR where they may share documents and discuss management of such patients.

Expert opinion has become easier to obtain with the help of technology, especially for providers located in remote areas.[183] Teleradiology and tele-pathology are established fields, with the respective doctors frequently providing their reports from remote locations. Primary care providers and internists often seek ECG readings from cardiologists and X-ray opinions from ortho consultants in their friends circle or hospital groups.

Teleconsultations with new patients have seen limited uptake by doctors.[184,185] Most doctors respond to new online patient queries with the equivalent of the age-old "Take two aspirins and call the clinic in the morning." They might suggest a medication or two for urgent symptoms but mostly advise patients to follow-up in a healthcare facility for a face-to-face consultations.

Busy doctors often feel they have no incentives to adopt or even try teleconsultations. Only a few fields of medicine have actively taken up teleconsultations for new patients—geriatrics, psychiatry, dermatology, and rural primary care physicians. Emergency care physicians have been guiding paramedics remotely for several decades now.[186]

The next section discusses why doctors continue to be averse to advising new patients over remote technologies and wary of using technology in ways described earlier.

Limitations of teleconsultations from a doctors' perspective

Navigating the legal requirements,[a] state policies, restrictions, and guidelines around teleconsultations is a major barrier, especially considering that the doctor needs to study and follow said legalities of all the places where his/her patients are calling from. Some places require an informed consent from the patient before using any teleconsultation platform, the format of which varies from place to place. Other places have restrictions on whether doctors can e-prescribe to patients they have not seen face to face before. California even has restrictions on the kind of agreements teleconsultation service providers can have with doctors.

Reimbursement of teleconsultations remains a challenge. Many health systems are actively promoting telemedicine, with reimbursements for doctors for each call. In most other areas, payment for teleconsultations majorly comes from patients paying out of pocket. Lack of clear reimbursement structure may make it challenging for a practice or a hospital to invest in telemedicine infrastructure.

Technical issues may affect quality of care. Seamless video conferencing requires very fast connectivity at both ends, and gaps in communication due to poor connectivity may result in poor treatment decisions. Lack of familiarity with the software tool or the telemonitoring gadgets at either end may result in missing vital information. Telemonitoring tools often generate a huge load of data, which may get overwhelming for the doctor to process without in-built analytical tools. Even if present, they may not be directly relevant to the particular doctor's needs. A market oversell quiet often raises expectations, and when the product does not perform to these unwarrantedly raised expectations, there are long-term problems with a wariness and even refusal of incorporation of newer advances in day-to-day work.

[a]Discussed in detail in Chapter 13.

All this is reflected in most doctors feeling untrained for the use of telemedicine in their respective practices. There may be cultural reasons behind this—a type of aversion to technology or even an inability to do something beyond what was taught in medical school. The fear of litigation is definitely there and has been played up greatly by the media, so the Indian Medical Association recently described telephonic consultations a strict no-no.[169]

Several studies have raised questions regarding quality of care delivered over telemedicine. Reduced ability of accurate diagnosis over remote tools results in a higher use of broad-spectrum antibiotics, although this was refuted recently.[187] There are concerns that substandard providers are more likely to try to equate their better peers using telecare and are more likely to resort to unethical means.

Use of telemedicine may not necessarily free up precious resources. Triage apps tend to be conservative, and often suggest a visit to a clinic or hospital, including when none may be needed. Health systems using triage apps have not seen a reduction in clinic or hospital visits.

Lastly, ethical questions need to be answered. Teleconsultations are likely to result in fragmentation of care, doctor shopping, and lack of continuity in patient records. How do we address these? A deeper trust is developed in an in-person consultation, and the strength of the patient-doctor relationship plays a big role in compliance and outcomes. If teleconsultations are necessarily of lower quality than in-person consultations, are we justified in offering them to the more vulnerable populations?

Facilitating doctors' adoption of teleconsultation

The authors feel that there need to be several systematic changes for teleconsultations to become mainstream.

We need to define the minimum quality of infrastructure, connectivity, and software capability needed for a quality consultation. To ensure patient safety, every clinical speciality should define patient scenarios, in which video conferencing is adequate against those which mandate in-person consultation. We need more training programs for both doctors and patients and more trained personnel assisting at the patient end in certain situations. We need to train doctors to avoid overprescription and overtesting.

The patient's integrated health records should be available to the doctor at the time of teleconsultation, and the doctor's notes and prescription should become part of the same integrated record.

Every health system and payor should define its payment policy for reimbursement of teleconsultations.

Every country should adopt national telehealth and/or telemedicine standards, guidelines, and policies, incorporating the previous factors and enforce them. Ideally, these national standards conform to international standards and guidelines. These should be regularly updated to keep abreast with rapid advances in technology. Deeper qualitative research is needed to better understand teleconsultations and how they result in changed workflows, a new kind of patient-doctor relationship, and ultimately impact patient outcome.

There is no doubt about the potential of teleconsultations in transforming delivery of healthcare. With the advances in technology the following issues still need to be addressed:

- Changing over from a physical documentation to ICT-based systems needs **additional learning** and used to be a source of rejection of the new technology. Much of the staff would be reluctant to change, but alongside, there was a fear that they may be replaced by younger persons. Deliberate attempts to sabotage have occurred in many projects include those managed by the author.
- ICT systems used to be **expensive** and hence reserved for use by the senior staff, the very same persons who needed additional training.
- ICT systems are **obtrusive**—pop ups ask questions and passwords repetitively leading to stoppage of work. They act as a master rather than a slave to the clinician.
- The few practitioners who successfully overcome the previously mentioned issues over control of the ICT systems would also find irrelevant side benefits like games and social media to be **engaging**, sometimes enough to cause **addiction** and obstruct day-to-day work.
- Even if not addicted, there are **distractions and diversions** through irrelevant components and systems not performing to expectations. Patient care has suffered as a result.
- Continuing and better documentation means **transparency**, which, while much needed, can be a cause of concern as information becomes easily accessed by competition and tax authorities. Private doctors especially in a few developing countries where cash payments are the norm prefer to avoid paying tax!
- **Hacking** and viruses are general fears but controllable.
- **Issues of patient privacy** are genuine concerns. Health data is being sold for USD 60 per person in the United States! In India, a new law (DISHA) assumes the doctor is at fault for leakages when it could just be a hacking.

There is an agreement that eHealth has to remain a support system for well-defined needs and not be pushed as an engineering solution to health.[20]

Telemedicine for community healthcare workers

Charles Umeh/Shashi Gogia

The availability of human resources (HR) has been recognized as a fundamental determinant of health provision.[188] Their lack has undermined the development of essential medicinal services particularly in the sub-Saharan Africa.

In low-resource settings, community health workers (CHWs) are frontline providers, who with proper training and now with access to technology can be a replacement for the lack of fully trained personnel like doctors and nurses. Their need and utilization is best explained by an Indian proverb, which is in *Hindi* "Andhon Mein Kana Raja"—the meaning is "Among the blind, the one eyed is king." In this context, the people, specially in remote and underdeveloped areas may be considered as blind, that is, unaware of what they can and should do for their healthcare, CHWs are the one-eyed people with some knowledge, which now is being constantly upgraded through technology, who can assist the community for health provision.

CHWs are typically volunteers prepared to give preessential medicinal services and counselling to enhance group well-being. Located in the village or community, CHWs provide first line contact for a majority of health needs of the community shouldering the bulk of the health service delivery burden.

CHWs provide preessential medicinal services in numerous areas of the world, including Brazil, Bangladesh, Ethiopia, and Pakistan. Contingently, CHWs give administrative support and instructions to the population on many topics starting from Maternal and Child Care, HIV and some common diseases. Since they are, as of now, individuals from the same community, there is an expanded level of trust, which originates from prior connections. This can be used to give the best care conceivable.

CHWs are commonly volunteers offering their administrations in their constrained available time. Their capacity to successfully screen and analyze ailments is related to (1) inadequate exposure and training and (2) lack of relevant instruments and gadgets.

WHO recommends a half year of training prior to being employed and another half year on the job training. But training and capability varies. For example, while India, despite having a provision of trained male and female CHWs in Subcentres and PHCs since long, it recently added the Accredited Social Health Activist (ASHA) worker. They were initially conceived to ensure that deliveries were conducted in hospitals but have now been inducted for very many activities. Payment, though through government agencies, is based upon services rendered, but their role has become so widespread that patients prefer to use them for general counselling in almost all health needs.

CHWs teach groups and individuals about family planning, nutrition, ante-natal and postnatal care, common diseases and their prevention, and many other applicable points. Utilization and availability of biomedical tools such as smart mobiles can be a great help in providing the care. These assist not only monitoring and support for care provision but also on the job training with a further possibility of AI-based support[b]. One example showing outcomes is the e-Mamta program in Gujarat, India,[189] which resulted in significant reduction in neonatal and maternal mortality.

CHWs serve many capacities, including direct home visits, evaluation and treatment of illness, information accumulation, instruction, and guiding and referrals. They can assist prophylactic strategies, help and assist the infirm and older generation individuals, oversee treatment of tuberculosis and AIDs, and manage groups coordinating care like for adolescence ailments.

Most CHWs, at least in developing countries, are remote based, which themselves are associated with the constraints posed by the lack of connectivity and of a constant power supply. PC-based systems are hence ruled out, so most applications for CHWs are necessarily dependent on mobiles.

CHWs advance a broad range of health aims throughout the globe, particularly maternal and child health, HIV/AIDS, and sexual and reproductive health. Most commonly, CHWs use mobile technology to collect field-based health data, receive alerts and reminders, facilitate health education sessions, and conduct person-to-person communication. Programmatic efforts to strengthen health service delivery focus on improving adherence to standards and guidelines, community education and training, and programmatic leadership along with management practices. Studies evaluating program outcomes have provided some evidence that mobile tools help community health workers to improve the quality of care provided, efficiency of services, and capacity for program monitoring.[190]

A few examples of such care provision are provided next.

Purpose of care support

Specialists from the College of Washington,[191] and Berkeley, California,[192] have built up a cell phone-based programming called CommCare that guides CHWs for disease management. Examples include screening for TB and diarrhea management. Here, exact further instruction on how to ensure hydration and also provide safe drinking water is provided. The program records follow-up visits and also monitors new births or deaths. It enhances CHW adherence to SOPs and treatment rules.

CommCare likewise creates an excellent workflow and trip management plan for the CHWs besides allowing automatic and convenient upload of the data to servers; training of CHWs is part and parcel, as are constant upgrades of the application itself.

[b]See section on AI.

Fast diagnostics

Images of blood smears can be sent to hematologists, of skin lesions to pathologists and dermatologists, slit lamps and retinoscopes to eye surgeons,[193] oral cavity, nasoscope or rhinoscope with dental and ENT surgeons and so on to assist diagnosis, and opinion on the necessary next steps. These can be shared directly from a mobile phone camera too like the previously mentioned.[191]

Adherence

Portability, ease of use, constant access to Internet, and information help fortify adherence. There is also a certain pressure associated with responding to messages, which flow in from higher quarters. The CHW hence remains informed and can follow and further spread well-being instructions of the community. Many CHWs function as adherence guides for those with tuberculosis (TB) or HIV. For instance, in Cape Town, South Africa, a specialist has made a database of his TB patients' mobile phone numbers, and his PC regularly conveys a customized instant message that reminds them to take their pharmaceuticals.[194]

In India, CHWs working under an organization called *Operation Asha*[195] provide TB medicines to patients in the field so that the required daily visits to the health center do not disturb day-to-day work. The program ensures e-compliance[c] through Iris and fingerprint scanners available through the mobile device they are carrying. They are now expanding to other diseases like mental health and hemophilia detection.

Many other innovations in care program are occurring. To help engage and additionally teach patients, there is incorporation of jokes and way of life tips in the writings. Instructions on physical exercise, nutrition, avoiding hazardous sexual practices, etc. are provided.

Ensuring health equity

Extraordinary financial, social, and basic disparities exist on the planet today. Dispersion of social insurance, which is omnipresent in the richer countries, exists only on paper, if at all, in the lower income countries especially Africa and South Asia. Of the 163 million births every year, 34 million infants die within a month, and 10.6 million children do so before achieving the age five. Global maternal mortality ratio (MMR) is 530,000.[196] More than 17 million deaths occurred due to cardiovascular illness worldwide in 2010, with over 60% happening in developing nations. The quantity of individuals living with HIV worldwide is 33.3 million.[197]

[c]https://en.wikipedia.org/wiki/Operation_ASHA.

In 1988, the Brazilian Programa Saude da Familia (PSF) was created. This model offers essential care administrations for families.[66] It has one family specialist, one medical caretaker, along with an administrative head who nurtures around six CHWs. Every family well-being group is in charge of a particular geographic zone and observing 3000–4500 individuals. CHWs visit every family in their geographic territory once per month, to report on illnesses and any other health problem with constant follow-up till the medical problem is settled. PSF gathers statistic and well-being data, which can be pinned to a particular geographic area through GPS mapping.

A few components that help shape a fruitful CHW program are hereby listed. *Firstly*, group cooperation is fundamental to secure members. They need to be participants and understand the needs of all the program components. Second, they should have satisfactory and dependable assets, for example, legislative and political help. Thirdly, they should preferably be from within the community—they will need some further training. Fourthly, they have to be close to the administration so that their motivation and engagement becomes known, which helps in keeping the program alive. Most selections should preferably be done through village health councils (VHCs). Fifth, a motivating bundle needs to be orchestrated, including pay and other incentives. SATHI's program for teleophthalmology succeeded thanks to the above measures.[147]

Many difficulties exist for those attempting to accomplish these five components of an effective CHW program. But it can be truly said that mHealth and eHealth are progressively changing the way healthcare and its administrations is being provided.

Evidence suggests mobile technology presents promising opportunities to improve the range and quality of services provided by community health workers. Small scale efforts, pilot projects, and preliminary descriptive studies are increasing, and there is a trend toward using feasible and acceptable interventions that lead to positive program outcomes through operational improvements and rigorous study designs. Programmatic and scientific gaps will need to be addressed by global leaders as they advance the use and assessment of mobile technology tools for community health workers.

Tele support for nurse practitioners

Bipinkumar Rathod

Introduction to primary healthcare nurse practitioner role

Primary healthcare is utmost important for any government healthcare delivery programs as it promises promotive, preventive, and initial care to large populations with minimal infrastructure. With nurses constituting the largest segment of human resources in healthcare, their role in the primary care setting needs to be further amplified in the changing environment of technology-enabled healthcare.

While in a hospital setting, the nurse provides care on the direction and guidance of the doctor; in remote areas, they have mostly to work independently. Most nurse practitioners working remotely serve as the single point of contact catering to large geographical areas in difficult terrains, for example, the north eastern states of India, rural Brazil, interiors of Australia, and Canada. Besides clinical nursing practices, care delivery, medical cares across the care continuum, and the nurse practitioner role hence becomes expanded to provide some interim help and even medications while waiting for the doctor.

Most countries adopting universal health coverage have stated a role of facilitating care delivery in last mile in its policy framework. This strengthening of primary care is best done by adoption of new technology. Telehealth has been slowly appearing in nursing practice since 2000. In some countries, many clinics run stand-alone through them. It has a special role for pre- and postoperative assessment of patients undergoing elective surgery.[198–200]

Nurse practitioners are already leaders in delivering extended healthcare support in developed and developing countries. For example, India is now emphasizing the role of the nurse practitioners in areas where specialist doctors are not available, such as many rural and interior locations.[201]

The typical primary nurse practitioners' role is to liaise among the families, physician, pharmacist, hospital nurses, and community health nurse team and social support team.

Communication in primary care: Telehealth a better solution

Primary healthcare team communication has become complex in the advent of multilayered referral systems, health insurance coverage, transition of care settings, follow-ups, and chronic care management in an ever changing dynamic of treatments/therapeutics/preventive care models. Emerging telehealth technology and tools can address this issue effectively. Telehealth can easily be integrated in primary care nurses' daily workflow to render care in wider geographical areas.

Telenursing can address many issues if used effectively in the primary care nursing environment, that is, maintaining continuity of care, multidisciplinary care environment, and outreach service.

Team communication and timely efficient decisions are utmost importance in delivering effective primary healthcare.

Dynamics of primary nursing care where there can be a role of telehealth intervention are mentioned in Table 1.

TABLE 1 Typical use cases scenarios of telenursing interventions.

S/no	Primary nursing care scenarios	Issues/challenges	Telehealth intervention[a]	Outcomes/impact
1	Early cancer detection	Early screening by nurses/referral suspected cases at village/health center	Video/high-resolution image of cancer signs, immediate evaluation by experts sitting remotely	Mass screening by experts/detection of breast and cervical cancer improved
2	Early assessment of new-born babies (http://unicef.in/Video/24/Meet-Barmer-s-E-ASHA-)	Detection of abnormalities	Auxiliary nurse midwife with tablet visit homes	Early detection and intervention and referral
3	Maternal health services	Remote areas/rainy seasons/road conditions	Routine ante-/postnatal visits via female health workers connected to primary care physician	Improved compliances/early intervention for complications
4	Health/diseases/surveys by primary health workers	Geographically scattered population, quick survey in endemic area	Mobile health application to collect questionnaire responses	Quick effective survey with direct responses from affected population
5	Disability screening by health visitors	Random and purposive data collection for health programs and social benefits	Photos/video for functional assessment and records	Rapid screening, holistic approach to disables
6	Child healthcare	More frequent visit to ER for home treatable conditions/concerns	Primary health nurses can deal with common ailments	Less pediatrics referral to ER
7	Mental health/addiction at rural level	Tech-savvy youth can avail more personalized counselling	Counselling/suppose services/youth in crisis/stress	Easy access to personalized mental health services
8	Geriatric care	Home/bed bound old-age population	Counselling/occupational therapy training/drug supply/treatment compliance	Reduced ER referrals/improved compliance
9	Chronic disease care management at home via telehealth	Noncommunicable disease burdens care/compliance	Primary care/therapy/counselling/assessment/training	Well controlled diseases/low complication rate

[a]Telehealth includes mHealth, telemedicine, and telenursing.

III. Telemedicine

Nurse lead telehealth primary nursing practice development: A new care model[202]

The International Council of Nurses Telenursing Network aims to seek, educate, support, and collaborate with nurses and nurse supporters from across the globe who have an interest in telenursing and promote nursing involvement in the development and use of telehealth technologies, with the goal of improving the timeliness, quality, and access of a broad range of healthcare services for individuals, their families, communities, and countries.

Primary health nursing care scenarios: How to plan telehealth intervention?

1. Identify and prioritize the care needs of community, that is, cancer care/postoperative follow-ups.
2. Choose most feasible telehealth solution.
3. Observe local health administration protocol of treatment and interventions for telehealth.
4. Follow general nursing care principles like, maintain privacy and dignity of beneficiaries during telehealth interventions.
5. Proper documentation of telecare rendered.

Way forward to establish telehealth nursing services at country level

1. Creation of strategic guideline to develop telenursing services in state/country.[202]
2. Creation of local health policies, nursing services guidelines, and ethical and legal framework of nursing practice.
3. Social, technological, economic, and political environment considerations.
4. Local nursing councils should create a nursing practice and service framework.
5. Nursing education: institute education and training facilities for conducting telenursing training.
6. Telenursing role and service development for nursing professionals by country's nursing councils.

Tele support for wounds, ulcers, and lymphedema

Shashi Gogia

Minor chronic but treatable problems of the limb include wounds, swelling, and pain secondary to venous and lymphatic diseases as well as diabetes. These are extremely common and best managed on an ambulatory basis by local care providers, preferably a primary care practitioner (PCP) or a nurse practitioner (NP) (See Fig. 1). There are many reasons why these clinics are at the top of the list of situations requiring telecare, including:

- These are chronic problems requiring repeated procedures, for example, dressing, but can be done by suitably trained health workers. Lack of such skills or specialized equipment means they need to go to a hospital. However, frequent travel is expensive as these patients are also disabled, even if temporarily.
- Care is on an ambulatory basis, but monitoring is required.
  - Most problems are minor but can have serious repercussions like infection.
  - Ischemia and cancer can appear similarly, which require specialist support.
- Consultation and backup is hence frequently necessary.
  - Some special materials or equipment may be required but the same can be sent.
  - Actual time of care is fraction of time taken for to and fro travel.
  - Travel to the specialist adds to cost on an exponential basis (see Fig. 1).

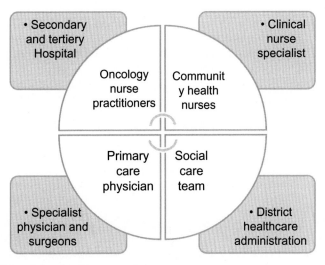

FIG. 1   Participants involved in a wound care program.

- Problems are not severe enough to stimulate relatives and care givers to leave their day-to-day work for travel as accompanying persons.
  - Problem restricts mobility—at least, for problems in the lower limb, support is required.
- Need for privacy and secrecy—with a wish against travel.
  - Wounds and ulcers are a source of smell and disgust.
  - Disfigurement and effects on gait are another source of embarrassment.
- Most problems are very visible.
  - Easy to share digitally.
  - Videos of gait and use of the hand also allow functional assessment.
  - Tele-mentoring of minor procedures like dressing and bandaging is possible.
  Another related issue is the sheer magnitude of the problem.

Venous diseases affect almost 10% of the global population and around 50%–70% will suffer from ulcers if not managed well. The city of Perth in 1991 reported an overall 0.6% of ulcers, which rose to 2.3% with increasing age.[203] Daily care of ulcers is best done on an ambulatory basis with regular monitoring (Fig. 2).[204]

Lymphoedema most commonly is due to filariasis, which affects 40 million globally.[205] Other causes like cancer, trauma, and venous disease are contributing to a possible 100 million affected.[206] Seventy percent of Lymphoedema care is self-care, 20% by a local counselor or therapist with only 10% requiring specialist intervention[207] (Fig. 3).

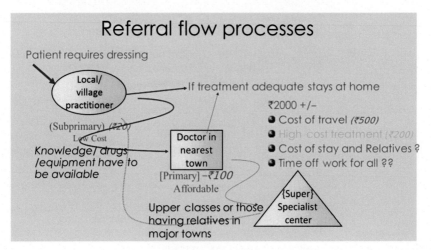

FIG. 2   A dressing done at a specialized time increase the cost exponentially. Figures are in Indian Rupees (INR) but would be roughly similar across the globe.

Level of intervention for lymphedema

With education and awareness, 70–80% can be self-managed

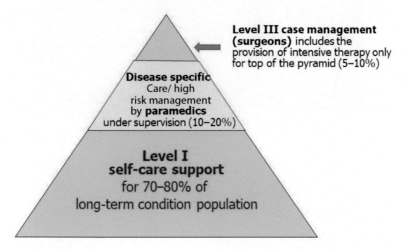

FIG. 3   Breakup of how a patient with lymphedema needs to be managed.

Diabetic foot affects around 10% of people with diabetes, which by itself affects 8.5% of the global load of 415 million cases in 2014.[208]

Confounding the care is the frequent chances of serious problems like arterial ischemia and infections mimicking or overlapping the above relatively minor problems. Hence, supervision and monitoring is a must, which is easily possible through sharing of data, photos, etc. Software and apps, which can tender advice and measure wound size, limb volume, etc., have led to solutions which make wound and limb care the highest ranking telesupport system.

Specialized wound and limb care clinics have come up in many hospitals. The emphasis, however, is on ambulatory care, use of nurse practitioners with offline and online support by clinicians.

The support is on a follow-up and daily homecare basis, like for any other chronic problem. Initial diagnosis and emergency care has to be managed by a surgeon preferably, which like all complicated procedures, would need a physical visit (Fig. 4).

The working of the telehealth component for ulcers is fairly simple. For routine ulcers, patient would need support higher than the PCP only for special situations, say the wound has not healed in a couple of weeks or there is a suspicion of an underlying cause. Otherwise, especially in emergencies, a specialist would be handling his problem, but both the patient

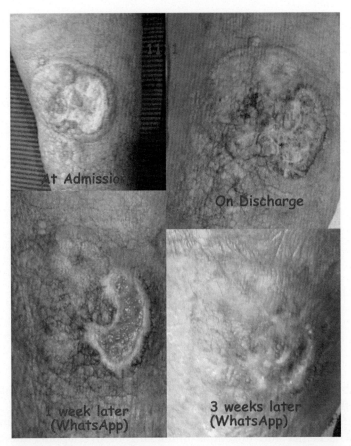

FIG. 4   This patient had come from outside Delhi—the top two images were taken during the physical visit—and after a few days went home to continue the compression therapy. She was happy to share her wound images via WhatsApp.

and the clinician may prefer not to wait for the wound to completely heal before sending them home. Communication between the PCP and the specialist would be in the form of sharing the photos, sometimes wound size, progress notes, smell, and other reports. They get a feedback about the next steps and may occasionally need to order for special dressing materials. Most care will remain local with a need to transfer with appointment for a surgical procedure. Sometimes the patient can directly share the information as shown in Fig. 4. Some learnings or instructions for a change in the method of dressing can be done during a video call.

Lymphedema management is similar. It is a chronic problem that requires with a great role of self-care through simple leg cleaning, emollients, etc. Like for chronic limb ulcers, there is a role for compression therapy, which needs special materials and some special training—both for the local care practitioner and the patient, as well as the use of a machine called the intermittent pneumatic compression pump (IPC). Most of this care is administered remotely. Specialist help is only asked for problems or for nonimprovement. Volume and other data can be shared through e-mail. Training on how to apply compression as well as the use of the machine is easily possible online through a video call. Measurements of limb volume are possible through software.[209]

The author recently treated 147 cases in a remote endemic area[210] through two camps and the limb volume reduction as well as the patient satisfaction rate was similar, if not better, than that of the patient attending the author's own tertiary care clinic (*yet to be published personal results*). The reasons for a better improvement are exemplary about the need for tele-care in lymphedema: (A) continuity of care is more possible remotely and (B) the patients presenting at the village level had presented at an earlier stage, which meant a higher chance of near complete recovery.

Many open source, shareware, and commercial applications are available to assist easy management like for measuring and monitoring wound and ulcer size, limb volume.

A commercial example is https://woundworks.com/technology- 3d-wound-imaging.

And an open source one is http://med.insofe.edu.in:8282/.

Telecare within different specialties

Magdala de Araújo Novaes

Telehealth Center, Clinics Hospital, Center of Medical Sciences, Federal University of Pernambuco, Recife, Brazil

Introduction

Magdala de Araújo Novaes

Telehealth applications enable the improvement of care, the flow of health information, and patient referral to healthcare providers. Use of telehealth facilitates access to specialized medical services, overcomes geographic barriers, reduces the time spent between diagnosis and therapy, and helps in the early identification of health problems, especially in developing countries.[211]

Modalities for health provision differ across the world in line with the consideration that there are different systems for health provision in various countries. In general, these systems are composed of healthcare facilities with different complexities and practices. In most countries, primary care facilities are the gateway to the patient in the health network, and from them, patients are referred for specialized care in clinics and hospitals or for lab tests and image exams. For example, let's imagine the following scenario:

CLINICAL CASE

Mrs. M.N.R., 42 years old, arrives at the Basic Care Unit of her neighborhood for a routine consultation. In the consultation the patient reports a different mole on their skin, which appeared a few months ago and has been increasing progressively. When examined by health professionals, they noticed an asymmetric spot and uneven edges. As a conduit, they were referred to a dermatologist for examination by a specialist. After the dermatologist's evaluation, the hypothesis is raised to skin cancer, and the patient is referred to an oncologist and referred for a biopsy. When the diagnosis of advanced skin cancer is confirmed, the specialist doctor directs the patient to surgery and appropriate chemotherapy. After the procedures the therapeutic course was prescribed, and the patient was referred to continue the postoperative care with the nursing team. When she was discharged from the hospital, she was referred to primary care, to evaluate the dressing and to monitor the side effects of chemotherapy, if they occur.

In the scenario described, telehealth can be present in all steps. The family doctor conducts a clinical discussion with a dermatologist by videoconference before referring the patient. The dermatologist suggests that a biopsy be carried out before receiving it in the office. The patient goes to the laboratory to do the biopsy, and at the time the images are sent by a telehealth platform for specialists to confirm the report (telediagnosis). Upon receiving the patient in the office, the dermatologist already has in hand by means of the electronic record of the patient all the clinical data of the first consultation and complementary examinations and, after discussion with the oncologist by videoconference, confirms that it is an aggressive skin cancer and recommends the immediate removal of the lesions, referring the patient to a hospital. During the procedure at the hospital, the surgery is transmitted by videoconference to other professionals (telesurgery) for an online second opinion. The video of the surgery is made available in virtual learning environment, so that students discuss the case with their academic preceptors (teleeducation). After the procedure the patient returns home and receives care from the surgical site by nurses, who monitor it through the smartphone with regular sending of images and vital signs (telemonitoring) and regular consultations by video call (teleconsultation). After discharge the patient returns to the dermatologist for follow-up. The outcome is forwarded to the family health doctor of the patient through a telehealth platform attaching all clinical data. From now on the family doctor will monitor with the patient the appearance of new lesions.

In summary, several practices or modalities of telehealth (teleconsultation, telediagnosis, telemonitoring, teleeducation, etc.) can be used during the care cycle, involving different technologies and actors. This diversity of telehealth modalities can be used in different contexts and specialties. Those who strongly use medical imaging, such as radiology, or at the other extreme that do not need a sophisticated technological infrastructure, such as psychiatry, are the ones that use telehealth the most.[212]

Teleradiology, for example, deals with the transmission of radiologic images (X-rays, tomography, and resonances) to have the radiology report by specialists in other places or even countries.[213]

Qualifying the patient for referral to specialized care along with remote delivery of test reports are among the possibilities of this technological advance in care delivery. Telecardiology, for example, facilitates the performance and evaluation of cardiac exams, the issuance of reports, and closure of diagnoses remotely by cardiologists, who are not physically present in the clinic or hospital where the examination was carried out.

As a result of these advances, telehealth or telemedicine allows a greater interaction between specialists, health services, the patient, and his family. It is important to emphasize that good health practices demand the adequate use of standards that allow the interoperability of systems and respect existing ethical and legal aspects.

Since specialties are concerned more with care, this chapter deals more with telemedicine along with occasional mention of training and teleeducation. For interest of the readers, at least in the United States, the specialties most likely to use direct physician-patient interaction are radiology (39.5%) followed by psychiatry(27.8%) and cardiology(24.1%),[214] while those using tele for contact with fellow professionals were emergency care(38.8%), pathologists (30.4%), and again radiologists (25.5%).

Teleradiology

Arjun Kalyanpur and Feroz Latif

Overview

Teleradiology is a word that today epitomizes innovation in healthcare technology and symbolizes efficiency in healthcare delivery. Due to the fact that radiologic imaging has for the most part been digital since approximately the turn of the millennium, the advantage of being able to transmit radiologic data over networks has made this technology innovation extremely valuable in bridging the gap between the demand for and supply of radiologist expertise. There is a critical global shortage of radiologists. In parallel, there is increasing utilization of medical imaging, driven by the increase in prevalence of lifestyle-related diseases requiring repeated imaging, increased speed and resolution of imaging technologies, and rising standards of care. Teleradiology, with its foundations based on digital imaging/DICOM, secure image encryption, and broadband telecommunications, provides a technology solution to bridge this gap. It has a major impact in decreasing report turnaround time and in improving service levels in the emergency setting. It has significant benefit in improving access of remote areas to high-quality and timely diagnostics. Standard protocols for communication levels between clinicians and radiologists ensure that service levels remain high, commensurate with on-site radiology. By using the centralized reading room coupled with the night-day model, radiologist productivity is increased, and healthcare costs can be reduced. Current and future trends including cloud, workflow analytics, and artificial intelligence are discussed.

Concepts and applications

Technology adoption in teleradiology today is much more than just for image transmission and report distribution in comparison with when commercial teleradiology started off about a decade and a half ago. This is seen by the industry embracing advances in healthcare information technology and information technology in general, in areas like cloud computing, machine learning, and artificial intelligence very early on.

Fig. 1 shows the flow of information in a typical form of teleradiology. Please note in Fig. 1 that not all components shown here are a must, nor is this an exhaustive list. Some of these devices may also be combined into a single device. For example, in some setups, a unified threat management (UTM) device could replace firewall and router.

The primary source of radiologic studies for teleradiology is digital imaging modalities such as digital X-ray [computed radiography (CR) or digital radiography (DR)], CT scanners, MRI scanners, ultrasound scanners, PET-CT scanners, gamma cameras, and angiographic data, which are typically forwarded to digital PACS systems.

DICOM versus Non-DICOM

Most of the newer modalities support DICOM standards and can communicate with any other device that conforms to DICOM standards. For older modalities that do not support DICOM, the images that could either be films or in digital form have to be converted to DICOM format before transmission to the teleradiology provider.

Secondary capture

Secondary capture images are images that are converted from a non-DICOM format to a modality independent DICOM format.[215] For legacy devices that use films, high-end digital scanners are used to digitize the films and convert them to DICOM. Some modalities like X-ray can also be retrofitted with computed radiography (CR) to enable DICOM output. For modalities that already have digital output in the form of images and videos, specialized software is available to convert them to DICOM format. This apart, documentation like prior reports, lab reports, and requisition, can be digitized and converted to DICOM so they are available to the radiologists along with the images while reading.

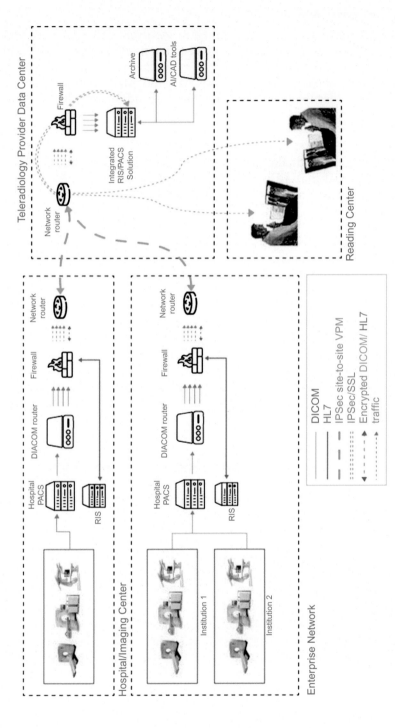

FIG. 1 Data flow in teleradiology.

Image transmission

The flow of images from the source to the teleradiology servers and further to the reading radiologists' workstation has to be fast, secure, and reliable. Several strategies are used to make this transmission smooth, staying within the boundaries of DICOM standards, which can be classified for this discussion into ones related to speed, security, availability, and integrity.

Speed

For emergent reads the turnaround time is usually within minutes, and it is critical that all images from the current study and any relevant prior examinations are made available to the reading radiologist at the shortest possible time. This is even more challenging as the amount of data produced by the newer generation of modalities keeps increasing. Speedy transmission of images is achieved in many ways. The most common method is to use compression. DICOM provides mechanisms for support of various compression algorithms, both lossy and lossless, such as JPEG2000, RLE, and even JPEG-LS. The type of compression protocol used can be found from the transfer syntax tag of the DICOM file. This built in support for compression in DICOM allows for the transfer of data between DICOM devices from different manufacturers.

Multithreaded or parallel transmission is commonly used to further speed up the transfer time in addition to compression. This is where specialized DICOM routers or gateways play an important role. Though most of the PACS support multithreaded transmission, these DICOM routers are designed to optimally utilize the available bandwidth and ensure fast and reliable transmission.

Many vendors provide proprietary algorithms to speed up transmission, but this would only work between nodes that use their software. The transmission of images between teleradiology servers and the image viewing software at the radiologist's workstation is again using DICOM protocols. In recent years, many vendors have implemented proprietary protocols of this to ensure all necessary images are available to the radiologists within seconds, if not minutes.

Security

As DICOM data contain a significant amount of metadata related to patient, study, etc., apart from the actual pixel data, ensuring confidentiality during transmission is a must, and many country- or region-specific laws need to be adhered to. HIPAA/HITECH act, rules, and regulations are one such set of regulatory compliance that needs to be achieved for teleradiology workflow in the United States of America.

This is achieved by ensuring all data in transit and at rest are encrypted and there are processes and procedures in place ensuring data security and availability only to authorized users. Usually an IPSec VPN tunnel is built between the hospital network and the teleradiology provider's datacenter. This ensures that all transmission is secured. DICOM also provides mechanism for encryption using the DICOM TLS protocol, usage of which is becoming common in the recent years.

Availability and integrity

Availability here refers to both the availability of data when required by an authorized user and also the availability of the teleradiology services whenever hospitals send studies for interpretation. For this, effective disaster recovery and business continuity plans and procedures have to be in place. Redundancy has to be built in for power, networks, application, database, etc. to ensure zero downtime.

It is important to maintain the integrity of the data and ensure accuracy and consistency of data. Data must remain intact during transit, and it must be ensured that it cannot be altered by unauthorized people.

Image management, viewers, and workflow

Management of images in terms of storage, further transmission to radiologists, and at times long-term archive is relatively challenging considering the huge amount of data. Design of this infrastructure should be guided by the information security availability, integrity, and confidentiality (AIC) triad. This is especially true in today's world of distributed computing and cloud architecture.

Once images are available on the radiologist's workstation, they can be viewed using DICOM viewers. These viewers can be in the form of a desktop application that can provide advanced features like 3D reconstruction, segmentation, and volume rendering or browser-based viewers that render the images in the web browser itself without having to install any software on the system. Web-based medical imaging is made possible by DICOMWeb, which is a DICOM standard and is a set of RESTful services. Some viewers are integrated with CAD/AI tools that can assist radiologists with a diagnosis on demand.

Analytics and AI tools also help with workflow. Tools that monitor a radiologist's report using natural language processing (NLP) and flag potential errors in laterality, body part, gender, etc. are one example on how technology can assist radiologists avoid discrepancies and improve efficiency. These tools can even alert the radiologist about calling the ordering physician to communicate critical findings.

Reports are usually distributed using HL7 messages. In the United States the practice of faxing back reports to the emergency department is still prevalent. Image transfer depends on the DICOM standard, which is already explained in Chapter 4.

Emergency applications

The origins of teleradiology lie in emergency diagnosis,[216] and till date the greatest impact of teleradiology has been in the area of medical emergency diagnosis. The clinical entities that are most greatly impacted by emergency teleradiology include the most life-threatening conditions[217–219] such as acute stroke, major trauma, pulmonary thromboembolism and aortic dissection, in all of which the cost of delayed diagnosis can be catastrophically high. By creating a framework whereby all emergency scans are reported within a 30-min timeframe, with further electronic prioritization of critical examinations as STAT priority, teleradiology has allowed for immediate diagnosis of such conditions, which in turn facilitates early intervention and superior patient outcomes.

The primary value proposition offered by emergency teleradiology is in decreasing report turnaround times. Within a radiology practice the implementation of teleradiology ensures rapid on-call response. These benefit both the patient and the treating physician, with special significance within emergency care.[220,221]

In the setting of emergency teleradiology, most communication occurs via two media, electronic and verbal (telephonic). The physical distance of the teleradiologist does not detract from the level of interaction.[219] Verbal communications of critical values are frequent in emergency teleradiology[222,223], given that the clinical spectrum is primarily directed towards acute care.

Teleradiology optimizes radiologist efficiency and diminishes healthcare costs

The practice of teleradiology is geared towards reporting efficiency, given that its primary goal is to generate and deliver an accurate and comprehensive report in the shortest possible time. This, in turn, promotes the most efficient usage of that most valuable commodity, radiologist's time, which has the potential to greatly decrease systemic healthcare costs.[224] Distribution of the caseload across the teleradiology enterprise ensures that radiologist time is most efficiently utilized, never wasted, while at the same time accommodating for spikes and troughs in the workload.

The reduction of healthcare costs by teleradiology can be facilitated by the day-night model wherein teleradiologists are geographically based diametrically across the globe from the hospitals where they provide services. This "follow the sun" model ensures that the radiologist does not need to stay awake at night, obviating the need for night shifts, which sometimes used to be every alternate week, thereby significantly enhancing radiologist productivity.[222,223] Other successful international models involve using radiologists who are of commensurate qualification in other geographic regions to reduce report turnaround time in a daytime outpatient clinic environment.[225]

Elective/subspecialty imaging: Another clinical application of teleradiology is in delivering specialized images to the subspecialist most qualified for their interpretation. For example, the imaging of a rare neurodegenerative condition in a newborn is best analyzed by subspecialist pediatric neuroradiologists, who are few in number worldwide. Similarly the use of telemammography can enhance the quality of a breast cancer detection program by directing images to a specialized mammographer. Virtual colonoscopy is another such specialized technique. Thus the use of teleradiology can be utilized to facilitate transfer of advanced imaging data to subspecialists and enhance reporting quality.[226–228]

Teleradiology services to remote areas

Deployment of teleradiology systems in remote and inaccessible locations where imaging equipment has been installed but no radiologist is available can be a lifesaver. With the exception of ultrasonography, which for regulatory and quality reasons requires physical presence of a sonographer, and interventional radiology, which for obvious reasons requires an onsite radiologist presence, all other radiologic modalities can be remotely interpreted. In remote locations, interpretation of radiologic images by qualified radiologists becomes challenging without teleradiology. In remote areas, such deployments done through public-private partnership between state governments and teleradiology providers can transform healthcare delivery.[219,229] Teleradiology can also be used to enhance screening programs for diseases of public health importance in endemic areas, as in the case of pulmonary tuberculosis.[230]

Virtual 3D Lab model: Postprocessing of imaging data is a labor-intensive and time-consuming task. If performed in a remote virtual environment, this can add efficiencies, reduce costs, and improve after hours turnaround.[231,232]

Quality and regulation

Teleradiology standards, such as those defined by the American College of Radiology, address the issues of image capture, transmission, review, and reporting while defining quality metrics for each of these processes.[233] Similarly the European Society of Radiology and separately the UK's Royal College of Radiologists have defined standards for the practice of teleradiology in their respective geographies.[234] Quality assurance driven by peer review is the keystone of good teleradiology practice.[235–237] The ACR RadPeer protocol presents a scoring framework for peer-review driven analysis of radiologist reporting quality.

Various standard organizations such as the US Joint Commission also regulate the practice of teleradiology. For international teleradiology, practice radiologists are required to be board certified (or recognized equivalent) and hold relevant licensure at the site of origin of images. The potential for malpractice litigation in the practice of teleradiology also requires appropriate insurance coverage that protects the practitioner at the site of image origin. As long as the regulatory requirements are complied with, the location of the interpreting radiologist is immaterial.[238]

Current and future trends

The cloud is a rapidly evolving phenomenon in recent years impacting most industries. Healthcare is no exception.[239,240] What this translates to in teleradiology is that patient images are leaving the server rooms of hospitals and beginning to reside on virtual networks of datacenters. This trend allows for three primary benefits: (a) extreme redundancy, as the images are distributed over a virtual network of servers that may be spread over different geographies, no longer a risk of the hospital PACS server "going down," traditionally a significant cause of loss of productivity in radiology departments worldwide; (b) decreased infrastructural costs that benefit smaller institutions/radiology practices—the cloud-based service can be utilized on a SAAS or a pay-per-use model, without high start-up infrastructural costs; and (c) most importantly, universal access to image data, without having to penetrate individual hospital firewalls, while still being HIPAA compliant. By this means the number of duplicate and unnecessary scans that are performed today can be drastically reduced, especially when patients are transferred from one healthcare facility to another.

Workflow and analytics: The teleradiology software of today has evolved considerably beyond routine image viewing and reporting features and incorporates new intelligent tools that route images seamlessly across networks to the most highly qualified radiologist, collaboration tools that allow a radiologist to interact online with a clinician and highlight lesions on radiologic images in a virtual environment, and analytic tools that allow every productivity and quality measure in an organization to be tracked in real-time mode.[241]

Mobile: New handheld devices with their high-resolution screens lend themselves to teleradiology on the go. Of greatest value for busy neurosurgeons, cardiologists, oncologists, etc., this allows physicians to quickly check their patient's images while commuting, between consultations, and even while on vacation, without having to drive to work and log in to a cumbersome workstation. For radiologists too, there are many evolving applications in the emergency arena, such as acute stroke and appendicitis, where mobile technologies can deliver benefit.[242-244]

E-training: To rapidly increase the pool of trained radiologists and address the current critical shortage of radiologists, drastic and innovative measures are needed, and e-training has proved to be one such game changer.[245] This is the educational tool of the future, with profound implications for healthcare education overall, not just in teleradiology, although given the virtualization and globalization of teleradiology, this is where e-training delivers maximum value.

Deep learning and artificial intelligence: The crux of all teleradiology is rapid report turnaround time (TAT).[244] The quality of a teleradiology provider is gauged by how tight TAT can be compressed, in the interest of enhancing patient care, while still maintaining the highest quality of interpretation. Tools that facilitate more speedy or accurate interpretation of images such as CAD, for example, for pulmonary embolism or lung nodules therefore can potentially enhance the teleradiology reporting process. A host of such algorithms driven by machine learning technologies, including tools for lesion detection, case prioritization, lesion segmentation and measurement, and report text generation, have recently been introduced, and many more are in development, which will be transformational in healthcare delivery as radiologist time and productivity will both be benefited. Teleradiology in that sense is at the dawn of a new era, as is all of clinical medicine.[246]

Since the beginning of teleradiology, a large number of benefits have been identified and described in the scientific literature.[216] Teleradiology is a branch of telehealth; its success is representative of the future of telehealth as a whole.

Telepathology

Sanjay Bedi

Overview

Pathology being an image rich specialty has immense possibilities of use of modern telecommunication technology to transfer images at a long distance to facilitate diagnosis education and research. Faster modes of connectivity and better resolution cameras have widened the possibilities. These may be a part of a complete patient record, that is, the EHR or components through mobile apps. Telepathology can be used for remotely rendering primary diagnoses, second-opinion consultations, quality assurance, education, and research purposes.[247]

Concepts and applications

Pathology as a subject involves gross specimens and microscopic images that are enhanced through various types of stains. It is hence largely image based and very amenable to digitalization. There is a patient history that is correlated with the images, and various diseases are accordingly diagnosed.

Telepathology mainly involves leveraging the enhanced capabilities provided by the better resolution provided by modern digital cameras with added maneuverability along with the ability to transfer the images over long distances provided by fast Internet connections mainly involving intraoperative telediagnosis, second-opinion teleconsultation, reference case archives, remote data and image processing, and quality assessment.

One of the earliest instances of telepathology took place in Boston in 1968. An academic pathologist, Dr. Ronald S. Weinstein, now described to be as the "father of telepathology" in a 1986 editorial outlined the actions that would be needed to create remote pathology diagnostic services. In Norway, Eide and Nordrum implemented the first sustainable clinical telepathology service in 1989.[13] This is still operational though decades have passed.

A digital slide is a classical whole slide image formed by imaging an entire physical (glass) slide, field by field, and then "knitting" these fields together to form a seamless continuous image that can be manipulated for morphometry, magnification, and color detection. One of the best known virtual slide collection is the "Juan Rosai's collection of surgical pathology seminars," curated by USCAP (see http://USCAP.org). However, now with availability of digital scanners, this is going to be more and more widespread, and multiple sites and institutions are making them available. With some display software, for example, aperio, one can scan and zoom around the image set.

Telepathology technologies

Digital pathology: It is an image-based information environment enabled by computer technology that allows for the management of information generated from a digital slide. Digital pathology is enabled in part by virtual microscopy, a method of capturing microscopic images and transmitting them over computer networks. This allows independent viewing of images by large numbers of people in diverse locations.

Pathology specimen slides are scanned, and high-resolution digital images are created for transmission. The image may be of an area of interest or larger like a whole slide imaging (WSI).

Telepathology enables a faster diagnosis. Patients in remote rural areas can be tested and diagnosed in a single trip to the nearest healthcare facility and obviate travel to a larger center, which is required often more than once, for example, for initial assessment and other investigation, on the date of the biopsy procedure, and later for results and ancillary procedures prior to definitive treatment. This delay in diagnosis can sometimes be fatal. This is not uncommon in traditional pathological systems due to logistical difficulties of coordinating the transfer of a patient.

The main categories of telepathology are as follows:

- Static image-based systems—images are captured from a digital camera connected to a microscope. An image area is selected and transmitted.
- Virtual slide systems—pathology specimen slides are scanned/videographed, and high-resolution digital images created for transmission.[1]
- Real-time systems—the operator remotely guides a robotically controlled motorized microscope. The consultant pathologist has complete control and can adjust the slide position, zoom, etc. so that the area of interest is brought under view and transmitted.
- Whole slide imaging (WSI)—digitization and scanning of a glass slide to generate a large sized digital image that can be viewed in parts in a manner that simulates microscopy.

Other benefits of telepathology are the following:

- Medical professionals in different locations can view images simultaneously and discuss diagnoses through teleconferencing.
- A doctor can consult with a pathologist who specializes in the patient's area of concern, such as liver pathology or lung pathology.
- A healthcare provider can get second opinions more easily.
- Patient data can be synchronized across various electronic health information systems.
- Once implemented a telepathology system is less expensive to operate than the traditional system.

Both telepathology and teleradiology are image-intensive branches. However, in teleradiology, the digital image is usually black and white, and hence transfer through electronic networks of at least the static image is easier due to smaller file size. On the other hand, in telepathology, the images on the microscope have to be captured using a special camera, and the point of lesion is sometimes not well identified at proper magnification. There is large color variation. Very-high-resolution images are needed to highlight the relevant color contrast and may also require different stains. The arrival of slide scanners, better cameras, higher bandwidth, and better viewing software, however, are allowing easier transfer of image transfers over long distances with substantial outcomes. Besides standard diagnostic work, the field of pathology education has especially benefited.

Mobile phones are now ubiquitous. With improved resolution of in-built cameras and better applications, a new world of mobile phone-based telepathology applications is emerging. Through specialized attachments, mobile cameras can easily capture images from microscopes and transmit them anywhere, allowing access to specialized opinion at point-of-care

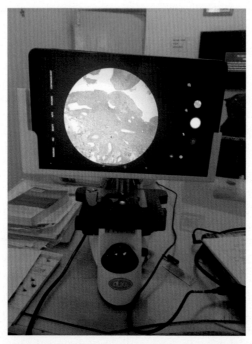

FIG. 2   An example of a modern microscope with a tablet replacing the eyepiece and providing all the functionality with global linkage via internet.

locations even in remote areas (Fig. 2). The equipment required is relatively inexpensive (except the phone). A request for consultation is possible from anywhere across the globe and include a simultaneous real-time correlation of both face to face and of the microscopic images. Social media tools like WhatsApp and Facebook are allowing pathology networks over the Internet as a real-time collaboration between multiple experts discussing pathology over mobile phones[248] (Fig. 2).

Even in low resource settings, better availability of high-speed networks is facilitating basic telepathology requirements through a simple microscope and a good mobile phone only. Image transfer can be done for the gross specimen and of the slides. Smart mobiles are making the previous investments in expensive systems, like those which allowed remote slide manipulation and zoom, infructuous.

Current and future trends

Artificial Intelligence (AI) is gradually making its entry into pathology with image processing software and automatic cell counters.[249] While this has been available for particle counting since long in hematology, now new arrivals on the scene are bringing image analyzers for tumor diagnosis in hematology, Pap smears, special stains and counting of nanoparticles in viral genomes.

Teleophthalmology

Manoj Rai Mehta

History

Ophthalmology was arguably the first branch of medicine to use technology of digital imaging and transferring of information through electronic communication channels for clinical and research application. It all started with the monitoring of retinal circulation during travel into space by astronauts during the Apollo missions.

Concepts and applications

Visual disability and blindness are major handicaps that disallow easy movement. Going for treatment is a challenge as they need to be accompanied by a caregiver. In a vast country like India where geographic terrain challenges are compounded by a skewed distribution of knowledge resources, teleophthalmology is proving to be a vital part of solution of taking high-quality medical care to the masses in areas with poor transport connectivity. Professional skills of paramedical personnel can be enhanced through online and offline interactions with skilled medical personnel and empower them to take certain decisions on ground zero and also plan timely referrals to the concerned lead facilities.

Key essential enablers

The **fundamental principles** of teleophthalmology are similar to other branches. These include acquisition of information by digital means, for example, an image through a slit lamp or fundus camera, transfer to a concerned person or organization, get relevant feedback, and use it to manage the patient. Besides a computer and connectivity, which can even be a smart mobile phone with inbuilt connectivity, one requires relevant software and hardware for acquisition of data. The available historical analog images can also be digitized before further transfer.

Hardware includes anterior and posterior segment cameras, tele-ERGs (electroretinography), adaptors for mobile phone cameras, etc. Software, including DICOM, may be required for transfer of images in different formats. A dedicated stand-alone or cloud-based server (public, private, or hybrid) is required for data storage. Additional software may be used for data retrieval and analysis. Mobile apps are going to be a game changer in due course.

Besides the traditional seeking of opinion from peer or expert group, which is important in anyone working alone, there is a special role for remote or otherwise poorly accessible areas. It can compensate for a shortfall of trained professionals. It can allow remote teaching and skill acquisition of not only the eye surgeon—whose work including surgery can be remotely supervised—but also the desired personnel in related fields such as ophthalmic assistants. Community-based care and research projects can be initiated, which includes the phenomenal outcomes of Aravind Eye Care System.[3]

Making a success of telecare for management of eye diseases depends on training. It also requires a challenging attitudinal change among the medical fraternity to break off the traditional mold. It is not an esoteric science and works like an adjuvant to the existing healthcare delivery system.

Case study 1[147]

Our team created a prototype model with scalable operations with the possibility of universal application (worldwide). This model was created under the aegis of National Program for Control of Blindness for the state of Mizoram as a tripartite agreement among the major stake holders:

(1) state health services
(2) provider of connectivity and support services
(3) Society for Administration of Telemedicine and Health Informatics (SATHI) as knowledge and lead operational partner

A hub-and-spoke model for the delivery of services was planned by the eye department of District Hospital Aizawl. The district hospital played a lead role in the planning and execution of surgeries and coordinated with the peripheral vision centers situated in geographically remote areas with limited access to surface transport.

Vision center concept and definition

The Vision Center (VC) was operationally headed by a paramedical person, who is trained in operating equipment and software; performs routine eye testing; dispenses, manufactures, and fits spectacle lenses; identifies and diagnoses main causes of decrease in vision; and specifically screens for cataract and diabetic retinopathy. VC was also nerve center for dissemination of education, information, and counseling of patients regarding eye care and common eye problems. The paramedical staff employed in the centers were from different streams—ophthalmic assistants, pharmacy graduates, and optometrists. A local project coordinator was stationed in Aizawl to take care of logistics and support and data collation. The Department of Ophthalmology at District Hospital Aizawl was identified for technical support and carrying out cataract surgeries. A tertiary care facility at New Delhi was identified for on- and offline consultation of specific cases as well.

Operational landmarks

- Setting up of VCs at chosen sites

  The sites were geographically remote but with a possibility of a fairly robust connectivity. The VC-in-charge staff were expected to live within the premises to ease travel and safety considerations as well. All VCs were provided with standardized equipment plan and operational manuals. Besides routine management and telecare, they also did school camps and surveys (Fig. 3). Machines for fitting spectacles lenses were also included in the program.

- Training of the VC-in-charge staff

  Perhaps the most crucial aspect of success was training of the staff. Induction training was held off-site in Delhi at a tertiary care eye center. A rigorous 15-day module was prepared to reorient the para medical staff towards learning and imbibing new set of skills.[146] A compressed clinical training capsule was created based primarily on pictorial teaching aids. There were short modules on general

FIG. 3   During the SATHI Project in Mizoram, eye camps done by the ophthalmic assistants helped create awareness as well as collect data.

management, accounting, social skills, and social marketing as well. A 2-day skill development workshop on cutting and fitting of spectacle lenses was arranged at the premises of a leading international manufacturing company. All the trainees were given extensive training on image capturing, running the software, and data transfer. Online training continued as well as refreshers courses during the project period.

- Kick-starting the program
    Two senior mentors from SATHI went to Aizawl to start the program. Three VCs were started immediately and three more within a fortnight.
- Monitoring and fine-tuning
    The program was monitored from the head office and periodic reports updated. SATHI mentors from Delhi visited from time to time to iron out operational problems and provide continual training and skill enhancement.

The total number of consultations in the first year was 3928, which crossed 10,000 over the 3 years of the sanctioned project period. The project was handed over to the state government after successful implementation of the pilot program. The project was accorded with an award for "Best Medical IT Project in the North East in 2014."

Case study 2

The Pan African Telemedicine Project[12] was conceived to help increase the skills of the medical fraternity of the African continent and to help exchange ideas between certain hospitals in Africa and tertiary care centers in India. Teleophthalmology was a part of this project. Teaching sessions on fluorescein angiography and management of diabetic retinopathy were organized for the University of Cairo, Egypt. Regular online consultations were arranged for Seychelles, Kenya; Tanzania, Egypt; and other countries on a mutually agreed timetable. Live streaming of surgeries was also a part of the program.

There are several teleophthalmology projects running concurrently in India. Sankara Nethralaya, Chennai; Arvind Hospital, Madurai; and LV Prasad Eye Institute, Hyderabad, are some of the leading organizations that run their own programs through their own dedicated staff.

Conclusion

Teleophthalmology is a "financially viable" adjuvant to the existing medical care delivery systems. However, it requires an innovative approach in the implementation with reorientation of the medical caregivers. From classical tenets of direct examination, one has to move towards image analysis, remote interview, and remotely controlled interventions.

Teledermatology

Keila Taciane Martins de Melo Oliveira and Magdala de Araújo Novaes

Overview

Teledermatology utilizes the application of ICT to allow on-site special-ized doctor intervention, since it has a large visual component converted easily to a digital format. There are additional benefits to the traditional methods of dermatological assessment, as it supplies the health profes-sional with diagnosis assistance, assessment of the progress of chronic conditions and therapeutic responses, tracking of increasing injuries, pa-tients monitoring, and health promotion.

Concepts and applications

Like other specialties, teledermatology can obviate the need of on-site physician intervention for dermatological patients. However, besides be-ing a remote care solution, it also helps add efficiency, practice, and lower costs. Furthermore, it has potential to stimulate health planning, clinical case discussions, and health research, besides providing dermatological care to populations in remote areas with poor access to in-person special-ist consultations.

Teledermatology is the third largest user of telemedicine, behind telera-diology, and telepathology.[250] The methodology is sending digital images along with a complete anamnesis, and physical examination results to a dermatologist teleconsultant for opinion and feedback. Though store-and-forward or asynchronous mode is preferred, this can also be performed in real time using a videoconference between the doctor, the patient, and the teledermatologist. There are also hybrid teledermatology practices, which combine synchronous and asynchronous elements. Teledermatology has of late moved forward to mobile applications too. Visual examination can be combined with teledermatoscopy, which allows tracking and sorting of dermatological conditions, including malignancies (Fig. 4).

Although real-time teledermatology provides better potential to clar-ify doubts, this modality maybe inconvenient due to its need for coordi-nation of visit timings and schedule. More than 80% of teledermatology programs in the United States use the asynchronous form. It provides greater accessibility and lowers service costs in the management of skin lesions with a reliability (diagnostic concordance) similar to synchronous systems.[251]

A component teledermatology is teledermoscopy, which has shown promise for screening of melanoma, besides allowing collaboration for di-agnosis and management of various cutaneous lesions. Teledermoscopy

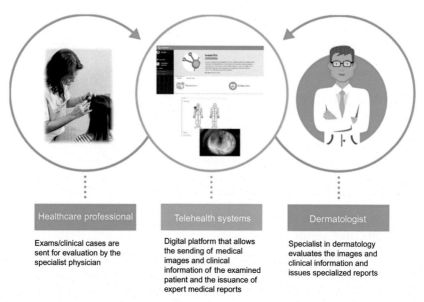

Healthcare professional

Exams/clinical cases are sent for evaluation by the specialist physician

Telehealth systems

Digital platform that allows the sending of medical images and clinical information of the examined patient and the issuance of expert medical reports

Dermatologist

Specialist in dermatology evaluates the images and clinical information and issues specialized reports

FIG. 4　Flowchart of information in a typical teledermatology setting.

combines conventional dermoscopy with digital image capture and allows long-term storage of pathological features. The physician gets to visualize and monitor changes in the morphological structures over time based on the stored content, allowing better correlation between clinical macroscopic examination and microscopic analysis. There can be further aggregation with concomitant use of teledermatopathology and telecytology, resulting in the increase of diagnosis accuracy. Considering economic and geographic factors, and as well as better clinical reasoning, teledermatology has gained increasing importance as an innovative method of professional aid besides being fundamental to enable wider health access.

Studies suggest that clinicians and teledermatologists have full or partial agreement in terms of diagnosis and injury management in over 75% of cases.[252] In pigmented skin lesions also, values of over 75% have been shown as per a concordance analysis between the pathological examination and teledermoscopy. This involved 43 pigmented skin lesions (11 melanomas, 23 melanocytic nevi, 3 basal cell carcinomas, 3 simple lentigines, and 2 seborrheic keratoses).[253]

In fact, teledermoscopy offered better diagnostic accuracy when compared with in-person dermatoscopic examination. In a recent study, teledermatology reached considerable levels of agreement when compared with standard attendance for clinical diagnosis of multiple skin lesions. Piccolo and colleagues compared the diagnosis of 66 pigmented skin lesions of macroimage and dermatoscopic with in-person clinical diagnosis. Another study found 91% correlation between teledermatology associated with teledermoscopy and on-site clinical evaluation of the lesions.[254] However, more clinical trials are needed.

Teledermatology requires a certain infrastructure to assure quality. Besides the technological infrastructure (the presence of computer and equipment for remote diagnostics at the health units; capture and storage of clinical data; and access to an adequate electronic system for teledermatology records, Internet, etc.), there are issues related to physical environment (guarantee of privacy, lighting, and comfort), and doctor-patient-teleconsultant relationships (guarantee of safety and confidentiality).

Finally the need for adequate training of the teledermatology professional regarding photodocumentation process cannot be overemphasized. This process aims to standardize the capture and storage of images targeting its quality and reliability to allow an assertive diagnosis to the teleconsultant.

Current and future trends

Teledermatology has emerged as an important support tool towards diagnosis and management of skin diseases, expansion of dermatologists' reach, reduction of waiting time between appointments, contribution to disease tracking, and health promotion.

It is also useful in the primary care for screening patients and qualifying patient's referrals, with a resultant reduction in unnecessary referrals. Recent research shows that this practice has the potential to reduce by 50% the number of specialized in-person consultations, with reports that over 85% of patients were satisfied, related to faster access to the expert without a need to spend on transportation.[250]

In 2010, 38% of the countries of the world had some kind of teledermatology program, and 30% had governmental agencies dedicated to this practice. Countries with higher economic power showed greater initiatives towards this. In the United States, teledermatology was developed by the army. And in around roughly two decades, the network has saved approximately US$ 30.4 million in travel costs. Since 2012, military teledermatologists from 40 locations have held about 40,000 consults.[255] Highly integrated systems, such as Kaiser Permanente in California, and countries where healthcare provision is the states' responsibility are far ahead in teledermatology.

In developing countries on the other hand, many patients never see a dermatologist, despite a disproportionate burden of skin disease. In sub-Saharan Africa, skin complaints represent up to 24% of medical visits, while only 14% of sub-Saharan African countries have trained dermatologists.[250]

Teledermatology can help in correcting the uneven distribution of dermatologists across the globe, mostly with the use of asynchronous teledermatology. It can lower costs and is very viable. An example is Africa Teledermatology Project, operating since 2007. It allows clinical discussions of neglected patients in Africa, by dermatologists from the United States, Europe, and Australia. Besides clinical services the project allows training of health professionals through teleeducation using local cases as examples.[255]

In Brazil a country of continental dimensions and a predominantly tropical climate, the population gets a high amount of sun exposure and increased risk of skin cancer. Teledermatology can play a key role in supporting cancer diagnostics and overcome the shortage and uneven distribution of specialists. Some reports are hereby provided.

The first such attempt was *Telederma*, a joint project between the Hospital of the Federal University of Rio Grande do Sul (UFRGS) and the Telemedicine Department at the University of São Paulo (USP). 95.8% diagnostic agreement was achieved, boosting the promotion of new strategies, such as the teledermatology of Santa Catarina State Integrated Telemedicine and Telehealth System, Amazon Protection System, and Telemedhansen, focusing on leprosy diagnosis.[256] More recently, the Telehealth Center of the Hospital das Clínicas of the Federal University of Pernambuco has started teledermatology and teledermoscopy programs for the diagnosis of skin cancer for the patients from remote areas.

Many advances are yet to come with artificial intelligence and powerful image analysis software. These technologies associated with teledermatology can increase the quality and speed of diagnosis and, for example, perform predictive analyzes for the diagnosis of cancer, with greater long-term availability of patient data.

Telecardiology

Sunita Maheshwari, Praveen K., and Sejal Shah

Overview

An increasing incidence of heart disease accompanied by a chronic shortage of cardiologists, especially in rural and remote areas, makes telecardiology an exciting new method bridging the patient-cardiologist gap. Telecardiology, as of today, includes not only televideo consultations with a cardiologist but also technology platforms that allow transmission of electrocardiograms (ECGs), echocardiograms, and angiograms. In addition, the teleconsult with the cardiologist has moved beyond just audiovisual communication to the usage of the digital stethoscope so cardiologists can see the patient, hear their heart sounds, view their reports, and finally give them an opinion and recommend management.

Thus telecardiology has moved from the video consults a decade ago to a full-fledged cardiac assessment from afar. Cardiac diagnosis at a distance is the way of the future, and this subchapter aims to highlight the current status of telecardiology.

Concepts and applications

The Global Burden of Disease 2015 study estimated 422 million cases of cardiovascular diseases (CVD) in 2015, showing that CVD still remains a major cause of health loss for all regions of the world. Cardiovascular disease is the world's No. 1 killer with 17.5 million people dying each year from CVD, an estimated 31% of all deaths worldwide.[150,151] In poorer countries the effects of CVD are even worse. For example, the Indian subcontinent is home to 20% of the world's population and among the regions with the highest burden of cardiovascular disease in the world. The Indian rural population and urban poor are facing a "double burden" with acute CVD illness in addition to a rapid growth in incidence of chronic disease. It is not just the poor who are affected. With unhealthy lifestyles, decreasing physical activity, increasing stress levels, and increasing intake of saturated fats and tobacco, the rise of CVDs is seen in the economically privileged population as well.[152,257]

Children, too, are afflicted with heart disease. With a global incidence of 1%,[153,154] nearly 180,000 children are born with heart defects each year in a country such as India. Of these, nearly 60,000 to 90,000 suffer from critical cardiac lesions requiring early intervention. Approximately 10% of present infant mortality in India may be accounted for by congenital heart diseases alone. The burden of rheumatic fever and rheumatic heart disease (RHD) currently falls disproportionately on children and young adults living in low-income countries with an incidence of an average of 0.9/1000 and accounting for 233,000 deaths annually.[258]

Where are the cardiologists? Based on a WHO report released in November 2013, the global health workforce shortage that was 7.2 million in 2013 is expected to reach 12.9 million by 2035. This is expected to have serious implications for the health of billions across the world, if not addressed. For instance, several countries in Asia and Africa face a challenge of shortage in trained healthcare personnel at all levels, especially in the rural areas. There is only about 1 doctor for every 1700 people in India, and it faces more than a 60% shortfall of specialists at the community health center level. There is a shortfall of 600,000 doctors and 1,000,000 nurses to reach the WHO recommendation of 1 doctor for every 1000 people. The situation is even worse when it comes to cardiologists. India trains only about 200 new cardiologists every year, an inadequate number, given the disease burden.[259,260] The same is true for many parts of Africa and the world.

There is a shortage of adequately trained specialists, technicians, and nurses for adult and pediatric cardiology to cater to noninvasive diagnosis and invasive and medical management. As a result, mortality from cardiovascular disease remains high.

One solution for the inequitable distribution of specialists is telecardiology. This encompasses teleechocardiography, tele-ECG, teleconsultations, and teleeducation. Imagine a cardiologist in a traffic jam in a major city utilizing his or her time to review an echocardiogram of a patient in a remote town, giving a diagnosis and directing therapy. With telecardiology, this is now possible. The advantage is that specialist advice is available for patients in remote areas eliminating the need and expense of unnecessary travel. Cardiac diagnosis at a distance is the way of the future.

Some telecardiology solutions are detailed in the succeeding text:

Digital stethoscope

Hearing the heart sounds is an integral part of cardiology and is now possible remotely as well. Studies have shown that the digital stethoscope may be more sensitive than the conventional stethoscope.[261] Using it for remote hearing makes it a valuable tool in telecardiology. Digital stethoscopes (Fig. 5) are compact electronic stethoscopes combining a high-resolution visual display with traditional auscultation. Using the device, medical professionals can perform dynamic remote auscultation. In addition, the visual waveforms presented in the format of the classical phonocardiogram can be transmitted to the specialist at the remote end for analysis and validation.

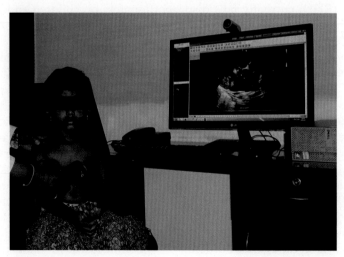

FIG. 5   Digital stethoscope.

Teleechocardiography

Echocardiograms, which are the most used diagnostic modality in cardiac structural and functional evaluation, need experts interpreting them to arrive at an accurate diagnosis. While technicians and physicians can be trained[262] to acquire echocardiographic images, many times a skilled cardiologist is needed to give an interpretation and plan management. Most recent echo machines are DICOM compliant, so transmission of these images is possible using a cardiovascular PACS. One issue in the transmission of echocardiogram images is its size as many are cine files, which requires robust compression techniques without losing the quality of the images.

CardioSpa (Telerad Tech, Bangalore) is one example of a cardiovascular PACS system, which has the ability to provide the cardiologist a seamless platform receiving all types of cardiac evaluations on a single platform from which they can interpret and report. The platform uses compression techniques, which brings the size of the images down by 40% for the ease of transmission that is then decompressed at the specialist end making teleecho possible without loss of image quality. The platform can also accept standard formats of ECG that can be transmitted through its workflow platform to be remotely read and reported by cardiologists. There are several other technology platforms available such as CARESTREAM Vue web-based PACS and UltraLinq. Many cardiac ultrasound manufacturers have developed dedicated cardiac workstations such as EchoPACS from GE and Q station from Philips.

Tele-ECG

An electrocardiogram (ECG) is the first line of diagnosis for cardiac diseases, and this has an important place in telecardiology.[156] ECG is a useful diagnostic tool in the diagnosis and management of ischemic heart disease and cardiac arrhythmia, and its availability in the primary care setting is now common.[262]

However, interpretational skills are not universally available at the primary care level, and obtaining rapid, accurate ECG reports with specialist input remains a challenge. The lack of reliable ECG testing and reporting under these circumstances may mean that some cardiac conditions are being missed. Routine availability of ECG interpretation at the primary care level can facilitate early referrals to secondary care while reducing unnecessary referrals where appropriate. This can be facilitated via telecardiology.

Transmission of ECG can be performed by either scanning the ECG and transmitting it or interfacing the ECG machine with a telecardiology software platform or to the existing cardiac PACS. There are now several products available in the market that can transmit ECG data directly from the device to the cloud, which can then be sent to the cardiologists on their smartphones for quick reporting. Research on low-cost devices for usage in poorer countries is imperative. In India the Bhabha Atomic Research Center has developed a 12 lead credit card-sized tele-ECG that can be connected via Bluetooth to a mobile or PC.[263] iMMi Life (www.immilife.com) a commercial venture has arrangements to send ECGs done by an empaneled doctor anywhere to five different cardiologists—including one in the vicinity to get a report on the possibility of myocardial infarction within minutes, so that emergency measures like aspirin and even streptokinase can be initiated.

Given the high prevalence of cardiovascular diseases and the limited number of cardiologists in small and remote towns in Brazil, telediagnosis of electrocardiogram is an important tool to face this shortage. The Brazilian Telehealth Program, since 2007, provides remote diagnostics service of electrocardiogram (tele-ECG) as the most important examination for clinical support for the primary care settings. Several states of the country offer this service using a 12-lead electrocardiogram, from large states like Minas Gerais with 853 towns to smaller states such as Pernambuco with 185 municipalities. In Minas Gerais, since the beginning of the service in 2005 until January 2016, 2.5 million ECGs were performed, in addition to 1024 Holter exams, and in Pernambuco, from 2016 to 2018, more than 21 thousand were performed[264] (Fig. 6).

Recently, tele-ECG has moved from the domain of hospitals and health centers directly to the patient home as well. Single-channel cardiac event recorder devices integrated into iPhones or Android smartphones allow

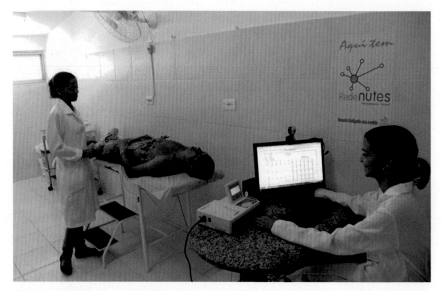

FIG. 6 Example of a tele-ECG performed at family health facility in a rural area. Telehealth Center, Clinics Hospital, UFPE, Brazil.

for automatic analysis, storage of ECG, and transmission to the patient's personal physician for review. The AliveCor Kardia Mobile ECG is one such FDA-approved device. Zoll, Philips, and other such companies also have products in this space.

Teleconsultation

Telemedicine technology can be leveraged to connect with people/ providers who need a specialist consultation. Simple and traditional audio-video technology can help cardiac patients to reach out in time to the right people and make a significant difference in the outcomes. Although adoption of telemedicine technology has been relatively slow worldwide due to many factors, this is changing, and its increased usage will help obviate the shortage of specialist cardiologists in remote and rural parts of the world.

Teleteaching in cardiology

There is an acute shortage of teaching manpower in the existing medical colleges and training programs especially in Asia and Africa, particularly at the postgraduate level. There is a similar shortage of trained pediatric cardiologists available to interpret pediatric echoes and direct care, especially in rural and remote areas. The training of pediatric cardiologists is key to improving outcomes of children with heart disease.

Current and future trends

Telecardiology is an innovative solution that can help address the issue of specialist shortage for teaching, clinical diagnosis and disease management worldwide.

Telecardiology can thus be a bridge between the patients and the specialists or between the primary physician/caretaker and the specialists. It can be in the form of diagnosing a new illness, treating a cardiac illness, closely monitoring the progress, providing educational material, counseling, etc. The following are some situations wherein teleservices can make a difference in the healthcare scenario:

- New patient evaluation. With the help of clinical history and clinical examination including using a digital stethoscope, telecardiology can help the team make a tentative plan including decision about the investigations needed and counseling regarding the possible diagnosis.
- Follow up to review the investigations advised and confirm the diagnosis and advice regarding the management.
- Follow-up after surgical or catheter intervention to review clinical outcome.

- Basic support in a triage prior to shifting the patient to a tertiary cardiac center, thus ensuring a more stable patient and an improved outcome.
- Handling nonemergency situations like chest pain in a stable patient.
- Diagnosing critical heart disease in the antenatal period and helping in advising immediate postnatal care or reassuring an expectant mother.

Advantages of telecardiology

- Saves time: Early consultation with specialists becomes feasible, and an inbuilt appointment system reduces long waits at clinics or hospitals.
- Reduces travel time: No travel needed for the patient especially when mobilization is difficult like in elder patients or even sometimes doctors. Cardiologists increase their reach to patients not in their immediate geographic location.
- Helps improve quality: Improves the knowledge of the referring general physician and reduces missed diagnosis due to the lack of specialist input. It also can provide a platform for teaching the medical fraternity and reduce professional isolation. In contrast to telephonic conversation or email opinions, video communication helps the patient, and the specialist sees each other helping them to understand the nonverbal gestures like body language.

Teleobstetrics/prenatal telemedicine service

Danielle Santos Alves and Magdala de Araújo Novaes

Overview

Obstetric telemonitoring is a promising area in which real-time tracking of biomedical parameters aims to improve the quality of the assistance provided, reduce unnecessary referrals, improve education in health, and reduce maternal fetal morbidity and mortality. Beyond this, combined with a shared EHR, it could support more timely problem detection by health professionals, pregnant women, and family.

Concepts

Pregnancy is a period with significant physical, psychological, and social changes not only in a women's life but also of the companion and family. In this context, doubts and insecurities may appear.[265] In many countries, there is a lack of qualified professionals to provide minimal gestational follow-up as per WHO recommendations.[266,267] This is even more critical among women of low socioeconomic strata, rural zones, and places far from the specialized health centers.[268,269] Early detection of complications is crucial to avoid maternal and fetal repercussions. It is intrinsically related to an improvement in the quality of the care provided, starting from the first prenatal consultations until the postnatal period.[267,270–272]

In this way, teleobstetrics or a distant obstetric practice mediated by information and communications technologies could be an alternative to reduce the distance between primary care health professionals and specialists, as could help the pregnant women.

Applications

Teleobstetric applications can benefit different healthcare processes across different levels of care. Primary care professionals (PCPs) manage the patients at home and in health clinics, and their referral/follow-up by the specialist is required only for cases in which the PCP has some doubts, which could be that the pregnant woman presents with some complication or factors of risk, which are not within the primary level's attributions. Many strategies are used: smartphone applications for health education, assistant support, "gestational daily," high-risk pregnancy monitored by devices who collect biomedical parameters (e.g., maternal and fetal cardiac frequency), among others.

Obstetric telemonitoring is understood by the exchange of information in the monitoring of maternal and fetal parameters that occurs in a virtual way (i.e., by devices, desktops, and/or smartphones).[273,274] It aims to improve healthcare, provide early detection of injuries, ensure local intervention before dislocation or even hospitalization,[273] and reduce unnecessary referrals, besides providing education in health and reduction of maternal and fetal morbidity and mortality. Obstetric telemonitoring is seen as an efficient alternative to decrease the distances between health professionals in primary care and specialists, ensure quality referrals, reduce costs as well as unnecessary hospitalization.[266,269,275–277]

The use of "gestational daily" could facilitate the information exchange between health professional and pregnant women, besides to stimulate the more timely access of healthcare by the women.[274] Some applications are related to health education, recommending the women's "active protagonism" in healthcare actions.[278,279]

Another advance is in the use of wireless devices to capture and track home-based data through smartphone applications which is then shared with the specialist. These include bracelets with sensors to get the vital signs, telephone oximeter, electrodes for monitoring uterine contractions, detection and reading of fetal heart rate, and portable urine analyzer.[280–283]

However, one limiting factor for the use of this technology is the lack of access to all of these devices for the less affording populations, due to high costs (relative to income). An additional issue is that the applications currently in use concentrate on the prenatal period. Few applications exist in relation to labor or the postpartum period. The few identified are related to the uterine contractions during the labor and breastfeeding recommendations. Important parameters like fetal heart rate, maternal BP, and fetal movement are not typically captured.

Global experiences in gestational telemonitoring

In a systematic review of the literature, successful follow-up teleobstetric experiences of women and relatives were observed in developed countries[281,284] with less experience in developing countries.[266,269,273,285] Several articles have proposed new technologies for home-based monitoring during pregnancy.[284,286]

In Australia a study was carried out using a portable respiratory device for the control and monitoring of asthma and other respiratory problems in pregnant women, found good results, and reduction in the number of cases of more severe seizures by early detection.[287] In California (the United States),[280] detections of changes in the urine (used in the preeclampsia/eclampsia anamnesis) were performed using a portable monitor within an iPad. In Turin, Italy, an application has been developed that collects and stores data on the daily life habits of pregnant women (diet, physical activity, and hydration), allowing healthcare professionals to remotely monitor and act when necessary.[279]

A study carried out in South Africa[286] works as an example of experiences in developing countries for the early detection and treatment of preeclampsia during home visits for pregnant women. Collected clinical data was translated into a scale of points, which could offer a possible diagnosis with options of therapeutic interventions. In Pakistan an application has been developed that monitors information from pregnant women and issues medication and healthcare alarms.[266]

Different devices with a diversity of parameters have been evaluated. These include monitoring the respiratory pattern of pregnant woman,[287] urinary alterations,[280] blood pressure, and oximetry[286] as well as uterine contractions.[282] A study conducted in the Netherlands conducted global gestational analysis wherein uterine contractions, fetal heartbeat, maternal heart rate, and fetal electrocardiogram were evaluated.[284]

Regarding fetal follow-up, it has been observed that there is less diversity of equipment for this function, with a focus only on the baby's heart rate,[284,288] leaving gaps regarding aspects such as evaluation of fetal movement and fetal biophysical profile. The main features preferred for fetal heart monitoring included special acoustic sensor to capture the

BCF, USG doppler,[288] portable electrodes for detection of BCF, and portable monitor for cardiotocography.[284]

Current and future trends

Many women seek information and advice on the Internet or via "pregnancy help" applications at the major virtual stores (Google, Apple, Amazon, etc.). But this information is not always based on scientific evidence.[272] It is important to develop virtual and safe environments for the access of information by pregnant women and family members. A worldwide trend is the use of mobile personal health record (mPHR) for health interventions, since smartphones have advanced technological capabilities and a growing ubiquity of use in the health profession.[274,277]

Preliminary cost-benefit studies have obtained encouraging results in reducing expenses for health provision with lower levels of complexity and are closer to users. Some advances such as the use of mobile devices connected to smartphones are restricted to developed countries. There are not enough reports from developing countries where maternal and fetal morbidity and mortality rates are higher.

Regarding fetal health, there have been weaknesses in the follow-up. Better correlation with maternal health is required for complete fetal evaluation. It is essential that both be monitored together. All gestational aspects need to be connected in the developed applications.

The primary focus of most studies has been largely restricted to gestation with few reports focusing on childbirth and the puerperium phases. These too need to be better researched, since although the prenatal period is critical and easy to perform, follow-up period also needs to be addressed since there is a high incidence of complications and mortality in relation to childbirth and puerperium.

It is necessary to address the entire network of care to pregnant women, especially for the portion of the population that faces the problem of access to basic health services. From a structuring of the service to holistic monitoring, integrating the different levels and services of healthcare can bring a paradigm change in obstetric and neonatal care.

Telecare in geriatrics

Gunnar Hartvigsen

Overview

Telecare is about getting access to the patient and/or his/her data from a remote location to support independent living, often in the patient's own home. The population of elderly, in particular, those suffering from chronic disease,[289] has increased, and often multimorbidity has increased need for care on a longterm basis. However, better as well as a bigger range of telecare equipment is available.[290] Simultaneously, limited access to healthcare personnel makes telecare a key component in offering adequate healthcare services to the population at large.

Applications

Telecare has gradually been accepted as an important tool within contemporary 21st century healthcare systems. Lack of clinical evidence, however, is a problem inhibiting widespread use. One reason for the unavailability of evidence is that it is technology dependent, and many components are commercial off-the-shelf (COTS) products. There is an inherent conflict of interest leading to refusal of publications.

Another reason is that many advances are only published as internal reports and/or in national languages. One example is the telecare project in Alta, Norway, in 1999.[13] The project was initiated to test how future mobile communication could improve home care services. To test this a broadband radio network was established, and a mobile version of an electronic health record (EHR) was implemented. This enabled access to the central EHR with the possibility of sending messages to community doctors, dermatologists, and pharmacies.

Both the home care nurses and the patients' experiences were positive. The nurses were very pleased with the possibility of updating the EHR together with the patients in the patients' homes. The easy access to information reduced potential problems of simultaneously memorizing several things with a reduced need for memo systems and thereby potential sources for errors. Another experience was that the patients could take part in the nurses reporting in a positive way. By taking pictures of patients' ulcers, the nurses could document the progress of the ulcer treatment. The solution also supported joint study of ulcer pictures. This also improved the nurses' knowledge of ulcer treatment. With email service the nurses did not have to keep waiting on the telephone. Instead, they could send requests asynchronously, and the doctors could respond after completing their other consultations. In addition, the email contact with the local pharmacy was positive. Majority of these requests were questions regarding prescriptions.[13]

Similar telecare services can be successfully installed in nursing homes. Online access by nursing homes can improve healthcare support for the elderly. When Kroken nursing home and two assisted living homes in Tromsø, Norway, in 2003 were connected to the Norwegian Healthnet, it became the first online institution for elderly in Norway.[291] The goal of the Kroken project was to connect a part of the care sector in Tromsø municipality to the Norwegian Healthnet and to offer the staff at Kroken nursing home the same services as those that had been offered within specialized healthcare. The project established electronic communication between nurses and supervisory physicians to exchange questions and answers via secure email. In addition, it was an established electronic communication between the nursing home and the university hospital for answers to lab tests and received discharge summaries. The experiences were positive. Both the staff at Kroken and the regulatory doctors reported that such a service was required. They preferred to use email instead of telephone to contact the regulatory doctors in between regular visits. A limited negative effect was the need to change the routines and to learn to use the new tools.

A more recent example of telegeriatrics in small rural hospitals describes how a telegeriatric service model can be used to overcome the long distance from hospitals with geriatrician-supported comprehensive geriatric assessment and coordinated subacute care. The components of this service included[292]

- geriatrician consulting done from remote location using wireless, mobile, high-definition videoconferencing
- a trained host nurse at the rural site
- structured geriatric assessment configured on a web-based clinical decision support system
- routine weekly virtual rounds
- support from a local multidisciplinary team that was established to overcome these barriers"

The earlier model was found feasible and sustainable even beyond the study period. Based on their findings, Gray et al.[292] conclude that their telegeriatric service model seems appropriate for use in small rural hospitals.

Teleoncology

Mariana Boulitreau Siqueira Campos Barros, Magaly Bushatsky, and Magdala de Araújo Novaes

Overview

Cancer is one of the leading causes of morbidity and mortality worldwide, with about 14 million new cases in 2012.[293] It was responsible for 8.8 million deaths in 2015, and with nearly one in six deaths due to neoplasms, it is the second leading cause of death globally. For the next two decades, the incidence is expected to rise by about 70%.[294] Teleoncology, defined as telehealth applied to oncology, emerges as a strong strategy to narrow the gap between oncology specialists and other health professionals by providing support in genetic counseling, surgeries, radiation, bone marrow transplantation, palliative care, and the construction of a therapeutic project with a multiprofessional approach, sharing images of examinations or slides of pathology by teleconference, as well as professional oncologists and patients, by teleconsultations for chemotherapy administration supervision or oral medications, nutritional or emotional support.[295,296]

Concepts and applications

The first teleoncology connection on record, occurred in 1995, when an oncologist working in the University of Kansas in the United States, was linked to a rural medical center located more than 250 miles away.[297]

In the United States, in 2013 and 2014, a randomized controlled study of prostate cancer patients after radical prostatectomy compared consultations conducted through telehealth with office visits and found equivalent efficiency between these variables: waiting time, total time dedicated to care, and "face time." There was also equivalent satisfaction between the patient and the oncologist; however, whether the cost reduction between the two groups is significant, needs further analysis.[298]

Currently, there is a diversity of models for the teleoncology practice in health services, which we highlight

- Face-to-face visits complemented by teleoncology for the consultation and supervision of the chemotherapy administration.
- Consultation and supervision of oral medicines by telemonitoring. Cancer patients were given the option of electronic monitoring of their symptoms so that health problems could be resolved quickly and effectively through an electronic device called a "health buddy."[a] This device can be connected to phone or mobile applications giving them immediate access to their care coordinators.
- Replacement of face-to-face visits by teleconsultations for evaluation and chemotherapy administration supervision in home care (Fig. 7).

- Discussions of clinical cases in meetings of multiprofessional team, by web or videoconference.[299]
- Training of health professionals' experts and those in remote locations through videoconference or distance learning platforms.

As per protocol, teleoncology is only adopted after the initial assessment visit and preferably once first dose of chemotherapy has been delivered by the tertiary care centers. It is only after these first contacts and with the greatest engagement of the patient in their care that remote practices

[a] Source: https://wmhin.org/wp-content/uploads/2016/02/Solway_Health-Buddy_WIN2016.pdf.

FIG. 7   Teleoncology for evaluation and chemotherapy administration supervision in home care. *From https://www.saltlakecity.va.gov/features/The_next_step_in_tele-health.asp.*

are initiated. Subsequent care is through tele, preferably from the patient's own home, but always as an accompaniment to traditional care depending on the patient's criticality.[300]

After consent for treatment a brief overview of telemedicine is explained to the patient. Once the patient feels familiar with the system, the specialist continues with the anamnesis, assisted by the doctor at the remote location with physical examination, review of X-rays, and laboratory results, and finally discussing diagnosis and treatment plan.[297]

While the specialist provides clinical supervision of patient care, teleoncology practice is a collaborative effort from the outset when local health staff identify and consult patients who need special care. In addition, the role of community nurses is critical to effective and efficient coordination of patient care. The clinical support, education, and management of medicines provided by telehealth nurses aim to increase drug adherence, decrease readmission rates, and prevent chronic complications of the disease.[297]

At the cancer center in Townsville, Australia, from 2007 to 2009, oncologists use videoconferencing to perform follow-up services and specialized consultations for 20 other rural hospitals. In this model, when the patient is evaluated to begin chemotherapy treatment, oncologists prescribe and send the telehealth care plan to the places where chemotherapy and therapy are administered by competent nurses.[300]

Under telesupervision, one needs to understand adopted strategies to train doctors, nurses, and health interns who work far from referral centers or for training in modern techniques of care. However, in addition to videoconferencing, platforms for asynchronous storage and transmission and mobile applications can and should also be used. These strategies contribute to the early detection of cancer and professional updates regarding new clinical protocols.[300]

An example of adopting multiple models simultaneously was carried out in Brazil in the years 2015–17. A quasiexperimental study used teleoncology in childhood cancer prevention and in the regulation of suspected cases for referral centers, with telehealth as a driving force for the local healthcare network. Over 4 weeks, PCPs participated in a videoconference course on early diagnosis of pediatric cancer. After this educational intervention, they were encouraged to refer the suspicious clinical cases to the higher unit. In 2 years, eight teleconsultations were generated, four of which were clinical cases and had their referrals qualified, none needed to be regulated to the reference unit, ruling out the diagnostic hypothesis of cancer.[264]

Current and future trends

Early detection of cancer favors a greater chance of cure, survival, and quality of life for the patient. Stimulating the screening of some types of cancer, such as breast cancer and cervical cancer, for example, should be performed at all levels of healthcare. Likewise, caring for patients already diagnosed requires close monitoring of the team, and psychological aspects need to be considered. Teleoncology presents itself as a strong strategy to face these challenges.

The use of new technologies such as cloud-based services and mobile technologies is increasing. These services facilitate remote practices and bring together providers, professionals, and patients, but the adoption of well-established clinical protocols associated with safety, ethical, and legal issues in the practice of teleoncology is necessary.

Other relevant aspects are the continuous training of the professionals involved in the care and the costs involved in the treatment. In many countries, access to chemotherapy or other care is limited, so the associated use of teleoncology to traditional services can improve patient care conditions.

There is overall population growth, particularly of the aged, contributing to a rising contribution of neoplasms in the global morbidity and mortality scenario. The question arises whether existing models of care in various global health systems are prepared to provide sufficient access to preventive, curative, rehabilitative, and palliative aspects of oncology-associated care and also able to meet the growing demand. Without teleoncology, it is unlikely that dedicated cancer units can manage all categories of patients, that is, those needing a firm diagnosis and those needing treatment or palliative care for various types of neoplasia.

Thus it is important to implement a line of care for suspected cases of cancer, with teleoncology as a strengthening of the reference network and counter reference.[264]

Teleneurology

Shivani Ghoshal

Overview

Neurology has changed remarkably over the last 20 years, and there is an increasing demand for timely neurological evaluation in both acute and outpatient settings. The disparity between the need for neurologists and the availability of local neurological care is growing, particularly in rural and underserved areas. Teleneurology is a technologically feasible solution that allows neurological expertise to be delivered to remote locations to supplement or replace in-person neurological care and bridge the current gap between neurological supply and clinical demand. As it has developed, teleneurology serves as a viable practice extension whether practicing in an inpatient setting—as a neurohospitalist, stroke specialist, or neurointensivist—or as an outpatient neurologist.

Concepts and applications

Teleneurology has demonstrated feasibility in evaluating general and subspecialty neurology outpatients including those with dementia, headache, epilepsy, movement disorders, neuroophthalmologic disorders, neurocritical care issues, and stroke.

Telestroke is a subset of teleneurology that focuses on the evaluation of patients with acute stroke syndromes for possible IV tPA administration or other emergency stroke treatments such as interventional clot retrieval. In the current standards of practice in neurological care, the decision to treat patients with acute ischemic stroke with IV tPA must be made within 3–4.5 h of symptom onset; more timely treatment equates to better patient outcomes and less complications from medication administration. Availability of neurological expertise is crucial to this process; in a survey of 278 ED physicians from 24 hospitals, 65% of physicians reported feeling uncomfortable giving IV rtPA without a consultation.[301]

Telestroke evaluations can be performed with a videoconferencing camera or using a complex, third-party robotic device that integrates videoconferencing with advanced optics and neuroimaging integration. In several clinical studies, telestroke has shown both feasibility and safety, as well as comparable interrater reliability of the virtual and bedside neurological examinations.[302] Notably, patients treated with IV tPA after remote evaluation by telestroke had outcomes that were similar to patients who were treated by bedside evaluation[303]; earlier treatment with IV tPA resulted in a greater probability of good functional outcome.[304] From its implementation, telestroke services have increased thrombolysis treatment rates, improved clinical outcomes, and cultivated opportunities for referring centers to gain stroke center designation status.

Teleneurocritical care

Not infrequently, critically ill patients require urgent consultations for neurological problems other than stroke, though the supply of neurologists and specialized staff trained specifically in neurocritical care issues are few. The critical care unit is another domain where robotic telepresence or teleneurology serves to monitor critically ill patients, evaluate unexplained coma, and respond quickly to unstable patients. Availability of remote monitoring of patients in the intensive care unit (ICU) by telemedicine enables ICUs without availability of neurocritical care expertise to expand and improve coverage, especially in disorders such as coma and status epilepticus, which may require continuous EEG monitoring. Disorders such as spinal cord injury, severe traumatic brain injury, and subarachnoid hemorrhage show better patient outcomes with specialized expertise and early intervention.[305] A metaanalysis of studies that compared outcomes before and after instituting tele-ICU found reductions in patient mortality and hospital lengths of stay with tele-ICU.[306] In another single-center study of a large academic medical center involving 6290 patients, the application of tele-ICU showed improved patient outcomes and fewer medical errors and greater adherence to best practices.[307]

Outpatient teleneurology

Though teleneurology is best known for its impact as telestroke in emergency room and inpatient settings, teleneurology has been successfully applied to outpatient evaluation of many nonacute neurological conditions as well. Often, teleneurology is useful for follow-up visits after an initial in-person evaluation. Remote evaluation of movement disorders, multiple sclerosis, epilepsy, headache, and dementia is feasible and regularly performed. In a neurological patient for whom mobility is impaired or travel is difficult, this may help with long-term follow-up and treatment adherence. In particular for patients with Parkinson's disease (PD), several large networks have successfully cared for patients with PD by telemedicine; remote standardized assessment of motor function in PD is well accepted and correlates well with in-person evaluation.[308]

Continuing medical education and research

Teleneurology may be helpful for purposes beyond traditional patient care. Educational opportunities for both patients and healthcare professionals alike can be provided over a telemedicine source. Through telemedicine, in rural areas, local neurologists may benefit from consultation with subspecialists at tertiary care hospitals and from a wider network of community neurologists. By establishing a wider network of neurologists in practical communication, teleneurology may help improve standardized examinations used in remote monitoring and care.[304]

Future trends

Teleneurology reflects opportunities for neurologists to help bridge the supply and demand mismatch between available providers and the clinical need. Though teleneurology is best known currently for its efforts in stroke care, teleneurology is rapidly growing beyond telestroke to supply neurological services to rural hospitals and areas with limited or no neurological coverage, from inpatient, to outpatient, to critical care services. The extension of teleneurology may be helpful for remote recruitment of patients into acute stroke and critical care treatment trials and study follow-up of recruited patients.

Telestroke remains one of the best-studied and validated models for telemedicine, aided by stroke's standardized National Institutes of Health Stroke Scale (NIHSS) metric for examinations. The variability that often accompanies subjective signs in neurological disorders may require further research to better standardize teleexamination and symptom assessment. More studies are needed to explore the limits of telemedicine for neurological diagnoses other than stroke. Standardized scales for neurological examination will likely improve both utilization and interrater reliability within teleneurology.

Telediabetes

Gunnar Hartvigsen

Telediabetes is one of several telemedicine services that has proven to improve patients' health and the delivery of health services to people with diabetes.

Concepts and applications

The main goal of diabetes treatment is to optimize glycemic control for which, over the years, clinical studies have suggested a number of possible action points, including

- increased frequency of visits to a multidisciplinary diabetes clinic resulted in lower HbA1C[309]
- more frequent regulations of insulin dosage[310]
- continuing training of people with diabetes[311]
- improved diabetes education[312]

In 2004 a report about a 10-year-old telediabetes program found sustainability with three indicators of success[313]:

- the administration took a long-term view of the value of the telemedicine service;

- Telediabetes enabled structured use of staff time and facilities;
- Service delivery followed national diabetes standards and a well-defined cycle of care within a long-term quality improvement program.

According to the International Diabetes Federation,[314] we still have a long way to go before every diabetes patient has reached his/her treatment goals.

A 2015 review of telemedicine intervention in the management of diabetes (telediabetes), gestational diabetes, and diabetic retinopathy identified 73 articles, published between 2005 and 2013, that met the criteria for inclusion in the final analysis. They looked for evidence based on the following factors: feasibility/acceptance, intermediate outcomes (e.g., the use of service and screening compliance), and health outcomes (control of glycemic level, lipids, body weight, and physical activity.)[315]

Variations in the definition of telediabetes and diabetes subtype, setting, technology, staffing, duration, frequency, and target population existed, as also differences in the measurement of outcomes. However, the authors did find evidence that telemonitoring and telescreening had positive effects in glycemic control and reduction in body weight and contributed to an increase of physical exercise. Another effect of telediabetes was its potential for changing diabetes control and prevention behaviors, in particular for type 2 and gestational diabetes. The review concluded that "there is strong and consistent evidence of improved glycemic control among persons with type 2 and gestational diabetes as well as effective screening and monitoring of diabetic retinopathy."

Several studies have proven that telediabetes is equivalent to clinical visits.[316–318] One paper reported that 79% of the patients did not find problems related to not meeting the physician in real life.[319]

Self-management of diabetes is a complex task, which involves maintaining healthy blood glucose levels through a balanced diet, physical activity, and medication (insulin) and success depends on extensive monitoring of these parameters.[13] A large number of tools have been developed for self-management of diabetes.[320,321] We also have experienced that patient groups have taken initiatives themselves to develop advanced tools that are not (commercially) available.[322]

One of these interactive mobile tools is the Norwegian Few Touch application/the Diabetes Diary/"Diabetesdagboka," to support people with type 1 and type 2 diabetes to manage their health.[323] Blood glucose and physical activity data is captured wirelessly from sensors, and tagged with nutrition data and insulin usage through a simple user interface. The data is processed and presented to the user. Users can easily view progression of daily blood glucose levels, their physical activity, and how they are doing as compared with their set goals for blood glucose level, diet, and physical activity.

An important design goal has been to present the data in a simple and user-friendly manner. To optimize usability, blood glucose and physical exercise data are transferred automatically to the user's smartphone running the Diabetes Diary. Users may choose to record only the time of their meals, or they can easily add a rough description of what kind of food they had. The user can also find information about diabetes and some practical advice. A model has also been developed to transfer the health values to an electronic health record (EHR) or make the data from the Diabetes Diary available for healthcare personnel.[321]

The functionality of the Few Touch application is described[323]:

- *Automatic data transfer*. To capture blood glucose data and exercise data, the Few Touch application uses a blood glucose meter and a step counter. To optimize usability, data from these sensors is automatically transferred using a "no-touch" principle. This means that the users do not need to initiate data transfer from the sensors; the sensors set up short-range communication to the smartphone automatically. A more recent version of the diary includes the possibility to record data from CGMs.
- *Entry of nutrition data*. The users can record their food intake using two different levels of detail: (a) a simple choice of the kind of meal (breakfast, lunch, etc.) or (b) choosing the kind of food they eat (bread, pasta, etc.). This design has been chosen to make the data entry process as easy as possible, enabling the user to decide on the level of detail to record. Thus the process requires only two or three screen touch or navigation moves. Summary reports appear after each entry, for example, the current status of their nutrition habits.
- *Motivational information*. By including daily tips and information related to practical situations, that is, information that is sufficiently "down to earth," the aim is to motivate and educate the user. Newer functionality includes the possibility to reflect upon the development of the glucose level.

Current and futures trends

Since 2008 nutrition has become a focus area for diabetes control. A major issue is identifying the appropriate nutritional value of food items, for example, those typically found in Norwegian supermarkets.

By the use of the included camera, the users can take pictures of their meal for later examination. In a pilot study,[324] the image included the following information: time, date, activity, blood glucose measurements before and after the meal, the insulin dosage (in insulin units), and optional comments from the user. A Diabetes Diary has been used in several clinical studies.[325,326] User feedback from the 6-month user intervention demonstrated good usability of the tested system, and several of the participants adjusted their medication, food habits, and/or physical activity.[323]

Of the five different functionalities, the cohort (of initial users) considered the BG sensor system the best.

In 2015 the former Few Touch Application was renamed "Diabetes-dagboka" (Norwegian) or "Diabetes Diary" (English). There is also a Czech version. Diabetesdagboka is available on smartphone (Android and iOS) and smartwatch (Pebble). The Diabetes diary has its own website and Facebook page.

Many test users still appreciate the system and are regularly using despite 10 years having passed. There are approximately 4000 users in Norway. New functionalities have been added, for example, a color bulb that switches between yellow above 10 mmol/l, green between 4 and 10 mmol/l, and red below 4 mmol/L according to the connected person's blood glucose level. If the person uses a CGM, the bulb will be updated whenever the user's phone receives a new blood glucose value. Another add-on is a panel mounted in the user's home that constantly shows all the user data recorded in the patient diary.

A systematic review of telediabetes services within indigenous communities based on findings from the United States, Canada, Australia, and India identified several enablers of telemedicine,[327] including

- the use of cultural and spiritual elements
- acknowledgement of local beliefs and traditions
- *and* appropriate community engagement

Another success factor was the participation of indigenous health workers since they spoke the local language and could help clinicians to better understand the local community.

The main barriers of telediabetes services included

- potentially high fail-to-attend rates
- lack of technical skills associated with the operation of telehealth equipment
- *and* lack of availability of local staff

They argued that the understanding of the enablers and barriers related to healthcare services in indigenous communities is essential when planning a telediabetes service.

Telepsychiatry and telemental health

Rodrigo da Silva Dias and Magdala de Araújo Novaes

Overview

The practice of telepsychiatry encompasses a large number of activities through ICT with transfer/exchange of a range of medical information including EHR, images, and video. These activities may focus on: psychiatric evaluations, therapy (individuals, group or family), patient and provider education as well as medication management. The exchange of data can involve patients, primary care providers, specialists, and health care managers. Telepsychiatry has been identified as one of the key elements to improve treatment and expand care in mental health by the WHO. Due to its ubiquity, telepsychiatry can be made available in extreme situations, for example, war zones and humanitarian shelters. It is progressing towards becoming a model of hybrid care, with technology platforms getting associated with conventional care to bring great benefit to patients.

Concepts and applications

Telepsychiatry uses mobile devices, phone, email, chat, text, and two-way videoconferencing to deliver psychiatric care over a distance. Primary telepsychiatry practice includes psychiatric evaluations, therapy—be it individual, group, or family—patient education, and medication management. It covers other activities like consultations for primary care providers, other specialties, healthcare managers, and exchange of medical information (EHR, images, videos, etc.).[328,329] The telepsychiatry ecosystem has established technical and safety standards with proper certifications (e.g., HIMSS and HIPAA) enabling the adoption of this practice both in public and in private healthcare environments.

Telepsychiatry is one of the key elements to improve treatment and expand care in mental health within the WHO's Grand Challenges in Global Mental Health Initiative.[330] Telepsychiatry processes are varied with as many different approaches. When there is a real-time exchange of information (e.g., videoconference), it is named synchronous telepsychiatry; otherwise, it would be termed as store-and-forward (e.g., recorded material sent by email or other platform for an expert comment) or asynchronous telepsychiatry. On a regular basis, telepsychiatry is performed in medical facilities (hospitals, outpatient clinics, and nursing homes), but can also be performed in military and correctional institutions, and even in schools. These not only are restricted to patient care but also include training, supervision, and evaluation of health teams and managers, whether specialized or not in mental health. Due to its ubiquity, telepsychiatry can be made available in extreme situations like war zones and humanitarian shelters. Cultural and ethnic differences can be minimized.

Although the studies have generally been conducted with small population samples and other methodological limitations, the results have been positive towards use of telepsychiatry.

Considering the age range and the type of mental disorder, we find some scenarios where telepsychiatry shows efficiency. There is great acceptance among children and adolescents in general. Telepsychiatry has been found efficient in the follow-up of autistic spectrum disorder[331] and attention deficit hyperactivity disorder (ADHD)[332] as well as in psychiatric emergency services.[333] There is also positive evidence in the approach towards obsessive compulsive disorders (OCD), conduct disorders, eating disorders, paranoia, anxiety, or PTSD.[334,335] Among the elderly the cognitive and mental functions assessments showed promising findings.[332]

In adults, telepsychiatry has shown a comparable accuracy and reliability with face-to-face evaluation in different disorders: depression, anxiety, posttraumatic stress disorder, eating disorders, substance abuse, and schizophrenia.[332,336] A significant role of telepsychiatry has been observed in suicide prevention and in emergency rooms.[328,337] A post 2004 tsunami telemental health program started by SATHI (Fig. 8) is still continuing and even expanded in scope to general patients long after the disaster aspects had been well managed.[120]

The main technology used in telepsychiatry is the videoconference. The appropriate virtual environment for service has the objective of obtaining the best possible therapeutic bond. This should be well illuminated so that you have a good view and quiet enough that the communication takes place in the most natural way possible. The space should be minimally decorated and without the activities of other people to avoid distractions and ensure privacy. The technical specifications of the equipment should provide the best quality of interaction between the two poles: transmission

FIG. 8 Photos from SATHI's telemental support program. The psychiatrist (top right) is advising health workers and the patient (below), while the happy boy with his sister on the left was nearly suicidal before undertaking the treatment. *Photographs curtsey SATHI and OXFAM India Trust.*

band ensuring synchronicity, camera with good lightning, and sensitive microphones. Preferably, they should allow up to three people to be seen, especially in childcare. Equipment that provides a more open field of vision for observing motor or specific activities is required in special situations, such as testing and assessing interactions between people. Flat screens guarantee eye contact. During the attendance, both ends must always check the perfect understanding of the information exchanged. Identification of the participants and the confirmation of authorization for participation in the consultation are standard procedures. In the case of care being focused on children and adolescents, parents should also give this authorization.[334-336] In Brazil, initiatives in telemental health already occur throughout the country. Videoconferencing is widely used for specialists to interact with the family health team to discuss clinical cases of patients with mental disorders (Fig. 9). Video and web conferencing are also used as tools for training in mental health care for non-specialized staff to reduce referral of patients to a specialized network and provide clinical support for patient management.[338]

Another significant point is the establishment of technical and safety standards and certifications (e.g., HIMSS and HIPAA) enabling the adoption of this practice both in public and in private healthcare environments. The activity of telepsychiatry must still be in accordance with the legislation, norms, and conducts that regulate the exercise of the activities related to healthcare. It is also necessary to follow the technical guidelines suggested by the associations and telehealth entities of each country. However, we still find a great variation of norms and laws.

FIG. 9 A web telepsychiatry session, connecting a hospital psychiatrist to a nurse in primary care facility. Telehealth Center, Clinics Hospital, UFPE, Brazil.

III. Telemedicine

In some countries, such as Brazil, there are more restrictions on medical activity and greater freedom and structuring for psychotherapeutic care.[338] Recently, rules and procedures for due financial reimbursement are being guaranteed as in the United States. Ethical issues are still being debated regarding the licensing and professional boundary concerns and the online therapeutic relationship.

Current and future trends

Like any other activity involving the incorporation of new technologies in health, telepsychiatry presents innumerable possibilities. The incorporation of new media with the use of mobile apps and physiological and behavioral data collection technology (e.g., sensors and wearables) shows great promise.[334] Mobile apps, despite financial barriers related to smartphone costs—which in any case are decreasing—are very well accepted by patients. The apps allow ecological momentary assessment (EMA) techniques and are developed for different actions in the care of mental disorders such as psychoeducation, communication, context sensing, and interventions.[334] More recently, augmented reality and virtual reality headsets have been incorporated as well. Passive data collection methods (geographic location, voice, and chat content) also with smartphones are being researched more recently. There is still a lack of studies on the effectiveness of the applications and their development and incorporation into the care workflow.[339]

It is clear that the evolution to a model of hybrid care, where platforms using technologies associated with conventional care would be the model of care bringing great benefit to patients. These platforms would gather the data collected (actively and passively) via web, mobile phone, sensors, and self-reports. It is still inclusive because it allows the participation of caregivers, family members, or otherwise.[334] The incorporation of artificial intelligence (AI) has also shown promise as a decision support tool both at a distance and/or at the consultation point. The use of robots both as an assistant of the health team and for assistance of patients has been growing, especially in dementia and autistic spectrum disorders.[340]

Telesurgery

Shashi Gogia

Overview

Telemedicine has been largely concerned about providing a remote opinion about a health condition, and telehealth has added components regarding medical education, public health, and administration. Surgery by its very nature is procedure related. Assuming that more general aspects would be discussed elsewhere, this subchapter restricts to specific components pertaining to procedures.

Concepts and applications

Telehealth in the surgical arena helps in enabling distance-based support for pre and postoperative care, teleeducation, telementoring of actual procedures, and telerobotics—that is, the performance of the procedure through remote means.[b]

Preoperative preparation

Assuming that the surgeon is present at a different location than the patient or his PCP, most patients are referred to him with a summary note on the problem. They may or may not be accompanied by phone call. There would be a tentative diagnosis—for example, a breast lump or lymph node for which a biopsy is required or a definite indication for surgery like a hernia, hydrocoel, and appendicitis. Notes are text, but there can be photos, measurements, and preliminary tests that can be shared through a store-and-forward platform.

The remote surgeon may elect to reconfirm the diagnosis by a remote examination through VC (Video Conference) or by sharing of photographs. Further tests may be ordered like a CT and MR, with special views etc., to not only confirm the problem but also to help in the planning of the surgery. General preoperative checkups like BP, blood sugar, chest X-ray, ECG, and viral markers can also be routed through the PCP. Appointments are then provided so that the patient reports directly to the OR for a day care surgery and, even if not, ensuring minimal duration of preoperative stay.

Operative procedure

ORs are designed for efficient management of the procedure. It is a strictly physical encounter. Comfort and convenience of the patient and efficiency with sterility are the key deciding factors. IT (Information Technology) and related automation that has crept in so far has been largely to ensure a no-touch technique like opening and closing doors, taps for scrubbing, light adjustment etc. Patient monitors ensuring safety of the patient by itself do generate data, but any action has to be performed on the spot by the anesthetist.

Remote presence and telecare have been ushered in with increasing use of endoscopy. Overall movement and control of the instruments is maintained by the surgeon, with constant viewing done through the

[b]There is a separate subchapter on this in Chapter 12—Ed.

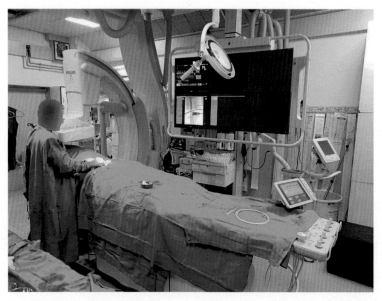

FIG. 10 Modern operating room with monitors, medical images support, electronic patient record access, with possibility of remote assistance by others physicians. *Photograph curtsey Dr Shoab Padaria.*

monitor (Fig. 10). The addition of physical as well as geographic distance and of robotic control of movements has been the next step.

Postoperative care

Once the patient is out of intensive care and all tubes are removed, there is little justification in making the patient stay in hospital. Early discharge allows for decrease in costs besides reducing the need for relatives to take time off work to stay nearby or make regular visits. Option of a video or telephonic consult ensures that there is safe, cost-effective, and quality care provision in a more homely environment.

Constant interaction between the PCP and the surgeon ensures quality care with little or no travel. Stitch removal, dressings, even the removal of a urinary catheter, etc. can easily be done by a PCP. Ensuring safety during transit is important. Also the surgeon has to be acquainted with the capability of the local care provider, besides availability of particular required equipment and drugs. For example, though removing of surgical staples (https://www.wikihow.com/Remove-Surgical-Staples) requires a special instrument, it can also easily be done a small mosquito forceps. Some telementoring may be required, for example, the author himself regularly teaches village health workers on how to tie a multilayer bandage for ulcers and lymphoedema.[c]

[c] Discussed under Wound Care and Lymphedema in Chapter 9.

Training of a surgeon

Most medical teaching is didactic. Training of a surgeon requires a more hands-on approach. Besides attending the OPD or wards, trainees have to be a part of the OR team with the rule—(1) *see* first, then (2) *assist*, and then (3) *do under supervision* before being allowed to operate independently. Medical colleges in the 20th century used to have viewing windows above the OR (Fig. 11) for step 1. Currently, systems exist to train a surgeon virtually. These are (1) *video-based learning* for step 1, (2) *simulation techniques* for step 2, and (3) *telementoring.* for step 3. In the first two steps, there is no physical contact by the student with the patient or anything else in the OR. Hence, safety and sterility are ensured.

Video-based learning

This is part of any CME or surgical conference these days. Either live streaming from the OR, or a recording of the live procedure is provided. The same can be viewed from anywhere across the globe using tools and sites like Livestream (www.livestream.com), WebEx (www.webex.com), Citrix (www.gotomeeting.com), and Zoom with methods to ask questions during live or real-time viewing. The cameras can be made to zoom; multiple cameras allow shots from different angles and focus on areas of importance. Automatic recording of procedures is standard, which allows one to freeze, reverse, fast forward, etc. like any other video. Thus video-based learning is far more flexible than any live viewing of a procedure.

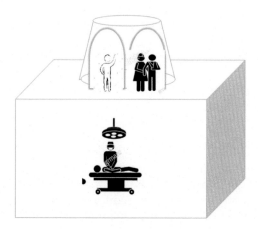

FIG. 11 OR design of teaching hospitals in the 20th century. These provided for glass windows on the roof for viewing of the procedure by students.

Computer-based simulation

These are methods similar to training of pilots with a focus towards operating on the human body. The user can hold instruments and manipulate them while viewing the TV monitor. Most common is the one used for training of endoscopy procedures. The earliest laparoscopy trainer was a simple plastic box covered with a rubber screen; from there the instruments were inserted. One could view from the outside or through the scope. Telescopic cameras with a light source make the experience more authentic. The latest trainers use and replicate actual normal and pathological anatomy through holograms and allow instruments to dig in, that is, virtual surgery is now possible (http://www.echopixeltech.com/). Stereotactic 3D imaging can be useful in the planning of surgery.

Telementoring of procedures

For procedures being done at a remote area, a less trained surgeon can be *teleguided* by a more experienced surgeon. Telementoring would require real-time connectivity for obvious reasons.

Mentoring and training nurses on how to do a particular dressing or to remove a drain is now fairly routine (*see previous text*). One of the earliest examples of mentoring an actual surgical procedure was in 2005 from India—a medical officer posted at the Guruvayoor temple in Kerala managed to insert a chest tube for a tension pneumothorax in a pilgrim with remote guidance from a surgeon at Amrita hospital in Kochi.[341]

Telementoring by radiologists for diagnosis of inadvertent intraoperative lung injury and pneumothorax or other problems is well described. The surgeon uses a special probe and uploads through his smart mobile.

On the higher end, even an experienced surgeon may occasionally call up a colleague or senior when in trouble like severe bleeding or unable to find the parathyroid tumor. Though mostly these calls are on the phone, live video sharing would make it better. Videos would be ongoing if an endoscopic procedure is in progress. For nonendoscopic procedures, special equipment has to be setup with extra effort and time wastage so there has to be ample justification.

Regulation and future trends

In summary, different modalities of telesurgery and remote practices can help the surgeon across the board, that is, from surgical planning, right up to postoperative care. Teleeducation—which does not require any extra infrastructure can be a constant accompaniment to allow basic training and professional updating. There are still issues related to the regulation of surgical practices at a distance in countries where restrictions are applied. On the other hand the use of artificial intelligence in surgical planning and monitoring is growing, as well as the use of robots and portable devices to monitor the patient during the whole cycle from pre- to postoperative care.

Teleotorhinolaryngology

Arindam Basu

Overview

Teleotolaryngology refers to the surgical discipline of distance-based practice of ear-, nose-, and throat (ENT)-related surgery. The ENT discipline includes surgical, diagnostic, and treatment procedures such as external (external otitis), middle (otitis media, perforation, and withdrawal of tympanic membrane), and inner (including hearing and balance and skull base ears) ear diseases; diseases attributed to nasal cavity and surrounding sinuses (septum, meati, frontal, and maxillary sinuses) and nasopharynx; and diseases of the oral cavity, palate, oropharynx, tonsils, adenoids, larynx, and esophagus.

Clinical applications

Clinicians commonly utilize a "scope"-based diagnostic procedures in ENT surgery: here the clinician projects light in "cavities" and then directly observes or projects the sometimes magnified image on a screen, with a choice of printing or further processing. For example, a handheld otoscope is a device that has an inbuilt light source and a magnifying lens. For diagnosis of pathologies in the external ear or the tympanic membrane, the clinician would insert the otoscope inside the external ear cavity, project light that reflects off the tympanic membrane, and reveal the anatomical details of the tympanic membrane. Thus the clinician is able to identify pathological lesions inside the external ear, perforations in the tympanic membrane, distortions in the tympanic membrane reflecting changes in the middle ear, accumulation of fluid, and/or the presence of cavities. The clinician can also video record these images for further clinical decision-making. Similarly, for examination of the nasal cavities and sinuses, the clinicians use fiberoptic endoscopes that can project light into the recesses of the sinuses (the maxillary sinuses), and using these devices, it is possible to diagnose diseases and pathological lesions within the nasal cavity. The fiberoptic endoscopes also enable the clinician to photograph or video record the lesions. In the larynx, or in the deeper recesses of larynx, the clinician can use laryngoscopes or video laryngoscopes to view and record lesions.

Clinicians also use another set of diagnostic procedures in ear, nose, and throat surgery: different forms of "functional recordings" of the organ systems. *Hearing* is recorded in the form of an audiogram using audiometry. An audiologist produces sound waves of variable frequency and intensity using either sets of tuning forks or sounding machines to the patient, and the patient in turn indicates the threshold at which he or she can perceive the sensation of sound. This results in recording an *audiogram*; interpretation of the audiogram provides an assessment of the hearing loss (conductive hearing loss or sensorineural hearing loss). The audiogram can be printed or can be recorded electronically. *Tympanometry* is a procedure where sound waves and pressures are projected on the tympanic membrane and the pressure measurements are recorded in the middle ear. These measurements indicate the pressure within the middle ear and the presence or absence of fluid for diagnostic purposes. *Electronystagmography* evaluates the performance of the vestibular organs, that is, the cochlea within the inner ear by mapping rapid eye movements and assessing the performance of the muscles that control eye movements. *Posturography* is another series of tests that are used to study balance of patients with vestibular dysfunction. Those who have problems of ringing in the ear ("tinnitus") and sensation of fullness in the ear with vertigo or dizziness undergo electrocochleography (a recording of the electrical activities of the inner ear organs) as diagnostic tests for Meniere's disease. *Video stroboscopy* is a procedure to study the movement of the larynx.

Each of the earlier procedures indicate that ear-, nose-, and throat-related diagnoses are dependent on a range of tools that can record images and electrical activities or other forms of information that can be transmitted over long distances, thus facilitating remote diagnoses for patients. Likewise, clinicians can use the results of these tests to diagnose and plan clinical management of patients who are located at some distance, or using store-and-forward technology, it is possible for clinicians to diagnose disease conditions and plan management of patients with diseases in the head and neck region. This practice of remote diagnosis and management of patients with diseases in the head and neck is referred to as teleotolaryngology.

Indications are situations where the practitioners are located remotely or in places not easily accessible or in extreme weather situations, as well as in military operations.[342–344]

In combination with the nature of anatomical and diagnostic processes that rely on either imaging or recording functions, a series of innovative processes and tools have enabled the use of teleotolaryngology. Smartphone-based devices that can record and image eardrums are tested.[345–347] Remote consultations where tertiary consultants work together with primary care providers or family practitioners and general practitioners are useful in the management of common conditions.[348,349] Examples of robotic surgery within ENT are mentioned in the relevant chapter

Future trends

In summary, teleotolaryngology provides opportunities for extending conventional diagnostic tools to aid distance-based diagnoses; they are useful in situations where remote care is needed and can be inaccessible. New tools are available using handheld devices such as mobile phones in a range of disease conditions. On the horizon are transoral surgeries, and tonsillectomies by robotic surgery provide an opportunity to extend the scope of telecare in ENT for situations such as emergency management of peritonsillar abscess, foreign body retrieval under expert guidance, and telementoring of emergency ENT procedures in primary care settings.

Teledentistry

Ana Estela Haddad, Denise Garrido Silva, and Ana Emília Figueiredo de Oliveira

Overview

Teledentistry proposes the use of telecommunication technology to provide dental education and dental care, not only for underserved populations or in distant locations, but also offering support to patients and a second opinion for dentists, whenever necessary.

Concepts and applications

The use of information and communication technologies (ICT) applied to health, whether in healthcare, education, or related to management or research activities, has to do with the emergence of telehealth. The concept of "teledentistry" proposes the use of telecommunication technology to deliver dental care across geographic distances to underserved patient populations.

"Teledentistry" was described in scope and meaning by Folke from the University of Texas in 2001.[350] However, the roots of teledentistry are same as other forms of telemedicine and highlight the definition adopted by the Association of American Medical Colleges: it is the use of telecommunications to send data, graphics, audio, videos, and images between localities and people distant from each other for clinical purposes. Chan et al.[334] suggest the adding of oral healthcare and education to the definition in the previous texts. The early notions of teledentistry were outlined in 1989, at a conference of the Westinghouse Electronics Systems Group in Baltimore.[351] An American Army project in 1994 called "Total Dental Access" had used data transmission over a telephone line, both synchronous and asynchronous (store and forward), as one of the pioneering projects in teledentistry. Soldiers serving in remote areas requiring dental care could be referred to and get further advice from specialists.

Teledentistry is also useful to supplement traditional teaching methods in dental education and in long-distance continuing educational providing new opportunities for dental students and dentists.[352] Teleconsultations can be real time or store and forward.

A multicenter study investigating the use of ICT in dentistry in Latin America analyzed 94 questionnaires answered by teachers and researchers and 221 questionnaires by clinical dentists. Teachers emphasized the importance of using ICT to promote collaborative learning and a series of innovations in education. They also identified the use of the electronic patient record in Brazil, Uruguay, and Colombia.[353]

There is a good applicability of teledentistry, for attending to the oral health of populations in remote regions. Its use by dentists and patients is very well accepted. However, payment for teledentistry services is still a critical issue for sustainability.[354]

Teledentistry is implemented in some developed countries and needs to be encouraged. Teledentistry in Brazil has developed in a similar manner to other fields. In the public health sphere, there have been two decisive aspects: the first was related to the fact that the Unified Health System (SUS) implemented by the Ministry of Health included dentistry since 2003, making it a participant and beneficiary of the national health policy; the other was following the recommendation of the World Health Organization Resolution WHA 58.28/2005,[355] Brazil adopted eHealth as a strengthening tool for Unified Health System (SUS) and started the Brazilian Telehealth Program.[240] Later the Open University of SUS was created. Under the Brazilian Telehealth Program, dentistry is a part in the range of offerings of teleconsultations and discussions related to oral health, in parallel to other topics in medicine, nursing, and other health areas. These are held for medical professionals, nurses, dentists, dental technicians and auxiliaries, technicians and auxiliaries in nursing, and community health agents, who work in primary healthcare.

A growing body of evidence supports the use of teledentistry, in particular, for early detection of dental diseases.[356] A role in specialist restorative care has been described in the Highlands and Islands of Scotland (HIT)[357] with the greatest benefits and cost savings, being recouped if patients had to travel long distances to visit the hospital. Teledentistry is especially suitable for management of referrals of older dependent adults with oral mucosal disease.[358]

In Alaska the Dental Health Aide Therapist program makes use native dental therapists and telemedicine to address inequity in access to dental care. The program began in Alaska as an expansion of the Community Health Aide Program. Alaskan Natives were trained and employed as dental health aide therapists with an expanded scope of practice to perform prophylaxes, restorations, and uncomplicated extractions and provide preventive care in Alaska Native villages.[359]

Teledentistry has the potential to improve access to oral healthcare and eliminate the disparities in rural areas and urban communities. Interdisciplinary communications will improve dentistry's integration into the larger healthcare delivery system. Implementing teledental applications necessitates full comprehension and consideration of the healthcare environment and also a commitment to completely integrate teledentistry within that environment.[360]

Recently a cost-effectiveness analysis was conducted comparing the use of teledentistry in delivering specialist dental services for rural patients as against the traditional method of consultation in Australia. The results showed that teledentistry is a cost-effective method to deliver dental care and an alternative to face-to-face consultation.[361]

Future trends

Teledentistry will be used in many other ways, such as quality and safety assessment, clinical decision support, medication e-prescribing, consumer home use, and simulation training. Although dentistry maintains a separate history, context, and identity within the wider scope of telehealth, it merges well with related applications and in the principle of integral healthcare, which is better achieved through interprofessional work and training in health. It is important for professionals, professors, researchers, and stakeholders to take this view into consideration. Such articulation of teledentistry within the scope of telehealth and related public health concerns helps in strengthening health systems, leading to the benefit of the whole population.

Teleemergency service

Kriti Gogia

Preamble

Twenty years ago, I recall a series of frantic calls to the doctor, a rushed cab to the hospital, and almost a month of painful dressings for my cousin when she burned her foot. Then 5 years ago, in a similar episode,[362] telehealth accelerated the healing process for a friend. His first response was a Google search for treatment options, followed by forwarding a picture of the injury to his physician, for further advice.

He was required to make a physical visit only once, progress being monitored through later exchange of photographs.

Concepts and applications

Telehealth is especially useful in emergency care, where time is of the essence. In 1995 the Global Emergency Telemedicine Services was launched collectively by the Ministries of Health in France and Italy.[363] That initiative was aimed at providing an immediate telemedicine-based response to any emergency situation globally. Since then, applications of telemedicine in emergency medicine have progressed from improving emergency response in rural settings[364,365] to reducing patient load in urban hospitals[364,366] thereon to video consults directly to the patient's home.

A recent survey in the United States observed emergency to be the second most frequent application of telemedicine.[367] With the severe and time-sensitive nature of ED-related injuries, a simple teleconsult can often be lifesaving. Rural areas in particular suffer from the drawback of lack of access to timely care. The same survey also observed that rural areas had a higher tendency than urban areas to utilize telemedicine in emergency care.[367] Telemedicine can go a long way towards addressing this socioeconomic gap.[341] Examples of successful applications of telecommunications in emergency response situations can be found across the globe.[341,368]

Teleradiology or transmission of digital images was one of the earliest and most effective applications of telehealth in emergency.[341] Another popular application is teleconsults to specialists from emergency departments in an effort to improve patient care and decision-making regarding transfers to a specialized trauma center.[364,366] Vitals of the patient in an ambulance can now be remotely monitored by the hospital, saving crucial time and enabling the hospital to provide the best possible care in the shortest possible timeframe.

Telemedicine has been found to be particularly successful for treating wounds and other minor injuries remotely.[366,368] One particular hospital in New York, the United States, introduced teleconsultation as an option in the ED.[369,370] Once a patient is checked into the ED, if the severity of his condition is not too high (e.g., for wounds, rashes, and upper respiratory infections), he/she is given the option of seeing a physician remotely. The history, vitals, and routine tests are still conducted by an in-person nurse/ assistant; however, the attending doctor converses with the patient via videoconferencing in a room in the hospital (Fig. 12). The advantages of this process are that it significantly cuts down on the wait time for the patient (as much as 75% sometimes), decreases burden in the ED, and frees time for the on-call doctors to see more urgent cases. Early surveys have shown high satisfaction scores among patients with this process.[369,370] A number of hospitals in the United States are now implementing similar programs in their emergency departments.

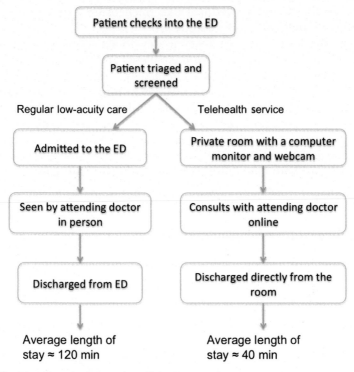

FIG. 12   Flowchart depicting telemedicine intervention.

Software and apps now exist that make even a visit to the ED unnecessary. It is now possible for the patient to connect with an ED physician from his home and receive a consult within minutes. If the symptoms are sufficient for the physician to make a diagnosis, the patient can skip any tests or hospital visits and directly pick up a prescription from the pharmacy, saving time and cost, decreasing burden in the ED, and allowing appropriate care delivery to the sicker patients. Such an app was recently launched in a New York hospital.[370] The On Demand Virtual Urgent Care App provides patients with immediate access to an ER physician for a teleconsult. The physician can then further advise them on the necessity of making an ER visit.

Current and future trends

A 2015 report of a survey done in Pondicherry, India, found emergency telemedicine systems to be cost-saving, time-saving, and as effective as in-person examinations by both healthcare providers and patients.[371] They performed telementoring for emergency procedures by residents. There are other similar examples of nonmedical persons instructed on emergency life-saving procedures like tracheostomy and putting in a chest tube for tension pneumothorax.[341]

Recent studies on teleemergency in developed countries have shown high levels of user satisfaction for the patients and the healthcare professionals, in terms of quality of care, interaction, and health outcomes.[364,366] The rate of return to the ED, after evaluation through a teleconsult, was observed to be similar to a regular visit, indicating similar rates of success.[366,369] These studies however have been limited in their approach due to the dynamic nature of the ED and limitations of scales for measuring qualitative patient outcomes. While these studies hypothesize an expected cost-benefit for both patients and providers, in terms of reduced visits to the ED with increased teleconsults, the same is yet to be evaluated. More rigorous and methodological studies are needed to identify both strengths and limitations of the current approaches in teleemergency; however, early results have been undeniably positive.

Tele-ICU

Rohit Raghav Gupta

Overview

Tele-ICU refers to the use of integrated audiovisual communication and electronic health systems to remotely monitor and manage patients in the intensive care unit (ICU). Also referred to as virtual ICU, remote ICU, or eICU, these systems are increasingly being integrated into academic and private institutions with over 13% of adult ICUs in the United States having some form of tele-ICU coverage.[372]

Depending on institutional resources, location, and bed capacities, Tele-ICU can offer powerful solutions for a variety of challenges. In geographic regions that have been traditionally medically underserved, tele-ICU can provide a workforce solution, where hiring an in-house staff intensivist might not be a viable alternative. For health systems having multiple satellite facilities, tele-ICU can help, by implementing best practices across facilities improving infection morbidity and mortality outcomes. By securing access to specialist intensivists, patient interventions can be planned in advance; triage decisions, leading to referral to higher care centers can be done in a safer and more expeditious manner. Conversely, inappropriate transfers can be minimized by providing expertise, guidance and close follow-up remotely.

Tele-ICU models

Several tele-ICU models exist that offer flexibility in terms of their input and resources for hospital systems to consider.[373] For most health systems, tele-ICU models exist as a hybrid from among these models.

In the continuous care model, tele-ICU physician monitors and manages patients in real time over predetermined time shifts. This can serve to provide night coverage remotely, while the onsite intensivist provides care in the daytime or alternatively provide 24/7 coverage. In the continuous care model, the teleintensivist would serve as the primary attendant who would work typically with on-site physician extenders or hospitalists to implement a plan of care.

In the scheduled care model, tele-ICU teams offer periodic consultation to the primary team caring for the patients. These are typically scheduled as planned consults during rounds once or twice a day.

In the responsive care model, tele-ICU consults are obtained in an unscheduled manner in response to clinical changes, in lab alerts, or for other unanticipated reasons.

Tele-ICU logistics and resources

Investing in a robust tele-ICU infrastructure is critical for the success of any program. This includes access to reliable secure Internet access with adequate redundancies for ensuring stable communication channels. A well-integrated electronic medical record system allowing the intensivist to review hospital labs, imaging, consult notes, and data from prior visits is required. Finally, it needs technological solutions for teleconferencing capabilities not only to communicate with the onsite medicine team but also with patients and their families.

All these resources can be located in a defined centralized facility where the tele-ICU staff would be located. This is commonly seen in tele-ICU facilities that provide continuous coverage to multiple hospital locations simultaneously. An alternative is a decentralized structure where tele-ICU staff provides care from flexible locations like their homes and offices using the Internet.

Staffing for tele-ICU teams can vary depending on the model of coverage and patient population. The tele-ICU team includes an intensivist physician who can be joined by critical care nurse practitioners (NP), registered nurses (RN), pharmacists, and registered nurse (RN), pharmacists, data entry staff, and quality management consultants. Depending on the program design, tele-ICU patient-to-RN ratio of 30:1 and patient-to-physician ratio of 50–150:1 can be implemented.[374]

Challenges

Several factors exist in the implementation of a successful tele-ICU program. It is important to have close integration between the tele-ICU and onsite hospital team. This includes a clear delineation of responsibilities, defined workflow pathways, and algorithms for escalation of processes.[374]

The idea of tele-ICU is to strengthen and support the onsite medical team rather than serve as their replacement. Building trust between teams requires close involvement of nursing and physician leadership and through close collaboration and joint training sessions.

Alongside these measures, special focus needs to be placed on documentation, patient data confidentiality, patient and family counseling, and quality improvement metrics.

Some of the challenges facing tele-ICU include credentialing, licensing, and malpractice regulatory requirements that are yet to catch up with the advancement in the field.[375] Another barrier to more widespread adoption is the current limitation in the ability to bill and secure reimbursements for tele-ICU services. These are gradually changing as regulators recognize the scope and potential of tele-ICU services.

Impact and future trends

As tele-ICU services have grown, more data has become available to assess their impact. Two recent metaanalyses have shown reduction in ICU mortality but with conflicting data on hospital mortality and length of stay.[376,377] Given the heterogeneity of tele-ICU models and multiple other factors affecting outcomes, more studies would be needed to conclusively determine overall trends. More significantly the use of tele-ICU teams for best practices like the ventilator care bundle and central line and urinary catheter utilization has shown to lead to reductions in duration of mechanical ventilation and ICU length of stay.[378]

Over the coming years, tele-ICU is expected to expand and provide a greater role in managing critically ill patient population. The use of a thoughtfully designed proactive integrated tele-ICU program will serve to improve patient safety and hospital outcomes while simultaneously offering avenues for cost reductions.

Teledialysis

Gunnar Hartwigsen

The idea of supporting dialysis patients at remote satellite stations or even at home started to evolve in the late 1980s/early 1990s. In Italy the first teledialysis services included follow-up care for every session in local and remote stations.[379] In 2003, Edefonti et al. concluded that teledialysis is useful in detecting and solving the clinical and technical problems of automated peritoneal dialysis.[380]

In Northern Norway, teledialysis started in September 2000 as a project to connect the university hospital to two remote satellites.[381] Based on the positive results from the project, Teledialysis has continued as a routine service since then and even spread to several places in Norway.

Dialysis in Norway is primarily offered as hospital-based hemodialysis (dialysis center).[13] This means that patients have to visit the renal unit three times a week for up to 5 hours. Many patients live far from the hospital and may have to spend up to 6–8 hours on commuting to and from the hospital 3 days per week. Long distances make it appropriate to decentralize dialysis treatment as much as possible. This is achieved either as "satellite dialysis" provided by smaller hospitals or nursing homes or by home dialysis (either hemodialysis or peritoneal dialysis).

The University Hospital of North Norway (UNN) in Tromsø, Troms County, has the medical and administrative responsibility for patients undergoing dialysis in the neighboring county of Finnmark. With a total population of 75000 in an area of 50000 km, the challenges in offering specialist healthcare services for the population are huge. UNN has the responsibility for three hemodialysis satellites in Finnmark.[381]

The aim of the teledialysis service was to improve the quality of patient care by providing patients and nurses at the satellite units with the same quality of follow-up care and support as that received by patients and healthcare staff at UNN.[13] With the help of telemedicine, they wanted to establish a joint workplace by incorporating staff at the satellites into UNN's everyday routines. Thus the nurses at the satellite centers had to be integrated into the daily routines at the nephrology department at UNN. The quality of patient care was improved by doing patient rounds in Alta and Hammerfest from UNN over a real-time video link. Before teledialysis became a routine, all communication between health staff at the satellites and UNN took place via telephone, paper documents were sent via traditional mail, and the nephrologists visited the satellite locations every fourth week. The patients from Alta and Hammerfest also had to travel to UNN every third or fourth month for follow-up.

The Norwegian Healthnet had installed a 2-Mbit/s network between all three sites. For security reasons a virtual private network (VPN) connection was used for all data transmission except videoconferencing (VC). Different VC solutions were evaluated. Equipment was chosen based on technical requirement specifications such as knowledge and experience analysis, support for both internet protocol (IP) and Integrated Service Digital Network (ISDN), built-in Multisite Conference Unit (MCU) menu and operating manual in Norwegian, and the possibility for connecting biomedical equipment and external camera to the VC equipment. In the system selected, also the expressed wish from the healthcare staff for a portable system and a rack for this purpose (codec, camera, and monitor) was met, even though the VC equipment did not qualify as biomedical equipment. Traditional VC equipment together with/connected through medical isolating transformers (in accordance to the technical standards IEC 60601-1) allows the use of VC in patients' room. VC use is as follows[13]:

- The nurses have day-to-day contact from Monday to Saturday. Here, current problems are discussed every day in a 15-min session to each satellite.
- Doctor and nurse have rounds every 14 days, alternating between Alta and Hammerfest. The rounds include review of all the patients and patient rounds. Ultrasound apparatus is used if required.
- At UNN, they have in-house training once every 14 days.
  The satellites participate in the in-house training through videoconferencing.
- The system is also used for emergency problems if needed.

In addition to VC, transmission of heart and lung auscultation and fistula murmurs was part of the telemedicine system. An electronic stethoscope was connected, but the quality of the transmitted heart or lung sound was not considered good enough for medical purposes. On the other hand the possibility of connecting the stethoscope to a PC and transmitting the sound to the doctor using a secure email solution was found to be more attractive. Ultrasound support was desired for providing guidance for inserting needles in deep blood vessels and for training new nurses on how to insert needles. Its direct use and a doppler sometimes outside the telemedicine context helped the diagnosis of pathological conditions in the blood vessels and fistulas and displayed "difficult" blood vessels.

Dialysis machine software is an online therapy data management system. PCs with software were installed at all sites to monitor the hemodialysis machines and to achieve a common electronic patient record system. The software provided the following capabilities for the clinician working at a remote location: direct downloading of dialysis parameters such as arterial, venous, and transmembrane pressure; conductivity; temperature; ultrafiltration rate; data on blood volume; and data storage of laboratory test results; nurses' reports; medication taken; blood pressure; and weight.[13]

For data security reasons and to enable simultaneous access to other hospital electronic sources such as digital radiographs and the main patient record systems, the server with the dialysis software was installed within the UNN's network with a VPN to the satellite units. This gave the nephrologists simultaneous access to other information sources provided by the hospital (digital X-rays and the patient's main electronic health record). In addition, all the necessities of data security could be achieved. For UNN the technology has improved the reliability of the advice given by its staff. For the satellites the faster response and higher information quality add to the reliability of the care they provide.[13]

The technological solutions together with new service delivery routines have strengthened cooperation between UNN and the satellite units. Patients benefit from greater continuity in checkups, follow-up, and treatment, as well as the opportunity to talk to UNN health professionals directly. The technology has improved the reliability of the advice given by its staff. In particular, the audiovisual contact both with the health staff before the rounds and with the patients during the rounds has contributed to this improvement. Both health staff and patients report this. A number of acute problems can be solved via telemedicine, and this could avoid the need for several emergency admissions. In addition, admissions for checkups are no longer necessary. Follow-up now takes place in almost the same way as for patients at UNN. For the satellite stations, it appears to be easier to fit VC into day-to-day routines. The software can also be used to allow nurses to do other things in the office while they monitor the machines via the PC screen.[13]

Annual costs included investments in teledialysis and broadband as well as time costs for specialists and nurses participating in the service. Both doctors and nurses must set aside time for teledialysis. Time is needed for the transmissions themselves and to prepare as well as do follow up work. The office service also needs to spend extra time for updating the electronic health record. Access to technical staff when needed is also important. Costs are saved because patients no longer need to travel to UNN four times a year for regular checkups. Now the necessary tests and procedures were performed at the satellite units. Travel costs and costs of overnight stays at the hospital are avoided. Costs are also saved for emergency admissions. In addition, the specialist's travel to Alta and Hammerfest has decreased to every 6 weeks instead of every 4 weeks.

The patients have been positive to this service and the staff satisfied with the experience of using teledialysis applications. They were most satisfied with the VC equipment and the electronic health record. Some of the staff at UNN thought that the electronic health record was as useful as the VC, because the record enabled computer-mediated communication. Ultrasound apparatus and the stethoscope were barely used, due to sound problems, less experience, and fortunately the lack of relevant medical problems.

Organization of teledialysis at the responsible institution needs to be individualized as per the needs of a particular hospital, depending on the number of doctors and nurses, where the equipment is located, etc. Before starting the program, it is recommended that plans and routines be drawn up for scheduling the connection and the content of the transmissions, for example, a weekly plan in which all activities and its responsible staff is plotted. The doctor and nurse responsible must be designated in the roster for the department. VC demands fixed schedules, as all the parties involved, that is, the patient, nurses, and the specialist as applicable, need to be available in synchronicity. There is a need for constant communication between the parties involved throughout. The possibility to use VC outside the scheduled timetable as per need also has to be catered to.[13]

The limitations of the system lie in the possibilities for diagnosing complex clinical conditions in which advanced diagnostic aids such as contrast X-rays are needed, or where the technical quality of the telemedicine equipment does not make it possible to differentiate between various potential diagnoses (e.g., with auscultation of the lungs: pulmonary congestion or pneumonia). When teledialysis is well established between sites, it is very important that all health staff members involved know who has the responsibility for the equipment and the network. Even so, it is recommended to identify a "super user" at each site in addition to this. It is also important to ensure access to technical personnel such as biomedical, information technology, and telecommunication staff.[13]

Some basic recommendations are the following:

- Before start-up, it is recommended that plans and routines be drawn up for scheduling the connection and the content of the transmissions.
- Establish a service that is as simple as possible, both technically and in relation to costs (depending on what you want to achieve).
- Ensure that the network is fast enough and as reliable in operation as possible.
- Take security considerations into account.
- Provide access to a common electronic patient journal that is up to date (should include laboratory data, X-ray result, and possibly images).
- Establish audiovisual communication such as videoconference.
- Ensure access to technical support personnel, such as biomedical, information technology, and telecommunication staff (for service and support when the system does not work).

The following were identified as unnecessary:

- online monitoring software of the hemodialysis machines
- electronic stethoscope (due to the quality of the transmitted audio)
- ultrasound

Telerehabilitation

Ganesh A. Joshi

Overview

Telerehabilitation overcomes the barrier of distance and time and provides access to patients having temporary and permanent disabilities for accurate diagnosis and prescription by physiatrist (physical medicine and rehabilitation or PMR specialist). A physiatrist can bring the patient in terms with his realistic potential through telerehabilitation and thus mitigate hazards of unscientific miraculous cures that trap doctor shoppers.

Telerehabilitation offers regular communication between the members of the rehabilitation team and realtime assessment of the patient's environment. Thus it improves the patient satisfaction and quality of life cutting down the cost and labor of accessing healthcare. Telerehabilitation facilitates realizing the goals of mainstreaming persons with disabilities in broad aspects beyond the scope of healthcare.

Concepts and applications

Disabilities of permanent and temporary nature affect every alternate household, but physiatrists are unevenly distributed across the globe. Telerehabilitation facilitates the physiatrist to reach out to many more patients to provide diagnosis and management through virtual mode than it was possible sitting in his clinic/institution/home visit. It is also possible to monitor the progress of treatment with better and continuous communication with the paramedical staff involved in rehabilitation. The two-pronged approach of rehabilitation management, namely, person with disability and his/her environment, is made possible through telerehabilitation in a very economical way providing 24X7 access to health for persons with disabilities at their location.

Physiatry is a medical specialty concerned with diagnosis and treatment of temporary or permanent disabling conditions through multiple interventional strategies. It aims to minimize morbidity and maximize quality of life with the objective of achieving optimal independence. The physiatrist treats persons with traumatic conditions like spinal cord injury, traumatic brain injury, amputation, and limb deformities; neurological disorders like stroke, parkinsonism, and multiple sclerosis; painful conditions like arthritis and osteoporosis; cardiopulmonary disabilities; cancer complications; disabling conditions of vision, hearing, speech, and intellect; and habilitates children with developmental disorders like cerebral palsy and autism. Physiatrists thus handle long-term and mostly lifetime care for all age groups from pediatric to geriatric. Physiatrist typically undertakes problem-based approach to rehabilitation management considering the patient's priorities and provides healthcare at primary, secondary, and tertiary level of prevention and emergency management.

Disability and rehabilitation

The WHO defines disability as an umbrella term, covering impairments, activity limitations, and participation restrictions.[382] Rehabilitation is a set of measures that assist persons with disabilities to achieve and maintain optimal functioning in interaction with their environments. It must address physical, psychological, social, educational, vocational, and recreational abilities of the person in a given environment. Rehabilitation processes need to work on two fronts (1) the person with disability (physical and psychological) and (2) the environment (living and nonliving).

Problem statement

People with disabilities are often seen as different from so-called "normal" humans. In fact, functioning and disability coexist in all human beings. The WHO made an effort to clear this issue by creating the International Classification of Functioning, Disability and Health (ICF) in the year 2001.[383] It is an integrative biopsychosocial model (Fig. 13) that provides a common language for all healthcare personnel that can be adapted for telemedicine applications.

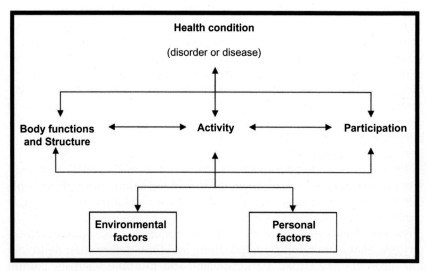

FIG. 13   Interactive model of ICF.

The WHO report on disability, 2011, indicates that 1 billion people globally experience disability, that is, every alternate household has a person with disability.[382] The underdeveloped countries and rural areas have a higher prevalence of disability but have less or no access to a physiatrist. The WHO has targeted better health for people with disabilities during its action plan 2014–21[384] that states the following:

- Half of persons with disabilities cannot afford healthcare, but they are 50% more likely to suffer catastrophic health expenditure.
- They have the same needs of general healthcare as others but are
  - twice more likely to find inadequacy in the health provider's skills and facilities,
  - thrice more likely to be denied healthcare,
  - four times more likely to be treated badly in the healthcare system.

Applying telerehabilitation

The following advantages of telerehabilitation make it very useful for healthcare of persons with disabilities:

- cutting short the time and distance between the patient's home and clinic
- overcoming accessibility problems of transport and healthcare center
- reducing cost of healthcare including consultation, therapy, equipment, admission, diet, referrals, transport, etc.
- mitigating communication barriers due to language and literacy level
- safeguarding patients from unscientific claims and miraculous cures

Telerehabilitation is available at any location and at any time and thus overcomes the following problems of rehabilitation management:

- unguided rehabilitation services offered by paramedical and rehabilitation personnel at remote locations without physiatrist's diagnosis and prescription
- difficulty in following a complex physiatric prescription at home including dose and timing of drugs, exercises, self-care activity, diet, and the use of assistive devices
- financial and psychological stress caused by lengthy admission periods
- access by the physiatrist to the home and work environment of the patient in real time to suggest necessary modifications

Diagnosis

Telerehabilitation provides a facility for the physiatrist to reach out to the patient at his home or nearby healthcare facility for specialist diagnosis. The person with disability may have difficulty in giving history due to difference in dialect, literacy level, dysphasia, mental illness, deafness, autism, blindness, intellectual deficiency, etc. As compared with only one informant who was escorting the patient in clinic but may not be well versed with the full extent of patient's problem, in the home care setting, a number of family members and friends are likely to be available to obtain the problem details and corroborate the same further.

The facility to record and retain these oral interactions translated to various languages makes it very useful for diagnosis. Thus a deaf patient may communicate his symptoms in sign language that can be interpreted and conveyed to the physician more accurately and recorded for future use. Under expert guidance over telerehabilitation, palpation and maneuvers can be conducted by the family physician within the comfort of the patient's own home while inspection and auscultation can be transmitted digitally. While a video clip of the gait and any episode of seizure is a logical tool that patients are already using to obtain a medical opinion, some forms of physical examination like manual muscle testing, range of motion, and functional independence measure can be done by paramedical staff at the bedside, and the recording transmitted digitally. Comparing the findings with older reports is essential for the diagnosis of conditions like postpolio syndrome. These findings also help to decide the line of management and to fulfill legal obligations like disability certification. Some questionnaire tools for screening of developmental disabilities can be used over telerehabilitation and thus help in early diagnosis. Investigations like electrocardiography and pulmonary function tests done bedside and transmitted in digital format help in confirming diagnosis. After having seen the doctor once, patients with less mobility find it easy to provide pathology and radiology test results over electronic media like smartphones, email, or through videoconferencing.

Physiatric prescription

The physiatric prescription includes pharmacotherapy, surgical intervention, therapeutic exercises, retraining in daily activities, assistive devices, diet, and environmental modification. Counseling the patient to follow all components of the physiatric prescription ensures success of the rehabilitation management. This is customized for each patient according to his health condition, expectation, and environment. Telerehabilitation provides direct access to the sociocultural and topographic environment of the patient at home, school, work, or any other section of his society in real time. Real-time assessment of environment through telerehabilitation makes it easy to prescribe necessary changes on a continuous basis without the need of a physical visit.

Treatment and monitoring

The physiatric prescription is executed by multiple members of the rehabilitation team that includes paramedical and rehabilitation professionals. Therapists provide exercise therapy, pain relief, gait training, speech therapy, psychotherapy, activities of daily living training, etc. Many more personnel like special educators, mobility instructors, and vocational trainers are also involved. The highly sophisticated component of the care is provided at the specially equipped rehabilitation center for a limited time period. Then these treatments continue at home by the patient himself or family and other caregivers or maybe engagement of domiciliary paramedical staff. Physiatrist can monitor the treatment on a regular basis through telerehabilitation and guide the healthcare personnel and/ or caregiver(s) for faster and directed rehabilitation. This supervision by the physiatrist lowers the complication rate with better handling as and when the complications do occur. Efforts towards direct psychotherapy, speech therapy, and physiotherapy through telerehabilitation are also under way. IoT can help monitoring of cardiorespiratory fitness during exercise schedules and alarm for maintenance of prostheses and implants like baclofen pump, and ventriculoperitoneal shunt. In this era of neuroprosthesis like functional neuromuscular stimulation and cochlear implants, the fine-tuning and maintenance of the devices can be effectively done through IoT. Reminders can be set for daily routines like drug intake, diet, exercise time, and clean intermittent catheterization.

Assistive devices

The assistive devices prescribed by physiatrist include orthoses, prostheses, mobility aids, and assistive technology. IoT can help the patient to control his environment with the help of various assistive devices. With handheld devices, CAD and CAM, bedside virtual cast can be taken from the patient's body part transmitted digitally to fabricate orthoses and prostheses in workshop at distance. The physiatrist can be present for fitment and checkout over a telerehabilitation link, and the records can be retained for future use. Mobility aids like crutches and wheelchairs can be prescribed and supplied with better suitability to the patient and his environment. The assistive technology for daily activity, mobility, communication, or environmental control can be prescribed based on the evaluation of the individual patient and his environment over the telerehabilitation link. The augmentative alternative communication devices used for autism, cerebral palsy, dysphasia, etc. can be provided, and training sessions can be arranged over telerehabilitation. A global repository of assistive technology shall make it possible to share appropriate devices for use.

Referral

Telemedicine provides a peer-to-peer referral link between family physician, physiatrist, and other specialists to improve knowledge sharing during the treatment. The referral to physiatrist is useful in pre-, peri-, and posttreatment stages in various medical and surgical conditions. For example, the presurgical planning of amputation level is essential for the success of prosthetic fitment. During various long-term illnesses, prevention and management of pressure ulcers can be best achieved with physiatric advice. Post spinal injury patients may have life-threatening complications like autonomic dysreflexia that can be managed by simply removing the inciting stimulus like impacted stools. In a similar way, referral from the physiatrist to various medical and surgical specialists over telemedicine link can facilitate rehabilitation management. AIIMS, New Delhi, India, regularly runs telerehabilitation consultations for its hospitals in rural areas and Andaman and Nicobar Islands. It also undertakes teleeducation classes for African countries to teach physiatry to, thus filling the gap of the faculty.

Community-based rehabilitation

Rehabilitation makes the person aware of his realistic potentials and enables him to decide what is best for him and thus empowering him for better inclusion in society. Community-based rehabilitation (CBR) provides suitable interventions by using community resources. CBR is the practicable modality of providing rehabilitation services at the remotest areas and is facilitated by telerehabilitation. Telerehabilitation serves to handle all the five axes of CBR[211] (Fig. 14). Health axis is managed through telemedicine as given earlier. Education axis is handled through teleeducation using hardware and software allowing special education. Livelihood axis involves skill training and upgradation, obtaining and retaining employment that is made possible through information communication technology. Social and empowerment axes involving marriage, recreation, culture, justice, advocacy, and self-help groups are already taken care by social media, but much more can be done. Thus telerehabilitation serves to be a solution for composite and comprehensive habilitation and rehabilitation of persons with disabilities.

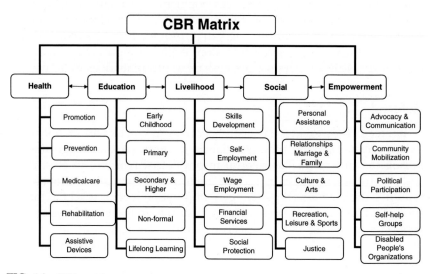

FIG. 14   CBR matrix.

Telecare during travel and for special situations

Gunnar Hartvigsen[a], Shashi Gogia[b]

[a]University of Tromsø—The Arctic University of Norway, Tromsø, Norway,
[b]Society for Administration of Telemedicine and Healthcare Informatics (SATHI), New Delhi, India

Introduction

The previous two chapters discussed situations in primary and specialized care, wherein remote support could be used to provide speedy care and efficiency while decreasing the need for travel for specialized support. The provider and the patient were in a place of their own, and for them, telecare was an add-on option to normal methods of care. We now move on to situations wherein health needs erupt outside one's own home, that is, during travel or when one is forced out of home—due to work, imprisonment or maybe even a disaster.

Before the 16th century, travel was known to be hazardous and done only out of dire necessity, like a search for food and water or an attempt to occupy new areas. Nomads or armies used to travel in large hordes wherein the health provider was always in tow. Colonization widened the scope and frequency of travel, but the focus was always work or business. From the 20th century onward, travel for tourism, adventure, and other means of enjoyment became common. As of now, tourism is a key earner for many countries. However, travelling has some special challenges related to health. There are chances of infections by newer bugs to which one has never been exposed, and hence less likely to be immune to. Different regions have different social, cultural, and economic conditions and commiserate food habits. Jet lag, when travelling in the east to west direction and changes of temperature when travelling north to south, is a cause for stress, as also the cramped conditions one undergoes while travelling.

255

The health provider in the remote locations may not be of the requisite skill and/or in all probability less aware of the social and economic conditions of the traveller. Brands and medicines differ, and tackling of insurance reimbursements is tricky. Travel-related health emergencies are special situations. One has to search for the right doctor, as your condition may not be a common one for the provider.

Then, there are situations like emergencies occurring during the travel or while on an expedition. Here, for smaller teams, retaining a full-time doctor is more expensive than actually shifting the patient for the occasional emergency. However, even this occasional need for shifting can be far costlier than providing telesupport, which can and should be attempted.

During expeditions—an example of the arctic is provided here, but it could be mountaineering, the Antarctic or other remote regions; solo long trips; etc.—any evacuation for medical reasons would mean a premature end to the same, and the adventure would be deemed as a failure. Having a doctor as part of any expedition—it is a requirement above a certain number of people—means he/she should be as competent in undertaking the adventure over and above the medical capability. The health provider will need to be given relevant training as good as any of the expedition members. But no doctor can cover all possible emergencies, so a need for remote support will always be there. Since there is going to be a lack of medical equipment and facilities—in the example provided (Box 1)—little could be done besides early evacuation, there are high chances that such functions could easily be covered remotely.

However, currently, like in the Arctic, the example provided in this chapter, as well as other remote situations, the conditions are better. The era of explorations is almost over, replaced by more or less permanent settlements. There are also excellent communication links, and hence, telecare has become somewhat mainstream.

BOX 1

BEING PHYSICALLY PRESENT DID NOT HELP MUCH!

Shashi Gogia (expedition doctor)

In the late 1970s, I used to travel with mountaineering teams as an expedition doctor. Once when one of the climbers got a frostbite, all that could be done was to assist evacuation of that person back to the base camp and further down. Being physically present did not really help the team, but did help me get acquainted to mountaineering!

Within this chapter, while the earlier sections pertain to direct health-care delivery or what would be better described as telemedicine, the last two pertain to situations outside day-to-day health delivery wherein ICT has a role. One is medical tourism where the travel itself is done for medical purposes and the other one is about how ICT helps in managing healthcare after disasters.

Maritime telemedicine

Gunnar Hartvigsen

"Telemedicine" or *medicine through telephony* came around with international shipping in the early 1920s. Its commencement was in ships that were not carrying any doctor or, at best, paramedics on board, during the voyage. This needed development of telecommunications (at that time radio communication) to address the need for physician consultations during the long travel. Immediate attention could be given with the realization that it would be hours or even days for a ship to come to shore.

The first such formalized recognition came with the International Radiotelegraph Conference in Washington in 1927. General Radio Regulations and the Additional Radio Regulations were revised. In addition, a table for the allocation of frequencies to the various services, including the broadcasting service, was established. This was subsequently expanded in the Madrid Convention of 1932.[385]

There have been significant changes during the last half century affecting the health and work safety of seafarers These include globalization of the shipping industry, automatization and mechanization, reduced number of crew in ships, increased use of short-term contracts, reflagging of ships, and multicultural crews.[386]

Telemedicine assures health provision for remote locations and tries to provide virtual support in the absence of a doctor. Improved communication has made it possible to receive telemedical advice in all parts of the world's oceans.

As per the Maritime Labour Convention (MLC), all ships carrying over 100 personnel—read crew members and/or passengers—must have a medical doctor on board if the voyage is greater than 3 days. However, most ships have 25 or fewer crew members. It is also likely that even if the doctor is present, he will need further help as many problems would be beyond his control.

In a survey done of over 100 seamen, 68% had experienced at least once, that their vessel was diverted as a consequence of a medical emergency. The average cost of such a diversion is a phenomenal 180,000 USD. Most of those surveyed, did think that the availability of expert medical advice, even on a phone, may have avoided a fair number of such evacuations.[385]

High-speed network communication between maritime activity and healthcare personnel onshore is becoming increasingly important.

Internet-based communication is essential to provide an efficient tool for improved healthcare services for seafarers. However, even though we experience a growing number of fishermen and other seafarers, access to offshore telemedicine and healthcare facilities are absent.[387,388] This could be a result of lack of adequate communication networks, absence of competent healthcare personnel (paramedics) besides a shortage of maritime, and offshore enhanced telemedicine equipment.[389] But the need is felt especially during problematic weather and when there is a fair distance increasing the time required for search and rescue (SAR) helicopters to reach a site, with reduced possibility of MEDEVAC. Seventy percent of the 100 seamen who participated in the earlier survey had additionally been on a vessel where there had been a need for a medical evacuation. They agreed that evacuation, though cheaper than a full diversion, was nevertheless far more expensive than full provision of the healthcare remotely through a telehealth system.

Emergencies experienced at sea include severed limbs, broken bones, gunshot wounds, tropical diseases, allergic reactions, and even cardiac arrest. The following telemedicine services within remote accident and emergency were found to be common. The various means of communication used included satellite, mobile, and radio[389]:

- telepresence, teleophthalmology, tele-EMS, and teleambulance (32%)
- teleconsultation (27%)
- telecardiology (12%)
- teleradiology (8%)
- teledermatology (7%)
- telemonitoring (5%)
- tele-ENT (3%)
- teleeducation (3%)
- radio medical advice (3%)

TMAS

The International Labor Organization (ILO) convention 164[390] states that all seafaring nation shall have a center for maritime Telemedical Assistance Service (TMAS), which offer medical advice on a 24/7 basis: "The competent authority shall ensure by a prearranged system that medical advice by radio or satellite communication to ships at sea, including specialist advice, is available at any hour of the day or night" (Article 7).

TMAS have been organized differently by the seafaring nations that have ratified the ILO convention. For example, Italy and Spain have established dedicated organizations for telemedicine service for ships. In countries like Norway, Sweden, Denmark, and Germany, designated physicians work in hospital units called Maritime Rescue Coordination Center (MRCC) to offer the service.

Radio Medico Norway

Radio Medico Norway provides medical assistance to ships in need of help for diagnosing and treatment of diseases and injuries. The service is free of charge and accessible 24/7 and offered to everybody independent of nationality. Medical assistance is offered in English and Norwegian. The first contact is done by voice/phone. If possible, e-mail with attachments and video consultations may be used after contact with the physician. In 2015, Radio Medico Norway did more than 3500 consultations and treated over 1200 patients worldwide.

Radio Medico Norway is a part of Norwegian Centre for Maritime Medicine at Haukeland University Hospital in Bergen, Norway. Physicians are on duty for one week at a time. As per need, all specialist departments at the Haukeland University Hospital can be made available through Radio Medico Norway. The more relevant departments also have in-house equipment for video consultations. Radio Medico Norway may be contacted directly, and all calls will be answered. However, most of the calls are routed through Rogaland radio (https://telenorkulturarv.no/en/rogaland-radio). There is a great interest in using two-way video between shore and ships. Inmarsat BGAN offers streaming of video with a binary speed of 385 kb/s, which is satisfactory for high-quality live pictures.

According to Radio Medico Norway, software solutions that can organize a consultation with filing of case record, pictures, ECG, and vital parameters such as oxygen saturation, pulse, and blood pressure are available on the market. However, they are not yet widely available onboard ships. The number of calls differs from zero to six/seven consultations per day with an average of three. Most of the calls could be managed by a GP since more than 95% of calls are trivial in nature. The remaining 5% call is for problems of a higher grade—generally accidents and injuries.

Even if the medical problems arising on board a ship mostly are trivial, the physician must have a solid insight in the special conditions prevailing in seafaring. He/she must know the possibilities and the limitation of therapeutic options, the medicines and equipment present on board, and the possibilities for evacuation of personnel in all waters and must be well trained in communication technique, especially maritime communication.

Telemedicine in commercial aviation

U.S. Mohalanobish

Historically, DELAG, Deutsche Luftschiffahrts-Aktiengesellschaft, was the world's first airline. It was founded on November 16, 1909, and operated airships manufactured by the Zeppelin Corporation. Its headquarters were in Frankfurt. The first fixed wing scheduled air service was started on January 1, 1914, from St. Petersburg, Florida, to Tampa, Florida. The four oldest airlines that still exist are Netherland's KLM (1919), Colombia's Avianca (1919), Australia's Qantas (1921), and the Czech Republic's Czech Airlines (1923).[391,392] The need for telemedicine use within commercial aviation came about in its post-World War 2 expansion following the development of the jet engines, bigger planes, and longer flights.

Incidence

Statistics of in-flight medical problems are somewhat difficult to come by. The exact incidence remains unknown because minor events do not need to be reported and there is, as yet, no central data repository cataloguing all events that require medical care.

The US National Transportation Safety Board requires that only those in-flight events that resulted in hospitalization for more than 48 h, a major fracture (except finger, nose, or toe) or injury to an internal organ, need to be reported as an accident. An FAA study found that 1132 such medical emergencies occurred during flights in the United States during 1996 and 1997, correlating to an incidence of more than one and a half per day.

Reported common problems included the following:

1. vasovagal attacks (syncope) (22%)
2. cardiac (20%)
3. neurological (12%)
4. respiratory (8%)
5. gastrointestinal (8%).

Of these 1132 incidents, 145 flights resulted in an emergency diversion. Fifteen (1.3%) were fatal, and the cause in all, but two, was cardiac in origin.[393]

The influence of space medicine

Manned space flights opened up the world of telemedicine in its fullest sense. Medical management and monitoring of all body parameters in all manned space flights including the long voyages on the Mir Space Station has been made possible through telemedicine.

All astronauts and cosmonauts are indoctrinated in fundamentals of medicine and made familiar with the limited medications and drugs they carry on board. However, in case of any ailment developing in flight, regular teleconsultations over voice line or video calls where available are resorted to for resolving medical ailments. Besides, all space crew undergo extensive monitoring of their physiological and psychological parameters on a daily basis. All parameters are sent to earth by telemetry in real time in most cases for subsequent processing.

India has had only one cosmonaut in space so far. That was Sqn Ldr Rakesh Sharma in 1984. Like all, his ECG and other parameters were telemetered. In addition, his vectorcardiogram (VCG) reports were collected and stored in flight and analyzed after return of the spacecraft to earth.[394]

The change

Communication links between airplanes and ground control have been a necessity for flight control and safety since long. Wi-Fi availability through satellite links is now routinely offered to passengers. Though links are still uncertain and possibly erratic, a passenger or onboard physician can consult a telephysician mid-flight. The least would be facilitation of an early pickup of the prescription though an airport pharmacy once the plane lands.

Limitations of telemedicine in aviation

There are few fundamental challenges to telemedicine in commercial flights, namely,

1. the legal issues
2. state of technology for telemetering live records in real time
3. availability of medically trained manpower onboard aircrafts
4. limited availability of medicines and medical equipment on board

Legal issues

Medical practice is legally restricted within a specific geographic zone for a doctor, normally within a country and in some larger countries like the United States, even within states of the same country. There have been no changes yet made to these legal regulations to cover cross border care (see Chapter 13).

With millions of people flying on thousands of flights each day, there is a real opportunity for provider expansion, bringing telehealth to passengers across the world. Some companies have begun to offer certain contracted telehealth services for airline crews and emergencies. By the mid-1980s, MedAire had become the world's largest provider of telemedicine service for commercial and general aviation. It provides in-flight emergency medical kits and crew training.[395]

The business models in this type of service are as follows:

Model 1: Telehealth for flight staff, including aircrew, cabin crew, and other flight personnel. The contracts are made with the airlines directly. Contracting airlines are provided health cover for their staff working through long shifts, during flights, and layovers in unfamiliar cities and airports with provision of online consultations for routine ailments, besides emergencies. Telehealth is an obvious convenience for this population. The individual can take medication on return, without filing a sickness report, whereas the airline gets the benefits of low absenteeism and fewer sick days. Economically, this may be more beneficial for the airline rather than hiring fixed ground-based healthcare support, which most airlines/employers in any case provide for. Minor ailments and emergencies are covered from a single source telehealth provider.

Model 2: Offering in-flight telehealth services directly to passengers. This needs technology support and with a broadband Internet on board. This model takes the same business approach as existing on-ground direct-to-patient interactions, only that it is in flight. The restrictions of this model have already been discussed earlier, but, at least, the passenger has a prescription that can be serviced at the airport of landing. This, more or less, is a replacement for on-site attendance. Commonly heard in-flight announcements like "Is there a doctor on board?" get minimized. The telehealth physician would be available to provide expert opinion and oversight of the trained airline crew to better manage the patient until the plane lands. The patient benefits with a greater care oversight that only a telemedicine emergency physician can offer. The airline benefits by promoting this innovative health and safety measure to its passengers and crew.

None of these potential models are mutually exclusive, and the telehealth provider can possibly build an arrangement combining all elements. Regardless of the business model chosen, there are two problems already discussed earlier:

(a) Licensing issues for the telehealth provider. That is, licensing is valid only for specific and predefined geographic locations and does not transcend national and sometimes even state boundaries.
(b) Privacy and security. Maintaining the privacy and security of patient health information, which is mandated under several state and national law of the country where the flight is. The comfort of personal communication with a doctor in person can never be fulfilled.

Even with these drawbacks, with more people travelling, longer flights, and advancements in technology, the opportunity for in-flight services will continue to increase. Taking telehealth to the airline industry is just one of the opportunities that providers of healthcare services can leverage to ushering in current models of telehealthcare and bring the doctor to the patient.

Arctic telemedicine

Andre Henriksen

Alaska (the United States), Finland, Iceland, Norway, Greenland (Denmark), Russia, Canada, and Sweden make up the eight Arctic countries. Together with Antarctica, they have some of the harshest weather conditions on the planet, which may include heavy snow, high-speed winds, extreme low temperature, and permafrost. The polar day, a period when the sun does not set for several months in the summer, and the polar night, when the sun does not rise for several months during the winter, are another characteristic of the Arctic and Antarctic regions. When implementing telemedicine services in these regions, additional challenges exist and must be addressed.

The distance between communities in these regions can be very long, and travel time to the nearest hospital can take a long time or even be impossible during the extreme cases of bad weather. In 2008 a person stationed at the Antarctica Troll research station[396] suffered a complicated leg fracture. With no operating room and limited surgical equipment, the team doctor, assisted by the cook who acted as a makeshift nurse, operated the broken leg with assistance from doctors at a Norwegian hospital via a satellite phone. Because of extremely bad weather, it took 2 weeks before a plane could land and evacuate the injured man to a hospital in Cape Town for further treatment.

In 2000 the Arctic Telemedicine Project Final Report—a project run by the Arctic Council—felt that acceptable healthcare in the Arctic regions is possible through telemedicine.[397] However, it felt the need for more work in the following four areas before trying to implement any telemedicine services in Arctic communities: physical infrastructure, training structures, interoperability guidelines, and community interface.

The available *physical infrastructure* must be carefully considered to make sure it is adequate for the planned service. In addition to stable power, working and online communication lines, with sufficient bandwidth, must be available. Extreme weather and the cold climate may interfere with transmitting equipment. The polar regions also suffer from multiple issues due to the curvature of the earth. Solar flare interference (i.e., aurora borealis/aurora australis) gathers on the poles and can render radio and radio telephones useless for extended periods. Similarly, during the polar day, satellites will often be directly in front of the Sun, further interrupting communications. In addition, the signal strength of passing satellites is often weaker close to the poles, which can make it necessary to install large and expensive receiving equipment.

A *training structures* plan, taking the time, cost of continuous education of new, and existing local health providers into account, must also be in place. In order for any telemedicine service to work over time, it is paramount that knowledge about how to operate the equipment is available at the Arctic location.

Interoperability guidelines for successful and secure transfer of health record and patients' health data must also be considered and implemented. Standards, especially medical coding, help avoid confusion and consequent delays in treatment. From the clinician's viewpoint safe and secure transfer of patient health records are also important.

The *community interface* is also an important focus area. This includes training of locals who will need to service the equipment, finding the optimal solution for local health providers to utilize the service, understanding cultural differences in what is considered healthcare, identifying the actual healthcare need of the local population, and aligning oneself with local cultural agents who will speak warmly of the provided service, to name a few. In short, it is important to find ways to make sure the receiving population will embrace the service and receive the best possible benefits from it.

A high number of telemedicine services have been successfully implemented in the Norwegian Arctic,[398] even while several other Arctic regions have a huge potential for similar services. Five challenging areas that need to be addressed have been identified to improve access and quality of care to Arctic residents. These are to (1) identify relevant services, (2) use recognized health ICT standards, (3) use suitable solutions for system interoperability, (4) identify funding opportunities, and (5) focus on privacy.

A systematic review of telemedicine services implemented in the arctic regions in 2016[389] found deployment of a large range of telemedicine services. These included teleinterpretation, teleambulance, teleconsultation, teleradiology, teleeducation, teledermatology, tele-ENT, telemonitoring, and telecardiology. It discussed additional challenges of Arctic telemedicine systems like extreme weather, lack of adequate communication networks, lack of trained personnel, and lack of appropriate equipment specialized for Arctic usage.

One example of a successful implementation of an Arctic telemedicine system for sharing patient data and providing medical consultations in acute medical situations is the videoconferencing acute medical conference (VAKe) telemedicine service.[399,400] At the remote location, VAKe consists of a wall-mounted camera, a remote-controlled ceiling camera, and microphones. At the acute unit at the University Hospital of North Norway (UNN), sound, video, and vital signs from the patients are received in real time. VAKe was used in August 2011 when a polar bear attacked a camp of youths from the British School Exploring Society (BSES) in Spitsbergen (Svalbard, Norway). One was killed and four sustained severe injuries. The surviving youths were helicoptered to Longyearbyen hospital, a small hospital not equipped for major surgeries. The flight to the Norwegian mainland is 1.5h, so using the VAKe system, a team of specialist surgeons at UNN assisted local doctors at Longyearbyen hospital to perform surgery on several head and neck injuries.[401,402] Outcomes of this tragic polar bear attack, would likely have been worse if this telemedicine service (VAKe) had not been in place.

Most successful implementations of Arctic telemedicine are onshore solutions. When working offshore (e.g., on oil rigs or fishing boats), existing Artic challenges are enhanced with long travel distances over water, poor communication, and extreme weather. As such, travel time for search and rescue helicopters to the Arctic takes a long time, reducing the time the rescue team has to find and assist people in need. During extreme weather conditions, these trips can be very dangerous or even impossible.[403]

Arctic telemedicine has been provided in one shape or another for almost as long as the telephone became available in Arctic/Antarctic regions. The downward trend in the amount of published literature on telemedicine in Arctic and extreme weather locations between 1995 and 2015[403] has not been accompanied by the same reduction, in other related fields like "maritime and offshore" and "remote accident and emergency." With improvement in communication technology like bandwidth and communication stability, these services will inevitably also encompass the Arctic and Antarctic regions too in upcoming years. Interest in these regions is increasing, from academic and government circles with a continuous presence through research stations. Commercial interests also rule alongside, related to increasing activity in both the oil and fishing industries in these regions. A concomitant increase in the need of health services is inevitable and can only be supplied through telemedicine services.

Telemedicine for prison populations

Suzanne Bakken and Anthony Pho

Background

Prisoners have higher rates of health problems than the general population including chronic diseases such as high blood pressure, asthma, and arthritis.[404] The most common health problems in prisoners include mental health (e.g., anxiety/depression); addiction and substance use; and communicable diseases such as HIV/AIDS, hepatitis C, and tuberculosis.[405,406] While, in some countries such as the United States, prisoners have a constitutional right to healthcare. Overcrowding and limited availability of healthcare professionals such as registered nurses, nurse practitioners, social workers, and doctors make healthcare delivery a considerable challenge in the prison setting.

Telemedicine

Telemedicine (also known as telehealth) is an innovative solution to delivering healthcare to prisoners. The Institute of Medicine[407] defines telemedicine as the use of electronic information and communication technologies to provide and support healthcare when distance separates the participants. Telemedicine may be synchronous, whereby a real-time two-way audio and video connection replaces the in-person, face-to-face visit.[408] It may involve asynchronous or delayed communication as well. For example, a medical provider might take a photo of a skin lesion and send it to a dermatologist with expertise in diagnosing skin conditions for assistance in determining what the lesion is and how to treat it. Telemedicine is a cost-effective solution for prison health because it enables prisons to address the needs of prisoners without the need of adding healthcare staff within the prison. Some examples of telemedicine solutions for the most common health problems in prison populations are discussed in the succeeding text.

Mental health

The lack of proper psychiatric services in prisons can lead to inmate populations with higher numbers of untreated mental illnesses, which can lead to increased violent behavior. This can have direct impact to the well-being of prisoners and prison staff alike. Telepsychiatry is a version of telemedicine focused on the delivery of mental healthcare. This care delivery method could involve a psychiatrist or other mental health professional remotely providing talk therapy using audio and/or video technology. Telepsychiatry has been implemented in prisons in at least six states (Arizona, California, Georgia, Kansas, Ohio, and West Virginia) in the United States increasing the number of inmates served. For example, a telemedicine services unit in the California prison system was able to treat 4400 prison inmates annually in 27 prisons (California Legislative Analyst's Office, 2007). Studies show that telepsychiatry is an effective means of delivering mental health services to those who would otherwise be difficult to reach.[404]

Substance abuse

There is a high rate of substance abuse and dependence in both incarcerated males and females.[409] Substance abuse treatment using telemedicine has been validated with multiple interventions.[410] Substance abuse treatment generally requires repeat sessions with a clinician over an extended period. In the prison setting, this becomes challenging if there is no clinician onsite with substance abuse treatment expertise or only one clinician for many prisoners who need treatment. Moving large numbers of prisoners to another treatment facility is usually not tenable. Delivering multiple sessions via telemedicine is more cost-effective and logistically feasible than previous strategies.[411]

Communicable diseases

HIV/AIDS, hepatitis C, and tuberculosis are communicable diseases that are prevalent among prisoners. Each of these conditions require specialized care, and prisons may lack appropriately certified and trained healthcare providers. HIV/AIDS is particularly prevalent in prison populations with rates about three times that of the general population.[412] A complicating matter for inmates with HIV is the fact that transporting inmates with HIV to healthcare providers with appropriate training may be cost prohibitive for the prison system. A study showed that care delivered by HIV specialists over video telehealth was superior to care delivered in person by providers without HIV specialty training when considering disease outcomes such as viral suppression.[413]

Emergency care

Incarcerated individuals may require emergency care in prisons. Studies have shown that telemedicine is effective for evaluating prisoners and preventing unnecessary emergency department visits.[414] The combination of a nurse in consultation with a physician via telemedicine enables the provision of limited emergency care in remote prison settings. Moreover, telemedicine decreases wait time for patients with emergent conditions.[415]

Conclusion

Prison populations clearly have a number of obstacles to receiving care for their health problems. With limited numbers of healthcare professionals providing care to many incarcerated individuals, solutions that maximize existing resources are ideal. Telemedicine is an innovative strategy that has been proven to provide remote healthcare without sacrificing quality.

Medical tourism

Anandhi Ramachandran

In summary

Medical tourism is an emerging trend where patients travel to overseas destinations for specialized procedures and other forms of medical care.[416] Medical tourism, health tourism, and medical travel are somewhat interrelated terms[29] related to a variation in the amount of motivation, procedure(s) performed, and the involved stakeholders, the biggest motivation being the spiralling cost of healthcare in developed countries. Lower pricing for most procedures, aided by technological advancements, Joint Commission International (JCI) accreditation, aggressive and targeted marketing to customers, travel insurance availability, and offer of quality and personalized services are contributory factors influencing medical tourism, which are, in turn, integrated into the wider tourism industry. Culture, social beliefs, value-added services, government policies, and availability of care also influence medical tourism behavior. Affordable cross border travel aids these movements. Another key driver is the access to healthcare information and advertising provided by the Internet.

Introduction

Medical tourism is a combination of two service industries, healthcare and tourism. The terminology is generally interchanged with the term "health tourism,"[416] though there is a slight difference between the two. Medical tourism described as medical outsourcing is the act of travelling from one's home country to another country to receive medical care that includes advanced treatment and procedures like cancer treatment, knee replacement, heart surgery, dental treatment[417] and cosmetic care at a cheaper cost and combining this with a vacation in the country they are visiting. Health tourism is related to health and wellness care like spa, yoga, and meditation. People are taught how to relieve stress, how to have healthy eating habits, and how to prevent sports-related injuries. Health tourism is defined as the organized travel outside one's local environment for the maintenance, enhancement, or restoration of an individual's well-being in mind and body. Traditionally two decades ago, people used to travel to developed countries to receive high-quality medical care. Currently, there is a change in the scenario with more people travelling from developed countries to developing countries like Thailand, Singapore, Brazil, Greece, Jordan, Malaysia,[418,419] Hong Kong, Hungary, India, and Israel to receive medical care. Asian countries are the main preferred medical tourism locations.

Reasons for growth of medical tourism

The most cited motivation for such travel is lower cost of treatment at the visited locations compared with the tourist-generating countries. The motivation increases when the problems faced are either not covered by insurance—say cosmetic surgery or dental treatment—or when there is an unnecessarily high waiting period for a procedure, more relevant for countries like the United Kingdom and Canada.

Medical tourism can be of two types: obligatory or elective. The former occurs when treatment is unavailable or illegal in the place of origin. The latter includes elective procedures, which, although available at the place of origin, may be delivered more quickly or in a more cost-effective manner in another location.

Hospitals in the visited countries adopt a number of branding strategies to attract medical tourists.[416] An important one is hospital accreditation. The most sought after form is the Joint Commission International (JCI)[420]—a not-for-profit American organization that provides standards and qualifications for medical facilities. This needs to be in addition to accreditation from their own medical boards. For example, India has National Accreditation Board for Hospitals and Healthcare Providers[421] (NABH) and Thailand has The Institute of Hospital Quality Improvement and Accreditation[422] (HQIA). Other motivating factors are availability of third-party insurance (medical and travel), better medical infrastructure facilities, governmental activities to improve quality of hospitals, and promotion of tourist attractions. Technological advancements of medical devices, fascination for alternative treatment, changing patient demography, affordable cross border travel facilities, and plethora of specialized websites targeting medical tourism are further pushing the patients to look for medical visits outside their countries. Major chunk of the medical tourists are uninsured individuals maybe because of retirement or nearing retirement. Another major push factor is that the healthcare system in Western countries is beginning to crack under pressure due to rising costs and changes in health policies.

Pros and cons of medical tourism

There are many advantages of booming medical tourism both to the country providing the facilities and to the individual seeking the facility. The host country gets an increase in foreign exchange earnings, improvement in quality of care provision, increased strategic alliances with other organizations both within and outside the country, greater employment opportunity, information, technology and knowledge sharing, growth of tourism industry side by side, social and cross-cultural experience, global marketing and medical trade relations, brand image of nation as world class healthcare destination, and improvement in medical infrastructure facilities.[423] The advantage gained by the individual is that they get quality care at low cost and in a relaxed environment. Many undergo recuperation after medical treatment in relaxing and luxurious spots in the host country.

While there are many benefits associated with undergoing medical treatment in foreign countries other than own, there are few disadvantages too.[424] If the medical tourist does not have full information regarding the treating doctors and the hospitals or if they opt for hospitals and providers based only on low cost, they might be at risk. In addition, in many countries, the medical licensing may not be regulated properly, and the lack of requisite legal procedures to address the issues may cause problems. Most of the hospitals offering medical tourism facilities do have an ethics board, grievance redressal mechanism, and SOPs for patient safety and quality of care. However, in any event of glitch during the care especially because of procedure—which is what they have come for—they try to placate the patient. Creating a legal issue in the way it would be handled in his or her own country is challenging for the patient. Being new to the country, such medical tourists are at a disadvantage in recruiting the service of an appropriate legal advisor in case of malpractice. Being on a budget or limited stay plan, any unforeseen complications like blood clots or pulmonary embolism, which may be related to inadequate postoperative care or travelling back to their own country too early, can have devastating consequences.

Medical tourism stakeholders

The major stakeholders are providers (hospitals and physicians), payers (healthcare insurance companies and third-party administration), drug manufacturers (clinical research and bulk drug outsourcing), and pharmacy chains in addition to the patients. Another significant stakeholder is the growing population of intermediaries (medical tourism companies). Opportunities are diffused by word of mouth and through targeted advertising and marketing.

The profile of the patients (age, gender, and education), their social and cultural beliefs regarding treatment, and their purchasing power all need to be considered while providing healthcare. The type of package includes core medical services like health plans, A-Z surgeries, and at times value-added services like airport pickup and drop facility, arranging stay for the patient's attendant, availability of a translator, availability of ethnic food, prayer room, and gym. Services like pretravel guidance, preoperative investigations, consultations and medications, and understanding of admission process to discharge facilities are other value-added services offered. Differential pricing strategy customized for the patients are used for targeting the medical tourists.

Telehealth/telemedicine and medical tourism

The benefits of telemedicine to medical tourism are plentiful. Telemedicine offers preventive and curative healthcare services from a distance through E-consultations, E-diagnosis, e-mail exchanges between physicians, and remote surgeries.[425] Before the patient travels a preevaluation encounter can be carried out with the exchange of complete medical records. Appointments can be scheduled, and the patients can get to know the services offered by the hospital where they plan to undergo treatment. As the patient is new to the medical tourism offering country, there are third-party organizations that coordinate and arrange the patients travel and stay through teleconsultations. While the patient is undergoing treatment, the primary care physician can participate in all care process and can be an observer of the surgeries remotely. Similarly, telemedicine allows for follow-up remote monitoring and consultation after the patient goes back.

Fast-growing mobile technologies, cloud services, web-based real-time communication, large wireless networks, virtual care solutions, improved videoconferencing technology, and wireless sensors all have enabled and promoted the use of telemedicine-based remote monitoring and care provision. Medical devices and wireless sensors connected to servers and worn by the patients or installed at home that can measure, track, and report patient's vital signs and conditions in real time are used. The information is then transferred wirelessly or via the Internet to medical databases and the healthcare professionals. Cloud based systems—which are the current norm, make the data more accessible. Patients can access their clinical data and carry it to any doctor in the system. The system allows sharing of high-quality medical photographs, X-rays, CT scans, MRI scans, PET scans, and other images among doctors and specialists, and thereby help to provide an insight into the patient's diagnosis. Telemedicine is not just for physical conditions, but also for mental health patients, Alzheimer patients who need treatment, but cannot receive the treatment due to a lack of mental health professionals in their area, can be helped beyond physical borders. Development of telemedicine facilities and data standards is an important factor for implementation. With the dynamic expansion of digital technology, it is expected that there will be plethora of user-friendly telehealth platforms that will give a further boom to the growing medical tourism industry.

Conclusions

Medical tourists travel to other countries for medical treatment due to low costs or insufficient availability as compared with within their own country. However, cheaper costs alone are insufficient to attract such tourists. Other factors like provision of health services at par with the tourist-generating countries offered range of service (e.g., Ayurveda in India), quality of the care, accreditation, and value-added services, and all are important factors to be considered when attempting to develop such a service. Nevertheless, medical tourism has become a growing industry in parallel with other forms of tourism. Use of mobile-based monitoring, cloud computing, and wireless sensors are contributing to the growth of telecare and of medical tourism.

Telehealth in disasters

Shashi Gogia

Disaster management is an exceptionally important application of telemedicine. This section discusses how ICT helps to manage the consequences of cataclysmic events such as natural disasters and terrorist attacks on the health of populations.

Disasters (*synonyms: cataclysm, calamity, tragedy, act of God, etc.*) are sudden accidents causing great damage or loss of life. These can be of the following types:

- **Natural disasters**: Pompei in Italy is an example of how the *volcanic eruption* wiped out the entire population of a town. Fortunately the houses and roads remained as is, so the place is an excellent tourist spot describing life during the Roman empire.[426] *Earthquakes* and *tsunamis* are consequential of the continuous migration northward of the tectonic plates from Gondwanaland,[427] which started around 200 million years back. Whether the movement is being accelerated by humans is debated. But others like *floods, hurricanes, landslides, and fires* are related to human activity directly or through climate change, with some a direct result of human error, like forest fires or a dam breach.
- **Environmental emergencies** include technological or industrial accidents occurring during production, utilization, or transportation of hazardous material. The Bhopal gas tragedy (1984) and Chernobyl nuclear leak (1986) are among the most well-known.
- **Complex emergencies** involving a breakdown of authority; looting; and attacks on strategic installations, including conflict situations and war.
- **Pandemics**—SARS, ZIKA, Ebola, bird and swine flu, etc.

As per the United Nations charter, a disaster can be defined as a serious disruption in the functioning of a community or a society, which exceeds an ability to cope from within its own resources. All disasters have health concerns, and the last groups (pandemics) are direct public health concerns. Some diseases like PTSD—first described after the first Gulf war—are directly linked with disasters.

Disaster management can be defined as organization and management of resources and responsibilities for dealing to lessen the impact of disasters. Disasters, by nature, are chaotic, and hence, health provision to the large numbers affected in a timely fashion is a challenge. The need for health support goes beyond any systems' capabilities, and alongside, any existing capability may already be comprised by the disaster itself. Once we understand that the main contributions of ICT to healthcare are through increasing reach, providing speedy access along with improvement in efficiency, the role of telecare in disasters becomes apparent (Fig. 1).

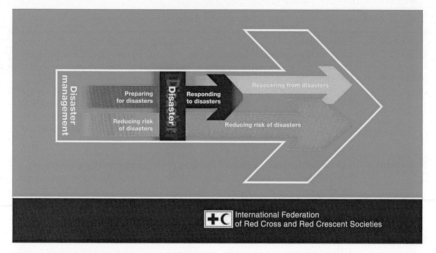

FIG. 1 Systematic approach to disaster management. Graphic curtsey International Federation of Red Cross (www.ifrc.org).

Disaster management has traditionally been divided into four phases and Health ICT has a role in all. The accompanying Table 1 describes these in detail.

Recent coordination of efforts to control disasters has been successful. The older concern that "More people die of aftereffects of natural disaster than the disaster itself" is no longer true. Deaths beyond the first 2–3 days are also relatively uncommon, at least in the developed countries—nowhere was this more exemplified when one compared the number of deaths in Haiti earthquake in 2010 (230,000) with that occurring following the Chile earthquake (708) in the same year.

However, disaster management is a challenge. Disasters are chaotic; whatever infrastructure existed before has broken down; there is a dire need for evacuation of affected personnel, a reverse flow of a specialized type of transport, while the existing population is short of supplies with a mismatch between needs and services.

ICT systems help in weaving though this chaos. The Sahana[428] project— initiated as a web-based public service by IBM after the 2004 tsunami in Sri Lanka—is an example. It has since been used in many other disasters and included as a core element of the disaster response coordination council of the Philippines government. Its main modules include the following:

- Sahana Missing Person Registry
- Sahana Organization Registry
- Sahana Shelter Registry
- Sahana Request/Aid Management System
- Sahana Volunteer Coordination System
- Sahana Situation Awareness

TABLE 1 Stages of disaster management and where does ICT have a role.

Phase	Description *Key care provider*	Components	How can ICT contribute
Mitigation	Prevent or minimize effects of disaster. *Government/local bodies*	Building codes and zoning, vulnerability analyses (high-risk individuals/communities), public education	Population and health facilities database with GPS localization. Personal and campaign level education through the Internet
Preparedness	Planning how to respond *Specialized agencies/ government*	Plans, emergency exercises and drills, training, warning systems. Evacuation in anticipation	Virtual simulations, scenario creations, support for evacuation, tele-training creating an ICT-enabled emergency workforce
Response	After the disaster. Three phases, **immediate** (0–2 days), **intermediate** (3–15 days), and **late** (15–60 days) *(All) large and small NGOs especially relief agencies, individuals, and governments*	*Immediate:* search and rescue, emergency relief, need-based evacuation and referral to hospital, *intermediate* food and sanitation supplies, temporary shelters, treatment camps, *late* continuation of intermediate and monitoring, PTSD	*Immediate*—GPS locators, sensors, teleconsults, telementoring, assisted evacuations, keeping hospital ready, *Intermediate*—monitoring of health indices, supply chain management. *Late*—see succeeding text
Recovery or rehabilitation	Two months to two or more years *Governments and local bodies*	Temporary housing, grants, rehabilitative care. Learnings to help transfer back to mitigation phase	Disease prevention, Creating a balanced health infrastructure, telesupport for long-term effects like PTSD, public health support, supply chain

Later supplementary efforts by Sahana include support for mental health especially children, but for this, the efforts by SATHI,[429] planned as telemental support project for those affected by the 2004 Tsunami in India, are better known. SATHI did an initial survey that clarified that a need for mental health support exists through needs assessment, did orientation, capacity building, etc. to result in online consultations and care by psychiatrists 400 km away. The efforts continue to this day as a telepsychiatry project run by the concerned psychiatric hospital run by the Schizophrenia Research Foundation (SCARF). The project faced many issues like lack of connectivity and absence of trained relief workers who could identify incumbent PTSD in the community. However, the hard work paid off with great satisfaction and suicide reduction.[a]

The work by SATHI underlined how breakdown of existing telesystems by the disaster affects the relief process. Telephone exchanges had got flooded. The introduction of mobile connectivity 4G has improved the situation of late but did not exist at that time.

Due to infrastructure constraints, ICT, supposedly an equalizer, allowing developing countries to leap frog to the modern era, has, in many places, actually increased the gap between the haves and have nots, not only between nations but also within communities.

The 2015 Chennai floods in India resulted almost overnight, in many online solutions for managing its general and health aspects. However, issues related to power failure and poor reach of networks which made online access impossible, surfaced much later. The better connected people had better online access, could go faster to places and also articulate their needs through social media like Facebook, Twitter, and WhatsApp.[430] Thus worse off areas remained relatively ignored, at least initially.

Chennai's spontaneous efforts through social media seemed to call for a response only. However, the full cycle of mitigation, preparedness, etc., had been missing. There was a lack of coordination especially between the locals and those trying to help from beyond the affected area. Many offered solutions were irrelevant to needs.[431] Sent food had prescriptive advice of preliminary good washing notwithstanding that clean water availability was a bigger problem than the food! Online solutions for disaster relief, like Sahana,[428] did help, but gaps in utilizing ICT to the fullest extent were evident.[20]

In summary

An existing ICT infrastructure with support personnel trained in its use especially telecare, can help early recovery from the health problems associated with disasters.

[a]See note and photograph in the telepsychiatry section in the previous chapter.

12

Mobile health (mHealth)

Sriram Iyengar
University of Arizona College of Medicine, Phoenix, AZ, United States

Introduction

One of the most exciting technological developments over the last few years has been mobile health, also known as mHealth. Various definitions of mHealth exist. According to the United States' National Institutes of Health "mHealth is the use of mobile and wireless devices to improve health outcomes, healthcare services, and health research."[433] The World Health Organization defines mHealth very broadly as "The use of mobile and wireless technologies to support the achievement of health objectives."[434] mHealth has been enabled by a vast amount of progress over the last 10 years in miniaturizing phones and physiological sensors and combining communication devices and computers into highly reliable and very portable devices.

Today, mHealth is enabled by three kinds of mobile phones, so-called basic phones, feature phones, and smartphones, and a host of miniaturized devices that collect health-related data including activity measurement. Basic phones support only text messaging besides making calls. Feature phones add multimedia display capabilities in a small form factor. For example, the Motorola RAZR, one of the most popular feature phones, had a small color display about 15.2 cm squared in area. These phones, often based on the SYMBIAN operating system, had some limited programming capabilities.

On the other hand, smartphones are very powerful computers with high-resolution color displays and excellent graphics that also function as communication devices for voice, access to the Internet, and two-way transfer of video and image communications. There are additional add-ons, like connectivity through Wi-Fi, infrared and bluetooth, and special sensors that can be and are being used for health apps. These include cameras with a very high degree of clarity—25+ megapixels (on high-end phones) for still image and video capture, touchscreen, gyroscope (orientation sensor), accelerometer (or motion sensor), and location awareness (GPS).

277

In developed countries, basic phones and feature phones have largely been replaced by smartphones like the Apple iPhone, Samsung Galaxy, Google Nexus, and similar. Smartphones tend to be expensive, and so in developing countries, basic phones and feature phones still predominate. However, even here, smartphones mostly based on the Android operating system are rapidly increasing in ownership and usage. Although feature phones have limited computing capabilities, they can still be used to obtain and transmit health-related data. For example, text messages can be transmitted using short message service (SMS).

mHealth can be viewed as a form of telemedicine/telehealth since the phone can be used to transmit and receive health-related data over distances. The SMS feature of mobile phones enables patients and health workers located remotely to rapidly send text messages and images containing health data to remote medical facilities and specialists who can then respond with expert advice using the same means. Mobile phones enable this communication to occur from the location of the person needing medical advice, which could be anywhere, like their home or an injury scene, rather than having to transport the patient to a clinic. This "anywhere" capability is provided by basic mobile phones, feature phones, and, of course, smartphones. Advanced software on smartphones, such as WhatsApp, offer secure, fast, and easy two-way transmittal of images, text, and video. Secure communications provided by WhatsApp are particularly desirable in the medical context since it supports provider-patient confidentiality. It should be noted that in such an exchange, the medical knowledge/expertise is provided from a remote location.

However, since smartphones are essentially very powerful computers capable of storing large amounts (16–128 Gb or more) of data, a vast amount of medical knowledge can be stored in the phone itself in the form of apps and databases. This is a powerful capability enabling medical knowledge, advice, and expertise to be available not only anywhere but also anytime. This should be contrasted with some common kinds of telemedicine in which the person needing medical care is interacting directly with the medical expert by phone or by video conference. In such a scenario the telemedicine hardware and software enable geographical distances to shrink, while patient and medical specialist are in synchronous two-way communication, and the expertise is transmitted synchronously. Of course, this means that a busy medical specialist has to find the time to participate in the remote encounter with the patient or their local caregiver and could be delayed or unable to participate at the scheduled time due to unexpected events. In other words, scheduling time from a busy remote specialist or medical expert could be challenging. The local caregiver could be a physician, health worker, or a family member. On the other hand, making medical expertise available inside the smartphone itself enables *asynchronous* medical care scenarios. For example, if a frontline health worker needs to assess a patient's mental health state, instead of calling for help, describing the symptoms, and then getting advice, the health worker could bring up an app that executes the Suicidal Behaviors Questionnaire-Revised (SBQ-R)[435] consisting of four multiple choice questions. The health worker could obtain responses to the questionnaire from the patient on the spot and almost instantly get advice that helps in decision-making. Specifically, the app-score may indicate that the individual is at high risk and needs transportation to the nearest mental health clinic. Or the app could indicate low risk, and the patient's mental state could be alleviated by soothing his/her feelings with the assistance of family and friends. Certain benefits of mHealth can be identified in this scenario. One is that the care is immediate and possible anytime/anywhere. Second is that, since the SBQ-R is a validated scale, it has high probability of making correct assessments of suicidal tendency. This means that the decision-making of the health worker can be more appropriate than relying on unaided assessment. In turn, this means that the person, really in need to see a mental health specialist and requiring treatment as an in-patient, can be identified with high accuracy, while those who do not need to be so treated get to avoid unnecessary transportation and medical care costs. This also decreases the burden on the local healthcare system.

Of course, just as any other technology, mHealth on smartphones also needs to be used carefully and judiciously. A quick search on any medical topic in the app store will likely produce hundreds if not thousands of matching apps. Many of these may be from dubious sources that have not been validated scientifically. Only those apps that have been validated and approved for use by local medical authorities should be used.[436]

Apart from medical assessments such as the scenario described earlier, the powerful multimedia and programming capabilities of smartphones enable the creation of apps that describe how to do medical/surgical procedures. For example, in the military context, health workers called medics many a times need to handle trauma situations in remote and combat locations in the absence of physicians and surgeons, including performing invasive procedures like blood transfusions and crico-thyroidotomies. Apps containing step-by-step instructions that integrate voice, images, and video can assist the medic in performing these procedures. Although such medics typically receive two or more years of intensive training, they are expected to be knowledgeable in very many medical conditions and to perform more than a 100+ medical and surgical procedures. For example, the US Special Operations Forces Medical Handbook contains 150 medical topics, including behavioral and veterinary health. Clearly a medic cannot be expected to know the details of all of these topics and this knowledge, presented in easy to access, searchable, step-by-step media-rich formats on a smart phone, rather than on bulky paper materials, could be very useful.[437]

mHealth on smartphones, in general, supports task shifting from physician, specialists, and surgeons, to other kinds of providers like medics, as we have seen earlier, or community health workers.[438–440] Often the latter kind of providers are mobile professionals, going from village to village in rural areas or situated in rural clinics that have limited facilities and expertise. It typically takes 7–8 years of education and training to become a physician and several more years to become a specialist. On the other hand, in many parts of the world, primary healthcare is provided by health workers who do not receive such lengthy and expensive training. Using mHealth tools on smartphones, such health workers can function as "physician extenders" who handle routine cases anytime/anywhere, enabling physicians and specialists to handle the difficult medical cases.

Apart from phones the last 5 years have seen an explosion of highly miniaturized sensors, wearable and otherwise that continuously measure and monitor health and health-related data such as heart rate and pulse rate, activities such as the number of steps walked and hours and times slept. Note that such data can also be obtained by apps on smartphones and smartwatches. In addition, other physiological sensors such as glucometers and blood pressure gauges have become communications enabled using the Bluetooth[441] system. External devices—like a telescopic zoom or microscope attachment—can also be connected directly or wirelessly.

This means that the data can be transmitted instantly to a smartphone or a computer and automatically integrated into a database that provides a longitudinal record to enable health analytics. Rapid changes in physiological parameters can be tracked, and alerts issued to caregivers that the patient may need rapid medical intervention.

Benefits of mHealth

The key benefit of mHealth is within the name itself—mobility. An extreme example was initiated recently by www.tardigrade.in—a virtual doctor who only does house visits, not for emergencies but for routine care. A health assistant travels to the patient's house, notes the patients' complaint, takes pictures as required and sends to the doctor and further enables a video conference with him, and then provides, as well as explains, the medications back to the patient based on the prescription created by the doctor.

Many available accessories and sometimes tools within the mobile itself allow blood tests and a few investigations. There is convenience, easy reach, and with connectivity—through coming up of 3G and 4G—and seamless access to Wi-Fi wherever available, which means that one can get health support anywhere anytime. The cost of healthcare has come down, because phones are also inexpensive, easy to use, and available ubiquitously

Drawbacks and issues

The small screen makes typing difficult, and autocorrect sometime makes it worse. There is near total dependence on connectivity for any type of data access, leading to the lack of reliability. Cell phone towers, after all, incur a certain cost and hence will be provisioned for only where there would be adequate number of people. Signals cannot reach walled-off areas and basements. Mobiles do get lost and misplaced. More important than the monetary or personal data loss is the privacy breach that may ensue if somehow the data can be pried open. Whatever privileges the mobile owner had, can become the privilege of the finder! Remembering that a doctor, an insurance provider, or even a hospital medical record person has secure access to data of thousands of patients, this can and has been misused. Health data security breach has ramifications next to the seriousness of stolen credit card information!

Hot areas of research

There are as of now over 325,000 health apps[6] out of the overall 3 million worldwide, though only a few are being used.

Health bots and AI can replace or, at least to some extent, compensate for the lack of physicians. While some of these issues are discussed in Chapters 6 and 14, there is much scope on how a physician can make the mobile a complete single tool to diagnose and treat patients—it has access to the EMR and can work as a stethoscope; the flashlight provides light; the camera records and also provides a magnified view of hard-to-reach areas; a flexible endoscope can be further attached, for example, such a view of the vocal cords helps intubation so that even a lay person can do it. The possibilities are immense, including complete telehealth solutions like the example for teleradiology in Fig. 1.

mHealth in supporting health workers

Pramod David Jacob, Shashi Gogia

Health workers could be those serving in the community such as community health workers (CHW) to more specialized roles such as nursing staff in noncommunicable disease (NCD) clinics.

As mentioned earlier, CHWs work in field areas such as patient's residences in villages or in camps held in these villages. These could be rather remote or rural areas, where there may not be mobile or Internet connectivity. Lately, devices such as tablets and smartphones have been introduced to these workers rather effectively, with applications that facilitate their work in the field. It has been found that these CHW and

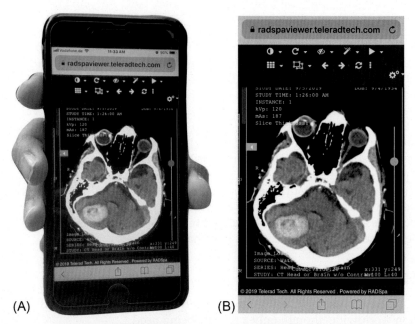

FIG. 1 (A) Axial noncontrast head CT image demonstrating an acute right cerebellar hematoma. Image is displayed on the RadSPA teleradiology workflow Zero-footprint viewer (TeleradTech, Bangalore) on a handheld mobile device (iPhone 7 Plus). (B) Mobile device screen capture of the same image (A). *Courtesy: Dr Arjun Kalyanpur, Teleradiology Solutions, Bangalore.*

other health workers are comfortable with android-based applications and thumb typing, as most of them have been introduced to technology via their own personal mobile or smartphones. So, they can be trained to work with applications that are tablet or smartphone based, as far as the application is intuitive, rather simple and user friendly. CHW can use such devices to carry out screening such as keep a track of BP, blood sugar, antenatal care, and vaccination records as well as other screenings for NCDs (Fig. 2).

Apps exist to enable the CHW to upload data to remote databases in real time if connectivity is available, or to store on the phone and upload later when connected. The uploaded data can easily be time and location-stamped. Use of the latter allows counterchecking, and validity of the information besides facilitating advanced processing of information like warning for alarming rises in incidence of particular problem in a certain area. Some aspects to cover are as follows:

1. No connectivity means that any application designed for these health workers will have to be housed completely in the device, including the decision support algorithms. Also, all the patient

FIG. 2 Health care worker saves patient information and related notes in a smart tablet app. *Curtsey PHFI, India.*

records of the CHW case load will have to be in the device, or if they are being loaded at regular intervals, then a process where the CHW loads the patient records of those patients she/he will be interacting on a given day or week will have to be preloaded before she goes out into the field, so that they can retrieve the record of a given patient to look at history, trend of health parameters, etc. They should then be able to enter new data into the respective patient's record into the device and store it. Also, they should be able to register new patients and start new records for them. When they reach connectivity, the new data is uploaded to the main server or cloud—in real time or batch mode once the CHW reaches her base—a process labelled as *synchronization.*

2. Application design should be in accordance with the workflow and related processes. Example tasks are creating of history, taking images, and measuring vitals including BP, blood sugar, and components of the antenatal chart, that is, simple work items, which are within the purview of the health worker. While CHWs may have simple straightforward applications, health workers such as NCD nurses may have more complex and sophisticated applications that include decision support and more depth in the information collected.

It is very important that the design of the applications and the screens move in congruence to the flow and relevance of their activities, without them having to toggle between screens to complete their tasks. Hence, before deployment of the app it is crucial to obtain user input during the design phase and also to test the app for usability, functionality, and compatibility with workflow.

Addition of AI through chatbots can help by asking related questions, for example, one can use the PQRST (Provocation/Palliation, Quality, Region/Radiation, Severity, and Time) chart for pain evaluation.[442] An image analyzer can be useful for skin lesions—an app that could assist diagnosis of venereal diseases, which however, when used by the author, it ran into problems related to patient privacy even though planned to be provided to female health workers only.

3. There may be local language capability required especially for patient reminders, alerts, and health education matter that are handed over to patients as printouts or sent via SMS or WhatsApp messages. This could be challenging in a country like India where there are numerous languages. Enabling the devices to input in local languages could be a requirement too (Fig. 3).

4. In many countries like India, there are regulatory bodies like Telecom Regulatory Authority of India (TRAI) that require the messages being sent to patients be vetted and authorized by them.

Developing apps for mobile devices

Sriram Iyengar

Today the landscape of mobile devices is vast, ranging from feature phones to smartwatches to small size phones to tablets that can range in size from a paperback book to a writing pad. Developing apps for feature phones is not typically possible for a third-party developer since most of these phones are closed environments: The apps on the phone are factory installed, and it is not at all easy for you and me to provide new apps. In fact the ability for people other than the hardware and software manufacturers to freely and easily add apps is what distinguishes a feature phone, such as the Motorola RAZR, from a smartphone such as the Samsung Galaxy. Similar to writing software for computers, anyone with the talent, skills, and knowledge can write a smartphone app and publish it in the major app stores. Anyone who likes the app can download it on to their smart mobile devices, sometimes after paying a small fee. Therefore, in this section, we will focus on developing apps for smart devices such as smartwatches, smartphones, and smart tablets.

App development is a complex topic involving many activities such as design, story boarding, user-experience design, programming, and

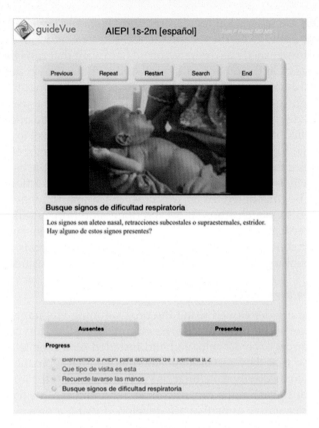

FIG. 3 Screen from a media-rich smartphone app to assist health workers in Spanish-speaking countries to use the World Health Organization's Integral Management of Childhood Illness guideline. Each screen also plays voiced instructions.

quality testing. A full description would take up several books of the same size as the current one and hence certainly beyond the scope of this chapter. Therefore we limit ourselves to providing only a high-level overview of this fascinating topic.

Smart mobile devices

Smart devices are essentially computers with additional capability of seamless two-way data and voice communication. Being computers, they need to have operating systems (OSs). Two operating systems, iOS, from Apple Inc., and Android, from Google, have the major market share among smart mobile devices with Windows Mobile at a distant third.[443] Android is most common in developing countries. iOS is used exclusively on hardware manufactured by Apple Inc. Google Inc. licenses Android OS to numerous manufacturers such as Samsung, LG, and Huawei. New versions of these OSs are released at regular intervals. It should be noted that since Apple owns both the hardware and the iOS software, you can expect your apps to perform exactly as designed on all hardware that runs the targeted iOS version(s). On the other hand, since Android can run on devices from multiple hardware manufacturers, there is a possibility that the app will function slightly differently, particularly with respect to the user interface, on different devices. Apps that function on multiple mobile operating systems are called cross platform apps. If an app is intended to execute on small to large format devices (phones to tablets), the developer must take care to acquire the screen size from the OS and then scale the user interface elements such as buttons, graphics, images, and text proportionately. This task cannot be considered trivial, especially since smartphones and tablets are designed to switch from landscape (long side horizontal) to portrait (long side vertical) mode and the app developer must make sure not only does the app continue to look good in all sizes and orientations, but there is seamless visibility of the buttons and easy help and use features.

Native apps versus HTML5 apps

Apps that are developed using the programming language of the mobile device, or to be more precise, its operating system, are called *native apps*. Such apps, once downloaded and installed on a mobile device, can be written so that they can execute stand-alone, that is, without needing continuous connectivity to cellular or Wi-Fi networks. If the app functionality calls for it, such apps can, of course, send and receive data to/from remote service native apps that are developed using a programming environment provided by Apple for iOS and Google for Android. A *cross platform* app is one that executes identically, or at least very similarly, on two (or more) operating systems. To make full-feature native cross platform apps, developers typically need to write code separately in the different development environments and different programming languages. On the other hand, if the app is intended to function in an environment relying upon continuous Internet connectivity, it can be developed using a method that essentially is equivalent to running the app under a web browser as a *web app*. Apps developed using this method typically use the HTML5 specification. A major advantage of such HTML5 apps is that they are inherently cross platform except for minor variations mostly due to hardware differences. The need for continuous Internet connectivity to function as intended becomes however its major drawback too and a likely problem in developing countries, which may be lacking widespread high-bandwidth Internet infrastructure. Hence, native apps tend to be preferred in these areas. Further the developer may need to target only Android apps in these countries. The website[443] provides current OS market-share information for specific countries and regions and can guide the developer in making OS choices.

Developing native apps

The procedure is similar for both Android and iOS.

(1) Register with and acquire a developer license from the OS owner. There are typically costs associated. In the case of Apple, at the time of writing, this license costs about U$100/year, and there may be additional license fees for specialized capabilities such as Apple watch or data storage.

(2) Download and install the app development environment, called a software development kit (SDK) on your computer. The SDK provides a visual interactive development environment (IDE) where you can design the user interface by dragging and dropping screen elements. The iOS IDE is known as "Xcode." The SDK uses a programming language to develop your app. In the case of iOS (Apple), the programming language Objective-C or another called SWIFT is used, while in the case of Android, the JAVA programming language is used. For Android development you can use the SDK provided by Google, called Android Studio. Other SDKs such as Eclipse are also available at varying costs. While the iOS SDK can execute on both Windows and Macintosh (MacOS) computers, it is preferable to create iOS apps using the MacOS SDK since a MacOS computer is required for final distribution of your iOS app. Android app development can be done exclusively on Windows computers. In either case, you need to become proficient in programming one of these languages. It is advisable to take formal courses and, of course, to learn the capabilities of the SDK(s) you choose to use. Excellent tutorials and courses are available on the web.

(3) After developing the app on your Windows or MacOS computer, you can transfer it from the computer via cable or Wi-Fi connection to the target mobile hardware for testing. On the mobile device you will observe how well the app works, its shortcomings, bugs, and capabilities. Having noted these aspects, you will go back to the SDK and fix your program and the user interface elements iteratively until results are to your satisfaction. Note that in commercial environments, app development is a complex multidimensional process that involves the active daily participation of programmers (coders), user interface and user-experience experts, graphic designers and artists, operating system and networking experts, quality assurance specialists, and others. This iterative process can take up considerable time and resources but is absolutely necessary to ensure the app works as intended and provides a pleasant experience to the target user.

(4) Whether in small one-person outfits or very large ones, a stage will come when the app can be released to the public by placing it in the app store. For iOS, this is the iTunes store, and for Android, it is uploaded to Google Play Store. In both cases the app has to be approved for distribution and placement in the store by Apple or Google. This approval process can take several days. Your app may be rejected because it does not meet acceptable criteria for performance, functionality, or content. Once approved the app will be available at the app store. You can choose to make it free, charge for it, make it available to everyone, or restrict to a private group.

(5) Typically, native apps designed to execute on iOS and on Android must be written in SWIFT or JAVA, respectively, and considerable effort must be expended in making sure that identical, or very similar, user experience and functionality are provided. If not, users may get confused, and there may be incompatibilities between the functionality experienced by users of the same app across the iOS and Android implementations. This means that two teams of programmers must be employed to develop and maintain the same native app on the two different operating systems. One way out of this dilemma is to use a *cross platform* environment. A system called XAMARIN, owned by Microsoft, enables this kind of development. Here the native programming language is called C# (C-Sharp). The IDE used is typically Microsoft's Visual Studio augmented with software tools that enable the development of highly compatible native iOS and Android versions of the same app. Of course, programmers using this system must become very proficient in C#, Visual Studio, and the nature and capabilities of iOS and Android. Note that some systems enable the development of native apps without programming. For example, Mobiloud Canvas[444] is able to convert certain kinds of websites to function as native apps. It is unclear whether the full range of mobile device features can be accessed with such tools.

Developing HTML5 apps

HTML5 stands for Hypertext markup language version 5.[445] Developing an HTML5 app is essentially the same as developing a website using the features and tools associated with HTML5. Teams that are proficient in developing websites can create mobile apps provided they use of HTML5 features and tools. These apps execute on the mobile phone within a web browser. Thus, as long as the web browser supports HTML5, the app will execute on iOS and Android with identical or very similar functionality and user experience. Proficiency in the JavaScript programming languages and HTML standards such as cascading style sheets (CSS) is needed for HTML5 app development. HTML5 apps are therefore cross platform apps, and, for the app developer, this route is an easy way to provide "write once, run on many platforms" capability. The app itself "lives" on a web server to which the browser on the mobile device connects. This means, of course, that the mobile device must have continuous web connectivity using either Wi-Fi or at least a 4G cellular data service. A major benefit of this approach is that any necessary app changes or updates can be made at the web server on which the app lives. All such changes will be reflected immediately to all users. However, there are certain deficiencies with this approach since HTML5 apps cannot access the full range of capabilities of the mobile devices such as access to the camera and microphone. This means that HTML5 apps may not be as powerful as native apps. If you do not need these capabilities and you can be assured that your target users will have continuous connectivity, there are many HTML5 app building tools available with powerful visual app building capabilities. A quick search on the web for "HTML5 development" will result in a plethora of tools. Choosing between these is often a function of personal taste, cost, and the anticipated learning curve associated with each product.

An aspect that used to be an issue in applications during the time of older mainframe computers but still of consideration specially in low resource areas is the classifying of the app features to front end (that is, what the user sees) and back end (that is, the actual storage and transfer of the information). In a completely web-based environment, both the screen and data reside on the remote system; in a native system, both may reside locally, but issues arise when the front end is local and the data server distant. Here the number of times the displayed data has to refresh or change for every entry while waiting for the back-end server to respond becomes a key issue. It also impacts upon the battery power expended by the mobile device. If the refresh is not complete, the cursor keeps spinning, and the screen remains unchanged while the user is literally twiddling his/her thumbs. Certain databases—the most famous being SQL Anywhere—allow data sharing on a synchronization basis, that is, the data currently in use are stored locally in a temporary albeit small memory slot within the mobile and then uploaded and synchronized with the bigger remote database as and when connectivity is considered good enough. Thus it behaves like a native app but allows functionality of a Web app even for less memory devices. Sometimes, this kind of an app is called a *hybrid* app.

Summary

Developers of apps for smart mobile devices typically need to make several decisions before embarking on app development. These include native apps versus HTML 5 apps, Android, iOS, Windows mobile, or cross platform, execute on smartphones and/or tablet, along with which database to use. Development of rich functionality apps typically requires the development of native apps and requires expertise in a variety of disciplines including interface design, programming, graphics, and user experience.

Persuasive technology and mHealth

Sriram Iyengar

Technology of various kinds plays an increasing role in modern life. This is especially true, even in developing countries, of information and communication technologies (ICTs) like mobile phones, including smartphones. Persuasive technology or PT is a vibrant emerging discipline that studies how technologies can be designed to encourage beneficial behaviors, of course, without coercion. The beneficial behaviors we are concerned with here relate to health, including encouraging health workers to use clinical practices that have been approved and shown to be effective, instructions from medical experts to patients to assist recovery from disease conditions, or advice and techniques for those who have no current health issues to improve and maintain wellness. In the case of smartphones and mobile/wearable sensors, the principles of PT can be used to design apps and technologies that help meet health goals.

Behavior change plays an important role in healthcare. Those who have chronic conditions like diabetes need to change their dietary habits, increase physical exercise, learn how to inject insulin, and monitor their glucose levels. People who are well may want to maintain or improve wellness by moderating intake of alcohol, quitting smoking, and losing weight. Health workers may need to modify the care they typically provide to their patients by adopting clinical care guidelines that have been recommended by authorities. For example, the World Health Organization has developed a set of clinical procedures called Integrated Management of Childhood Illnesses to guide community health workers in developing countries in diagnosing and treating health problems in children up to 5 years of age. Adherence to these can be aided by tools on smartphones.[438–440]

PT was originally developed by BJ Fogg,[446] who suggested that technology, especially computing technologies, can promote behavior change if they include one or more of the following attributes. These are sometimes known as primary task support principles.

1. **Reduction**: Complex tasks should be broken down into a series of smaller steps that the user can perform easily.
2. **Tunneling**: Users should be provided with guidance to navigate through the steps, especially if there is more than one step to be chosen from.

3. Tailoring: The information provided by the system should be designed to be compatible with their educational, cultural, and social background.
4. Personalization: The system should be very closely aligned with the needs and characteristics of the targeted individual
5. Self-monitoring: The users should be provided with feedback about their performance or status.
6. Simulation: Helps users understand the connection between the behavior change they are being asked to perform and the resulting benefits.
7. Rehearsal: Provides facilities for the user to rehearse the desired behavior change prior to putting it into practice.

These principles were extended and refined in the persuasive systems design (PSD) model,[447] which provides specific analytic and design principles for developing persuasive systems. In PSD, 21 such principles have been identified and divided into three categories:

1. Dialogue: Computer to human interactions directing humans toward target behaviors. Two important such principles are the self-explanatory rewards and reminders.
2. System credibility: Trustworthy systems can influence human behavior. Design principles here include verifiability of the process and a real-world feel.
3. Social support: Systems that leverage social factors such as cooperation and competition can produce the desired behavioral change.

The specific primary task support and persuasive systems design principles to be applied in a particular case depend on multiple factors including the culture, technology availability, economic status, educational attainments of the target users, and their environment. The following table provides an example in the mHealth context. Here the goal is to develop smartphone apps that assists community health workers in developing countries to follow the World Health Organization's Integrated Management of Childhood Illness (IMCI).[448] IMCI is complex and can be hard to learn since it covers a wide spectrum of childhood illnesses. mHealth solutions such as smartphone apps have the potential to replace bulky paper-based materials with a highly portable and interactive tool. However, these apps have to be designed carefully, taking into account multiple user and environmental challenges. The principles of PT described earlier provide a systematic conceptual basis and framework, rather than ad hoc methods with which to design such apps. One benefit of the PT approach is that design solutions based on PT are evidence based with a reasonably high expectation of success.

TABLE 1 Application of principles of persuasive technology in a mHealth app for a developing country.

User and environment challenge	Persuasive technology principle	Design solution for smartphone app
Literacy deficits among target users	Tailoring	• Provide images, video, audio in addition to text information • Media should be culture and language sensitive to target users
Poor Internet connectivity in user's environment	Tailoring	App should be able to function stand-alone
Training/educational deficits	Reduction	Break up the health information in the apps into small steps
Training/educational deficits	Tunneling	App should present clinical information as a series of steps and help user choose the next step
Performance feedback needed for improvement	Self-monitoring	App should document user activities and provide reports

Table 1 provides an example of the application of PT principles to the design of mHealth applications. The mHealth application is being designed to provide anytime-anywhere clinical decision support and procedure guidance for community health workers in a developing country. In Table 1 the first column describes the operating environment for the mHealth app. For instance the first row notes that the health workers have poor literacy in terms of reading complex medical terms and may, indeed, have only basic reading and writing skills. The app will then have to be "tailored" to enable them to overcome these literacy deficits. The design solution is to supplement the text content of the app using multimedia including voiced instructions, still images, and videos. Instructions using video are especially useful to enable understanding and skill development of medical procedures such as performing cardiopulmonary resuscitation (CPR) and dressing wounds. Providing video of medical conditions such as the various kinds of breathing distress (asthmatic wheezing, stridor, and so on) can improve diagnostic accuracy. Video of medical procedures enables health workers to perform these procedures accurately, following prescribed guidelines, and thereby include patient recovery.

The tailoring in row 1 in the succeeding text can benefit not only the health workers but also their patients. This is because in locations where health worker literacy is deficient, there patients themselves are also likely to be poor. The health worker could show the images and videos to patients to improve their knowledge about their condition and improve their ability for self-care, such as taking care of wounds. Iyengar et al provide examples.[438–440]

mHealth evaluation

Meghan Corin Bradway, Eirk Årsand

Evaluation of new and emerging ideas or devices in the medical realm—and mHealth is one such—offers challenges and opportunities. The approach you take to evaluation depends on what is being evaluated and why. It is incumbent upon the healthcare stakeholders involved to establish appropriate evaluation approaches that accounts for the priorities and input of all parties involved in the inception, idea, development, and usage of mHealth platforms.

The challenge of mHealth evaluation: Merging two independent environments

While mHealth technologies were originally intended for individual consumers, patients also often present these technologies and abundance of self-gathered data, to their healthcare providers. In response to mHealth, clinical practices need to adapt appropriately, and the medical world is calling for evidence that mHealth is safe and effective.

To look at the status and limitations of mHealth evaluation today, first we have to note that we are dealing with two environments that have evolved separately and are now trying to merge: clinical evidence-based medical care and commercially based mobile health (mHealth). While traditional healthcare and research depend on rigorously tested protocols and health standards developed over hundreds of years and generations of understanding, the commercial mHealth environment has evolved very rapidly—roughly between 2008 and 2018—in response to technological capabilities and the needs of individuals, providing near immediate self-management solutions.

The added needs of mHealth evaluation

To understand mHealth, we need to understand health behavior and motivation. Traditionally, evaluation of health interventions has been based upon noncontinuous or cumulative measures of health change, for example, HbA1c and lipid levels. The purpose of evaluation is to determine if a health intervention is safe and effective for end users. However, the concept of "effective" becomes a more complex issue than the traditional drug trial scenario in which the drug either works or does not work. Today, one must take into account the more frequently or even continuous accounts of a patient's unique self-management routine that are gathered via mHealth technologies. The concepts of safety and effectiveness for mHealth are based upon several questions in addition to changes in clinical measures. These include the following: Is the device relevant to the patient? Does the patient want to use it? Is it commensurate with that particular patient's health needs? Does it pose any risks? Does it meet the expectations of patients and their care providers? Therefore evaluation of mHealth requires not only traditional measures, such as resource use and changes in a medical condition, but also additional insight into what motivates a patient to choose to use mHealth technology, how they choose to use it, and what impact such use has on their health.

Racing against the clock to evaluate mHealth

While patients are increasingly more engaged in not only testing, even do-it-yourself (DIY) movements[449] and formal development, one main challenge still remains—time. Due to the rapid evolution of mHealth, by the time trials conclude,[450] the technology may become outdated. Fortunately the technology also allows researchers to collect the same continuous and relevant data that individuals choose to record—everything from steps taken to blood glucose to medication. Yet few are able to incorporate these "usage logs" and self-gathered data into conclusive clinical trials[451,452] due to the lack of evaluation standards for mHealth. Instead, most trials rely on changes in clinical health measures at, for example, 3-month intervals and standardized questionnaires, often reliant upon memory, which is prone to human error.

In response, governmental, research projects, health, and independent organizations, such as the FDA,[453] WHO and mTERG's mERA checklist,[454] FI-STAR,[455] PatientView, and online app stores, are also stepping up to propose more comprehensive frameworks and certifications for evaluation. Each approach is unique, with variations of target audience, intended level of evaluation, and the related capabilities of the assessors themselves. Some incorporate end-user reviewers, such as PatientView's App Directory (See http://myhealthapps.net/), provide assessment themselves as a service, such as the AppSaludable Quality Seal[456] or the NHS App Library,[457] or provide toolkits and recommendations for others to follow to formally assess mHealth technologies for clinical integration, such as the WHO's MAPS toolkit.[448] While the level of evaluations range from testing individual mHealth technologies to assessing a particular region's or health system's readiness for mHealth integration, most focus on common criteria including data security, reliability, and privacy as well as technical usability and user experience. Despite these efforts and increased patient engagement, there is little consensus on which methods or even which questions should be considered most important and relevant to answer the relevant needs of both, patients and their care providers. However, we can agree that each stakeholder group, from patients to care providers, not just health authorities and commercial developers, should have a role in mHealth evaluation—after all, they are the end users of these technologies.

Issues and future of telehealth

Medicolegal, ethical, and regulatory guidelines pertaining to telehealth

Maurice Mars

University of KwaZulu-Natal, Department of TeleHealth, Durban, South Africa

Telemedicine covers a wide range of activities in countries with different laws, health systems, regulations, needs, expectations, cultures, and approaches to ethics. This chapter explores legal, regulatory, and ethical issues of telecare. It is not intended to be a legal text or offer legal and ethical opinion, but aims to raise awareness in general.

There are many legal and ethical issues related to telecare. Interpretations and solutions will differ, based on local and national contexts. Because of such diversity, there will never be one "correct" approach to all telehealth matters, legal and/or ethical. The reader will need to analyze his/her own environment and the services offered to determine how these issues are addressed and the possible solutions, taking into account existing laws, regulations, and professional society guidelines. In the absence of ethical guidelines for telemedicine within a jurisdiction, it is suggested that the World Medical Association's 2009 "Statement on Guiding Principles for the Use of Telehealth for the Provision of Health Care" can be followed—their definition of telehealth includes telemedicine.[458]

As with other healthcare activities, health professionals have to comply with existing legislation, associated regulations, and the medical ethical guidelines adopted and followed in their country. Telemedicine may be covered in specific telemedicine laws or in aspects of other laws such as health, telecommunication, information communication, data security, and privacy. These may not always be called laws but may be found, for example, in directives within the European Union or guidelines and guidance in China.

297

Telemedicine law

Telemedicine law may be at a national or state/regional/provincial level. Malaysia was the first country to have such a law in 1997,[459] followed by France and Brazil. These three laws differ in their definition of telemedicine. Malaysian law refers only to teleconsultation; French law refers to teleconsultation, teleexpertise, telemonitoring, teleassistance, and telesurveillance; but in Brazil, teleconsultation allows for physician-to-physician or healthcare worker-to-physician consultation and explicitly excludes patient-physician consultation.[460] A similar situation exists in the United States. As of mid-2017, 44 states had over 200 telehealth-related pieces of legislation, many of which addressed remuneration, with no two states having concurrence.[461] The definition of telemedicine varies among states, with some excluding email, phone and/or fax from the definition, and in some instances store and forward telemedicine.

Regulations appear to be interpreted differently or made more onerous for telemedicine. Radiologists and pathologists can routinely report at a distance without the need for a prior doctor-patient relationship or even meeting the patient, but telemedicine regulations deem similar scenarios in other specialties unacceptable.[462] There are numerous concordance studies in various branches of medicine that report telemedicine diagnosis to be as good as or comparable with face-to-face diagnosis.[216,463,464] Many studies have reported that patients are satisfied with telemedicine consultation and diagnosis.

Data privacy and security rules called HIPAA[a] in the United States were initially created for health insurance purposes, but do hold relevance for telecare. In India, a draconian law called Digital Information Security for Healthcare Act (DISHA)[465] has been proposed, but fortunately not yet in place. It calls for high fines and even jail for a practitioner for any perceived breach of data privacy. The objection raised is that the healthcare practitioner is being assumed guilty even if the issue could be a software glitch or poor storage of the data.

Medical ethics and telemedicine

The term "medical ethics" was introduced by Thomas Percival, an English physician, in 1803.[466] Medical ethics are defined as the "moral principles that govern the practice of medicine".[467] They have evolved from at least the 4th century BC, with the Hippocratic oath dealing with two of the four foundations of modern medical ethics, beneficence (do good) and nonmaleficence (do no harm), to which respect for autonomy (the right of a competent person to make informed decisions about their

[a]See glossary for terms.

own medical care) and justice (fairness and equality) have been added. Modern medical ethics are largely a product of the mores of the developed world. The individual is recognized as an autonomous entity who must make informed decisions for him- or herself. But local culture and customs differ across the world. In patriarchal societies or those in which decisions about a person's health and treatment are made by the family or community, autonomy is not a priority. This needs to be considered when developing or assessing telemedicine ethics in different settings.

Commonly raised legal and ethical issues are as follows:

- Physician patient relationship
- Licensure
- Jurisdiction
- Quality and standard of care
- Continuity of care
- Consent
- Confidentiality
- Privacy
- Data security
- Authentication
- Remuneration
- ePrescription

The doctor-patient relationship

The doctor-patient relationship is considered a fundamental component of the delivery of high-quality medical care. The relationship is based on mutual respect, trust, and knowledge, and if absent, is considered to impair the physician's ability to make a full assessment of the patient, making the patient less likely to trust the diagnosis and management.[468] Regulators see the relationship, or lack thereof, as one of the major problems of telemedicine. Regulations in many jurisdictions require a prior relationship before there can be a telemedicine consultation, other than in an emergency. All states in the United States now allow a physician to establish a relationship with a new patient via telemedicine, and the American Medical Association has defined several ways in which a patient physician can be established for telemedicine, including VC-based examinations, a consultation with another physician who has an ongoing relationship with the patient, and meeting evidence-based practice guidelines for establishing a patient-physician relationship.[469] How this is to be achieved in store and forward telemedicine is not commonly addressed.

The WMA 2009 statement notes the challenge that telemedicine makes to the conventional approach to a doctor-patient relationship but does not identify this as a requirement, other than the need to comply with relevant legislation and professional guidelines.[458]

Licensure

Licensure has different components. The first is that the health professional has fulfilled the educational requirements to practice. In the United States, one has to qualify through the United States Medical Licensure

Examination (USMLE), while in many other countries, there is a need for a university qualification in medicine. Thereafter, health professionals must be registered or licensed with the relevant national or local medical council or board to legally practice in a given jurisdiction.

Should health professionals require separate licensure to practice telemedicine? This implies that they will require further education or training. Some argue that this is appropriate; others point out that the telephone has been used in clinical practice over distance for over a hundred years,[8] without the need for additional licensure. The WMA's stance is, "The physician providing telehealth services should be familiar with the technology" and "The physician should receive education/orientation in telehealth communication skills prior to the telehealth encounter."[458]

The second relates to jurisdiction. In the case of cross border consultation, be it between countries or jurisdictions within countries, should health professionals be licensed/registered to practice in the other country or state? There is need to reflect on Malaysian law that imposes severe fines and/or jail for health professionals who do not comply. What of international humanitarian services offered by nongovernmental organizations?

Jurisdiction

In part, jurisdiction has been covered under licensure. It also refers to where and under which laws legal action will be taken if necessary. It is usually held that the legal jurisdiction in telemedicine is that in which the patient resides. The WMA's principle of the duty of care notes, "The legal responsibility of health professionals providing health care through means of telehealth must be clearly defined by the appropriate jurisdiction."[458] It has been generally held that the referring doctor is responsible for the patient, as in the rescinded WMA 2007 Statement of Ethics for Telemedicine.[471] The WMA's 2009 position is now more explicit and also addresses continuity of care, "The physician needs to clarify ongoing responsibility for the patient with any other health care providers who are involved in the patient's care."[458] In the absence of jurisdictional regulations, this could mean that the legal jurisdiction could shift to that of the doctor being consulted.

Quality and standard of care

The Institute of Medicine's six aims for improving quality of healthcare are the provision of safe, effective, timely, efficient, equitable, and patient-centered care.[472] While telemedicine aims to achieve all of these, is a teleconsultation as good as a face-to-face consultation, and are treatment and management plans proposed as effective? This relates in part to concerns about a prior doctor-patient relationship. As stated, there are many concordance and satisfaction studies across a range of specialties using telemedicine that show teleconsultation to be comparable with face-to-face consultation. The effectiveness or outcomes of telemedicine are not as well researched, but ideally need to be monitored in all telemedicine services.[473]

Guidelines are a way of setting standards of practice and quality of care. These should follow existing clinical practice guidelines, which may need to be modified to meet telemedicine-specific circumstances. Guidelines should be developed by experts within the discipline and should be endorsed by the relevant professional body.[458] In addition, operational, technical, legal, and ethical guidelines should be developed.

Consent

Should there be a specific consent for telemedicine? Consent has been viewed in different ways. The extreme one is that telemedicine is new, different, and with potentially more risk to the patient, so the patient must be protected by being informed of all aspects of the telemedicine consultation process.[474] These include how a telemedicine encounter differs from traditional face-to-face consultation and care; how data is to be acquired, transmitted, and stored; what security is in place to ensure that it is not intercepted; who will see it at the other end; who will have access to it; how confidentiality will be maintained when others are present during a VC session; and how the patient and health professionals involved will be authenticated. Additionally, the patient should be informed of other options available. To ensure that this is done, informed consent should be written with records kept in the patient's file and a copy provided to the patient.

Others see video consultation as little different from face-to-face consultation and question the need for telemedicine-specific consent. The WMA takes a pragmatic approach, advising adherence to relevant legislation regulations, taking informed consent "to the extent possible," documenting the consent with consent following "similar principles and processes as those used for other health services."[458]

For informed consent to be valid, the patient must understand what he or she is consenting to. To explain data transmission and its security before, during, and after transmission by videoconference, mobile phone network, the Web, email, or instant messaging requires the doctor to have a sound knowledge of what has to be explained and makes the assumption that the patient has also fully understood this when they provide the consent. The problem exacerbates when translators gain consent. Recent studies have shown that less commonly spoken languages have not kept up with technology and do not have words for many aspects of ICT—especially the medical terms and that patients do not necessarily understand the words translated into their first language or in English.[475]

In the United States, 20 states as well as Washington DC have informed consent requirement, with two requiring written acknowledgement from the patient, as the Federation of State Medical Boards and the American Medical Association are promoting the requirement of informed consent for telemedicine.[462]

Confidentiality and privacy

The words confidentiality and privacy are often used incorrectly. Confidentiality refers to personal information about a patient that cannot be divulged by a physician without the patient's consent. Privacy refers to the right to control access to oneself. It includes physical privacy and privacy of electronic data. Privacy of electronic data entails ensuring data security, including encryption, during its acquisition, transfer, and storage, and control of who has access to the information. Access to data can be assigned and controlled using different levels of authentication including passwords, onetime pins, and biometric identification. Breach of physical privacy and confidentiality is possible when third parties, such as technicians, are present during VC consultations.

Authentication

Authentication is less commonly addressed: how can the identity, qualifications, and licensure/registration of the referring practitioners and the physician being consulted and the identity of the patient be confirmed? In some instances, services contracts and credentialing processes for the physicians can partly address this concern. For VC telemedicine, recognition of the person in view serves as a form of confirmation. Store and forward services may use a secure website with access controls and authentication. Digital signatures and certificates, which are the norm for government and legal documents, are not adopted for telehealth, but may be used in the future (remember that an image of the signature is very easy to emulate). But what of unsolicited email requests for telemedicine services or the more recent emergence of instant messaging telemedicine and direct to consumer services? Blockchain is being discussed as an answer too (see Chapter 14).

The ethics of telemedicine

In the developed world, concepts of medical ethics are well established. They are being refined as medicine advances and gives rise to new issues. Similarly, approaches to ethics related to telemedicine are evolving. Simplistically, all that is required is that health practitioners abide by laws and regulations. However, the situation can be complex and an ethical conundrum. Is it ethical to deny a patient a telemedicine consultation with a specialist when he/she is available, because of the absence of a prior doctor-patient relationship, there is uncertainty about data security, or even a lack of understanding of the technology to be used that may invalidate consent? Is it ethical to thereby subject them to diagnosis and management by a less qualified or relatively less experienced local practitioner?

Must a patient in snowbound remote northern Canada or Russia, isolated areas of Australia, or the Sahara desert travel long distances under adverse conditions and at significant cost to themselves or the tax payer, because of ethical concerns? In the developing world, the patient may not be able to afford the travel costs or face the risk of losing a scarce job because of absence from work, thereby also being denied quality care.

14

Disruptive technologies: Present and future

Magdala de Araújo Novaes[a], Arindam Basu[b]

[a]Telehealth Center, Clinics Hospital, Medical Science Center, Federal University of Pernambuco, Recife, Brazil, [b]School of Health Sciences, University of Canterbury, Christchurch, New Zealand

Introduction

Arindam Basu

Telehomecare, or telehealth applications in home-based care, seeks to offer new strategies to improve and expand access to care, using a range of distance-based digital practices. Such care may be associated with health promotion, prevention, and treatment of chronic diseases, for critically ill patients (acute or terminal) or for home-based rehabilitation. While home care is increasingly dependent on face-to-face interaction with humans (be it in real life or virtual spaces), it is a fact of life that robots and automation have replaced human workers in many fields and are threatening jobs everywhere. While the health sector has been a late entrant in IT, such replacement, so far, has been little, but that may not be true in the future. The pros and cons of the **use of robots** where handiwork is involved, that is, surgery is a high-impact topic worth studying. Tied to the concept of robotics is the concept of **artificial intelligence (AI)**—a field of computer science with high overlap of statistics and mathematics and can be called machine learning, which has advanced further to deep learning that the machines learn themselves. The role of AI in improving healthcare especially in underserved areas is being noted by international agencies like WHO. ISO as well as ITU.[578] **Virtual reality (VR)** is considered revolutionary within healthcare, due to new possibilities offered for interfacing (system/user); the use of multisensory devices; navigation in three-dimensional spaces; immersion in the context of the application;

sharing and interaction in real time; and extending the senses that previously were simple vision and hearing to three-dimensional manipulation using touch, pressure, and even smell enabled through the use of devices such as head-mounted displays (HMDs), gloves, or the user's own body. Last but not least, **blockchain** refers to a public decentralized ledger, where the valid peer-to-peer transactions are recorded in a distributed chain of blocks, with constant updation as long as some new approved transactions take place.[5] As soon as a block is appended to the blockchain, the update is transmitted to entire distributed structure, providing redundancy, transparency, and security.

Telehomecare

Magdala de Araújo Novaes

Overview

Telehomecare, or telehealth applications in home-based care, seeks to offer new strategies to improve and expand access to care, using a range of distance-based digital practices. Home care is characterized by the delivery of health services to the patient at home. Care may be associated with health promotion, prevention, and treatment of chronic diseases, for critically ill patients (acute or terminal) or for home-based rehabilitation. We will discuss here telehomecare by the home health agencies that provide health services to patients in their homes as an alternative to traditional hospitalization.

Concepts and applications

Home care is one of the fastest growing modalities in the world. By 2014 the number of home-based care agencies increased by 66%, and more than 4.9 million patients received healthcare from 12,400 HomeCare agencies between 2013 and 2014. More than half of the care assisted by these agencies was for continuation of care after hospitalization. With an aging population, the number of patients receiving home healthcare will increase, making HHC a major source of intensive care with concomitant lowering of hospital readmission.[476]

The prominence of home care emerged in the post WWII period of the 20th century as a palliative care strategy, to minimize infection risks and to reduce hospitalization costs. Its recent rapid growth can be partly explained by the rising health needs of an aging population with emergence of a rising number of persons with multiple chronic problems like cancer, COPD, and Alzheimer. With the transition of care from the hospital to home, the patient continues to receive care by a multidisciplinary team but at a place that allows greater comfort and contact with the family, often contributing to better treatment results.

The attending physician devises the home care plan for the patient, based on the patient's clinical profile. There is a need to take a comprehensive view of necessary infrastructure in place and coordination between the health team—physician, nurse, physiotherapist, nutritionist, social worker, and family members—who will provide care on a 24/7 or on a predefined support scale (Fig. 1). This scenario of geographically distributed care is very conducive to the insertion of distance health practices (telehealth), which in this context contribute to improve the performance of home care and enabling a less invasive and more personalized care.

Imagine a patient with advanced heart failure, renal failure, and motor weakness, with frequent calls for emergency services and several hospital admissions in 1 year. This patient is offered palliative care and is assigned to a HomeCare program. The healthcare team develops a specialized treatment plan tailored to the patient's needs. Nurses and physicians would come to the home through scheduled visits, conduct face-to-face assessments, and deliver instructions for the patient and family members regarding use of devices for collecting health information including vital signs and sending data via the internet to the facility. The information collected at home is grouped in an electronic health record (EHR), which is constantly accessed by the professionals involved. As a result the patient can possibly reduce the number of hospitalizations and emergency calls by 60% during the same period of time.

This is an example of 24-h home care that allows reflection on the scope, impact, and effectiveness of home care, showing positive results related to the improvement or nonaggravation of patients' health status. This is a situation where telehealth sensors and networked devices have enabled real-time clinical evaluation of patient(s) and continuous monitoring of their health parameters and consequently allow agile decision-making.

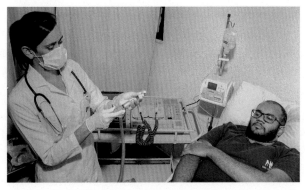

FIG. 1   Nursing care in the home. From Interne Home Care. (www.interne.com.br).

IV. Issues and future of telehealth

In telehomecare, alert systems located in the home of the patients send notifications to a telemonitoring center after collecting data on specific symptoms and signs of the patients at home. In the telemonitoring center, nurses and doctors analyze data in real time and deliver interventions aimed at avoiding complications or prevention of worsening of the health state of the patients. Messages can be transmitted over the phone or using other applications, directing specific behaviors to the patient's family members who are their carers at home or to the care team itself. Visits by physicians and supervising nurses may be performed from a distance, over and above scheduled appointments, thus improving patient safety. In addition, the use of an electronic patient record, coupled with applications and online interaction systems (chat or video calls), allows simultaneous access and hence engagement by all professionals involved.

Telehomecare can be applied in different scenarios, but they are especially suited in the setting of patients with chronic obstructive pulmonary disease, patients with heart and renal failure, those with NCDs, and the aged.

Results of supplementing traditional care with telehomecare are encouraging. Sahakyan et al.[477] analyzed data from 3513 patients in a telehealth program, 62% of whom had heart failure, 55% had COPD, and 29% had diabetes. Home care was associated with a significant reduction in the blood pressure levels of the patients monitored in the telehomecare program, with more pronounced alterations in patients with uncontrolled blood pressure.

Applications, websites, or online interactive systems can be used in home health monitoring. Jeffs et al.[478] have developed an application for home healthcare and have evaluated the usability, acceptability, and scalability of this application. Their application software allows monitoring of health status and has a patient-oriented user interface for loading information.

Impact and future trends

Home healthcare, administered either on-site or remotely, allows specialized care, which focuses on the patient and his particular needs, with benefits of reduced hospitalizations and consequent cost saving. The positive impact is perceivable both from an institutional perspective and the healthcare system in general. Laustbader et al.[479] has reported the impact of a palliative care program at home and reported that a $10,435 reduction for patients who received home care assistance compared with those who received traditional hospital care. In addition, the cost per patient during the last 3 months of life has been $12,000 lower.

The impacts of home care are even greater in the health system when associated with the use of wearable devices. Here the patient wears sensors that collect health parameters viewable on smartphones or in the monitoring centers. It is a worldwide trend related to the strong growth of mobile technologies around the world. Patients can, for example, see their heart rates in real time, or the patient's family can monitor the patient's location in case of mental illness. With such devices, it is possible for larger hospital equipment and numerous monitoring devices to be dispensed with.[480] An example of a prophylactic wearable is the Spire device, which is attached to the patient's garment by a clip; the sensor identifies changes in the user's breath and sends a notification to their smartphone.[481]

The potential to reduce health spending from the home care and use of these technologies has already been discussed, with possible reduction of the need for periodic reassessments and frequent medical consults: physicians monitor the data, and the patient requests an on-site visit only when some abnormality has been identified.[481]

Despite the great benefits brought by telehomecare, there are challenges to be overcome, such as the adequate training of professionals and the development of systems that ensure greater patient safety, which evaluate not only isolated symptoms but also a wider range of health aspects, as well as adapting to the local infrastructure where the patient is located.[482] False alarms constitute a major chunk.

The applications of telehomecare are expected to expand particularly in developing countries where traditional services are limited and potential of hospital-induced infections is high. Clear guidelines and protocols ensuring quality of care, are needed, along with training, and guidance of the professionals involved to make telehomecare increasingly effective when it is presented as an alternative or as a supplement to traditional care.

Tele-robotics in healthcare including in surgery

Shashi Gogia

The 2008 movie *WALL-E* (https://en.wikipedia.org/wiki/WALL-E) highlighted a possible redundancy of human hands or feet in the robotic era, with retention of only the brain and eating capability. Interestingly, however, IT was conceived more to emulate and replace brain functions.

Robots and automation have replaced human workers in many fields and are threatening jobs everywhere. Since the health sector has been a late entrant in IT, such replacement has so far been little, but may not be so in the future. This subchapter discusses the pros and cons of the use of robots where handiwork is involved, that is, surgery.

We start, however, by briefly describing an entirely different set of telepresence robots that are more general, not any specific procedure related. The first is a static bedside robot that provides emotional care for patients. The second wheel-mounted one offers teleconsultations especially for the ED, OPD, and inside the ICU where patients can be prescribed streptokinase and other relevant medications after remote physical examination by cardiologists and neurologists[483] within the golden period after ensuring confidence of the diagnosis. These so-called point-of-care (PoC) robots have been found to extremely beneficial as per a recent review from Korea.[484]

"Big surgeons make big incisions" was an adage of yore. In those days a generous incision allowed the surgeon flexibility to safely complete a delicate dissection and manipulation through a complete view. It ensured that crucial structures were left unharmed even while stopping inadvertent bleeding. Prolonged postoperative pain was felt to be an acceptable consequence. What is called minimally invasive surgery (MAS) is essentially working towards conservative skin incisions, manipulation, and dissection being restricted to only those tissues that need to be removed or repaired. The term was introduced when manipulation was added to stereotactic access and to endoscopy of all possible body orifices (nose, mouth, rectum, and urethra) and of body cavities, that is, laproscopes, thoracoscopes, arthroscopes, etc. The benefits of pain reduction even lead to an artificial manipulation space being created (retroperitoneal for kidney, extra peritoneal for hernia, Carpal tunnel, face, etc.) or use an existing albeit, pathological one—the hydronephrotic kidney.

Surgery is a highly skilled technique requiring brain and hand co-ordination. One may have an inclination to learn the skills, but no further DNA exists that one can be a borne surgeon. Even the famous YouTube video about a 7-year-old boy performing surgery in a village described him using a book for reference! (https://www.youtube.com/watch?v=23wuWZWgC5U).

> It takes 5 years to learn when, why, and how to do a surgical procedure, another 10 years to learn **when not to do** the procedure. *(Anonymous)*

Basic procedure techniques like tissue handling, ensuring the lack of tension, and knot tying are general skills that one learns over time. With the introduction of newer techniques especially MAS, the entire scene changed. Many additional skills needed to be imbibed like manipulating the scope to zoom and catching a bleeder even while looking at the screen etc. Use of lasers to coagulate the gall bladder bed had a short tenure but complications including inadvertent perforations by instruments not under vision persisted. Complication rates reached an all-time high during the 1990s.[485]

Even if basic and extra skills are imbibed, there are additional issues that automation can correct. A surgeon could be tired, sick, or simply unavailable when the need arises due to a multitude of reasons. Manipulating instruments and even their steady holding for long periods is tiring, which becomes less ergonomic when doing endoscopy. Endoscopic manipulation is done in all directions, but visualization is in 2D, and mostly, the person moving the camera is someone else. Working with a new or different assistant has additional issues. Finally, doing the same job day in day out is boring.

Computers and robots do not get fatigued, never get bored, can configure multiple levers (hands), and coordinate many different visions. Configuring, interestingly, is extremely easy if the task is unvarying and repetitive. Robots are preferred for activities that are repetitive, can be dangerous for the user (e.g., danger of radiation), or need access to difficult-to-reach spots. The automotive sector, the leader in robotics, uses it, for example, for material handling, spot welding, and painting. Bomb disposal squads were among other first-level users.

Added advantages that make robotics score higher than humans include a possibility of 360* vision; auto zoom; special sensors, for example, temperature; color filters that can distinguish a cancer cell from normal, multiple attachments; and most importantly quick coordination between all these. However, getting all this together is a slow learning process and expensive. One also has to consider that any mishap can be a life-and-death issue with little clarity on whom to fix responsibility for the said mishap—see the separated positions between the patient and surgeon in Fig. 2. In an actual scenario the distance can be much more—even across the globe.

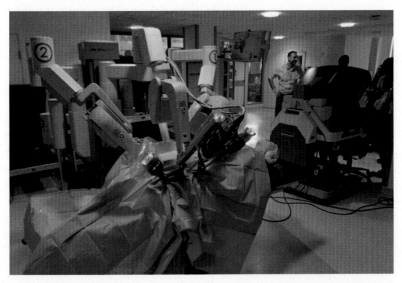

FIG. 2   The Da Vinci Robot operating on a dummy while the surgeon is sitting in the right side.By Cmglee—Own work, CC BY-SA 3.0, https://commons.wikimedia.org/w/index.php?curid=39154360.

On the other hand, once the software and skills are embedded and fine-tuned, there is no need for any extra training or effort. Replication is a cinch and can be done to an unimaginable scale that also brings down costs.

Initial skill acquisition by such IT systems has to be an amalgamation of many minds—computer engineers, surgeons, anatomists, etc. Each advance requires testing, learning, and coordination. Surgeons have to be trained to utilize the robotic system, including taking over after recognizing when and where system is failing. Changes have to be incremental.[a] But these are early days yet. Automation is not yet complete and needs supervision by humans, who, in turn, needs to be trained on the particular machine so that the supervision is effective. As of now, robots show significant promise, but robust evidence base supporting its use remains lacking.[486]

Robotics is expensive. Still, it has become routine in many surgical fields especially if there are endoscopic procedures that require remote manipulation. Hard-to-access areas needing standardized but repetitive action top the list. Examples are prostatectomy, neurosurgery, cardiac surgery, and vascular surgery. Telepresence also permits telementoring of novice surgeons. Joint implants are a special case as each newer implant has very precise anatomic specifications but would require high level retraining of the surgeon. Training a robot is a onetime replicable affair.

Laparoscopic and thoracoscopic procedures have some constraints, and robotics has been an attempt to correct them. These were a need for a stable camera platform with flexibility of zoom and broader field of vision; conversion of the two-dimensional view into something that allowed depth appreciation; stability of the holding and retracting instruments—that is, inserted from the third and fourth ports; and finally a need for better ergonomics of not only single-handed laparoscopic instruments but also a comfortable, sitting operating position.

The first operating robot was a voice-activated AESOP. It was funded by NASA to help service its space shuttle while in orbit. It was cleared, by the FDA in 1994, for use as a surgical assistant, maneuvering the endoscopic camera while the surgeon was controlling other instruments, essentially replacing the cameraperson to facilitate solo-surgeon laparoscopic operations.

Movements though slow and expected to improve over time, were very precise, nonjerky, and without any tremor. Response time for the rare mishap, given the precision movement, was in nanoseconds as opposed to milliseconds in humans.

---

[a] Read the section comparing evolutionary and revolutionary changes in Chapter 1.

This further extended to taking charge of other instruments and coordination and resulted in what was now called ZEUS. After animal testing, ZEUS carried out a tubal reanastomosis in 1998 and later a coronary artery bypass surgery (CABG). The daVinci Robotic system came up separately, but both have now been merged.

The daVinci system has been found successful for almost all types of laparoscopic procedures. However, a special role is mentioned only for a few select procedures like hysterectomy, transoral and velopharyngeal surgery in the head and neck,[487] radical and sometimes even standard transurethral prostatectomy (TURP), and CABG; besides some other conditions that mean prolonged surgery; and other hard-to-reach areas as explained earlier. For most procedures, however, currently, the expense is unjustified. Also, there is a cost on training on using daVinci itself, and the complication rate has not really decreased.

RoboDoc is another one that came up for orthopedic surgery, specifically total hip and now knee arthroplasty. It is in widespread use outside of the United States as it has yet not received FDA clearance.

Neurosurgery

Neurological surgery is well suited for the incorporation of robotic assistance. Bony superstructure meant small holes for manipulation—spurring a growth in stereotactic surgery. This minimally invasive neurosurgery became possible once CT scans allowed for pinpoint localization of lesions. That one had to work between tight anatomical confines, and large veins were a further incentive along with understanding of potential harm related to even the slightest mishap. Even nonstereotactic, procedures are microsurgical in nature. However, the many and varied steps involved in localization, access, and surgical execution would require distinct "robotic competencies." The CyberKnife is an image-guided robotic technology for noninvasive cancer surgery to provide radiosurgery (e.g., a gamma knife uses gamma rays) for lesions anywhere in the body when radiation treatment is indicated. It has a special role for hard-to-reach brain tumors like meningiomas of the skull base.

Safety aspects

Auto-driven cars have killed people,[488] the 2018 Lion Air Crash in Indonesia[489] killed 189 people. It was due to two separate flight automation control systems working against each other—the pilot was not even aware of the problem or the solution, which was to simply switch off the computer! One hundred forty-four deaths in the United States have been linked to robotic surgery.[490] An inquest after a botched surgery death in

Newcastle, England, revealed how the robot first made a wrong stitch during a mitral valve replacement procedure—but additional stitches to correct the same made matters worse. At one stage, there was so much blood clogging the camera that the controlling surgeon could not see anything. Action has been taken against the surgeon.[491]

The biggest issue is fixing responsibility for such unwarranted deaths. In the case of the Lion Air Flight, the Boeing company has been sued as the pilot also died. Such an end, fortunately or unfortunately, is unlikely during a surgical procedure unless the surgeon gets a heart attack horrified at the turn of events!

In conclusion, there is a possibility that robots may better the surgeon in the future, but there is need for caution. Complications have occurred and may rise further. Even if it is, hopefully, far less than the cases of medical negligence we face today, the issue of fixing responsibility will be extremely complex.

Artificial intelligence and IoT in healthcare

Abhishek Gattani

What is AI?

The term intelligence has very diverse meanings including spying! For our purposes, it can be a form of deductive reasoning or a method of "communicating complex ideas, acting on them, and holding conversations."[492] Narrowing this broad concept of the purposes of computation and telehealth, it also can be a form of reasoning or critical thinking.

Artificial intelligence (AI) is a field of computer science with high overlap of statistics and mathematics and can be called machine learning. AI is a broad term and often misunderstood.

AI's history and evolution

Birth of AI happened in the 1940s and 1950s with its winners and setbacks.[493,494] Notable successes in the health domain[b] included MYCIN,[78] ePrescriptions, and CDSS especially using Arden Syntax.[79] A big change since 2011 has been the advent of deep learning leading to exponential growth. AI is being described as the new electricity and data the new oil. Companies like Google, Apple, Amazon, and Facebook are investing heavily in AI labs. So have the governments of China, the United States, and Europe—in hundreds of billions of dollars to ensure that they do not

[b]These are discussed in Chapter 5.

lag behind economically and also sadly militarily. The tools of warfare are changing to precision kills![495]

What is deep learning

Logic is the basis of programming within computer systems. A simple If/Then/Else example—**IF** (the drawn object having four lines and perpendicular margins) **all lines are equal, THEN** (it is a) **Square** (, or) **ELSE** (it is a) **Rectangle.** There are many variations that are largely mathematical in nature and depend on calculations. Now, let us take this logic further into machine learning. A cube or a rectangular block has six sides; out of them, only three can be visible. And even among these entities, it is unlikely that their rectangular representation, a 2D figure, will have appropriate angles or sizes of the lines. With machine learning, nevertheless, accurate measurement can be made available for the visible lines and angles—also extrapolated for invisible ones to surmise a cube, cuboid, irregularity, etc. CT scans are that way reconstructs of multiple 2D images in a different plane or in 3D.

Deep learning goes beyond such reconstructs. It literally self-learns from conclusions, and uses them for further analysis, which means using data and the surmises, that is, outcomes of a clutch of data to further create the association and reasoning used to create a certain predictivity. Unlike machine learning where all the inputs are manual, deep learning takes in existing inputs and hence depends on much higher volumes of data. In machine learning and deep learning, the accuracy and sanctity of data are important though deep learning is somewhat more flexible.

A good way to describe AI would be its similarity to a child. A child's learning comes by regular associations between pictures and moving objects like a dog, cat, or table. Then, over time, children develop patterns and can recognize these objects on their own. AI works similarly; essentially, it is a class of computer programs that can learn patterns from data. The contention is that computers, in the domain of artificial intelligence, can serve as "intelligent agents" mimicking if not matching humans in thought processes and reasonings; it is possible for computers to emulate human cognitive behavior. Such cognitive performance systems would eventually be closer to the notion of human "intelligence."[496]

Just like a parents' understanding that quality education (kind of school, teachers, books, etc.) helps long-term career building, AI systems also need emphasis and detail on the quality of training, as well as the training methodology (kind of data, kind of labels, frequency of these examples, etc.). In a sense, AI is quite different from traditional software. In traditional software, engineers write algorithms, logic, heuristics, and patterns to convert data and information towards knowledge and wisdom. Today's AI instead tries to derive wisdom by ascertaining patterns within the data that are fed in. What makes it interesting and super capable is its close coordination with the internet to capture more data as per need and hence the relevance here to describe Internet of Things or IoT in the same chapter. Alexa and Google Home are good examples. One of the initial responses from them are "I am still learning" as it starts analyzing the voices of its masters and also their favorite objects and searches.

"Intelligence is largely determined by genetics. Critical thinking, though, can improve with training and the benefits have been shown to persist over time. Anyone can improve their critical thinking skills. Doing so, we can say with certainty, is a smart thing to do."[496] A deep learning model is designed to continually analyze data with a logic structure similar to how a human would draw conclusions.

Why the hype?

To understand why this sudden surge in AI research, funding, and applications, let us take AI application in telemedicine as an example, that is, skin-lesion recognition. The idea is to be able to use a mobile phone camera to screen for various blisters, macule, melanoma, etc. For years the steps of building such an application included collecting lots of images of various lesions, writing computer programs to extract features from those images, and using machine learning to learn how these features combine for a lesion type. Vaguely speaking, AI will learn that, if for the lesion (A) asymmetry is high, (B) border is irregular, (C) diameter is greater than 6 mm, and (D) it is pigmented, then most likely the image is of a melanoma.

Note that writing good detectors for all the earlier features (pigment, asymmetry, etc.) is essential and took years of research. Not only is feature engineering expensive, but also it takes years of work to get good accuracy with human engineered features. With deep learning, feature engineering is learnt from the images. This dramatically reduces the years of R&D needed for an AI application and also results in higher accuracy. Deep learning systems have consistently beaten the state-of-the-art results in various domains like face recognition, OCR, and speech recognition (see Fig. 3).

AI scores greatly over human learning in many ways. Even while a computer without electricity is dead and without information, it gets access to information at nanospeeds when it is switched on. The memory resource is billions of computers and other devices worldwide. Hence, learning never has to go through the cycle of birth, schooling, readjustment, failure, and death. What one device learns can be replicated instantly. Transfer between individuals has to be either relearning or through genes that can take generations! No need for DNA or reverse transcriptase. The initial learning is slow and laborious. Unlike humans, there is no feedback or

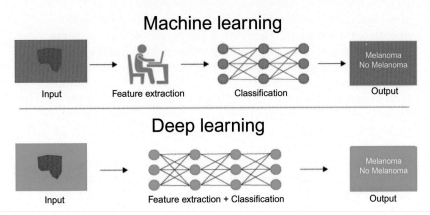

FIG. 3 Feature extraction is done by machines themselves in deep learning.

even penalty on how effective or harmful it will be. That will be and always remain to be a slow manual process.

Applications of AI in healthcare

Because of the dramatic increase in the amount of data, increase in computing power, and reduction of costs in building an AI system, deep learning-based AI is finding many new applications in healthcare. Here are a few examples:

Diagnosing diseases: AI systems can learn to see patterns similar to the way doctors see them. Examples of such systems are many: breast cancer cell segmentation from pathology images (Fig. 4A and B), malignant lymphoma classification from biopsies, and pancreas segmentation from CT scans (Fig. 4C). To train these systems, one requires high-quality labeled data. Currently, one of the applications especially in telemedicine includes the ability to scan through lots

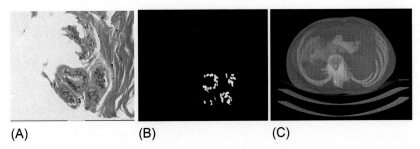

FIG. 4 (A) Breast cancer cell original (B) segmentation. (C) Pancreas segmentation from CT scans.

of X-rays, CT scans, and MR scans to provide a second opinion or reduce the workload. However, a key benefit of these systems, often overlooked, is that by training them on high-quality examples, we can now replicate best medical practices to all bringing a level of standardization and scale that is needed in healthcare. Though radiologists are especially at risk, it is unlikely that AI systems are going to replace doctors anytime soon. However, their potential in highlighting problems that assist the doctor to focus on the final interpretation is undeniable.

Developing drugs: Drug development is an expensive process. AI can be used at various stages of the drug development process such as identifying targets for intervention, discovering drug candidates, speeding up clinical trials, and finding biomarkers for diagnosing the disease. For instance, AI can help speed up trials by identifying suitable candidates by analyzing demographic and history data. AI can also detect early signs of a trial not going well so investigators can intervene sooner. For drug candidates, AI algorithms can analyze a molecule's structural fingerprints and descriptors to identify high-value prospect molecules.

Personalized care: How each of us reacts to a drug and treatment is different. Designing personalized treatment plans both at the care, as well as at the drug level is tedious and costly. AI can change how we prescribe drugs. Using data from electronic health records and the composition of a drug, AI system can predict which aspects might not react well with a patient and thus alter the treatment plan.

IoT?

IoT short for Internet of Things refers to interconnection of various day-to-day objects and devices such as a refrigerator, a watch, and an ultrasound scanner. to the internet enabling them to send and receive data. Let us consider just your future home, something which is current in many advanced countries, that is, the use of Alexa (Amazon©) and Google Home© to start music or the TV or search the net for answers. Since they can be activated remotely also, it has become possible to use these and other methods in what are smart homes to switch on the heater before reaching home. A smart refrigerator can check the available quantity of food and order the grocery directly. Similar connected devices can create data for healthcare purposes too with radical implications for ambulatory and outpatient care.

Applications of IoT in healthcare

The latest Apple watch has an EKG built in; this can be analyzed through AI. Body patches can live-stream vital signs. Weight can be accurately quantified and continuously monitored by sensors in your shoes.

Smart mattresses can relay information about how well you sleep. Wi-Fi routers can identify people by how they walk and even signal the hospital to send an ambulance in case they experience a fall.[497] More precise sensors can monitor breathing and heart rates with 99% accuracy. The sort of intelligent applications and devices that will be built using all these sensors is exciting but still vastly unexplored. Some examples are as follows:

Medication compliance: World-over, incorrect, or inconsistent intake of medicines is an issue. Even small improvements in compliance can dramatically save money and lives. Wi-Fi signal can help identify if the elderly is not making the required trips to the medical cabinet. Weight sensors in smart pill bottles or even sensors in the blister packaging can alert if doses of medication are being missed or an overdose is occurring.

Workflow optimization: IoT in healthcare means increased real-time visibility across the organization. Now, you have data about what the patient was doing, his vitals, and medication compliance before he visits the hospital and data about the patient flows through the hospital, for instance, when the tests were ordered, the images reviewed, and the ECG (report). AI can then be fed all these data, and healthcare providers can identify bottlenecks affecting patient wait times, reduce costs by avoiding unnecessary tests, and predict when would be the right time to discharge a patient.

Remote monitoring: The biggest application of IoT in healthcare is remote monitoring because of the tremendous cost benefits to health providers and the preventive nature of care to patients. By combining IoT and AI, we can also proactively intervene and save lives. Take congestive heart failure (CHF)—when a patient is discharged, a common problem is that CHF can resurface if swelling in the foot is not monitored properly. With IoT and AI, we can deploy sensors in socks or other wearable devices to monitor if the foot is swelling to alert the medical team to take action. Robots are already working and corresponding with specialists in stroke clinics and ICUs.[483] Fall detection in the elderly can be achieved by apps within the phone itself![498]

Challenges in AI and IoT

It is easy to get carried away and start imagining that these technologies can replace healthcare providers, but that, as of now, is a tall order, even for radiology, the first specialization possibly thought to be replaceable.[499] There are many challenges associated with these intelligent systems, listing here a few:

Bias: It is important for healthcare providers to evaluate the data that were used to train these systems and ensure that bias does not creep in. An AI polyp detection system trained using diagnostic data from a US population will not be as effective in identifying the peculiarities associated with the South Asian phenotype. Similarly, the data being used to train an AI system need to account for variations in ethnicity and environmental factors.

Black-Box: One drawback of deep learning-based AI is that patterns may not be understandable or visible. Very often, one cannot explain why a particular diagnosis was recommended by the system. This is an active area of research; until then, it is important to ensure that a human layer is present to help explain odd conclusion.

Failure: AI systems, just like humans, can fail. There is much technology behind it. And eventually, the key to continued use is a persistent personalized linkage, that is, the local Wi-Fi, Bluetooth, etc. to a provide access to the World Wide Web. Processing of information involves generally a linked mobile device, which mostly is also the mode of transmission. A failure to link or even a temporary loss of the connectivity can cause problems. The smaller devices may run on a battery, while the large ones like a refrigerator have no problem of electricity, etc. but in any case, if power goes out, the device is literally powerless!

Often, it is not the AI system that fails but failure results from human operational errors like deployment issues, training problems, incorrect software version, and incompatible hardware. In several accidents recorded by self-driving cars being tested in the United States, the operator had stopped paying attention to the system alerts because he wasn't driving!

Voice or emulated speech is used to communicate to the responder, sometimes, like for falls in the elderly, a phone call to the emergency. Other times, pop-up is displayed on a screen at the place where the relevant healthcare provider would be able to take action. There is always an issue of false alarms that is well described for fall systems,[498] besides ensuring that the relevant person is there at all times to answer calls. Both would be less of a problem once the systems mature.

Accountability: Robotic surgery had been linked to 144 deaths in the United States at the time of this writing.[490] Who is accountable when a death happens? The company, the developer, or the operator. AI and IoT warrant significant changes to our legal systems, privacy laws, and also employment agreements, and most of these are yet to happen. *You can jail Alexa if she makes a mistake, but you can be rest assured that even in jail, she will merrily continue talking without regret.*

It is well understood that the potentials of AI and IoT outweigh the risks. The right way to think of AI in healthcare is to design the perfect human-computer symbiosis. For example, instead of building an AI that replaces the doctor, how about we let an AI system ask intelligent questions and use IoT to collect the patients' data in near real time, process and summarize them, and then give the specialist all the information they need to make the diagnosis. p Learning?

Virtual reality in health

Amadeu Campos de Nutes

Virtual reality (VR) is not a new concept, but is nevertheless considered revolutionary for the development of applications in the health arena. This is related to the new possibilities it offers for the interfacing system or user; the use of multisensory devices; navigation in three-dimensional spaces; immersion in the context of the application; sharing and interaction in real time; and extending the senses previously linked to simple vision, hearing, and three-dimensional manipulation for touch, pressure, and even smell through the use of devices such as head-mounted displays (HMDs), gloves, or the user's own body.

In many situations, VR is confused with augmented reality (AR). While in VR, the user navigates, observes, and immerses himself in a three-dimensional virtual world in real time, in AR, the real world is used to visualize and interact with virtual objects, giving the illusion that the real world and the virtual world are mixed. Unlike virtual reality in which users immerse themselves in a virtual environment, augmented reality does not take a user into a virtual environment. Instead, AR lets the user view virtual objects within real environment, whether by the use of tablets and smartphones or devices such as glasses.

The origins of VR can be traced in 1838 when Charles Wheatstone's research demonstrated that the brain processes the different two-dimensional images from each eye into a single object of three dimensions. In Table 1, we can visualize the evolution of virtual reality concept over time.

After the 1990s, there were several unsuccessful attempts to further evolve the concept of VR technology. During the same period the internet became popular, diverting everyone's attention, and VR was temporarily forgotten, understanding that it was not easily accessible. This period of lapse and forgetfulness of VR started in the 1990s and lasted till about 2010.

After 2010, there have been significant and rapid advances in the development of virtual reality applications due to the emergence of mobile technologies, especially the rise of smartphones, which were small and powerful, but armed with high-density displays. Inbuilt 3D capability and other graphics features like virtual light enabled a generation of reality devices. In addition, the video game industry continued to drive the development of consumer virtual reality without interruption. Another

TABLE 1   Evolution of virtual reality over time.

VR technology	Years
The stereoscope	1838
The view-master	1839
The lenticular stereoscope	1849
Link trainer-the first flight simulator	1929
Science fiction story predicted VR	1930s
Sensorama	1950s
The first VR head-mounted display	1960
Headsight—first motion tracking HMD	1961
The ultimate display	1965
Sword of Damocles	1968
Artificial reality	1969
GROPE—force-feedback system	1971
VIDEOPLACE—artificial reality	1975
VCASS—visually coupled airborne systems simulator	1982
VIVED—virtual visual environment display	1984
BOOM box	1989
UNC walkthrough project	1990s
Arcade games and machines	1991
CAVE	1992
The lawnmower man	1992
SEGA VR glasses	1993
Nintendo virtual boy	1995
Google glass, cardboard, oculus rift	21st century

advancement of smartphones that contributed to the use of VR was high-end sensors like camera depth detectors, spirit level, proximity sensor, and motion controllers. Many can simulate natural human interfaces and are already a part of the daily tasks of human computing.

Nowadays, VR has been attracting much interest. Being a new user interface paradigm, it offers great benefits in many areas of application such as entertainment and gaming, flight simulators, data visualization systems or architecture,[500,501] modeling systems,[502] planning and design, teleoperation environments,[503] and collaborative systems.[504]

FIG. 5 Categorization of virtual reality application in health.

In health, virtual reality applications can be categorized according to their purposes such as, for example, qualification of the health professional in a given scenario, training of procedures, education, simulation, rehabilitation, treatment of phobias, and diagnosis of diseases. This categorization may still consider the target audience, as shown in Fig. 5.

Training of health professionals and teaching of procedures to medical students are among the most commonly used VR applications for health. These applications aim to prepare students, technically and psychologically, to develop real tasks, to assist the educational process in different age groups, to offer professionals the means to train new techniques simulating different generic situations, and to facilitate the teaching of how to behave while attending to patients. As an example, Ragazzoni et al.[505] used virtual reality to perform training and virtual simulation for infection control and management of Ebola virus treatment. In this context, virtual reality provided a realistic and effective educational structure and opportunity to provide virtual exposure to the public health operational skills that are essential for infection control and management of Ebola virus treatment. This training is designed to increase staff safety and create a safe and realistic environment where health professionals can acquire basic and advanced skills.

In the educational context, Izard et al.[506] developed a software to illustrate the potential of virtual reality in the learning the human anatomy. Virtual reality software uses stereoscopic glasses to allow users to have the feeling of being in a virtual environment, clearly showing in 3D the different bones and shapes that make up the skull. All content is accompanied by audio explanations. Another example that used VR as a support to the teaching-learning process was developed by Silva et al.[507] who researched the students' satisfaction with the use of an VR application based on serious games for teaching the digestive system. The application, in addition to using the VR goggles also used a control for better interaction and learning with the elements of the digestive system. The study showed

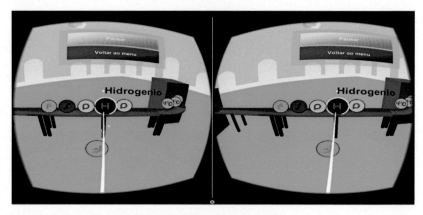

FIG. 6   Virtual reality application in the form of VR goggles.

there was evidence that the preference of all users in favor of using the VR platform as a teaching support tool relates it with its simplicity and the possibility of immersing within a virtual environment of the human body and viewing in 3D its elements (Fig. 6).

There is a growing interest in virtual reality-based programs designed to positively impact overall health and well-being. Of late, virtual reality has been used to facilitate rehabilitation through the exercise that aims to promote health. Campelo et al.[508] presented a model of virtual rehabilitation (VRehab) applied to the elderly, considering the promotion of health, rehabilitation, and injury prevention. In addition, Shin[509] in his studies added the strategy of digital games along with virtual reality for rehab exercises. These types of games can be classified into motion-based, serious game and virtual reality game.

In the field of medical procedures, educators began to introduce virtual reality in about 1997 as a tool with high potential of use for training of medical procedures and for treatment of several physical and cognitive deficiencies. They used VR to train medical students in practical experimentation and to improve their repeat practices. VR environments provide the opportunity to repeat a procedure at any time of the cycle and minimize the risk of being in contact with the patient and recreate instances of surgical tool related accidents. They had shown that training in virtual environments can improve the portability of information, reducing training time, cost, and errors.[510,511]

Virtual reality teaches surgical procedures to medical students better than the standard practice of video demonstration.[503] Gonçalves et al.[512] found advantages through use of VR allowing simulation of medical procedures. Their research focused on three-dimensional (3D) modeling of breast structures for the detection and diagnosis of breast lumps.

The training of psychomotor skills and surgical procedures of medical students and residents in distance surgery before entering the operating room is another area that has been using VR technology. The training is carried out through a virtual reality environment with the real-time transmission of high-resolution (8K) 360-degree videos from a surgical room environment for the teaching of resident physicians and undergraduate students in surgical procedures. Video recordings of surgical procedures are transmitted in real time over the internet and students can watch using VR goggles or smartphones.

Pulijala et al.[513] have developed Oculus Surgery, a virtual and immersive environment of an operating room for surgeons interning in maxillofacial surgery. The technology uses VR goggles, hand-motion tracking devices, high-resolution stereoscopic 3D videos, and 360-degree videos. This application allows a trainee to participate in a surgical procedure and interact with the patient's anatomy. Oculus Surgery is useful for surgical trainees as a visualization aid and for senior surgeons as a practice-based learning tool. Similar applications exist for surgeries where video is constant, for example, laparoscopic and endoscopic procedures.

In relation to the treatment of phobias, Monge et al.[514] proposed the VRPhobia, which is an interactive virtual reality system that improves the visual and auditory parts of the therapy, placing the patient in a virtual world that provides stimuli to face their phobias such as imagining scenes or situations they are afraid to face in the real world. In this virtual environment, they can learn the proper techniques to learn how to respond to anxiety triggers. The system is based on the techniques used by the therapists and the training that the patient undergoes. It works as a tool that improves the therapy process.

Blockchain

Fernando Sales

Transactions are the basis of the trust-based systems where people interact with each other, for example, healthcare and finances; however, the exact process of creating trust continues to evolve.[515] In general, financial operations must be registered for accounting purposes,[516] and formal recognition of a valid transaction between two parties, usually, needs attestation by a third party that in turn provides trust to the whole financial system.[517]

In health and medical care, data about health moves between patients and doctors/nurses/caregivers. This exchange is based on trust. Transactions need to be recorded and organized in a way so that they are not tampered with. Nodes in such transactions are patients, doctors/nurses/healthcare providers, and the points of care.

For example, suppose that a pharmacy company decides to publicize the prescription drug receipts for an educational campaign about antibiotic usage, some sensitive information like the personal identification data needs to be encrypted, but every other nonsensitive data can be allowed public access. This is a typical case for blockchain.

Every transaction is recorded as a block that is added to the blockchain, and any person interested in accessing the information may read it, without the need of previous authorization of the pharmacy company. Using blockchain, data from operations are safely stored, and some level of secrecy is kept for sensitive data. There are several additional examples of blockchain applications that may be found in this chapter references.

Blockchain is a public decentralized ledger, where the valid peer-to-peer transactions are recorded in a distributed chain of blocks, with constant updation as long as some new approved transactions take place.[518,519] As soon as a block is appended to the blockchain, the update is transmitted to the entire distributed structure, providing redundancy, transparency, and security.

The components of blockchain technology are

- nodes that contain the database of ledgers and current state of transactions
- ledgers themselves that include transactions
- contracts (smart contracts)—the consensus that governs the regulation of the transaction network; this eliminates the need for "trust" that is traditionally used in transactions such as banking and healthcare delivery and information exchange
- consensus networks that enable the contracts
- wallets—these manage the identity of the users in the network

Bitcoin (BTC) and Ethereum are examples of public blockchain. As of 2008, what could be called a revolution was initiated with the proposal of Bitcoin (BTC)[518] and its actual release the following year. BTC is an innovative electronic cash system to provide peer-to-peer trusted transactions without the need of a third-party validation.[517]

In the financial context the trust provider role was largely fulfilled by banks.[517] In the beginning of the third millennium, however, the internet and e-commerce brought about a new set of demands for digital operations with inbuilt technical challenges, largely associated with information security issues and a possibility of fraudulent and nontraceable transactions.[519] However, for long, this digital system kept on with the old assumption, and trust was provided by a restricted set of institutions.

The independence from a central authority to trust the transactions was a paradigm shift and the major contribution of BTC. It opened new perspectives to a wide variety of electronic transactions, not just limited to the financial system. However, one of the major concerns of BTC's creator was to protect the identity of the peers. To achieve this, sensitive data about the parties involved is encrypted and its hashkey—a sort of a signature code, used to attest the authenticity of the parties—is made public.

Even if a local block is tampered by any malignant system, it will remain different to the other branches of the redundant chain, reducing significantly the odds of a fraudulent transaction and providing certain level of security to the blockchain.

Based on these features, blockchain has been called "the trust protocol" and may be the technology responsible by the new internet generation: "the internet of value."[517] With blockchain technology, a new era of decentralized applications has risen, allowing peer-to-peer interactions, which are useful in the IoT context.[520] Smart contracts can be firmed between two different applications, providing new horizons to the machine interactions. For example, the logistics sector will be dramatically impacted, especially when automated delivery systems will be launched.[521]

In healthcare, several applications to blockchain have been developed, and new products and services are being created.[522–524] The important aspect is allowing the possibility of sharing medical data anonymously, which can allow new multicentric trials and unfettered access to clinical information, something very useful for clinical research.[525] There are fresh business opportunities in personal health data and their commercial exploration. Technology companies have joined the personal healthcare market, offering products and services for prevention and monitoring vital signals such as heart rate, pulse oximetry, blood pressure, and 1-lead electrocardiograms.[526–530] Data is stored in private clouds and maintained by companies who use them to build other products using machine learning techniques.[526,530–532] Even though maintained by the providers, such data that belonged to the patients could not be monetized previously. Now, there are possible revenue models that allow grant of access even while maintaining the required anonymity.[533]

Another example of blockchain-based healthcare applications is an online personal health record (PHR)[534] in which patients' data can be stored and made available, preserving privacy and allowing the data owners to provide access to their data. This example, also known as *omniPHR*, has interesting features because it uses *openEHR*[535] standard, which allows interoperability by means of other standards as *HL7*[536] and *SNOMED-CT*.[537] A performance assessment was performed, and *omniPHR* had an average response time below 500 ms, which can be used in real applications. Besides the previously mentioned, there are several other examples.[538–541]

Blockchain may be pioneering a new revolution, similar to the one enabled by the internet at the turn of the millennium, as described in the book by Chris Anderson *The Long Tail*,[533] which describes the impact on oligopolies by the digital revolution. Internet allowed new companies to enter consolidated markets by offering online services on demand, direct to the consumers. Amazon is a prime example—it started through online book publication but is now among the largest companies worldwide.

Despite its potential, blockchain does have some issues with relevant questions about the future of this technology: scalability and security[542,543] Bitcoin's transactions have been raised exponentially in the last years, with concomitant increase in the amount of data mining operations, electrical power consumption, and computational cost. In terms of security, blockchain is considered a secure application once it uses AES-256—Advanced Encryption Standard using 256 bits, an advanced algorithm for data encryption and decryption, the latest and best security standard, but how long it will remain is a moot question. Despite such risks, blockchain is already being used in different scenarios and in several applications, demonstrating a potential to change the way that data can be securely saved in the internet. The next section of this chapter, discusses big data a natural follower of this theme.

Big data

In line with Moore's law and faster communication, there has been an exponential growth in the amount of digital content generated and released online, leading us to the "information era." The term "big data," though widely used, lacks a formal definition. However, common sense dictates that "big data" refers to large amounts of data, around hundreds of terabytes (~100 TB), and unstructured formats and generally results from a continuous data flow.[544]

The term "big data" has become viral in the last 5 years. The concept was introduced in 2001 in a technical report written by Doug Laney of Meta Group that described the *three dimensions of data management*: volume, velocity, and variety.[545] Briefly, *volume* is related to increasing amount of data generated and collected, which needs to be processed and stored; *velocity* describes the speed of data transmission and performance of applications, which will necessarily be affected by rising amounts of data and how speed is retained. The third dimension, *variety*, is related to the diversity of data sources and the related need for standards to allow sharing and interoperability.

Additional dimensions have been added of late to this paradigm: *veracity* and *value*.[544] Both are contemporary themes, as it is important to address the authenticity of the information and, also, its value.

Healthcare is one of the sectors that produces large amounts of data from a variety of sources and needs to be quickly accessed for decision-making.

In clinical care, these sources make up the electronic health record, such as laboratory data, medical prescriptions, medical imaging data, genetic data, and prescription notes, along with the administrative data. Some potential applications of big data in health are related to predictive medicine, patient monitoring, clinical and administrative performance improvement, and production of genetic knowledge, among others. Big data's capacity in the health sector is defined as "The ability to acquire, store, process, and analyze large amounts of health data in a variety of ways and provide meaningful information to users, allowing them to discover business values and insights in a timely manner."[546]

The last few years have witnessed an increase in the variety and quantity of medical devices connected to the internet, some of which are in the form of "wearables." As of 2019, there are several biomedical signals and biomarkers being recorded and transmitted to the cloud for further analysis and to support a healthier living. This ongoing revolution includes individuals using devices to measure and quantify their daily health indexes, like the total number of steps traveled and the total duration of REM sleep every night.

Personal wearables have been feeding private large databases with personal health information. Worldwide, millions of daily users provide data that can allow large populations studies.[547,548] Inspired on this trend of personal healthcare monitoring, the *National Institutes of Health* (*NIH*) has launched the "All of Us Research Program," which aims to gather data from 1 million or more people in the United States for research purposes.[549]

Programs like this have the power to generate big data applications. They also permit analysis of different random subgroups with low bias, which can be helpful to establish causal inference,[550] which is defined as a statistical approach focused on studying the "cause and effect" relationships between variables. Using big data is more specific and more impactful than correlation through regression analysis,[551] especially when trying to establish new management strategies or new treatments.[552]

For example, the 100 million Brazilian cohort funded by several institutes gathered and integrated different data sets of personalized information to assess the impact of several social protection programs on health, education, and work, among others.[553] Cohort studies are valuable because inferring causality through confounding variables is challenging. Cohort studies are not easy to design if working on a prospective basis,[9,554] but do become possible if digital health data is utilized as exemplified by the NIH's "All of Us Research Program."[549]

Several approaches and new technologies have been developed to manage large data volumes, fulfill performance requirements, and integrate different data sets into large data lakes, to permit the data analysis process. The most used tools are open source,[555] for example, Hadoop[556] and Spark.[557] These are available in Python, one of the most popular programming languages for data science applications worldwide.

The conjunction of IoT, wearable medical devices, high-speed connectivity, and blockchain have been generating big data applications, where there has been a rising trend to use a business analytics approach, to learn from the data, from clinical trials to the local enterprise, a relatively new concept though predicted some decades ago by authors like Peter Senge,[558] who described the term "learning organizations," responsible for transforming several industries including the healthcare sector.

15

Worldwide initiatives

Christopher Pearce

Health and Biomedical Informatics Center, University of Melbourne, Parkville, VIC, Australia

Australian experience

Christopher Pearce

Australia is blessed with a high-quality health-care system, under-pinned by a universal health insurance scheme, designed to ensure equity of access for all Australians. Medicare provides a rebate for general practice consultations that are face to face, and the states deliver a network of public hospitals that provide free care to all citizens.

At the same time, we are cursed by a small population in a vast country. Eighty-six percent of the population live in cities, the vast majority clustered at the eastern seaboard. This has led to inequities in health-care outcomes between those in urban and rural environments and between indigenous and nonindigenous populations. For this reason, Australia has been both experimenting and alongside, delivering services by distance technology for 40 years.[559]

Commencing with ophthalmology and dermatology projects in Queensland, the use of telehealth has steadily grown over time (see Fig. 1). The state of Queensland still provides the bulk of services (40%) with mental health (22%) being the most popular speciality. Eighty-five percent of programs are provided by videoconferencing, the rest using store-and-forward technology.[560] Early reports suggest that the benefits are starting to accrue to patients and providers. Patients are benefiting from lower costs and reduced inconvenience while accessing specialist health services, improved access to services, and improved quality of clinical services. Health professionals are reported to have benefited from access to continuing education and professional development; provision of enhanced local services; and experiential learning, networking, and collaboration.[561]

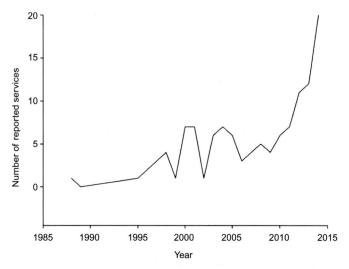

FIG. 1   Number of reported Australian telehealth services over time.[560]From Bradford NK, Caffery LJ, Smith AC. Telehealth Services in Rural and Remote Australia: A Systematic Review of Models of Care and Factors Influencing Success and Sustainability, vol. 16; 2016.

The types of benefits are varied—for services such as ophthalmology, benefits are in the form of quicker (shorter wait times), more timely decision-making and earlier intervention to highly specialized services and specialists usually only available in urban areas. In mental health and oncology, however, it may be the ability for participants to stay in their local support systems. Another benefit is the ability for professional development and advice to be delivered to remote practitioners, such as the Australian College of Rural and Remote Medicine's TeleDerm service.[562]

The significant change in the past 5 years has been the integration of telehealth services into the Medicare system, moving telehealth from a project basis to a care delivery model that can be accessed by any Australian, using medical professionals according to need, and meeting the standards required.[563]

Commencing in 2011 the federal government introduced Medicare item numbers to support specialists conducting video consultations with patients in rural environments and in residential aged care facilities. In addition, additional incentive payments were put in place to support doctors to develop telehealth capabilities.[563]

As of 2018 the program has supported a million consultations over 7.5 years, which, although encouraging, still represents a small amount of the total consultations covered by Medicare, and still therefore telehealth remains underutilized across the country. In 2017–18 there were 193 million "professional attendances" but only 188,000 telehealth services. Table 1 lists the actual uptake from government figures.[563]

TABLE 1   Services, providers, and benefits paid from July 1, 2011 to December 31, 2018.

Provider type	Services	Providers	Benefits paid $
Specialist	641,920	6427	114,137,847
General practitioner (includes practice nurse)[a]	284,792	11,887	21,348,555
Optometrist	2182	164	100,861
Midwife	207	33	10,243
Nurse practitioner	4763	123	260,845
Auxiliary (PN+AHW)[a]	5590	851	550,645
Total	**939,454**	**19,485**	**136,408,996**

[a] *Practice nurses and aboriginal health workers.*

The majority of specialists involved are consultant physicians (subspeciality unspecified) and psychiatrists. Combined with the earlier finding that the majority of programs funded by other means are in mental health, the largest area of telehealth activity remains in mental health.

In summary, telehealth remains a potential yet to be realized. The barriers to the uptake are many and varied, and there is no silver bullet to make it happen. Funding through Medicare focuses on the medical model and does not take into account modern team care arrangements (a fault with Medicare as a whole) nor supports store-and-forward services. The emphasis on videoconferencing excludes other models of care, using monitoring technologies or even combining a set of complementary technologies, including email and voice. To do so, we need

- single, seamless funding;
- invisible technology;
- digitally enabled generalists;
- health literate population;
- single shared health record;
- national medical registration at both ends;
- community need, for example, isolation/access/distance.

Despite this the vast size and low population density will continue to drive innovation. Geographic isolation should not be combined with information isolation.

Telehealth in Brazil

Magdala de Araújo Novaes

Brazil is a continental country that has undergone changes in its demographic, socioeconomic, and epidemiological profile in recent decades, accompanied by a change in the profile of illness and death. Its health system, Health Unified System (Portuguese: *Sistema Único de Saúde*, SUS), is one of the largest and most complex public health systems in the world, guaranteeing universal and free access to the entire population of the country, and promotes comprehensive health care, prevention and health promotion, and lifelong care.[66]

In this context, telehealth is presented as a strong strategy to overcome several problems, like poor distribution of health services and professionals in the territory causing long waiting lines for care, inadequate patient's referrals, risks in the displacement of patients and professionals, limited professional training, limited government investments for continuing education, limited local infrastructure for patient care, and increased system costs.

The World Health Organization recommended a need for a global digital health strategy in resolution WHA 58.28/2005,[564] which was reinforced recently in resolution WHA 71.7/2018. In line with the previous text, the Ministry of Health adopted digital health as a tool to strengthen SUS.[565] The Telehealth Brazil Program and the Virtual Blood Centers (RHEMO) were established from 2007 by the Ministry of Health and later on the Open University of SUS (UNASUS).[565] At the same time the University Telemedicine Network (RUTE) was created by the Ministry of Science and Technology in partnership with the Ministry of Education.

All these actions of telehealth together are public policies created to expand access to health, promote the permanent education of professionals, qualify patient care, optimize system costs, and promote research and innovation in SUS. Added to these initiatives are several telehealth products and services offered by complementary Brazilian health system through companies and by the third health sector. In the public sector, there are more than 20 telehealth centers of the Brazilian Telehealth Program operating in all the states of the country, more than 160 units of telehealth in school hospitals and units of the Brazilian blood center's network.

The Brazilian Telehealth Program began its activities integrating the primary care network to university referral centers in nine states of the country and currently operates throughout the country, offering teleassistance, teleeducation, and remote management for all SUS units. More than 3.5 million teleeducation sessions, 5 million remote diagnoses produced, and 800 thousand teleconsulting sessions are based on the best scientific evidences (Fig. 2).

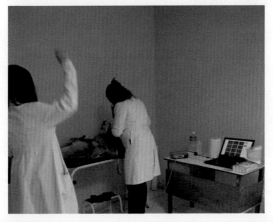

FIG. 2   Teleconsultations by web conference and telediagnosis of electrocardiogram by the Brazilian National Telehealth Network. Performed by the Telehealth Center (NUTES) of the Clinics Hospital of the Federal University of Pernambuco.

IV. Issues and future of telehealth

RUTE has implemented videoconferencing infrastructure to promote the integration of teaching service, and research, through Special Interest Groups (SIGs), and promotes clinical meetings and technical-scientific discussions between hospitals in a wide range of health specialties involving professionals, students, teachers, residents, researchers, and managers (Fig. 3A and B).

(A)

(B)

FIG. 3   (A) Videoconference sessions between hospitals through the RUTE network for the discussion of clinical cases and (B) monitoring of procedures. Telehealth Center (NUTES), Clinics Hospital of the Federal University of Pernambuco.

The country is preparing to advance further through actions that integrate all sectors of health, industry, providers and users of health care, research, and teaching, and management. From its strategic vision of digital health (eHealth), published in 2017, seeks to provide and use comprehensive information, in a precise and safe way, the action that aims at the constant improvement of the quality of services, processes, and health care.[76]

> By 2020, e-Health will be incorporated into the SUS as a fundamental dimension and recognized as a strategy for consistent improvement of health services through the availability and use of comprehensive, accurate and safe information that will speed up and improve the quality of care and of the processes in the three spheres of government and in the private sector, benefiting patients, citizens, professionals, managers and health organizations.

In addition to the wide use of telehealth in the public sector, the private sector is booming with companies providing distance medical reports (with emphasis on electrocardiography and medical imaging) and mobile applications (scheduling visits, medical second opinion, etc.), besides big data, artificial intelligence, and IoT applications. Hospitals are preparing for the delivery of health services at a distance. On the other hand Brazilian legislation (medical visits by videoconference are restricted), poor technological infrastructure (limited internet access in remote places), and billing and reimbursement issues represent barriers to a greater expansion of telehealth in the country.

Telemedicine/telehealth in Canada

Ed Brown

Canada has a land mass of 9.985 million square kilometers and a population of 37 million people, largely living in urban centers close to its southern border with the United States. As of July 2018, more than 32 million Canadians (86.4%) were living in 4 of Canada's 13 provinces and territories: Ontario (38.6%), Quebec (22.6%), British Columbia (13.5%), and Alberta (11.6%).[566] With 3.5 persons per square kilometer, Canada is one of the countries with the lowest population densities in the world. Some small remote communities can only be accessed by ice roads in the winter and by plane or boat in the warmer summer months. This distribution of the population and the geography of Canada present challenges in the distribution of health human resources relative to the population and results in the challenges of access to health services. As a result, digital and virtual technology plays an increasingly important role in the delivery of health-care services, and Canada has been recognized as a world leader in telehealth.

With its earliest beginnings over 30 years ago in Newfoundland and Labrador,[567] telehealth services exist in every province and territory in the country.[32] Through investments made by the provincial and territorial governments and supported through investments made by a federal government-funded organization, Canada Health Infoway, live two-way videoconferencing, both scheduled and on demand, is available across the country in various forms inclusive of both hardware- and room-based systems and increasingly through software-based solutions that can be used directly from the patient's home. The degree to which these solutions are used varies across the provinces. Ontario, with the largest population, has an organization dedicated to advancing the use of virtual solutions—the Ontario Telemedicine Network (OTN). It reported 894,375 clinical videoconferences in fiscal 2017–18. It is offering both hardware- and software-based videoconferencing solutions through a purpose-built platform along with virtual tools beyond simple videoconferencing.

Videoconferencing is being used for emergency care. TeleStroke in Canada was first implemented in Ontario in 2002 and is now available at scale in multiple jurisdictions across Canada. Since that time, emergency-based telehealth services have been implemented for virtual critical care, mental health crisis, for more timely response to communities that may be supported by nursing stations and for other applications.

Asynchronous modalities are also being used increasingly. Both general and specialized electronic consultation (eConsult) tools are being adopted by primary care practitioners who would like to receive consults and advice from specialists, reducing the need for face-to-face specialist visits and decreasing wait times for consultations. Specialty asynchronous modalities such as for dermatology and ophthalmology are used, as is secure messaging. Asynchronous modalities' adoption and penetration varies regionally but is growing significantly as tools become more ubiquitous and easier to use.

Direct-to-consumer telehealth is also on the rise. Remote patient monitoring and digital self-care management tools have been in use for over 10 years, particularly for patients with chronic obstructive pulmonary disease, congestive heart failure, and diabetes. They are being used at a provincial, regional, or program level in more than half of Canada's provinces and are resulting in decreased visits to the emergency department and admissions to hospital. The models of care to support this vary provincially and regionally.

While Canada has a publicly funded health-care system, increasingly, direct-to-consumer solutions are being offered by private sector companies. Clinical grade applications with evidence supporting their efficacy in delivering positive patient outcomes. They are already in use by some organizations while undergoing trials at a regional or provincial level in some cases. These solutions are also increasingly being offered to employees of large organizations through insurers. Employers and insurance companies alike are recognizing the value of delivering solutions to employees to empower them to manage their health care in a more convenient manner.

Private enterprise is also marketing direct-to-consumer primary care services using a variety of solutions. These range from the use of mobile apps to help consumers manage their chronic conditions (and additionally generate reports to providers) to interactive mobile apps that point consumers to an automated triage process and allow for increasing levels of interaction with a health-care provider up to and including a video visit.

Artificial intelligence, advanced analytics, and blockchain technology are also emerging in the Canadian health landscape, and these three areas are certain to play an increasingly important role in Canada's health system.

New models of care are emerging. The status quo bricks and mortar-based health-care system are being disrupted by advances in technology. However, policy and regulatory frameworks have not necessarily kept up to these advances. Government at the provincial, territorial, and federal levels is in the process of analysis, policy and regulatory evolution to ensure quality of care and patient safety, and appropriate economic models are in place to sustain the publicly funded health system, which is a source of pride for Canadians.

Digital and virtual means for health-care delivery and building capacity within the health system is vitally important to Canada. Focused leadership and continued development of our expertise will help us continue to be world leaders in this area.

India case study

Shashi Gogia

Besides being the second most populated country, India is understood to be the most diverse in the world from all contexts—geographic, linguistic, religious, and cultural—and of the types of health-care remedies that its population can avail itself. A demand for telecare exists due to wide income disparities and a largely rural population served by not only less number of, but also less qualified, doctors. There are also a fair number of people residing in remote and inaccessible areas, for example, the Andamans and Nicobar Islands in the Bay of Bengal and the Himalayan mountains. Poor roads are a common issue in most of the hilly regions like northeastern India.

Health is a state subject, but the central ministry provides guidelines and special funding for the poor. Despite the offers of free health care in government hospitals, most of the population prefers private care as the government hospitals are either overcrowded or lacking facilities and sometimes both.

India's initial forays in telemedicine were at the behest of Indian Space Research Organization (ISRO), which had ample support from the government and more importantly its own satellites.[11] Notable projects at the turn of the century included support for adventure travellers in the Himalayas and running a medical camp in the 2001 Allahabad Kumbh Mela from Lucknow.

Early projects could not be sustained, as soon cheaper and better technology and connectivity became available. But significant learnings of the value of telecare evolved. The learnings translated to more focused areas of work like the creation of eHealth standards,[568] a virtual e-learning platform,[148] and nationwide health grid with linkages between medical colleges. Telecare support has been offered to the neighboring developing countries as well as Africa.[12]

Lately, efforts to create a uniform e-identity for India's citizens called the Aadhar card[569] have allowed a nationwide EHR creation and better support toward health care for all. A nationwide health insurance scheme provisioning for reimbursement for the secondary and tertiary care called Ayushman Bharat for the poor riding on this has been launched.

Telemedicine in Africa

Charles Noble

Africa, and sub-Saharan Africa (SSA) in particular, face many challenges: astute poverty, asymmetric distribution of diseases, an aspirational citizenry, the lack of skilled personnel, and aberrant or absence of supply of health and other modern infrastructure.[570]

Specifically pertaining to eHealth, there is a lack of adequate communication infrastructure and adequate personnel who are trained in providing remote care and hence use this infrastructure. Admittedly, it can be done through teleeducation within the same telemedicine system.[571]

Scope of telemedicine and mobile health networks

- It improves patient-doctor communication.
- It provides acceptable methods for home-based health-care care.
- It provides convenience in accessing health services.
- It enhances simple retrieval of patients' medical records.
- It saves money and time
- Streamline workflow

The medical needs are immense. SSA constitutes 70% of the world's HIV burden; 2800 African residents die every day due to malaria. Other infectious diseases like dysentery, cholera, typhoid, chicken pox, and diarrhea consume millions. Under-five mortality is extremely high.

In this region, communication and the use of Internet are basically restricted largely to emails, with less use of specific health-related and telemedicine applications. Adding to it are social, economic, and political problems leading to a high index of corruption and bloodshed. ICT infrastructure is suboptimal in SSA notably so in 33 of its 48 countries hindering their all-round economic development. Internet penetration is 4.2% and broadband at 1.4%, a luxury. Wherever mobile communications exist, they face the issue of not having enough power to even charge the mobiles.

Ethiopia and South Africa are exceptions having well-developed telemedicine facilities, while Burkina Faso and Nigeria having almost none, constitute the other extreme.

Doctors are scarce: approximately 1 doctor for every 10,000 in 10 countries and 2 per 10,000 in 37. In comparison, Germany has 34, the United States 26, England 23, Canada 19, and India 6. Fourteen countries do not have more than a single radiologist. Specialists are present only in cities, and the persons working in rural areas also have to face health access problems related to poor roads and nonavailability of telephone, let alone internet and library access.[572,573]

As per ITU, developing the telecommunication infrastructure is going to be a challenge. Reaching adequate penetration with the rest of the word will mean expenditures of around 30%–40% of gross national product (GNP) versus 0.4%–0.8% in advanced countries.[574]

Conclusions

Telemedicine offers much in improving the health support systems. There is a huge cost in developing and implementing the telecommunication infrastructure, abridgement of eHealth activity, enabling legislation for telemedicine, and correcting the poor doctor-patient ratio. Special initiatives like the use of teleeducation will provide all-round development.

Summary of learnings

Table 2 summarizes the learnings from each country, in no particular order of priority or significance.

TABLE 2   Summary of learnings from various countries.

Complex technologies are not essential: simple text messages and email can be sufficient
Government funding does not guarantee widespread uptake
Telehealth can (and should) disrupt traditional models of care
Although overcoming the barriers of distance drives much of telehealth, it has applications in urban areas as well
Telehealth supports both primary care and secondary care and breaks down the barriers between them
Adequate funding of telehealth remains a barrier

A final word

If the case studies earlier teach us anything, it is that the path to good care involves telehealth in all its aspects and that need should tailor the technology and the funding. The variety of models and the persistence of effort demonstrate the importance of telehealth into the future.

Glossary

Used in the book to mean any emergency call (911) The emergency calling number of the United States is recognized world over thanks to Hollywood movies. These vary, for example, 000 is used in Australia and 108 in India.

Asymmetric digital subscriber line (ADSL) A data communication technology that enables faster data transmission over copper telephone lines than a conventional voiceband modem can provide.

Artificial intelligence (AI) Using computer processing to make decisions.

Augmented reality/virtual reality (AR/VR) Three-dimensional emulation—VR (see in the succeeding text), AR creates perceptions from 2D images. A mixed form (MR) is a combination.

Application Program Interface (API)

Kilo or megabytes per second [(k/M) bps] Transmission data speeds. In a typical network environment, upload, that is, data being sent away from a local to remote site and download—that is, the reverse speeds vary with the latter being faster.

Compact Disc (CD) A portable storage medium that can be used to record, store and play back audio, video and other data in digital form. It has a capacity of 80 minutes of audio, or 650 megabytes to 700 MB of data.

Computer-aided design/manufacture (CAD/CAM) AI in the publishing and manufacturing domain.

Capital expenditure (CAPEX) One-time fixed costs initially required to start a particular project. Hardware, software, land acquisition are examples.

Clinical decision support systems (CDSS) AI aiding a clinician in day-to-day work, DDSS or diagnostic decision support system is the most common form.

Continuous Glucose Monitor (CGM) A device to continuously monitor Blood Glucose levels report the same on a realtime basis.

The Internet cloud (Cloud) A near infinite set of connected server computers where all possible information is stored on a private or public basis with a capability to be viewed almost anywhere anytime.

Clinico pathology conference (CPC) Academic interaction between clinicians and pathologists following a diagnosis is obtained by the latter.

Chronic pulmonary obstructive disease (COPD)

Computerized provider order entry (CPOE) A type of CDSS that analyses prescriptive advice and checks for over or under dosage, mismatched drugs, interactions, redundancy etc.

Digital Imaging and Communications in Medicine (DICOM) International standard for communication of biomedical diagnostic and therapeutic information in disciplines that use digital images and associated data.

Digital Versatile Disc (DVD) An advanced form of the compact disc which allows between 4 to 18 Gb of data. It is more commonly understood as Digital Video Disc as it was largely used for playing high definition movies.

Data, information, knowledge, wisdom (DIKW) Information science of flow processes in computer systems—explained fully in Chapter 1.

Diplomate National Board (DNB) a medical specialty specific certification program in India.

Electro cardiogram (ECG)

Emergency room (ER) Hospital wing where incoming serious cases are first seen -also called casualty or **Emergency Department (ED)**.

Electroencephalogram (EEG)

Electronic health record (EHR) EMR and EHR are interchangeable terms—explained in Chapter 3.

Electronic medical record (EMR)

Fast Health Interchange Resource (FHIR) The latest version of HL7 is FHIR (pronounced "fire"). It allows interoperability between electronic Patient Administration Systems (PAS), Electronic Practice Management (EPM) systems, Laboratory Information Systems (LIS), Dietary, Pharmacy and Billing systems, and electronic medical record (EMR) or electronic health record (EHR) systems.

General practitioner (GP) The term FP for family practitioner is also used.

Global positioning system (GPS) Online maps guiding traffic. Can guide public health requirements. It helped extract persons stuck under buildings during the Haiti earthquake.

Health information exchange (HIE) A virtual place holder for sharing health-related information.

Home HealthCare (HHC) Care provision at the patients home delivered through various devices.

Hospital (Management &) Information System also Health Information and Management System [H(M)IS)] Comprehensive software solutions used in epidemiology and public health. Where H pertains to hospitals, it includes solutions that manage all the services within the hospital including an EMR.

Healthcare Information Management Systems and Societies (HIMSS) Organization which classifies and certifies hospitals for various levels of EMR adoption. The highest level is 7 (www.himss.org).

Healthcare Insurance Portability and Accountability Act (HIPAA) Active in the United States, similar rules required in India—IT Act is not specific to healthcare.

Healthcare information technology (HIT) IT solutions pertaining to health also known as HCIT.

Health Level Seven (HL7) With a name based on the seventh or (health-related) application layer networking, HL7.org is a not-for-profit organization supported by hardware and software vendors to allow computers to talk to each other.

Hypertext Markup Language (HTML) The language that lead to the birth of the Internet. Developed by Tim Berners Lee, it enabled seamless document sharing through a network of computers. HTML5 contains added audio and video.

International Classification for Diseases (ICD) Promoted by WHO, ICD started as a classification of the causes of death, but later morbidities were also added. Currently version 10 is being used globally. Version 11 is under development.

Information and communication technology (ICT) IT is data creation and processing, while C is about transmission and sharing. See Chapter 4.

Intensive care unit (ICU)

Integrated healthcare enterprise (IHE) An organization that is helping collaborations between health organizations.

International Health Terminology Standards Development Organization (IHTSDO) A not-for-profit association based in Denmark. It owns, maintains, and distributes SNOMED CT.

Internet of things (IoT) When devices talk to each other without involving humans.

Integrated Services Digital Network (ISDN) A set of communication standards allowing simultaneous digital transmission of voice, video, data, and other network services using standard telecommunication equipment.

International Standards for Organization (ISO) The specific technical committee (TC) for standards pertaining to telehealth and HIT is TC 215. TC 62 that works with medical devices is aligned closely.

Internet Protocol security (IPSec)

Indian Space Research Organization (ISRO) India's equivalent to NASA.

Information (and communication) technology (IT) See ICT earlier.

International Telecommunication Union (ITU)

Intravenous Tissue-Type Plasminogen Activator IV tPA Used for emergency clot dissolution as treatment of thrombotic events leading to stroke etc.

Local area network (LAN) Sharing digital information within an institution, home, or workplace using wired or wireless media.

Minimal access surgery (MAS) Doing surgery through natural orifices or small incisions—examples are laparoscopic and endoscopic approaches.

Multimedia Messaging Service (MMS) Largely replaced now by WhatsApp and WeChat that allows more options and is cheaper.

Memorandum of Understanding (MOU) An official legally binding agreement between two or more parties regarding a particular work plan.

National Aeronautics and Space Administration (NASA) Official agency from the United States that is doing space exploration and research.

Noncommunicable Diseases (NCDs) As opposed to communicable diseases—which (do not) have a transmissible pathogen.

Nurse practitioner (NP) Person providing care at the subprimary level. In ideal conditions, they should be trained nurses, but the same is being provided by many others—so the term is used here in a generic sense.

Operating expenditure (OPEX) Running or recurrent costs of—consumables, salaries, and rent are examples.

Operating room/operation theater (OR/OT) The dedicated location or room within a healthcare facility where procedures are performed.

Picture Archiving and Compression System (PACS) Filmless recording of medical images done through digitization. These are stored in hard disks and can be viewed from anywhere after being allowed access.

Primary care provider (PCP) Generally the GP can also be the nurse practitioners based on regulations in various locations.

Primary HealthCare (PHC) First level care.

Primary Healthcare Center (PHC) A government facility providing first level care.

Personal health record (PHR) An EHR under direct control of the patient.

Posttraumatic stress disorder (PTSD) Mental affects after going through a traumatic event like war or natural disaster. Telehealth has an important role.

Representational State Transfer (RESTful) An API that uses HTTP requests to GET, PUT, POST and DELETE data.

Software as a service (SaaS) Internet cloud-based platforms on a pay-per-use mode. The application runs on the server which you access during the same.

Society for Administration of Telemedicine and Healthcare Informatics (SATHI) A not-for-profit doing telemedicine projects in India—www.sathi.org.

Store and forward (S&F) A form of asynchronous telehealth where information is collected, stored, and then forwarded or used for health support.

Short messaging service (SMS) The oldest and still the commonest method to send text through mobile phones.

Systematized Nomenclature in Medicine (SNOMED) A semantic standard—a collection of health terminologies and phrases which transcends cultural and language barriers also called SNOMED CT with CT for Clinical Terminology.

Standard Operating Protocol(s) [SOP(s)] Guideline on the best method to be followed for any identified issue. SOPs are prescribed for disease management too, for example, an emergency triage.

Transmission Control Protocol/Internet Protocol (TCP/IP) The most common protocol used for data sharing and internet.

Universal Serial Bus (USB) The most common method for physical transfer of data between computer systems and peripherals. A memory stick uses a USB connection but is nevertheless called a USB (drive).

Unique Health (or Hospital) Identity (UHID) Records are indexed and later traced based on the UHID.

Video conferencing (VC) Face-to-face video telephone call. Can be one to one or multipoint.

Voice Over Internet Protocol (VoIP) Internet telephony which uses data streams (codecs) rather than analog signals. Interestingly includes video telephony too.

Virtual reality (VR) Simulation of real-time experience through computers or holography.

Wide area network (WAN) Information sharing across a wide area or even a country but within the same institution.

World Health Organization (WHO)

References

1. Manjhi D. *Wikipedia*. https://en.wikipedia.org/wiki/Dashrath_Manjhi.
2. *2014: 100000 flights per day*. https://garfors.com/2014/06/100000-flights-day-html/%09.
3. Chen S, Cheng A, Mehta K. A review of telemedicine business models. *Telemed J E Health*. 2013;19(4):287–297. https://doi.org/10.1089/tmj.2012.0172.
4. Oh H, Rizo C, Enkin M, Jadad A, Powell J, Pagliari C. What is eHealth (3): a systematic review of published definitions. *J Med Internet Res*. 2005;7(1):e1. https://doi.org/10.2196/jmir.7.1.e1.
5. Pennic F. *Survey: 76% of Patients Would Choose Telehealth Over Human Contact*. HIT Consultant; 2013. https://hitconsultant.net/2013/03/08/survey-patients-would-choose-telehealth-over-human-contact/#.XEv8olxKg54. Accessed January 26, 2019.
6. Research2guidance. *325,000 Mobile Health Apps Available in 2017—Android Now the Leading mHealth Platform*; 2017. https://research2guidance.com/325000-mobile-health-apps-available-in-2017/. Accessed January 10, 2019.
7. CIO Survey. *IT Project Success Rates Finally Improving*. https://www.cio.com/article/3174516/project-management/it-project-success-rates-finally-improving.html.
8. Aronson SH, Mackenzie C, Bell AG. The lancet on the telephone 1876-1975. *Med Hist*. 1977;21:69–87.
9. Bashshur RL, Shannon GW. *History of Telemedicine*. Mary Ann Liebert; 2009. ISBN 13 978-1-934854-11-2, ISBN e-book 978-1-934854-04-2.
10. Gupta RRR, Mitra M, Bera J. *ECG Acquisition and Automated Remote Processing*. Springer; 2014: pp. 214. ISBN: 8132215575.
11. Mishra SK, Kapoor L, Singh IP. Telemedicine in India: current scenario and the future. *Telemed J E Health*. 2009;15(6). https://doi.org/10.1089/tmj.2009.0059.
12. Mars M. E health in Africa. *Telemed J E Health*. 2012;18:3–4.
13. Hartvigsen G, Pedersen S. *Lessons Learned From 25 Years With Telemedicine in Northern Norway*. University Hospital of North Norway, Norwegian Centre for Integrated Care and Telemedicine Book; 2015. EBook Available from http://www.telemed.no.
14. WHO. *Atlas of EHealth Country Profiles*. 3rd ed. Geneva: World Health Organization; 2015.
15. Kimura M, Croll P, Wong CP, et al. Survey on medical records and EHR in Asia-Pacific region languages, purposes, IDs and regulations special topic: health IT in Asia-Pacific region. *Methods Inf Med*. 2011;50(4):386–391.
16. Payne TH, Corley S, Cullen TA, et al. Report of the AMIA EHR 2020 Task Force on the Status and Future Direction of EHRs. *J Am Med Inform Assoc*. https://doi.org/10.1093/jamia/ocv066.
17. Mishra SK, Kapoor L, Singh IP. Telemedicine in India: current scenario and the future. *Telemed J E Health*. 2009;15(6). https://doi.org/10.1089/tmj.2009.0059.
18. Neurology care "is lacking" for UK patients. *BBC News*. http://www.bbc.com/news/health-13665523. Accessed January 24, 2018.
19. Zhai Y, Zhu W, Hou H, Sun D, Zhao J. Efficacy of telemedicine for thrombolytic therapy in acute ischemic stroke: a meta-analysis. *J Telemed Telecare*. 2015;21(3):123–130. https://doi.org/10.1177/1357633X15571357.
20. Gogia SB, Maeder A, Mars M, Hartvigsen G, Basu A, Abbott P. Unintended consequences of tele health and their possible solutions. Contribution of the IMIA Working Group on telehealth. *Yearb Med Inform*. 2016;(1):41–46. https://doi.org/10.15265/IY-2016-012.

21. The patient will see you now, by Eric Topol. *NY Times*. https://www.nytimes.com/2015/02/15/books/review/the-patient-will-see-you-now-by-eric-topol.html. Accessed March 6, 2019.

22. C. Do. B. Judson *Telehealth and Telecare Aware*; 2017. http://telecareaware.com/tag/bruce-judson/. Accessed March 6, 2019.

23. H. Mack. Thirty-six connected health apps and devices the FDA cleared in 2016. *MobiHealthNews*; 2016. https://www.mobihealthnews.com/content/thirty-six-connected-health-apps-and-devices-fda-cleared-2016. Accessed January 23, 2019.

24. Fifty-one connected health products the FDA cleared in 2017. *MobiHealthNews*. 2017. https://www.mobihealthnews.com/content/fifty-one-connected-health-products-fda-cleared-2017. Accessed January 23, 2019.

25. TytoCare. *On Demand Medical Exams With a Doctor. Anytime. Anywhere*. https://www.tytocare.com/. Accessed March 7, 2019.

26. WHO. *Atlas of eHealth Country Profiles 2015: The Use of eHealth in Support of Universal Health Coverage*. Geneva: WHO; 2016.

27. *The Nightscout Project—We Are Not Waiting*. http://www.nightscout.info/. Accessed March 7, 2019.

28. *Live Better, Together!* PatientsLikeMe. https://www.patientslikeme.com/. Accessed March 7, 2019.

29. *About Health Level Seven International*. HL7 International. http://www.hl7.org/about/. Accessed March 7, 2019.

30. Gulliford M, Naithani S, Morgan M. What is "continuity of care"? *J Health Serv Res Policy*. 2006;11(4):248–250. https://doi.org/10.1258/135581906778476490.

31. Garth WJ. *Continuity of Care Starts With You*. Medscape; 2011.

32. Sutherland V, Deren M. Telehealth: Maximizing Health Care Resources to Serve Patient Needs Canada Health Infoway. https://www.infoway-inforoute.ca/en/209-what-we-do/digital-health-and-you/stories/387-telehealth-maximizing-health-care-resources-to-serve-patient-needs. Accessed March 7, 2019.

33. Poissant L, Pereira J, Tamblyn R, Kawasumi Y. The impact of electronic health records on time efficiency of physicians and nurses: a systematic review. J Am Med Inform Assoc 12(5):505-516. https://doi.org/10.1197/jamia.M1700.

34. Merrel RC. Geriatric telemedicine: background and evidence for telemedicine as a way to address the challenges of geriatrics. *J Healthc Inform Res*. 2015;21(4):223–229.

35. Shetty R, Sreekar H, Lamba S, Gupta AK. A novel and accurate technique of photographic wound measurement. *Indian J Plast Surg*. 2012;45(2):429. https://doi.org/10.4103/0970-0358.101333.

36. Gogia SB. A novel and accurate technique of photographic wound measurement. *Indian J Plast Surg*. 2012;45(2):429.

37. Tai-Seale M, McGuire TG, Zhang W. Time allocation in primary care office visits. *Health Serv Res*. 2007;42(5):1871–1894. https://doi.org/10.1111/j.1475-6773.2006.00689.x.

38. Hayrinen K, Saranto K, Nykanen P. Definition, structure, content, use and impacts of electronic health records: a review of the research literature. *Int J Med Inform*. 2008;77(5):291–304. https://doi.org/10.1016/j.ijmedinf.2007.09.001.

39. Leyens L, Reumann M, Malats N, Brand A. Use of big data for drug development and for public and personal health and care. *Genet Epidemiol*. 2017;41(1):51–60. https://doi.org/10.1002/gepi.22012.

40. Hartzband D, Jacobs F. Deployment of analytics into the healthcare safety net: lessons learned. *Online J Public Heal Inf*. 2016;8(3):e203. https://doi.org/10.5210/ojphi.v8i3.7000.

41. Brenson T. *Principles of Health Interoperability HL7 and SNOMED*. 2nd ed. London: Springer; 2012.

42. Yellowlees P. Telemedicine Enabled Homecare. Presentation at The American Telemedicine Association Fifth Annual Meeting, May 21-24, 2000, Phoenix Civic Plaza, Phoenix, AZ.

43. Mercy Health Unveils $54M Virtual Care Center. https://hitconsultant.net/2015/10/07/mercy-health-unveils-54m-virtual-care-center/#.XIHsuFwzY54. Accessed March 8, 2019.

44. Kaufman SB. *Shifting responsibilities in home care. FDA Workshop on Home Care Technology Trends*; 2001.

45. Mukherjee S. *Digital Health Care Revolution* Fortune; 2017. http://fortune.com/2017/04/20/digital-health-revolution/. Accessed March 8, 2019.

46. About American Well. https://www.americanwell.com/about-us/. Accessed March 9, 2019.

47. GIGO (Garbage In, Garbage Out) Definition. https://techterms.com/definition/gigo. Accessed March 8, 2019.

48. Belleti D, Zacker C, Mullins D, et al. Perspectives on electronic medical records adoption: electronic medical records (eMR) in outcomes research. *Patient Relat Outcome Meas.* 2006;12(1):29–37.

49. Hartvigsen G, Pedersen S. *Lessons Learned From 25 Years With Telemedicine in Northern Norway.* Tromsø: Norwegian Centre for Integrated Care and Telemedicine, University Hospital of North Norway; 2015.

50. Emergency Medical Communications Center (AMK)—Oslo University Hospital. https://oslo-universitetssykehus.no/avdelinger/prehospital-klinikk/akuttmedisinsk-kommunikasjonssentral-amk. Accessed March 9, 2019.

51. Coiera E. *Guide to Health Informatics.* 3rd ed. CRC Press; 2015. ISBN-13: 978-1444170498, ISBN-10: 144417049X.

52. Kuzmina OD, Fominykh AD, Abrosimova NA. Problems of the English abbreviations. *Med Transl.* 2015;199:548–554.

53. Woywodt A, Matteson E. Should eponyms be abandoned? Yes. *Br Med J.* 2007;335(6617):424. https://doi.org/10.1136/bmj.39308.342639.AD.

54. About IHE. *Integrating: The Healthcare Enterprise.* http://www.ihe.net/About_IHE/.

55. Pallin DJ, Chng Y-M, McKay MP, Emond JA, Pelletier AJ, Camargo CA. Epidemiology of epistaxis in US Emergency Departments, 1992 to 2001. *Ann Emerg Med.* 2005;46(1):77–81. https://doi.org/10.1016/j.annemergmed.2004.12.014.

56. Sander C. Genomic medicine and the future of health care. *Science.* 2000;287(5460):1977–1978.

57. Donabedian A. The quality of care. How can it be assessed? 1988. *Arch Pathol Lab Med.* 1997;121(11):1145–1150.

58. Tucker JL, Adams SR. Incorporating patients' assessments of satisfaction and quality: an integrative model of patients' evaluations of their care. *Manag Serv Qual An Int J.* 2001;11(4):272–287.

59. Haidet P, Paterniti DA. Building a history rather than taking one: a perspective on information sharing during the medical interview. *Arch Intern Med.* 2003;163(10):1134–1140.

60. Townsend A, Leese J, Adam P, et al. eHealth, participatory medicine, and ethical care: a focus group study of patients' and health care providers' use of health-related internet information. *J Med Internet Res.* 2015;17(6):e155.

61. Moore GE. Cramming more components onto integrated circuits. *Proc IEEE.* 1998;86(1):82–85.

62. Schaller RR. Moore's law: past, present and future. *IEEE Spectrum.* 1997;34(6):52–59.

63. Boucher JL. Technology and patient-provider interactions: improving quality of care, but is it improving communication and collaboration? *Diab Spectrum.* 2010;23(3):142–144.

64. Bragazzi NL. From P0 to P6 medicine, a model of highly participatory, narrative, interactive, and "augmented" medicine: some considerations on Salvatore Iaconesi's clinical story. *Patient Prefer Adherence.* 2013;7:353.

65. Hood L, Price ND. Demystifying disease, democratizing health care. *Sci Transl Med.* 2014;6(225):225ed5.

66. *Family Health Strategy (ESF)* [original in Portuguese] http://portalms.saude.gov.br/acoes-e-programas/saude-da-familia/sobre-o-programa. Accessed February 17, 2019.

67. Fadiman A. *The Spirit Catches You and You Fall Down: A Hmong Child, Her American Doctors, and the Collision of Two Cultures,* 1st pbk ed. New York: Farrar, Straus and Giroux; 1998.

68. Delfanti A, Iaconesi S. *Open Source Cancer. Brain Scans and the Rituality of Biodigital Data sharing. The Participatory Condition.* University of Minnesota Press; 2016.

69. Gogia SSB, Malaviya A. Patient care records through document template or EMR: the rheumatology experience part II—user satisfaction. *Indian J Med Inform.* 2013;7(1):1–15.

70. Katz SJ, Moyer CA. The emerging role of online communication between patients and their providers. *J Gen Intern Med.* 2004;19(9):978–983. https://doi.org/10.1111/j.1525-1497.2004.30432.x.

71. Sechrest RC. The internet and the physician-patient relationship. *Clin Orthop Relat Res.* 2010;468(10):2566–2571. https://doi.org/10.1007/s11999-010-1440-3.

72. Mesquita AC, Zamarioli CM, Fulquini FL, de CEC, Angerami ELS. Social networks in nursing work processes: an integrative literature review. *Rev da Esc Enferm da USP.* 2017;51.

73. Eckard C, Asbury C, Bolduc B, et al. The integration of technology into treatment programs to aid in the reduction of chronic pain. *J Pain Manag Med.* 2016;2(3):118. https://doi.org/10.35248/2684-1320.16.2.118.

74. Spasić I, Button K, Divoli A, et al. TRAK app suite: a web-based intervention for delivering standard care for the rehabilitation of knee conditions. *JMIR Res Protoc.* 2015;4(4):e122. https://doi.org/10.2196/resprot.4091.

75. Guseh JS, Brendel RW, Brendel DH. Medical professionalism in the age of online social networking. *J Med Ethics.* 2009;35(9):584–586.

76. Ministério da SAÚDE. *Visualização não encontrada. Brasil.* http://portalms.saude.gov.br/acoes-e-programas/digisus; 2018. Accessed March 29, 2019.

77. Lamar C. *Urine Flavor Wheels Helped Doctors Taste Patients' Pee Centuries Ago.* io9; 2012. https://io9.gizmodo.com/urine-flavor-wheels-helped-doctors-taste-patients-pee-c-5953234. Accessed March 30, 2019.

78. Copeland BJ. *MYCIN. Artificial Intelligence Program;* 2017. Encyclopedia Brittannica. https://www.britannica.com/technology/artificial-intelligence. Accessed January 16, 2019.

79. T. Vetterlein, H. Mandl, K.-P. Adlassnig. Fuzzy Arden Syntax: a fuzzy programming language for medicine. J Biomed Inform 2012;45(August 4):711:718.

80. World Health Organization. *Global Status Report on Noncommunicable Diseases 2014. Attaining the Nine Global Noncommunicable Diseases Targets; A Shared Responsicility;* 2014, ISBN: 9789241564854.

81. Valderas JM, Starfield B, Sibbald B, Salisbury C, Roland M. Defining comorbidity: implications for understanding health and health services. *Ann Fam Med.* 2009;7(4):357–363. https://doi.org/10.1370/afm.983.

82. Fix GM, VanDeusen Lukas C, Bolton RE, et al. Patient-centred care is a way of doing things: how healthcare employees conceptualize patient-centred care. *Health Expect.* 2018;21(1):300–307. https://doi.org/10.1111/hex.12615.

83. Stewart M. *Patient-Centered Medicine: Transforming the Clinical Method.* Cleveland, OH: CRC Press; 2003.

84. Frampton SB, Guastello S. Patient-centered care: more than the sum of its parts planetree's patient-centered hospital designation program. *Am J Nurs.* 2010;110(9):49–53. https://doi.org/10.1097/01.NAJ.0000388265.57051.e6.

85. Boyd CM, Lucas GM. Patient-centered care for people living with multimorbidity. *Curr Opin HIV AIDS.* 2014;9(4):419–427. https://doi.org/10.1097/COH.0000000000000073.

86. McDonald KM, Sundaram V, Bravata DM, et al. *Closing the Quality Gap: A Critical Analysis of Quality Improvement Strategies (vol. 7: Care Coordination).* Agency for Healthcare Research and Quality (US); 2007.

87. Institute for Healthcare Improvement. *Better Health and Lower Costs for Patients With Complex Needs: An IHI Triple Aim Collaborative*; 2015. September.

88. Wagner EH, Sandhu N, Coleman K, Phillips KE, Sugarman JR. Improving Care Coordination in Primary Care. *Med Care*. 2014;52(11 Suppl 4):S33–S38. https://doi.org/10.1097/MLR.0000000000000197.

89. Van Houdt S, Sermeus W, Vanhaecht K, De Lepeleire J. Focus groups to explore health-care professionals' experiences of care coordination: towards a theoretical framework for the study of care coordination. *BMC Fam Pract*. 2014;15(1):177. https://doi.org/10.1186/s12875-014-0177-6.

90. Ito M, Martini JSC, Iochida LC. *CPRM: a chronic patient's management model based on the concepts of customer's relationship*. In: *Proceedings of the 2008 ACM Symposium on Applied Computing* New York: ACM; 2008:1364–1368.

91. Ball M, Ballen S, Danis C, Concordia A, Jean M, Minniti M. *No Patient Engagement, No Chance for Adherence: A Case Study*.

92. Coulter A, Parsons S, Askham J. *Where Are the Patients in Decision-Making about Their Own Care?* 2008.

93. World Health Organization. Patient engagement: technical series on safer primary care. *World Heal Organ*. 2016;4(28). https://doi.org/10.1016/S0378-6080(10)32050-2.

94. Kickbusch I, Maag D, Saan H. *Enabling Healthy Choices in Modern Health Societies*. European Health Forum Badgastein; 2005:0–11.

95. Nutbeam D. Health literacy as a public health goal: a challenge for contemporary health education and communication strategies into the 21st century. *Health Promot Int*. 2000;15(3):259–267. https://doi.org/10.1093/heapro/15.3.259.

96. O'Donohue W, James L, Snipes C, eds. *Practical Strategies and Tools to Promote Treatment Engagement*. Cham: Springer International Publishing; 2017. https://doi.org/10.1007/978-3-319-49206-3.

97. Brown L. *Digital Literacy: Towards a Definition*. Oxford: Health Education England, NHS; 2016:1–28. https://www.hee.nhs.uk/our-work/digital-literacy.

98. Davis FD. Perceived usefulness, perceived ease of use, and user acceptance of information technology. *MIS Q*. 2006;13(3):319. https://doi.org/10.2307/249008.

99. Kayyali R, Hesso I, Ejiko E, Nabhani Gebara S. A qualitative study of telehealth patient information leaflets (TILs): are we giving patients enough information? *BMC Health Serv Res*. 2017;17(1):362. https://doi.org/10.1186/s12913-017-2257-5.

100. Granger BB, Bosworth HB. Medication adherence: emerging use of technology. *Curr Opin Cardiol*. 2011;26(4):279–287. https://doi.org/10.1097/HCO.0b013e328347c150.

101. Schumaker RP, Ginsburg M, Chen H, Liu Y. An evaluation of the chat and knowledge delivery components of a low-level dialog system: the AZ-ALICE experiment. *Decis Support Syst*. 2007;42(4):2236–2246. https://doi.org/10.1016/j.dss.2006.07.001.

102. Weizenbaum J. Joseph. ELIZA—a computer program for the study of natural language communication between man and machine. *Commun ACM*. 1966;9(1):36–45. https://doi.org/10.1145/365153.365168.

103. Looyestyn J, Kernot J, Boshoff K, Ryan J, Edney S, Maher C. Does gamification increase engagement with online programs? A systematic review. Amblard F, ed. *PLoS One*. 2017;12(3):e0173403. https://doi.org/10.1371/journal.pone.0173403.

104. Tang PC, Ash JS, Bates DW, Overhage JM, Sands DZ. Personal health records: definitions, benefits, and strategies for overcoming barriers to adoption. *J Am Med Inform Assoc*. 2006;13(2):121–126. https://doi.org/10.1197/jamia.M2025.

105. Irizarry T, DeVito Dabbs A, Curran CR. Patient portals and patient engagement: a state of the science review. *J Med Internet Res*. 2015;17(6):e148. https://doi.org/10.2196/jmir.4255.

106. Rigby M, Georgiou A, Hyppönen H, et al. Patient portals as a means of information and communication technology support to patient-centric care coordination—the missing

evidence and the challenges of evaluation. *Yearb Med Inform*. 2015;24(01):148–159. https://doi.org/10.15265/IY-2015-007.

107. Van Woensel W, Roy PC, Abidi SR, Abidi SSR. A mobile and intelligent patient diary for chronic disease self-management. *Stud Health Technol Inform*. 2015;216:118–122.

108. Schneider S, Stone AA. Ambulatory and diary methods can facilitate the measurement of patient-reported outcomes. *Qual Life Res*. 2016;25(3):497–506. https://doi.org/10.1007/s11136-015-1054-z.

109. Lyles CR, Fruchterman J, Youdelman M, Schillinger D. Legal, practical, and ethical considerations for making online patient portals accessible for all. *Am J Public Health*. 2017;107(10):1608–1611. https://doi.org/10.2105/AJPH.2017.303933.

110. Coughlin SS, Stewart JL, Young L, Heboyan V, De Leo G. Health literacy and patient web portals. *Int J Med Inform*. 2018;113:43–48. https://doi.org/10.1016/j.ijmedinf.2018.02.009.

111. Norman CD, Skinner HA. eHealth literacy: essential skills for consumer health in a networked world. *J Med Internet Res*. 2006;8(2):e9. https://doi.org/10.2196/jmir.8.2.e9.

112. Rao B, Lombardi A. Telemedicine: current status in developed and developing countries. *J Drugs Dermatol*. 2009;8(4):371–375.

113. Harzheim E, Gonçalves MR, Umpierre RN, et al. Telehealth in Rio Grande do Sul, Brazil: bridging the gaps. *Telemed J E Health*. 2016;22(11):938–944. https://doi.org/10.1089/tmj.2015.0210.

114. Lustig TA. *The Role of Telehealth in an Evolving Health Care Environment*. Washington, DC: National Academies Press; 2012. https://doi.org/10.17226/13466.

115. Dinesen B, Nonnecke B, Lindeman D, et al. Personalized telehealth in the future: a global research agenda. *J Med Internet Res*. 2016;18(3):e53. https://doi.org/10.2196/jmir.5257.

116. Free C, Phillips G, Watson L, et al. The effectiveness of mobile-health technologies to improve health care service delivery processes: a systematic review and meta-analysis. Cornford T, ed. *PLoS Med*. 2013;10(1):e1001363. https://doi.org/10.1371/journal.pmed.1001363.

117. World Health Organization. *Everybody's Business—Strengthening Health Systems to Improve Health Outcomes: WHO's Framework for Action*. Geneva: WHO; 2007. https://doi.org/10.1371/journal.pone.0013372.

118. Pagliari C. Design and evaluation in ehealth: challenges and implications for an interdisciplinary field. *J Med Internet Res*. 2007;9(2):e15. https://doi.org/10.2196/jmir.9.2.e15.

119. van Gemert-Pijnen JE, Nijland N, van Limburg M, et al. A holistic framework to improve the uptake and impact of eHealth technologies. *J Med Internet Res*. 2011;13(4):e111. https://doi.org/10.2196/jmir.1672.

120. Gogia SB. Providing tele mental health services after disasters-based on the Post Tsunami experience. In: Ada S, ed. *Cases in Managing E Services*. Pennsylvania: IGI Global; 2009:238–252.

121. Brasil, IBGE. *Tábua Completa de Mortalidade Para o Brasil—2016: Breve Análise Da Evolução Da Mortalidade No Brasil*. Rio de Janeiro: Instituto Brasileiro de Geografia e Estatística; 2017.

122. da S. Simões CC. *Relações Entre as Alterações Históricas Na Dinâmica Demográfica Brasileira e Os Impactos Decorrentes Do Processo de Envelhecimento Da População*. Rio de Janeiro: IBGE; 2016.

123. Ghosh R, Heit J, Srinivasan S. Telehealth at scale. In: *Proceedings of the First International Workshop on Managing Interoperability and Complexity in Health Systems—MIXHS '11* New York, NY: ACM Press; 2011:63. https://doi.org/10.1145/2064747.2064761.

124. Khatri KL, Tamil LS. Early detection of peak demand days of chronic respiratory diseases emergency department visits using artificial neural networks. *IEEE J Biomed Health Inform*. 2018;22(1):285–290. https://doi.org/10.1109/JBHI.2017.2698418.

125. Runkler TA. Introduction. In: Runkler TA, ed. *Data Analytics*. 2nd ed.Wiesbaden: Springer Fachmedien; 2016:1–3. https://doi.org/10.1007/978-3-658-14075-5_1.

126. Burke J. The world of health analytics. In: Kudyba SP, ed. *Healthcare Informatics*. Boca Raton: CRC Press; 2010:161–180. https://doi.org/10.1201/9781439809792-c8.

127. Chen H, Chiang RHL, Storey VC. Business intelligence and analytics: from big data to big impact. *MIS Q.* 2012;36:1165–1188.
128. Chaudhuri S, Dayal U, Narasayya V. An overview of business intelligence technology. *Commun ACM.* 2011;54(8):88. https://doi.org/10.1145/1978542.1978562.
129. Risch T, Canli T, Khokhar A, et al. Data warehouse. In: *Encyclopedia of Database Systems.* Boston, MA: Springer; 2009:657–658. https://doi.org/10.1007/978-0-387-39940-9_882.
130. Bhatt C, Dey N, Ashour AS. In: Bhatt C, Dey N, Ashour AS, eds. *Internet of Things and Big Data Technologies for Next Generation Healthcare.* vol. 23. Cham: Springer International Publishing; 2017. https://doi.org/10.1007/978-3-319-49736-5.
131. Ward MJ, Marsolo KA, Froehle CM. Applications of business analytics in healthcare. *Bus Horiz.* 2014;57(5):571–582. https://doi.org/10.1016/j.bushor.2014.06.003.
132. Charleer S, Mathieu C, Nobels F, et al. Effect of continuous glucose monitoring on glycemic control, acute admissions and quality of life: a real-world study. *J Clin Endocrinol Metab.* 2018;(January). https://doi.org/10.1210/jc.2017-02498.
133. Microsoft Corporation. *PowerBI.* https://powerbi.microsoft.com; 2018. Accessed January 29, 2018.
134. SAP. SAP Business Analytics.
135. Tableau Software. https://www.tableau.com/. Published 2018. Accessed January 29, 2018.
136. Muito AW. *Além Do Jardim de Infância: Temas de Educação Online.* Rio de Janeiro: Armazém Digital; 2005.
137. Anderson T, Dron J. Three generations of distance education pedagogy. *Int Rev Res Open Dist Learn.* 2011;12(3):80. https://doi.org/10.19173/irrodl.v12i3.890.
138. Kafer PR, Mikuski JC. *E-Book Princípios Da Andragogia Para Facilitadores: Em Pdf*; 2014. http://www.mkaplus.com.br/blog/andragogia/andragogia. Accessed March 21, 2019.
139. Mitre SM, Siqueira-Batista R, Girardi-de-Mendonça JM, et al. Metodologias ativas de ensino-aprendizagem na formação profissional em saúde: debates atuais. *Cien Saude Colet.* 2008;13(Suppl 2):2133–2144. https://doi.org/10.1590/S1413-81232008000900018.
140. Moran J. O Que é Educação a Distância.
141. Sabbatini RME, Cardoso SH. O Setor de Saúde e a EAD. In: Litto FM, Formiga M, eds. *Educação a Distância. O Estado Da Arte.* 1st ed.São Paulo: Pearson; 2011.
142. Litto FM. *As Interfaces da EaD na Educação Brasileira.* Rev USP, 2013:57–66.
143. Frenk J, Chen L, Bhutta ZA, et al. Health professionals for a new century: transforming education to strengthen health systems in an interdependent world. *Lancet.* 2010;376(9756):1923–1958. https://doi.org/10.1016/S0140-6736(10)61854-5.
144. Frenk J, Chen L, Bhutta ZA, et al. Health professionals for a new century: transforming education to strengthen health systems in an interdependent world. *Lancet.* 2010;376(9756):1923–1958. https://doi.org/10.1016/S0140-6736(10)61854-5.
145. Stevens DL. Appendix A: neurology in the United Kingdom—numbers of clinical neurologists and trainees. *J Neurol Neurosurg Psychiatry.* 1997;63(Supplement 1):67S–72S. https://doi.org/10.1136/jnnp.63.2008.67S.
146. Mehta MR, Phukan RB. Training module for tele-ophthalmology. *Indian J Med Inform.* 2014;8:34–37.
147. Phukan R, Mehta MR, Gogia S. Results and problems in executing teleophthalmology. *Indian J Med Inform.* 2014;8(2):32–33.
148. Institutions C. *Report of the working group on tertiary care institutions for 12th five year.* New Delhi: Yojana Bhawan, Govt of India; 2012.
149. IIT. *National Programme for Technology Enhanced Learning*; 2012. https://onlinecourses.nptel.ac.in/. Accessed March 14, 2019.
150. Roth GA, Johnson C, Abajobir A, et al. Global, regional, and national burden of cardiovascular diseases for 10 causes, 1990 to 2015. *J Am Coll Cardiol.* 2017;70(1):1–25. https://doi.org/10.1016/j.jacc.2017.04.052.
151. Goyal A, Yusuf S. The burden of cardiovascular disease in the Indian subcontinent. *Indian J Med Res.* 2006;124(3):235–244.

152. Xavier D, Pais P, Devereaux PJ, et al. Treatment and outcomes of acute coronary syndromes in India (CREATE): a prospective analysis of registry data. *Lancet*. 2008;371(9622):1435–1442. https://doi.org/10.1016/S0140-6736(08)60623-6.

153. Hoffman JIE, Kaplan S, Liberthson RR. Prevalence of congenital heart disease. *Am Heart J*. 2004;147(3):425–439. https://doi.org/10.1016/j.ahj.2003.05.003.

154. Shah B, Sharma M, Kumar R, Brahmadathan KN, Abraham VJ, Tandon R. Rheumatic heart disease: progress and challenges in India. Indian J Pediatr 2013;80 Suppl. 1:S77-86. https://doi.org/10.1007/s12098-012-0853-2.

155. India faces challenge in trained health care personnel at all level. *Deccan Hearld*. 2011; February 28 (Newspaper Article, Bangalore, India).

156. Maheshwari S, Zheleva B, Rajasekhar V, Batra B. e-Teaching in pediatric cardiology: a paradigm shift. *Ann Pediatr Cardiol*. 2015;8(1):10–13. https://doi.org/10.4103/0974-2069.149512.

157. Medical R. *NHS, The Information, Digital Directorate, Policy Health, The Unit, Informatics Colleges*; 2009.

158. D'Avila OP, Pinto LF da S, Hauser L, Gonçalves MR, Harzheim E. The use of the Primary Care Assessment Tool (PCAT): an integrative review and proposed update. *Cien Saude Colet*. 2017;22(3):855–865. https://doi.org/10.1590/1413-81232017223.03312016.

159. Sabik LM, Lie RK. Priority setting in health care: lessons from the experiences of eight countries. *Int J Equity Health*. 2008;7(1):4. https://doi.org/10.1186/1475-9276-7-4.

160. Bashshur RL, Shannon GW, Smith BR, et al. The empirical foundations of telemedicine interventions for chronic disease management. *Telemed J E Health*. 2014;20(9):769–800. https://doi.org/10.1089/tmj.2014.9981.

161. Bashshur RL, Howell JD, Krupinski EA, et al. The empirical foundations of telemedicine interventions in primary care. *Telemed J E Health*. 2016;22:342–375. https://doi.org/10.1089/tmj.2016.0045. https://www.ncbi.nlm.nih.gov/pmc/articles/PMC4860623/.

162. Center for Health Statistics (USA). National Hospital Ambulatory Medical Care Survey: 2010 Summary Tables; 2010. http://www.census.gov/population/metro/. Accessed March 2, 2019.

163. U.S. Department of Health and Human Office of Health Policy. Report to Congress: E-Health and Telemedicine. Washington, DC; 2016. https://aspe.hhs.gov/pdf-report/report-congress-e-health-and-telemedicine. Accessed March 2, 2019.

164. Moore MA, Coffman M, Jetty A, Klink K, Petterson S, Bazemore A. Family physicians report considerable interest in, but limited use of, telehealth services. *J Am Board Fam Med*. 2017;30(3):320–330. https://doi.org/10.3122/jabfm.2017.03.160201.

165. Ebell MH. How to find answers to clinical questions. *Am Fam Physician*. 2009;79(4): 293–296.

166. Wade VA, Eliott JA, Hiller JE. Clinician acceptance is the key factor for sustainable telehealth services. *Qual Health Res*. 2014;24(5):682–694. https://doi.org/10.1177/1049732314528809.

167. Schwamm LH. Telehealth: seven strategies to successfully implement disruptive technology and transform health care. *Health Aff*. 2014;33(2):200–206. https://doi.org/10.1377/hlthaff.2013.1021.

168. Schmitz CAA, Gonçalves MR, Umpierre RN, et al. Teleconsulta: nova fronteira da interação entre médicos e pacientes. *Rev Bras Med Fam Comunidade*. 2018;12(39):1–7. https://doi.org/10.5712/rbmfc12(39)1540.

169. Perapadam BS. Avoid telephonic consultation requests: IMA. *The Hindu*. 2018;(August 17):8.

170. Montgomery A, Hunter D, Blair E, Hendricksen M. Telemedicine today: the state of affairs. *Rev Bras Med Fam Comunidade*. 2015;12(39):1–7.

171. Singh K, Drouin K, Newmark LP, et al. Developing a framework for evaluating the patient engagement, quality, and safety of mobile health applications. *Issue Brief (Commonw Fund)*. 2016;5(1):1–11.

172. Santos M. *A Natureza Do Espaço: Técnica e Tempo, Razão e Emoção*. 4a. São Paulo, SP: Editora da Universidade de São Paulo; 2006. http://files.leadt-ufal.webnode.com.br/200000026-4d5134e4ca/Milton_Santos_A_Natureza_do_Espaco.pdf. Accessed March 2, 2019.

173. McIsaac M, Scott A, Kalb G. The supply of general practitioners across local areas: accounting for spatial heterogeneity. *BMC Health Serv Res.* 2015;15(1):450. https://doi.org/10.1186/s12913-015-1102-y.

174. D'Avila OP, da S Pinto LF, Hauser L, Gonçalves MR, Harzheim E. O uso do primary care assessment tool (PCAT): uma revisão integrativa e proposta de atualização. *Cien Saude Colet.* 2017; https://doi.org/10.1590/1413-81232017223.03312016.

175. Mash R, Almeida M, Wong WCW, Kumar R, von Pressentin KB. The roles and training of primary care doctors: China, India, Brazil and South Africa. *Hum Resour Health.* 2015;13:93. https://doi.org/10.1186/s12960-015-0090-7.

176. Andrade M, Maia A, Cardoso C, Alkmim M, Ribeiro A. *Cost-Benefit of the Telecardiology Service in the State of Minas Gerais: Minas Telecardio Project*; 2017.

177. Moreira AM, Marobin R, Rados DV, et al. Effects of nurse telesupport on transition between specialized and primary care in diabetic patients: study protocol for a randomized controlled trial. *Trials.* 2017;18(1):222. https://doi.org/10.1186/s13063-017-1954-z.

178. Weinstein R, Lopez A, Joseph B, Erps K, Holcomb M, Barker G. Telemedicine, telehealth, and mobile health applications that work: opportunities and barriers. *Am J Med.* 2014;127(3):183–187. https://doi.org/10.1016/j.amjmed.2013.09.032.

179. Advisory Board. *A Milestone: Kaiser Now Interacts More With Patients Virtually Than In-Person.* Advisory Board Daily Briefing, Washington, DC. https://www.advisory.com/daily-briefing/2016/10/13/kaiser-telehealth. Accessed March 2, 2019.

180. Bratovic MA. A digital revolution in health care is speeding up. *The Economist.* March 2017. https://www.economist.com/business/2017/03/02/a-digital-revolution-in-health-care-is-speeding-up. Accessed March 2, 2019.

181. Umpierre RN, Agostinho MR, Mengue SS, et al. Telehealth in Rio Grande do Sul, Brazil: bridging the gaps. *Telemed J E Health.* 2016;22(11):938–944. https://doi.org/10.1089/tmj.2015.0210.

182. Foley & Lardner LLP. Telemedicine and Digital Health Survey. 2017. https://www.foley.com/files/uploads/2017-Telemedicine-Survey-Report-11-8-17.pdf. Accessed March 19, 2019.

183. Sandberg J. How telemedicine is transforming health care. *Ortho Spine News.* 2016. http://www.orthospinenews.com/2016/06/28/how-telemedicine-is-transforming-health-care/. Accessed March 19, 2019.

184. Thomas L, Capistrant G. *Physician Practice Standards and Licensure.* 2017. https://utn.org/resources/downloads/50-state-telemedicine-gaps-analysis-physician-practice-standards-licensure.pdf. Accessed March 2, 2019.

185. Whitten P, Holtz B. Provider utilization of telemedicine: the elephant in the room. *Telemed J E Health.* 2008;14(9):995–997. https://doi.org/10.1089/tmj.2008.0126.

186. Dorsey ER, Topol EJ. State of telehealth. *N Engl J Med.* 2016;375(2):154–161.

187. Yao P, Gogia K, Hafeex B, Hsu H, Greenwald P. Antibiotic prescribing practices: is there a difference between patients seen by telemedicine versus those seen in-person? *Telemed J E Health.* 2019; https://doi.org/10.1089/tmj.2018.0250.

188. Kabene SM, Orchard C, Howard JM, Soriano MA, Leduc R. The importance of human resources management in health care: a global context. *Hum Resour Health.* 2006;4. https://doi.org/10.1186/1478-4491-4-20.

189. E-Mamta, Mother and child tracking system, Gujarat; 2013. http://informatics.nic.in/news/newsdetail/newsID/276. Accessed February 21, 2016.

190. Agarwal S, Perry HB, Long L-A, Labrique AB. Evidence on feasibility and effective use of mHealth strategies by frontline health workers in developing countries: systematic review. *Trop Med Int Health.* 2015;20(8):1003–1014. https://doi.org/10.1111/tmi.12525.

191. Switz NA, D'Ambrosio MV, Fletcher DA. Low-cost mobile phone microscopy with a reversed mobile phone camera lens. Pai M, ed. *PLoS One.* 2014;9(5):e95330. https://doi.org/10.1371/journal.pone.0095330.

192. Derenzi B, Borriello G, Jackson J, et al. Mobile phone tools for field-based health care workers in low-income countries. *Mt Sinai J Med*. 2011;78:406–418. https://doi.org/10.1002/msj.20256.

193. Mehta MR, Phukan RB. Training module for tele-ophthalmology. *Indian J Med Inform*. 2014;8(2):34–37.

194. Haji HA, Rivett U, Suleman H. *Investigating mobile graphic-based reminders to support compliance of tuberculosis treatment*. PhD Thesis, Department of Computer Science, Faculty of Science, University of Cape Town; 2017.

195. Sinha A, Batra S, Batra S, Ahuja S. Using biometrics to turn the tap off of multi drug resistant TB (MDR TB). *Indian J Med Inform*. 2014;8(2):38–41.

196. WPRO. *Child Health*. Manila: WPRO; 2017.

197. US Department of Health and Human Services. *Global HIV/AIDS Overview*. HIV.gov. US Department of Health and Human Services, Washington, DC. https://www.hiv.gov/federal-response/pepfar-global-aids/global-hiv-aids-overview. Accessed February 17, 2019.

198. Hwa K, Wren SM. Telehealth follow-up in lieu of postoperative clinic visit for ambulatory surgery. *JAMA Surg*. 2013;148(9):823. https://doi.org/10.1001/jamasurg.2013.2672.

199. Brice J. *Telehealth Safe for Some Postoperative Evaluations*. Medscape. 2013. https://www.medscape.com/viewarticle/807613. Accessed February 4, 2019.

200. Rimal D, Hui J, Fu H, et al. Our experience in using telehealth for paediatric plastic surgery in Western Australia. *ANZ J Surg*. 2017;27(4):277–281. https://doi.org/10.1111/ans.13925.

201. Shri J.P. Nadda launches new Nurse Practitioner courses and 'Live Register' for Nurses; 2018. http://pib.nic.in/newsite/PrintRelease.aspx?relid=146556. Accessed February 4, 2019.

202. ICN—International Council of Nurses; 2018. https://www.icn.ch/what-we-do/ehealth/. Accessed February 4, 2019.

203. Baker SR, Stacey MC, Jopp-McKay AG, Hoskin SE, Thompson PJ. Epidemiology of chronic venous ulcers. *Br J Surg*. 1991;78(7):864–867. https://doi.org/10.1002/bjs.1800780729.

204. Jopp-McKay AG, Stagey MC, Rohr JB, Baker SR, Thompson PJ, Hoskin SE. Outpatient treatment of chronic venous ulcers in a specialized clinic. *Australas J Dermatol*. 1991;32(3):143–149. https://doi.org/10.1111/j.1440-0960.1991.tb01779.x.

205. WHO. *Epidemiology*. Geneva: WHO; 2016.

206. Rockson SG, Rivera KK. Estimating the population burden of lymphedema. *Ann N Y Acad Sci*. 2008;1131(1):147–154. https://doi.org/10.1196/annals.1413.014.

207. Douglass J, Graves P, Gordon S. Self-care for management of secondary lymphedema: a systematic review. Fischer PU, ed. *PLoS Negl Trop Dis*. 2016;10(6):e0004740. https://doi.org/10.1371/journal.pntd.0004740.

208. WHO. *Diabetes*. Geneva: WHO; 2017.

209. Gogia K, Gogia SB. Limb measurement software for lymphoedema patients. *Indian J Med Inform*. 2014;8(2):48–49.

210. Gogia SB, Sathi S. Correspondence: elimination of lymphatic filariasis. *Natl Med J India*. 2016;29(1):37.

211. World Health Organization. *Telemedicine: Opportunities and Developments in Member States: Report on the Second Global Survey on EHealth 2009*. vol. 2. Geneva: World Health Organization; 2010. https://doi.org/10.4258/hir.2012.18.2.153.

212. Moser PL, Hauffe H, Lorenz IH, et al. Publication output in telemedicine during the period January 1964 to July 2003. *J Telemed Telecare*. 2004;10(2):72–77. https://doi.org/10.1258/135763304773391495.

213. Burute N, Jankharia B. Teleradiology: the Indian perspective. *Indian J Radiol Imaging*. 2009;19(1):16–18. https://doi.org/10.4103/0971-3026.45337.

214. Kane CK, Gillis K. The use of telemedicine by physicians: still the exception rather than the rule. *Health Aff*. 2018;37(12):1923–1930. https://doi.org/10.1377/hlthaff.2018.05077.

215. Digital Imaging and Communications in Medicin (DICOM). Overview. About DICOM. https://www.dicomstandard.org/about/. 2018. Accessed January 14, 2018.

216. Bashshur RL, Krupinski EA, Thrall JH, Bashshur N. The empirical foundations of teleradiology and related applications: a review of the evidence. *Telemed J E Health*. 2016;22(11):868–898. https://doi.org/10.1089/tmj.2016.0149.

217. Johnston 3rd WK, Patel BN, Low RK, Das S. Wireless teleradiology for renal colic and renal trauma. *J Endourol*. 2005;19(1):32–36. https://doi.org/10.1089/end.2005.19.32.

218. Kennedy S, Bhargavan M, Sunshine JH, Forman HP. The effect of teleradiology on time to interpretation for CT pulmonary angiographic studies. *J Am Coll Radiol*. 2009;6(3):180–189.e1. https://doi.org/10.1016/j.jacr.2008.09.013.

219. Kalyanpur A, Sivan C, Eigles S. Utilization of verbal communication of positive findings in an emergency teleradiology environment. In: *Radiological Society of North America 2009 Scientific Assembly and Annual Meeting. Chicago, IL*; 2009.

220. Lee JK, Renner JB, Saunders BF, et al. Effect of real-time teleradiology on the practice of the emergency department physician in a rural setting: initial experience. *Acad Radiol*. 1998;5(8):533–538.

221. Platts-Mills TF, Hendey GW, Ferguson B. Teleradiology interpretations of emergency department computed tomography scans. *J Emerg Med*. 2010;38(2):188–195. https://doi.org/10.1016/j.jemermed.2008.01.015.

222. Kalyanpur A, Weinberg J, Neklesa V, Brink JA, Forman HP. Emergency radiology coverage: technical and clinical feasibility of an international teleradiology model. *Emerg Radiol*. 2003;10(3):115–118. https://doi.org/10.1007/s10140-003-0284-5.

223. Kalyanpur A, Neklesa VP, Pham DT, Forman HP, Stein ST, Brink JA. Implementation of an International Teleradiology Staffing Model. *Radiology*. 2004;232(2):415–419. https://doi.org/10.1148/radiol.2322021555.

224. Rosenberg C, Kroos K, Rosenberg B, Hosten N, Flessa S. Teleradiology from the provider's perspective-cost analysis for a mid-size university hospital. *Eur Radiol*. 2013;23(8):2197–2205. https://doi.org/10.1007/s00330-013-2810-5.

225. Kalyanpur A, Singh J, Tan L, Goh T. Impact of teleradiology on clinical practice and workflow: benefits of a Singapore India teleradiology link. In: *BJR Congress Series*. Birmingham: British Institute of Radiology; 2008.

226. Leader JK, Hakim CM, Ganott MA, et al. A multisite telemammography system for remote management of screening mammography: an assessment of technical, operational, and clinical issues. *J Digit Imaging*. 2006;19(3):216–225. https://doi.org/10.1007/s10278-006-0585-9.

227. Fruehwald-Pallamar J, Jantsch M, Pinker K, et al. Teleradiology with uncompressed digital mammograms: clinical assessment. *Eur J Radiol*. 2013;82(3):412–416. https://doi.org/10.1016/j.ejrad.2012.03.004.

228. Lefere P, Silva C, Gryspeerdt S, et al. Teleradiology based CT colonography to screen a population group of a remote island; at average risk for colorectal cancer. *Eur J Radiol*. 2013;82(6):e262–e267. https://doi.org/10.1016/j.ejrad.2013.02.010.

229. Char A, Kalyanpur A, Puttanna Gowda VN, Bharathi A, Singh J. Teleradiology in an inaccessible area of northern India. *J Telemed Telecare*. 2010;16(3):110–113. https://doi.org/10.1258/jtt.2009.009007.

230. Coulborn RM, Panunzi I, Spijker S, et al. Feasibility of using teleradiology to improve tuberculosis screening and case management in a district hospital in Malawi. *Bull World Health Organ*. 2012;90(9):705–711. https://doi.org/10.2471/BLT.11.099473.

231. Swennen GRJ, Mollemans W, Schutyser F. Three-dimensional treatment planning of orthognathic surgery in the era of virtual imaging. *J Oral Maxillofac Surg*. 2009;67(10):2080–2092. https://doi.org/10.1016/j.joms.2009.06.007.

232. D'Sousa R, Kalyanpur A. Emergency teleradiology-based 3D-post processing services for a tertiary care medical center in the US from a remote 3D lab in India. In: *4th Annual Conference of the Society for Emergency Radiology and 5th Asia- Pacific Congress of Interventional Oncology, Delhi,* 2017.

233. Silva 3rd E, Breslau J, Barr RM, et al. ACR white paper on teleradiology practice: a report from the Task Force on Teleradiology Practice. *J Am Coll Radiol.* 2013;10(8):575–585. https://doi.org/10.1016/j.jacr.2013.03.018.

234. The Royal College of Radiologists. *Standards for the Provision of Teleradiology Within the Unkted Kingdom.* 2nd ed. London: The Royal College of Radiologists; 2016.

235. Agrawal A, Agrawal A, Pandit M, Kalyanpur A. Systematic survey of discrepancy rates in an international teleradiology service. *Emerg Radiol.* 2011;18(1):23–29.

236. Agrawal A, Koundinya DB, Raju JS, Agrawal A, Kalyanpur A. Utility of contemporaneous dual read in the setting of emergency teleradiology reporting. *Emerg Radiol.* 2017;24(2):157–164. https://doi.org/10.1007/s10140-016-1465-3.

237. Hohmann J, de Villiers P, Urigo C, Sarpi D, Newerla C, Brookes J. Quality assessment of out sourced after-hours computed tomography teleradiology reports in a Central London University Hospital. *Eur J Radiol.* 2012;81(8):e875–e879. https://doi.org/10.1016/j.ejrad.2012.04.013.

238. Wachter RM. International teleradiology. *N Engl J Med.* 2006;354(7):662–663. https://doi.org/10.1056/NEJMp058286.

239. Kharat AT, Safvi A, Thind S, Singh A. Cloud computing for radiologists. *Indian J Radiol Imaging.* 2012;22(3):150–154. https://doi.org/10.4103/0971-3026.107166.

240. Haddad A, da Silva D, Monteiro A, Guedes T, Figueiredo A. Follow up of the legislation advancement along the implementation of the Brazilian Telehealth Programme. *J Int Soc Telemed eHealth.* 2016;4:1–7.

241. Ridley EL. Teleradiology Requires Emphasis on Workflow Management. AuntMinnie.

242. Seong NJ, Kim B, Lee S, et al. Off-site smartphone reading of CT images for patients with inconclusive diagnoses of appendicitis from on-call radiologists. *AJR Am J Roentgenol.* 2014;203(1):3–9. https://doi.org/10.2214/AJR.13.11787.

243. Szekely A, Talanow R, Bagyi P. Smartphones, tablets and mobile applications for radiology. *Eur J Radiol.* 2013;82(5):829–836. https://doi.org/10.1016/j.ejrad.2012.11.034.

244. Eigles S, Panughpath SG, Kalyanpur A. Enhancing turn-around-time (TAT) on stroke protocol head CT reports via continuous quality improvement (CQI) methodology in a busy teleradiology practice. *Am J Exp Clin Res.* 2015;2(2):102–104.

245. Pinto A, Brunese L, Pinto F, Acampora C, Romano L. E-learning and education in radiology. *Eur J Radiol.* 2011;78(3):368–371. https://doi.org/10.1016/j.ejrad.2010.12.029.

246. Dreyer KJ, Geis JR. When machines think: radiology's next frontier. *Radiology.* 2017;285(3):713–718. https://doi.org/10.1148/radiol.2017171183.

247. Farahani N, Pantanowitz L. Overview of telepathology. *Surg Pathol Clin.* 2015;8(2):223–231. https://doi.org/10.1016/j.path.2015.02.018.

248. Dirilenoglu F. High-resolution image sharing (his) on whatsapp: a method to facilitate instant and high-quality case consultations in cytopathology. *Turkish J Pathol.* 2019. https://doi.org/10.5146/tjpath.2017.01450.

249. Fischer JR. First AI pathology diagnostic system up and running in clinical setting; 2018. https://m.dotmed.com/news/story/42613. Accessed March 17, 2019.

250. Moreno-Ramírez D, Romero-Aguilera G. Teledermatología, del debate a la calma. *Actas Dermosifiliogr.* 2016;107(5):366–368. https://doi.org/10.1016/j.ad.2016.01.006.

251. Naka F, Makkar H, Lu J. Teledermatology: kids are not just little people. *Clin Dermatol.* 2017;35(6):594–600. https://doi.org/10.1016/j.clindermatol.2017.08.009.

252. Berk-Krauss J, Polsky D, Stein JA. Mole mapping for management of pigmented skin lesions. *Dermatol Clin.* 2017;35(4):439–445. https://doi.org/10.1016/j.det.2017.06.004.

253. Piccoli MF, Amorim BDB, Wagner HM, Nunes DH. Teledermatology protocol for screening of skin cancer. *An Bras Dermatol.* 2015;90:202–210.

254. Walocko FM, Tejasvi T. Teledermatology applications in skin cancer diagnosis. *Dermatol Clin.* 2017;35(4):559–563. https://doi.org/10.1016/j.det.2017.06.002.

255. Coates SJ, Kvedar J, Granstein RD. Teledermatology: from historical perspective to emerging techniques of the modern era: part I: history, rationale, and current practice. *J Am Acad Dermatol.* 2015;72(4):563–566. https://doi.org/10.1016/j.jaad.2014.07.061.

256. MIOT HA. *Desenvolvimento e sistematização da interconsulta dermatológica a distância.* 2005. https://doi.org/10.11606/T.5.2005.tde-05092005-164704.

257. Hoffman JIE, Kaplan S. The incidence of congenital heart disease. *J Am Coll Cardiol.* 2002;39(12):1890–1900.

258. Mendis S, Puska P, Norrving B, eds. *Global Atlas on Cardiovascular Disease Prevention and Control.* Geneva: World Health Organization; 2011.

259. Voros K, Bonnevie A, Reiczigel J. Comparison of conventional and sensor-based electronic stethoscopes in detecting cardiac murmurs of dogs. *Tierarztl Prax Ausg K Kleintiere Heimtiere.* 2012;40(2):103–111.

260. Singh S, Bansal M, Maheshwari P, et al. American Society of echocardiography: remote echocardiography with web-based assessments for referrals at a distance (ASE-REWARD) study. *J Am Soc Echocardiogr.* 2013;26(3):221–233. https://doi.org/10.1016/j.echo.2012.12.012.

261. Schwaab B, Katalinic A, Richardt G, et al. Validation of 12-lead tele-electrocardiogram transmission in the real-life scenario of acute coronary syndrome. *J Telemed Telecare.* 2006;12(6):315–318. https://doi.org/10.1258/135763306778558204.

262. Backman W, Bendel D, Rakhit R. The telecardiology revolution: improving the management of cardiac disease in primary care. *J R Soc Med.* 2010;103(11):442–446. https://doi.org/10.1258/jrsm.2010.100301.

263. De A. BARC develops credit card-size ECG machine that will cost around Rs 4,000—Technology News. *India Today.* 2017.

264. Barros MBSC, Barros KMS, Santana JB, et al. Be alert: can be cancer! The telehealth as early suspicion tool to the pediatric cancer. In: Joint Event:19th Euro Congress on Cancer Science and Therapy & 25th Cancer Nursing & Nurse Practitioners Conference. vol. 9. Lisboa, Portugal: J Cancer Sci Ther; 2017. https://doi.org/10.4172/1948-5956-C1-106.

265. Osma J, Plaza I, Crespo E, Medrano C, Serrano R. Proposal of use of smartphones to evaluate and diagnose depression and anxiety symptoms during pregnancy and after birth. In: *IEEE-EMBS International Conference on Biomedical and Health Informatics (BHI)*; 2014:547–550. https://doi.org/10.1109/BHI.2014.6864423.

266. Suleman Z. Journey of a thousand miles: harnessing mobile communications technology to solve problems in maternal health and child mortality in Balochistan, Pakistan. *IEEE Pulse.* 2015;6(1):28–31. https://doi.org/10.1109/MPUL.2014.2366895.

267. Moreira MWL, Rodrigues JJPC, Oliveira AMB, Saleem K. Smart mobile system for pregnancy care using body sensors. In: *2016 Int Conf Sel Top Mob Wirel Networking, MoWNeT 2016*; 2016:1–4. https://doi.org/10.1109/MoWNet.2016.7496609.

268. de Oliveira RB, Melo ECP, Knupp VM de AO. Infant's deaths profile in the city of Rio de Janeiro according to birth weight, in the year 2002. *Esc Anna Nery.* 2008;12:25–29.

269. Blank A, Prytherch H, Kaltschmidt J, et al. "Quality of prenatal and maternal care: bridging the know-do gap" (QUALMAT study): an electronic clinical decision support system for rural Sub-Saharan Africa. *BMC Med Inform Decis Mak.* 2013;13(1):44. https://doi.org/10.1186/1472-6947-13-44.

270. Brasil, Ministério da Saúde, Secretaria de Atenção à Saúde, Departamento de Atenção Básica. *Atenção Ao Pré-Natal de Baixo Risco.* Cadernos d. Brasília - DF: Editora do Ministério da Saúde; 2012.

271. Organização Das Nações Unidas (ONU). *Transformando Nosso Mundo: A Agenda 2030 para o Desenvolvimento Sustentável. Agenda 2030 de Desenvolvimento Sustentável.* https://nacoesunidas.org/pos2015/agenda2030/; 2016. (Accessed April 30, 2018).

272. World Health Organization. *Maternal Mortality Ratio. Health Statistics and Information Systems.* Geneva: World Health Organization; 2017.

273. Idri A, Bachiri M, Fernández-Alemán JL, Toval A. Experiment design of free pregnancy monitoring mobile personal health records quality evaluation. In: *2016 IEEE 18th International Conference on E-Health Networking, Applications and Services (Healthcom)*; 2016:1–6. https://doi.org/10.1109/HealthCom.2016.7749501.

274. Bachiri M, Idri A, Fernández-Alemán JL, Toval A. Mobile personal health records for pregnancy monitoring functionalities: analysis and potential. *Comput Methods Prog Biomed*. 2016;134:121–135. https://doi.org/10.1016/j.cmpb.2016.06.008.

275. Tagliaferri S, Esposito FG, Ippolito A, et al. Telemedicine to improve access to specialist care in fetal heart rate monitoring: analysis of 17 years of TOCOMAT network clinical activity. *Telemed J E Health*. 2017;23(3):226–232. https://doi.org/10.1089/tmj.2016.0087.

276. Kuruvilla S, Bustreo F, Kuo T, et al. The global strategy for women's, children's and adolescents' health (2016-2030): a roadmap based on evidence and country experience. *Bull World Health Organ*. 2016;94(5):398–400. https://doi.org/10.2471/BLT.16.170431.

277. Bachiri M, Idri A, Fernández-Alemán JL, Toval A. *A preliminary study on the evaluation of software product quality of pregnancy monitoring mPHRs*. In: *2015 Third World Conference on Complex Systems (WCCS)*; 2015:1–6. https://doi.org/10.1109/ICoCS.2015.7483224.

278. Sajjad UU, Shahid S. *Baby+: a mobile application to support pregnant women in Pakistan*. In: *Proceedings of the 18th International Conference on Human-Computer Interaction with Mobile Devices and Services Adjunct. MobileHCI '16*; New York, NY: ACM; 2016:667–674. https://doi.org/10.1145/2957265.2961856.

279. Tommasone G, Bazzani M, Solinas V, Serafini P. *Midwifery e-health: from design to validation of "Mammastyle—Gravidanza Fisiologica"*. In: *2016 IEEE 18th International Conference on E-Health Networking, Applications and Services (Healthcom)*; 2016:1–6. https://doi.org/10.1109/HealthCom.2016.7749499.

280. Neumeyer J, Prince J, Miller A, Koeneman B, Figueria S, Kim U. Mobile urinalysis for maternal screening: frugal medical screening solution and patient database to aid in prenatal healthcare for expecting mothers in the developing world. In: *2016 IEEE Global Humanitarian Technology Conference (GHTC)*; 2016:569–575. https://doi.org/10.1109/GHTC.2016.7857337.

281. Moreira MWL, Rodrigues JJPC, Oliveira AMB, Saleem K. *Smart mobile system for pregnancy care using body sensors*. In: *2016 International Conference on Selected Topics in Mobile & Wireless Networking (MoWNeT)*; 2016:1–4. https://doi.org/10.1109/MoWNet.2016.7496609.

282. Sadi-Ahmed N, Kedir-Talha M. Contraction extraction from term and preterm electrohyterographic signals. In: *2015 4th International Conference on Electrical Engineering (ICEE)*; 2015:1–4. https://doi.org/10.1109/INTEE.2015.7416822.

283. Awiti AM, Shifferaw BM, Byamukama MB, Kizito R, Mwikirize C. Design and implementation of an android based digital fetoscope. In: *2016 IEEE-EMBS International Conference on Biomedical and Health Informatics (BHI)*; 2016:152–155. https://doi.org/10.1109/BHI.2016.7455857.

284. Vermeulen-Giovagnoli B, Peters C, Jagt MB, et al. The development of an obstetric telemonitoring system. In: *2015 37th Annual International Conference of the IEEE Engineering in Medicine and Biology Society (EMBC)*; 2015:177–180. https://doi.org/10.1109/EMBC.2015.7318329.

285. Mensah N, Sukums F, Awine T, et al. Impact of an electronic clinical decision support system on workflow in antenatal care: the QUALMAT eCDSS in rural health care facilities in Ghana and Tanzania. *Glob Health Action*. 2015;8:25756. https://doi.org/10.3402/gha.v8.25756.

286. Dunsmuir DT, Payne BA, Cloete G, et al. Development of mHealth applications for pre-eclampsia triage. *IEEE J Biomed Health Inform*. 2014;18(6):1857–1864. https://doi.org/10.1109/JBHI.2014.2301156.

287. Zairina E, Abramson MJ, McDonald CF, et al. Telehealth to improve asthma control in pregnancy: a randomized controlled trial. *Respirology*. 2016;21(5):867–874. https://doi.org/10.1111/resp.12773.

288. Kazantsev A, Ponomareva J, Kazantsev P. Development and validation of an AI-enabled mHealth technology for in-home pregnancy management. In: *2014 International Conference on Information Science, Electronics and Electrical Engineering*; vol. 2. 2014:927–931. https://doi.org/10.1109/InfoSEEE.2014.6947804.

289. Botsis T, Hartvigsen G. Current status and future perspectives in telecare for elderly people suffering from chronic diseases. *J Telemed Telecare*. 2008;14(4):195–203. https://doi.org/10.1258/jtt.2008.070905.

290. Botsis T, Demiris G, Pedersen S, Hartvigsen G. Home telecare technologies for the elderly. *J Telemed Telecare*. 2008;14(7):333–337. https://doi.org/10.1258/jtt.2008.007002.

291. Nyheim B. Telemedisin: Kroken sykehjem er på nett. *Sykepleien*. 2005;93(9):50–51. https://doi.org/10.4220/sykepleiens.2005.0003.

292. Gray LC, Fatehi F, Martin-Khan M, Peel NM, Smith AC. Telemedicine for specialist geriatric care in small rural hospitals: preliminary data. *J Am Geriatr Soc*. 2016;64(6):1347–1351. https://doi.org/10.1111/jgs.14139.

293. International Agency for Research on Cancer (IARC). *Biennial Report 2012–2013*. Lyon: International Agency for Research on Cancer (IARC); 2013.

294. World Health Organization. *Cancer Fact Sheet*. Geneva: World Health Organization; 2018.

295. MBSC B. *Câncer infantojuvenil: itinerário terapêutico a partir de duas unidades de referência no estado de Pernambuco—Brasil*; 2014.

296. Doyle-Lindrud S. Telemedicine in Oncology. *Clin J Oncol Nurs*. 2016;20(1):27–28. https://doi.org/10.1188/16.CJON.27-28.

297. Doolittle GC, Spaulding AO. Providing access to oncology care for rural patients via telemedicine. *J Oncol Pract*. 2006;2(5):228–230. https://doi.org/10.1200/JOP.2006.2.5.228.

298. Viers BR, Lightner DJ, Rivera ME, et al. Efficiency, satisfaction, and costs for remote video visits following radical prostatectomy: a randomized controlled trial. *Eur Urol*. 2015;68(4):729–735. https://doi.org/10.1016/j.eururo.2015.04.002.

299. Sabesan S, Roberts LJ, Aiken P, Joshi A, Larkins S. Timely access to specialist medical oncology services closer to home for rural patients: experience from the Townsville Teleoncology Model. *Aust J Rural Health*. 2014;22(4):156–159. https://doi.org/10.1111/ajr.12101.

300. Sabesan S. Medical models of teleoncology: current status and future directions. *Asia Pac J Clin Oncol*. 2014;10(3):200–204. https://doi.org/10.1111/ajco.12225.

301. Kleindorfer D, Xu Y, Moomaw CJ, Khatri P, Adeoye O, Hornung R. US geographic distribution of rt-PA utilization by hospital for acute ischemic stroke. *Stroke*. 2009;40(11):3580–3584. https://doi.org/10.1161/STROKEAHA.109.554626.

302. Gross H, Hall CE, Wang S, et al. Prospective reliability of the STRokE DOC wireless/site independent telemedicine system. *Neurology*. 2006;66(3):460. https://doi.org/10.1212/01.wnl.0000209203.87339.21.

303. Schäbitz W-R, Steigleder T, Cooper-Kuhn CM, et al. Intravenous brain-derived neurotrophic factor enhances poststroke sensorimotor recovery and stimulates neurogenesis. *Stroke*. 2007;38(7):2165–2172. https://doi.org/10.1161/STROKEAHA.106.477331.

304. Moulin T. Telestroke: the use of telemedicine in stroke care. *Cerebrovasc Dis*. 2009;27(Suppl. 4) [Supplement issue].

305. Wilcox ME, Adhikari NK. The effect of telemedicine in critically ill patients: systematic review and meta-analysis. *Crit Care*. 2012;16(4):R127. https://doi.org/10.1186/cc11429.

306. Lilly CM, Cody S, Zhao H, et al. Hospital mortality, length of stay, and preventable complications among critically Ill patients before and after tele-ICU reengineering of critical care processes. *JAMA*. 2011;305(21):2175. https://doi.org/10.1001/jama.2011.697.

307. Vespa PM. Multimodality monitoring and telemonitoring in neurocritical care: from microdialysis to robotic telepresence. *Curr Opin Crit Care*. 2005;11(4):133–138.

308. Dorsey ER, Deuel LM, Voss TS, et al. Increasing access to specialty care: a pilot, randomized controlled trial of telemedicine for Parkinson's disease. *Mov Disord*. 2010;25(11):1652–1659. https://doi.org/10.1002/mds.23145.

309. Kaufman FR, Halvorson M, Carpenter S. Association between diabetes control and visits to a multidisciplinary pediatric diabetes clinic. *Pediatrics*. 1999;103(5):948–951. Pt 1.
310. Shalitin S, Ben-Ari T, Yackobovitch-Gavan M, et al. Using the Internet-based upload blood glucose monitoring and therapy management system in patients with type 1 diabetes. *Acta Diabetol*. 2014;51(2):247–256. https://doi.org/10.1007/s00592-013-0510-x.
311. Lange K, Swift P, Pankowska E, Danne TISPAD. Clinical practice consensus guidelines 2014. Diabetes education in children and adolescents. *Pediatr Diabetes*. 2014;15(Suppl 20):77–85. https://doi.org/10.1111/pedi.12187.
312. Konrad K, Vogel C, Bollow E, et al. Current practice of diabetes education in children and adolescents with type 1 diabetes in Germany and Austria: analysis based on the German/Austrian DPV database. *Pediatr Diabetes*. 2016;17(7):483–491. https://doi.org/10.1111/pedi.12330.
313. Whittaker SL, Adkins S, Phillips R, Jones J, Horsley MA, Kelley G. Success factors in the long-term sustainability of a telediabetes programme. *J Telemed Telecare*. 2004;10(2):84–88. https://doi.org/10.1258/135763304773391512.
314. International Diabetes Federation. *IDF Diabetes Atlas*. 8th ed. Brussels: International Diabetes Federation; 2017. IDF Congress. IDF 2017. https://www.idf.org/our-activities/congress/programme-and-abstracts.html. ISBN: 978-2-930229-87-4. Online: www.diabetes-atlas.org.
315. Bashshur RL, Shannon GW, Smith BR, Woodward MA. The empirical evidence for the telemedicine intervention in diabetes management. *Telemed J E Health*. 2015;21(5):321–354. https://doi.org/10.1089/tmj.2015.0029.
316. Wood CL, Clements SA, McFann K, Slover R, Thomas JF, Wadwa RP. Use of telemedicine to improve adherence to American diabetes association standards in pediatric type 1 diabetes. *Diabetes Technol Ther*. 2016;18(1):7–14. https://doi.org/10.1089/dia.2015.0123.
317. Harris MA, Freeman KA, Duke DC. Seeing is believing: using skype to improve diabetes outcomes in youth. *Diabetes Care*. 2015;38(8):1427–1434. https://doi.org/10.2337/dc14-2469.
318. Levin K, Madsen JR, Petersen I, Wanscher CE, Hangaard J. Telemedicine diabetes consultations are cost-effective, and effects on essential diabetes treatment parameters are similar to conventional treatment: 7-year results from the Svendborg Telemedicine Diabetes Project. *J Diabetes Sci Technol*. 2013;7(3):587–595. https://doi.org/10.1177/193229681300700302.
319. Fatehi F, Martin-Khan M, Smith AC, Russell AW, Gray LC. Patient satisfaction with video teleconsultation in a virtual diabetes outreach clinic. *Diabetes Technol Ther*. 2015;17(1):43–48. https://doi.org/10.1089/dia.2014.0159.
320. Årsand E, Tatara N, Hartvigsen G. Wireless and mobile technologies improving diabetes self-management. In: Cruz-Cunha MM, Moreira F, eds. *Handbook of Research on Mobility and Computing: Evolving Technologies and Ubiquitous Impacts*. Hershey, PA: IGI Global; 2011. https://doi.org/10.4018/978-1-60960-042-6.
321. Issom D-Z, Woldaregay AZ, Chomutare T, Bradway M, Årsand E, Hartvigsen G. Mobile applications for people with diabetes published between 2010 & 2015. *Diabetes Manag*. 2015;5(6):539–550. https://doi.org/10.2217/dmt.15.40.
322. Bradway M, Grøttland A, Blixgård HK, Årsand AG. System for enabling clinicians to relate to a mobile health app: preliminary results of the Norwegian trial in the EU FI-STAR project. In: *Abstracts from ATTD 2016 9th International Conference on Advanced Technologies & Treatments for Diabetes Milan, vol 18*. Milan: Diabetes Technology & Therapeutics; 2016:A-1-A-140. https://doi.org/10.1089/dia.2016.2525.
323. Arsand E, Tatara N, Ostengen G, Hartvigsen G. Mobile phone-based self-management tools for type 2 diabetes: the few touch application. *J Diabetes Sci Technol*. 2010;4(2):328–336. https://doi.org/10.1177/193229681000400213.
324. Froisland DH, Arsand E. Integrating visual dietary documentation in mobile-phone-based self-management application for adolescents with type 1 diabetes. *J Diabetes Sci Technol*. 2015;9(3):541–548. https://doi.org/10.1177/1932296815576956.

325. Arsand E, Froisland DH, Skrovseth SO, et al. Mobile health applications to assist patients with diabetes: lessons learned and design implications. *J Diabetes Sci Technol.* 2012;6(5):1197–1206. https://doi.org/10.1177/193229681200600525.

326. Holmen H, Torbjornsen A, Wahl AK, et al. A mobile health intervention for self-management and lifestyle change for persons with type 2 diabetes, part 2: one-year results from the norwegian randomized controlled trial renewing health. *JMIR MHealth UHealth.* 2014;2(4):e57. https://doi.org/10.2196/mhealth.3882.

327. Wickramasinghe SI, Caffery LJ, Bradford NK, Smith AC. Enablers and barriers in providing telediabetes services for Indigenous communities: a systematic review. *J Telemed Telecare.* 2016;22(8):465–471. https://doi.org/10.1177/1357633X16673267.

328. Salmoiraghi A, Hussain S. A systematic review of the use of telepsychiatry in acute settings. *J Psychiatr Pract.* 2015;21(5):389–393. https://doi.org/10.1097/PRA.0000000000000103.

329. American Psychiatric Association (APA). What is Telepsychiatry? https://www.psychiatry.org/patients-families/what-is-telepsychiatry. Accessed April 20, 2018.

330. Collins PY, Patel V, Joestl SS, et al. Grand challenges in global mental health. *Nature.* 2011;475(7354):27–30. https://doi.org/10.1038/475027a.

331. Doyen CM, Oreve M-J, Desailly E, et al. Telepsychiatry for children and adolescents: a review of the prometted project. *Telemed J E Health.* 2018;24(1):3–10. https://doi.org/10.1089/tmj.2017.0041.

332. Chakrabarti S. Usefulness of telepsychiatry: a critical evaluation of videoconferencing-based approaches. *World J Psychiatry.* 2015;5(3):286–304. https://doi.org/10.5498/wjp.v5.i3.286.

333. Thomas JF, Novins DK, Hosokawa PW, et al. The use of telepsychiatry to provide cost-efficient care during pediatric mental health emergencies. *Psychiatr Serv.* 2018;69(2):161–168. https://doi.org/10.1176/appi.ps.201700140.

334. Chan S, Godwin H, Gonzalez A, Yellowlees PM, Hilty DM. Review of use and integration of mobile apps into psychiatric treatments. *Curr Psychiatry Rep.* 2017;19(12):96. https://doi.org/10.1007/s11920-017-0848-9.

335. American Academy of Child and Adolescent Psychiatry (AACAP). Clinical update: telepsychiatry with children and adolescents. *J Am Acad Child Adolesc Psychiatry.* 2017;56(10):875–893. https://doi.org/10.1016/j.jaac.2017.07.008.

336. Hubley S, Lynch SB, Schneck C, Thomas M, Shore J. Review of key telepsychiatry outcomes. *World J Psychiatry.* 2016;6(2):269–282. https://doi.org/10.5498/wjp.v6.i2.269.

337. Heravian A, Chang BP. Mental health and telemedicine in the acute care setting: applications of telepsychiatry in the ED. *Am J Emerg Med.* 2018;36(6):1118–1119. https://doi.org/10.1016/j.ajem.2017.10.053.

338. Dias RDS, Marques ADFH, Diniz PRB, et al. Telemental health in Brazil: past, present and integration into primary care. *Arch Clin Psychiatry.* 2015;42(2):41–44. https://doi.org/10.1590/0101-60830000000046.

339. Anthes E. Mental health: there's an app for that. *Nature.* 2016;532(7597):20–23. https://doi.org/10.1038/532020a.

340. Berrouiguet S, Perez-Rodriguez MM, Larsen M, Baca-Garcia E, Courtet P, Oquendo M. From eHealth to iHealth: transition to participatory and personalized medicine in mental health. *J Med Internet Res.* 2018;20(1):e2. https://doi.org/10.2196/jmir.7412.

341. Prabhakaran K, Lombardo G, Latifi R. Telemedicine for trauma and emergency management: an overview. *Curr Trauma Rep.* 2016;2(3):115–123. https://doi.org/10.1007/s40719-016-0050-2.

342. Faulkner J, Taylor E, Nessen S, Boedeker D, Boedeker B. Development of a tele ENT program to support distant military treatment facilities for the european regional medical command. *Stud Health Technol Inform.* 2014;196:101–106.

343. Woldaregay AZ, Walderhaug S, Hartvigsen G. Literatures review of telemedicine services in maritime and extreme weather. *Int J Integr Care.* 2016;16(5):S46. https://doi.org/10.5334/ijic.2597.

344. Malik AZ. TELE ENT: a step forward in providing specialist services in far remote areas. *J Rawalpindi Med Coll.* 2017;21(1):68–71.

345. Wu C-J, Wu S-Y, Chen P-C, Lin Y-S. An innovative smartphone-based otorhinoendoscope and its application in mobile health and teleotolaryngology. *J Med Internet Res.* 2014;16(3):e71. https://doi.org/10.2196/jmir.2959.

346. Milner TD, Montgomery J, Stewart M. Flexible nasendoscopy: the use of smartphones as an immediate light source. *Clin Otolaryngol.* 2018;43(1):399–400. https://doi.org/10.1111/coa.12696.

347. Shah MU, Sohal M, Valdez TA, Grindle CR. iPhone otoscopes: currently available, but reliable for tele-otoscopy in the hands of parents? *Int J Pediatr Otorhinolaryngol.* 2018;106:59–63. https://doi.org/10.1016/j.ijporl.2018.01.003.

348. Yulzari R, Bretler S, Avraham Y, Sharabi-Nov A, Even-Tov E, Gilbey P. Mobile technology-based real-time teleotolaryngology care facilitated by a nonotolaryngologist physician in an adult population. *Ann Otol Rhinol Laryngol.* 2017;127(1):46–50. https://doi.org/10.1177/0003489417745089.

349. Russo JE, McCool RR, Davies L. VA telemedicine: an analysis of cost and time savings. *Telemed J E Health.* 2016;22(3):209–215. https://doi.org/10.1089/tmj.2015.0055.

350. Folke LE. Teledentistry. An overview. *Tex Dent J.* 2001;118(1):10–18.

351. Cook J. SDN video conferencing in postgraduate dental education and orthodontic diagnosis. In: *Learning Technology in Medical Education Conference 1997 (CTI Medicine)*; 1997:111–116.

352. Chen J-W, Hobdell MH, Dunn K, Johnson KA, Zhang J. Teledentistry and its use in dental education. *J Am Dent Assoc.* 2003;134(3):342–346.

353. del C López Jordi M, Figueiredo MÇ, Barone D, Pereira C. Study and analysis of information technology in dentistry in Latin American countries TT—Estudio y análisis de la informática odontológica en países de Latinoamérica. *Acta Odontol Latinoam.* 2016;29(1):14–22.

354. Irving M, Stewart R, Spallek H, Blinkhorn A. Using teledentistry in clinical practice, an enabler to improve access to oral health care: a qualitative systematic review. *J Telemed Telecare.* January 2017:1357633X1668677. https://doi.org/10.1177/1357633X16686776.

355. World Health Organisation. In: *WHA58.28 eHealth. eHealth Resolut to 58th Meet World Heal Assem. (4)*; 2004:121–123.

356. Estai M, Kanagasingam Y, Tennant M, Bunt S. A systematic review of the research evidence for the benefits of teledentistry. *J Telemed Telecare.* 2018;24(3):147–156. https://doi.org/10.1177/1357633X16689433.

357. Nuttall NM, Steed MS, Donachie MA. Referral for secondary restorative dental care in rural and urban areas of Scotland: findings from the highlands Et Islands Teledentistry Project. *Br Dent J.* 2002;192(4):224–228.

358. Bradley M, Black P, Noble S, Thompson R, Lamey PJ. Application of teledentistry in oral medicine in a community dental service, N. Ireland. *Br Dent J.* 2010;209(8):399–404. https://doi.org/10.1038/sj.bdj.2010.928.

359. Williard ME, Fauteux N. Dentists provide effective supervision of Alaska's dental health aide therapists in a variety of settings. *J Public Health Dent.* 2011;71(Suppl 2):S27–S33.

360. Patel RN, Antonarakis GS. Factors influencing the adoption and implementation of teledentistry in the UK, with a focus on orthodontics. *Community Dent Oral Epidemiol.* 2013;41(5):424–431. https://doi.org/10.1111/cdoe.12029.

361. Teoh J, Hsueh A, Marino R, Manton D, Hallett K. Economic evaluation of teledentistry in cleft lip and palate patients. *Telemed J E Health.* 2018;24(6):449–456. https://doi.org/10.1089/tmj.2017.0138.

362. Maeder AJ, Gogia SB, Hartvigsen G. Next generation telehealth. Contribution of the IMIA Telehealth Working Group. *Yearb Med Inform.* 2011;6(1):15–20.

363. Case RB, Groth SJ, Anderson TM, Byrne GJ, Proctor JH, Kealy JA. Telemedicine in Emergency Medicine. Emergency Medicine Practice Committee. *Am Coll Em Phys*; 1998. http://armtelemed.org/resources/51-TM_in_Emergency_Medicine.pdf. Accessed January 14, 2018.

364. Mueller KJ, Potter AJ, MacKinney AC, Ward MM. Lessons from tele-emergency: improving care quality and health outcomes by expanding support for rural care systems. *Health Aff.* 2014;33(2):228–234. https://doi.org/10.1377/hlthaff.2013.1016.

365. Dharmar M, Romano PS, Kuppermann N, et al. Impact of critical care telemedicine consultations on children in rural emergency departments. *Crit Care Med.* 2013;41(10):2388–2395. https://doi.org/10.1097/CCM.0b013e31828e9824.

366. Ward MM, Jaana M, Natafgi N. Systematic review of telemedicine applications in emergency rooms. *Int J Med Inform.* 2014;84(9):601–616. https://doi.org/10.1016/j.ijmedinf.2015.05.009.

367. Ward MM, Ullrich F, Mueller K. Extent of telehealth use in rural and urban hospitals. *Rural Policy Brief.* 2014;2014(4):1–4.

368. Keane MG. A review of the role of telemedicine in the accident and emergency department. *J Telemed Telecare.* 2009;15(3):132–134. https://doi.org/10.1258/jtt.2009.003008.

369. Sharma R, Gordon J, Greenwald P, et al. Revolutionizing the delivery of care for ED patients. *NEJM Catal.* 2017. https://catalyst.nejm.org/telehealth-express-care-service-revolutionizing-ed-care. Accessed January 14, 2018.

370. Sharma R, Fleischut P, Barchi D. Telemedicine and its transformation of emergency care: a case study of one of the largest US integrated healthcare delivery systems. *Int J Emerg Med.* 2017;10(1):21. https://doi.org/10.1186/s12245-017-0146-7.

371. Kumaran M, Chittoria R, Elan, et al. Tele-Emergency: JIPMER Experience. *Austin J Emerg Crit Care Med.* 2016;3(2):1050. http://austinpublishinggroup.com/emergency-critical-care-medicine/fulltext/ajeccm-v3-id1050.php.

372. Bartolini E, King N. Emerging best practices for tele-ICU care nationally. *NEHI Issue Br.* 2013;2013(November).

373. Reynolds HN, Bander J, McCarthy M. Different systems and formats for tele-ICU coverage: designing a tele-ICU system to optimize functionality and investment. *Crit Care Nurs Q.* 2012;35(4):364–377. https://doi.org/10.1097/CNQ.0b013e318266bc26.

374. Davis TM, Barden C, Olff C, et al. Professional accountability in the tele-ICU: the CCRN-E. *Crit Care Nurs Q.* 2012;35(4):353–356. https://doi.org/10.1097/CNQ.0b013e318266bef4.

375. Rogove H, Stetina K. Practice challenges of intensive care unit telemedicine. *Crit Care Clin.* 2015;31(2):319–334. https://doi.org/10.1016/j.ccc.2014.12.009.

376. Young LB, Chan PS, Lu X, Nallamothu BK, Sasson C, Cram PM. Impact of telemedicine intensive care unit coverage on patient outcomes: a systematic review and meta-analysis. *Arch Intern Med.* 2011;171(6):498–506. https://doi.org/10.1001/archinternmed.2011.61.

377. Wilcox ME, Adhikari NKJ. The effect of telemedicine in critically ill patients: systematic review and meta-analysis. *Crit Care.* 2012;16(4):R127. https://doi.org/10.1186/cc11429.

378. Kahn JM, Gunn SR, Lorenz HL, Alvarez J, Angus DC. Impact of nurse-led remote screening and prompting for evidence-based practices in the ICU*. *Crit Care Med.* 2014;42(4):896–904. https://doi.org/10.1097/CCM.0000000000000052.

379. Formica M, Quarello F, Stramignoni E, et al. Informatics support and teledialysis. *Minerva Urol Nefrol.* 1994;46(1):11–16.

380. Edefonti A, Boccola S, Picca M, et al. Treatment data during pediatric home peritoneal teledialysis. *Pediatr Nephrol.* 2003;18(6):560–564. https://doi.org/10.1007/s00467-003-1147-8.

381. Rumpsfeld M, Arild E, Norum J, Breivik E. Telemedicine in haemodialysis: a university department and two remote satellites linked together as one common workplace. *J Telemed Telecare.* 2005;11(5):251–255. https://doi.org/10.1258/1357633054471885.

382. WHO. *Better Health for People With Disabilities: Infographic.* Geneva: World Health Organization; 2018.

383. World Health Organization. *International Classification of Functioning, Disability and Health (ICF).* Geneva: World Health Organization. https://www.who.int/classifications/icf/en/. Accessed April 2, 2018.

384. WHO. *Disabilities*. Geneva: WHO; 2017.

385. Radio Conferences. https://www.itu.int/en/history/Pages/RadioConferences.aspx?-conf=4.39. Accessed February 15, 2019.

386. Norwegian Centre for Maritime Medicine. *Textbook of Maritime Medicine* (Online text-book); 2013. http://textbook.ncmm.no/index.php/textbook-of-maritime-medicine. Accessed August 16, 2019.

387. Horneland AM. Maritime telemedicine—where to go and what to do. *Int Marit Health*. 2009;60(1–2):36–39.

388. Guitton MJ. Online maritime health information: an overview of the situation. *Int Marit Health*. 2015;66(3):139–144. https://doi.org/10.5603/IMH.2015.0028.

389. Walderhaug S, Granja C, Horsch A, Hartvigsen G. Telemedicine services for the arctic: a systematic review. *JMIR Med Inform*. 2017;5(2):e16. https://doi.org/10.2196/medinform.6323.

390. International Labour Organization. ILO Convention 164. Telemedical Advise to Ships; 1987. http://www.ilo.org/dyn/normlex/en/f?p=NORMLEXPUB:12100:0::NO::P12100_ILO_CODE:C164.

391. *Airline*. https://en.wikipedia.org/wiki/Airline.

392. World's First Commercial Airline The Greatest Moments in Flight Space. https://www.space.com/16657-worlds-first-commercial-airline-the-greatest-moments-in-flight.html. Accessed February 15, 2019.

393. Ruskin KJ, Hernandez KA, Barash PG. Management of in-flight medical emergencies. *Anesthesiology*. 2008;108(4):749–755. https://doi.org/10.1097/ALN.0b013e31816725bc.

394. Personal Info communications being associated with Soyuz T-11 mission.

395. *Medical, Security and Travel Safety Services* MedAire. https://www.medaire.com/. Accessed February 15, 2019.

396. Antartica Troll Research Station. https://www.tv2.no/a/2312685.

397. Hild CM. Arctic Telemedicine Project Final Report. Institute for Circumpolar Health Studies, University of Alaska Anchorage, Alaska; 2000. http://hdl.handle.net/11374/27.

398. Walderhaug S, Granja C, Horsch A, Hartvigsen G. Telemedicine services in Arctic environments—challenges for successful implementation. In: Granja C, Budrionis A, eds. *SHI 2015. Proceedings of the 13th Scandinavian Conference on Health Informatics* (15–17 June 2015, Tromsø, Norge). Linköping Electronic Conference Proceedings, No. 115. Linköping, Sweden: Linköping University Electronic Press; 2015:98–101. ISSN: 1650-3686 (print), ISSN: 1650-3740 (online), ISBN: 978-91-7685-985-8.

399. Bolle SR, Larsen F, Hagen O, Gilbert M. Video conferencing versus telephone calls for team work across hospitals: a qualitative study on simulated emergencies. *BMC Emerg Med*. 2009;9(1):22. https://doi.org/10.1186/1471-227X-9-22.

400. Bolle SR, Lien AH, Rolv Mjaaseth MG. *Videobased Emergency Medical Interaction*. https://tidsskriftet.no/en/2013/01/.

401. Skarvøy LJ, Jørgensen M. Legene opererte isbjørnofrene via videochat. [The doctors op-erated the polar bear victims via video chat] VG (online), Oslo, Norway; 2011. https://www.vg.no/nyheter/innenriks/i/V0P0J/legene-opererte-isbjoernofrene-via-videochat. Accessed March 4, 2019.

402. Hartvigsen G, Pedersen S. *Lessons Learned From 25 Years With Telemedicine in Northern Norway*. Tromsø: Norwegian Centre for Integrated Care and Telemedicine, University Hospital of North Norway; 2015.

403. Woldaregay AZ, Walderhaug S, Hartvigsen G. Telemedicine services for the arctic: a systematic review. *JMIR Med Inform*. 2017;5(2):e16. https://doi.org/10.2196/medinform.6323.

404. Wheeler J, Hinton E. Effectiveness of telehealth on correctional facility health care. *JBI Database Syst Rev Implement Rep*. 2017;15(5):1256–1264. https://doi.org/10.11124/JBISRIR-2016-002969.

405. Watson R, Stimpson A, Hostick T. Prison health care: a review of the literature. *Int J Nurs Stud*. 2004;41(2):119–128. https://doi.org/10.1016/S0020-7489(03)00128-7.

406. Restum ZG. Public health implications of substandard correctional health care. *Am J Public Health*. 2005;95(10):1689–1691. https://doi.org/10.2105/AJPH.2004.055053.

407. Institute of Medicine (US) Committee on Evaluating Clinical Applications of Telemedicine. In: Field MJ, ed. *Telemedicine: A Guide to Assessing Telecommunications for Health Care*. Washington, DC: National Academies Press; 1996.

408. Young J, Badowski M. Telehealth: increasing access to high quality care by expanding the role of technology in correctional medicine. *J Clin Med*. 2017;6(2):20. https://doi.org/10.3390/jcm6020020.

409. Fazel S, Bains P, Doll H. Substance abuse and dependence in prisoners: a systematic review. *Addiction*. 2006;101(2):181–191. https://doi.org/10.1111/j.1360-0443.2006.01316.x.

410. Young LB. Telemedicine interventions for substance-use disorder: a literature review. *J Telemed Telecare*. 2012;18(1):47–53. https://doi.org/10.1258/jtt.2011.110608.

411. Batastini AB, King CM, Morgan RD, McDaniel B. Telepsychological services with criminal justice and substance abuse clients: a systematic review and meta-analysis. *Psychol Serv*. 2016;13(1):20–30. https://doi.org/10.1037/ser0000042.

412. Maruschak LM. HIV in prisons, 2001-2010. *BJS Bull*. 2012;2012(September):1–12. https://doi.org/10.1111/j.1745-9133.2006.00116.x.

413. Patel MC, Young JD. Delivering HIV subspecialty care in prisons utilizing telemedicine. *Dis Mon*. 2014;60(5):196–200. https://doi.org/10.1016/j.disamonth.2014.04.001.

414. Ellis DG, Mayrose J, Jehle DV, Moscati RM, Pierluisi GJ. A telemedicine model for emergency care in a short-term correctional facility. *Telemed J E Health*. 2001;7(2):87–92. https://doi.org/10.1089/153056201750279584.

415. Fox KC, Somes GW, Waters TM. Timeliness and access to healthcare services via telemedicine for adolescents in state correctional facilities. *J Adolesc Health*. 2007;41(2):161–167. https://doi.org/10.1016/j.jadohealth.2007.05.001.

416. Wikipedia. *Medical Tourism in India*. https://en.wikipedia.org/wiki/Medical_tourism_in_India. Accessed July 8, 2019.

417. Gray HH, Poland SC. Medical tourism: crossing borders to access health care. *Kennedy Inst Ethics J*. 2008;18(2):193–201.

418. Saligram PS, Bhattacharjee A, Crooks VA, Labonté R, Schram A, Snyder J. Overview of the Medical Tourism Industry in Bangalore. India Centre for Public Health and Equity, Version 1.0. Research Team. Downloaded from http://www.sfu.ca/medicaltourism/. Accessed July 8, 2019.

419. Sarwar A. Medical tourism in Malaysia: prospect and challenges. *Iran J Public Health*. 2013;42(8):795–805.

420. The Joint Commission. www.jointcommissioninternational.org.

421. National Accreditation Board for Hospitals and Healthcare Providers. https://www.nabh.co/.

422. The Healthcare Accreditation Institute. https://www.ha.or.th/EN/AboutUs/History.

423. Health tourism and its impacts on host nation and hospitality industry. *The WritePass J*. December 12, 2012. https://writepass.com/journal/2012/12/page/18/. Accessed July 8, 2019.

424. The pros and cons of medical tourism. *Flux Mag*. 2018. https://www.fluxmagazine.com/pros-and-cons-medical-tourism/. Accessed July 8, 2019.

425. Hong YA. Medical tourism and telemedicine: a new frontier of an old business. *J Med Internet Res*. 2016;18(5):3–6. https://doi.org/10.2196/jmir.5432.

426. Pompeii. http://www.history.com/topics/ancient-history/pompeii.

427. Gondwana. https://en.wikipedia.org/wiki/Gondwana.

428. SahanaEden. SahanaWiki. 2012. http://eden.sahanafoundation.org/wiki. Accessed December 14, 2015.

429. Gogia SB. Providing tele mental health services after disasters—based on the Post Tsunami experience. In: Ada S, ed. *Cases in Managing E Services*. Pennsylvania: IGI Global; 2009:238–252.

430. Chennai floods: latest news, videos and chennai floods. *Times of India*, Delhi. 2015, December 6.

431. *FloodRelief-Healtheducationproject1*; 2015.

432. SahanaEden. SahanaWiki. 2012. http://eden.sahanafoundation.org/wiki. Accessed December 14, 2015.

433. HIMSS. Definitions of mHealth HIMSS. https://www.himss.org/definitions-mhealth. Accessed March 27, 2019.

434. World Health Organization. *MHealth Assessment and Planning for Scale Toolkit*. Geneva: WHO; 2015.

435. Osman A, Bagge CL, Gutierrez PM, Konick LC, Kopper BA, Barrios FX. The Suicidal Behaviors Questionnaire-Revised (SBQ-R): validation with clinical and nonclinical samples. *Assessment*. 2001;8(4):443–454.

436. Dellavalle RP, Brewer AC, Karimkhani C, Buller DB, Kamel Boulos MN. Mobile medical and health apps: state of the art, concerns, regulatory control and certification. *Online J Public Health Inform*. 2014;5(3):3. https://doi.org/10.5210/ojphi.v5i3.4814.

437. McDowell D. *Evaluation of special operations forces medical handbook content in a phone-based decision support application as an operational clinical support tool*. Report Prepared for US Army Medical Research and Materiel Command, 2011.

438. Gautham M, Iyengar MS, Johnson CW. Mobile phone-based clinical guidance for rural health providers in India. *Health Informatics J*. 2015;21(4):253–266. https://doi.org/10.1177/1460458214523153.

439. Iyengar SM, Florez-Arango MF. Decreasing workload among community health workers using interactive, structured, rich-media guidelines on smartphones. *Technol Health Care*. 2013;21(2):113–123. https://doi.org/10.3233/THC-130713.

440. Florez-Arango MF, Iyengar MS, Dunn K, Zhang J. Performance factors of mobile rich media job aids for community health workers. *JAMIA*. 2011;18:131–137.

441. Escobar E. What is bluetooth? https://www.scientificamerican.com/article/what-is-bluetooth/. Accessed July 12, 2019.

442. Keystone C. *PQRST Pain Assessment Method*. Crozer-Keystone Health System, PA. http://www.crozerkeystone.org/healthcare-professionals/nursing/pqrst-pain-assessment-method/. Accessed March 27, 2019.

443. StatCounter Global Stats. *Mobile Operating System Market Share Worldwide*. StatCounter Global Stats. Viewed February 25. http://gs.statcounter.com/os-market-share/mobile/worldwide; Accessed March 27, 2019.

444. Barron BS. How to Use MobiLoud Canvas to Convert Your Website Into a Mobile App Mobiloud; 2018. https://www.mobiloud.com/blog/how-mobiloud-canvas-helps-convert-your-website-into-native-apps/. Accessed March 27, 2019.

445. Frain B. *Responsive Web Design With HTML5 and CSS3*. Google Books, Packt Publ; 2012.

446. Fogg B. *Persuasive Technology: Using Computers to Change What We Think and Do (Interactive Technologies)*. 1st ed Morgan Kaufmann. Stanford, CA: Stanford University; 2002.

447. Oinas-Kukkonen H, Harjumaa M. Persuasive systems design: key issues, process model, and system features. *Commun Assoc Inf Syst*. 2009;24(March):28.

448. WHO. *Integrated Management of Childhood Illness (IMCI)*. Geneva: WHO; 2017.

449. Greene JA. Do-it-yourself medical devices? Technology and empowerment in American Health Care. *N Engl J Med*. 2016;374(4):305–308.

450. Saczynski JS, McManus D, Goldberg RJ. Commonly used data-collection approaches in clinical research. *Am J Med*. 2013;123(11):946–950.

451. Inglis SC, Donesky D, Disler RT, et al. Patterns of technology use in patients attending a cardiopulmonary outpatient clinic: a self-report survey. *Interact J Med Res*. 2015;4(1):e5. https://doi.org/10.2196/ijmr.3955.

452. Carter MC, Burley VJ, Cade JE. Weight loss associated with different patterns of self-monitoring using the mobile phone app my meal mate. *JMIR MHealth UHealth*. 2017;5(2):e8. https://doi.org/10.2196/mhealth.4520.

453. Brooke MJ, Thompson BM. Food and Drug Administration regulation of diabetes-related mHealth technologies. *J Diabetes Sci Technol*. 2013;7(2):296–301.

454. Agarwal S, LeFevre AE, Lee J. Guidelines for reporting of health interventions using mobile phones. *BMJ Br Med J*. 2016;352(8049):438.

455. Norwegian Centre for Integrated Care and Telemedicine, Tele-Health Network for Diabetes Patients: FI-STAR Project Use Case Trial. Tromso, Norway.

456. *AppSaludable Quality Seal*. http://www.calidadappsalud.com/en/distintivo-appsaludable/. Accessed March 27, 2019.

457. NHS Apps Library—NHS https://www.nhs.uk/apps-library/. Accessed February 23, 2019.

458. WMA Statement on Guiding Principles for the Use of Telehealth for the Provision of Health Care. Vol. 60. New Delhi. In: *Proc. 2009 Conference of World Medical Association*. https://www.wma.net/policies-post/wma-statement-on-guiding-principles-for-the-use-of-telehealth-for-the-provision-of-health-care/. Accessed March 3, 2019.

459. *Laws of Malaysia, Telemedicine Act 1997*. Malaysia: Malysia Govt.; 1997.

460. Brazil Law N. 12.871. Brazil.

461. Meltzer R. *Legal Barriers Are Limiting Telehealth's Reach, Experts Say*. FierceHealthcare; 2018. https://www.fiercehealthcare.com/tech/barriers-law-are-limiting-telehealth-s-reach-legal-experts-say; Accessed March 26, 2019.

462. Thomas L, Capistrant G. State telemedicine gaps analysis: physician practice standards and licensure. *Am Telemed Assoc*. 2017;84:9–10.

463. Bashshur RL, Krupinski EA, Weinstein RS, Dunn MR, Bashshur N. The empirical foundations of telepathology: evidence of feasibility and intermediate effects. *Telemed J E Health*. 2017;23(3):155–191.

464. Bashshur RL, Shannon GW, Tejasvi T, Kvedar JC, Gates M. The empirical foundations of teledermatology: a review of the research evidence. *Telemed J E Health*. 2015;21(12):953–979.

465. F.No Z-18015/23I2017-eGov. *Digital Lnformation Security in Healthcare, Act (DISHA)*. New Delhi, 2018.

466. Percival T. *Medical Ethics*. Cambridge: Cambridge University Press; 2014. https://archive.org/details/b21935014/page/n9.

467. Oxford English Directory. *Oxford Living Directories*. Oxford: Oxford University Press; 2018.

468. Kaba R, Sooriakumaran P. The evolution of the doctor-patient relationship. *Int J Surg*. 2007;5(1):57–65.

469. Farouk A. *Telemedicine Prompts New Ethical Ground Rules for Physicians*. Chicago, USA: AMA News; 2016.

470. Aronson SH. The Lancet on the telephone 1876–1975. *Med Hist*. 1977;21:69–87. https://www.ncbi.nlm.nih.gov/pmc/articles/PMC1081896/.

471. Association WM. *WMA statement on the ethics of telemedicine*. In: *58th WMA General Assembly, Denmark: Copenhagen*; 2007.

472. Baker A. Crossing the quality chasm: a new health system for the 21st century. *Br Med J*. 2001;323:7322.

473. Ekeland AG, Bowes A, Flottorp S. Methodologies for assessing telemedicine: a systematic review of reviews. *Int J Med Inform*. 2012;81(1):1–11.

474. Mars M, Jack C. Why is telemedicine a challenge to the regulators? *S Afr J Bioeth Law*. 2010;3(2):55–58.

475. Jack C, Hlombe Y. Language MM. Cultural brokerage and informed consent-will technological terms impede telemedicine use? *S Afr J Bioeth Law*. 2014;7(1):14–18.

476. Harris-Kojetin L, Sengupta M, Park-Lee E, Valverde R. Long-term care services in the United States: overview. *Vital Heal Stat Ser 3, Anal Epidemiol Stud*. 2013;2013(37):1–107.

477. Sahakyan Y, Abrahamyan L, Shahid N, et al. Changes in blood pressure among patients in the Ontario Telehomecare programme: an observational longitudinal cohort study. *J Telemed Telecare*. 2018;24(6):420–427. https://doi.org/10.1177/1357633X17706286.

478. Jeffs L, Jain AK, Man RH, et al. Exploring the utility and scalability of a telehomecare intervention for patients with chronic kidney disease undergoing peritoneal dialysis-a study protocol. *BMC Nephrol*. 2017;18(1):155. https://doi.org/10.1186/s12882-017-0557-y.

479. Lustbader D, Mudra M, Romano C, et al. The impact of a home-based palliative care program in an accountable care organization. *J Palliat Med*. 2017;20(1):23–28. https://doi.org/10.1089/jpm.2016.0265.

480. Rettberg JW. *Seeing Ourselves Through Technology: How We Use Selfies, Blogs and Wearable Devices to See and Shape Ourselves*. 1st ed. London, UK: Palgrave Macmillan; 2014. https://doi.org/10.1057/9781137476661.

481. Fantoni A. Dispositivos wearable para o campo da saúde: reflexões acerca do monitoramento de dados do corpo humano. *Temática*. 2016;12(01). http://www.periodicos.ufpb.br/ojs/index.php/tematica/article/view/27416. ISSN: 1807-8931.

482. Radhakrishnan K, Xie B, Berkley A, Kim M. Barriers and facilitators for sustainability of tele-homecare programs: a systematic review. *Health Serv Res*. 2016;51(1):48–75. https://doi.org/10.1111/1475-6773.12327.

483. *Stroke Telemedicine (Telestroke)—About*. Rochestor, Minnesota: Mayo Clinic. https://www.mayoclinic.org/tests-procedures/stroke-telemedicine/about/pac-20395081. Accessed February 16, 2018.

484. Suk Lee H, Kim J. Scenario-based assessment of user needs for point-of-care robots. *Healthc Informatics Rev*. 2018;24(1):12–22. https://doi.org/10.4258/hir.2018.24.1.12.

485. Duca S, Bălă O, Al-Hajjar N, et al. Laparoscopic cholecystectomy: incidents and complications. A retrospective analysis of 9542 consecutive laparoscopic operations. *HPB (Oxford)*. 2003;5(3):152–158. https://doi.org/10.1080/13651820310015293.

486. Khajuria A. Robotics and surgery: a sustainable relationship? *World J Clin Cases*. 2015;3(3):265–269. https://doi.org/10.12998/wjcc.v3.i3.265.

487. Remacle M, M. N. Prasad V, Lawson G, Plisson L, Bachy V, Van der Vorst S. Transoral robotic surgery (TORS) with the Medrobotics Flex™ System: first surgical application on humans. *Eur Arch Oto-Rhino-Laryngol*. 2015;272(6):1451–1455. https://doi.org/10.1007/s00405-015-3532-x.

488. Wakabayashi D. *Self-Driving Uber Car Kills Pedestrian in Arizona, Where Robots Roam*. New York, USA: New York Times; March 19, 2018.

489. Levin A. Lion air crash demonstrates unintended consequences of cockpit automation. *Insur J*. January 2018. https://www.insurancejournal.com/author/alan-levin/. Accessed May 1, 2019.

490. Robotic surgery linked to 144 deaths in the US. *BBC News*; 2018. http://www.bbc.com/news/technology-33609495. Accessed March 31, 2018.

491. Newcastle robot surgery inquest: "Risk of further deaths". *BBC News*; 2019. https://www.bbc.com/news/uk-england-tyne-46143940. Accessed May 1, 2019.

492. Bulter H. Is it better to be intelligent or a critical thinker? *Sci Am*. 2017. https://www.scientificamerican.com/article/why-do-smart-people-do-foolish-things/.

493. Turing A. Computing machinery and intelligence. *Mind: Q Rev Psychol Philos*. 1950;59(236):433.

494. Russel S, Norvig P. Artificial intelligence—a modern approach. In: *Series in Artificial Intelligence*. 3rd ed. Upper Saddle River, NJ: Prentice Hall; 2009 [chapters 3–4].

495. Robbins M. Has a rampaging AI algorithm really killed thousands in Pakistan? *The Guardian*. https://www.theguardian.com/science/the-lay-scientist/2016/feb/18/has-a-rampaging-ai-algorithm-really-killed-thousands-in-pakistan. Published February 16, 2016.

496. Steinberg R, Kaufman S. The evolution of Intelligence. In: Gabora L, Russon A, eds. *The Cambridge Handbook of Intelligence*. Cambridge: Cambridge University Press; 2011:328–350.

497. Kawale SR, Malwatkar GM. Fall detection system for elderly person using embedded system. *Int J Adv Sci Eng Technol*. 2016;4(3):94–97.

498. Igual R, Medrano C, Plaza I. Challenges, issues and trends in fall detection systems. *Biomed Eng Online*. 2013;12:66. https://doi.org/10.1186/1475-925X-12-66.

499. Birdwell RL. The preponderance of evidence supports computer-aided detection for screening mammography. *Radiology*. 2009;253(1):9–16. https://doi.org/10.1148/radiol.2531090611.

500. Birt J, Manyuru P, Nelson J. Using virtual and augmented reality to study architectural lighting. In: *Proc. 34th International Conference on Innovation, Practice and Research in the Use of Educational Technologies in Tertiary Education*. Toowomba, Australia: ASCILITE; 2017:17–21. https://research.bond.edu.au/en/publications/using-virtual-and-augmented-reality-to-study-architectural-lighti.

501. Xu Y, Zhou X. Research on application of virtual reality technology in architectural space design. *DEStech Trans Mater Sci Eng*. 2016. icmsme.

502. Hassan SS, Krämer M. Evaluating immersive virtual reality environment for facility management planning. 2017. Thesis for International Master of Science in Construction and Real Estate Management Joint Study Programme of Metropolia UAS and HTW Berlin. Submitted on August 25, 2017.

503. Harrison B, Oehmen R, Robertson A, et al. Through the eye of the master: the use of Virtual Reality in the teaching of surgical hand preparation. In: *IEEE 5th International Conference on Serious Games and Applications for Health (SeGAH)*; 2017; 2017:1–6.

504. Wongkoblap A, Vadillo MA, Curcin V. Researching mental health disorders in the era of social media: systematic review. *J Med Internet Res*. 2017;19(6):e224.

505. Ragazzoni L, Ingrassia PL, Echeverri L, et al. Virtual reality simulation training for Ebola deployment. *Disaster Med Public Health Prep*. 2015;9(5):543–546.

506. Izard SG, Méndez JAJ, Palomera PR. Virtual reality educational tool for human anatomy. *J Med Syst*. 2017;41(5):76.

507. Silva A, Valerio M, Albuquerque P, Campos Filho A. Anatomia Digital: Um ambiente virtual de apoio ao processo ensino-aprendizagem. In: *Brazilian Symposium on Computers in Education (Simpósio Brasileiro de Informática Na Educação-SBIE)*; vol. 28. 2017:745.

508. Campelo AM, Hashim JA, Weisberg A, Katz L. Virtual rehabilitation in the elderly: benefits, issues, and considerations. In: *2017 International Conference on Virtual Rehabilitation (ICVR)*; 2017:1–2.

509. Shin J-H, Bog Park S, Ho Jang S. Effects of game-based virtual reality on health-related quality of life in chronic stroke patients: a randomized, controlled study. *Comput Biol Med*. 2015;63:92–98. https://doi.org/10.1016/j.compbiomed.2015.03.011.

510. Chestnut JA, Crumpton LL. Virtual reality: a training tool in the 21st century for disabled persons and medical students. In: *Proceedings of the 1997 16 Southern Biomedical Engineering Conference*; 1997:418–421.

511. Brown DJ, Kerr S, Wilson JR. Virtual environments in special-needs education. *Commun ACM*. 1997;40(8):72–76.

512. Gonçalves VHL, Melo MTD, Costa HDR, et al. Computer simulation used in diagnostic procedures analysis of breast cancer. In: *2015 Pan American Health Care Exchanges (PAHCE)*; 2015:1–3.

513. Pulijala Y, Ma M, Ayoub A. VR surgery: interactive virtual reality application for training oral and maxillofacial surgeons using oculus rift and leap motion. In: *Serious Games and Edutainment Applications*. New York: Springer; 2017:187–202.

514. Monge JP, López G, Guerrero LA. Supporting phobia treatment with virtual reality: systematic desensitization using oculus rift. In: Duffy V, Lightner N, eds. *Advances in Human Factors and Ergonomics in Healthcare. Advances in Intelligent Systems and Computing*, vol. 482. Cham: Springer; 2017.

515. Miller MH, Upton CW. *Macroeconomics a Neoclassical Introduction*. Chicago: University of Chicago Press; 1986.

516. Barth ME, Landsman WR, Lang MH. International accounting standards and accounting quality. *J Account Res*. 2008;46(3):467–498. https://doi.org/10.1111/j.1475-679X.2008.00287.x.

517. Tapscott D, Tapscott A. *Blockchain Revolution: How the Technology behind Bitcoin Is Changing Money, Business, and the World*. Penguin Random House, UK: Penguin; 2016.

518. Nakamoto S. *Bitcoin: A Peer-to-Peer Electronic Cash System*. Working Paper, 2008.

519. Mukherjee A, Nath P. A model of trust in online relationship banking. *Int J Bank Mark*. 2003;21(1):5–15. https://doi.org/10.1108/02652320310457767.

520. Wang X, Zha X, Ni W, et al. Survey on blockchain for internet of things. *Comput Commun*. 2019;136:10–29. https://doi.org/10.1016/J.COMCOM.2019.01.006.

521. Marr B. How blockchain will transform the supply chain and logistics industry. *Forbes*. 2018;(March).

522. Casino F, Dasaklis TK, Patsakis C. A systematic literature review of blockchain-based applications: current status, classification and open issues. *Telematics Inform*. 2019;36:55–81. https://doi.org/10.1016/J.TELE.2018.11.006.

523. Vazirani AA, O'Donoghue O, Brindley D, Meinert E. Implementing blockchains for efficient health care: systematic review. *J Med Internet Res*. 2019;21(2):e12439. https://doi.org/10.2196/12439.

524. Kuo T-T, Kim H-E, Ohno-Machado L. Blockchain distributed ledger technologies for biomedical and health care applications. *J Am Med Inform Assoc*. 2017;24(6):1211–1220. https://doi.org/10.1093/jamia/ocx068.

525. Maslove DM, Klein J, Brohman K, Martin P. Using blockchain technology to manage clinical trials data: a proof-of-concept study. *JMIR Med Inform*. 2018;6(4):e11949. https://doi.org/10.2196/11949.

526. Park S, Chung K, Jayaraman S. Wearables: fundamentals, advancements, and a roadmap for the future. In: Sazonov E, Neuman MR, eds. *Wearable Sensors*. Academic Press (Elsevier); 2014:1–23 [chapter 1.1]. ISBN 9780124186620. https://doi.org/10.1016/B978-0-12-418662-0.00001-5.

527. Casselman J, Onopa N, Khansa L. Wearable healthcare: lessons from the past and a peek into the future. *Telematics Inform*. 2017;34(7):1011–1023. https://doi.org/10.1016/J.TELE.2017.04.011.

528. Lymberis A. Smart wearables for remote health monitoring, from prevention to rehabilitation: current R&D, future challenges. In: *4th International IEEE EMBS Special Topic Conference on Information Technology Applications in Biomedicine*, April 24–26, 2003. Birmingham, UK: IEEE; 2003:272–275. https://doi.org/10.1109/ITAB.2003.1222530.

529. Case MA, Burwick HA, Volpp KG, Patel MS. Accuracy of smartphone applications and wearable devices for tracking physical activity data. *JAMA*. 2015;313(6):625. https://doi.org/10.1001/jama.2014.17841.

530. Riazul Islam SM, Kwak D, Humaun Kabir M, Hossain M, Kwak K-S. The internet of things for health care: a comprehensive survey. *IEEE Access*. 2015;3:678–708. https://doi.org/10.1109/ACCESS.2015.2437951.

531. Gorny AW, Liew SJ, Tan CS, Müller-Riemenschneider F. Fitbit charge HR wireless heart rate monitor: validation study conducted under free-living conditions. *JMIR MHealth UHealth*. 2017;5(10):e157. https://doi.org/10.2196/mhealth.8233.

532. de Zambotti M, Goldstone A, Claudatos S, Colrain IM, Baker FC. A validation study of Fitbit Charge 2^{TM} compared with polysomnography in adults. *Chronobiol Int*. 2018;35(4):465–476. https://doi.org/10.1080/07420528.2017.1413578.

533. Anderson C. *The Long Tail: Why the Future of Business Is Selling Less of More*. Hachette Books; 2006.

534. Roehrs A, da Costa CA, da Rosa Righi R. OmniPHR: a distributed architecture model to integrate personal health records. *J Biomed Inform*. 2017;71:70–81. https://doi.org/10.1016/J.JBI.2017.05.012.

535. Curto-Millet D, Shaikh M. The emergence of openness in open-source projects: the case of OpenEhR. *J Inf Technol.* 2017;32(4):361–379. https://doi.org/10.1057/s41265-017-0042-x.

536. Noumeir R. Active learning of the HL7 medical standard. *J Digit Imaging.* 2018;(October):1–8. https://doi.org/10.1007/s10278-018-0134-3.

537. Sanz X, Pareja L, Rius A, et al. Definition of a SNOMED CT pathology subset and micro-glossary, based on 1.17 million biological samples from the Catalan Pathology Registry. *J Biomed Inform.* 2018;78:167–176. https://doi.org/10.1016/J.JBI.2017.11.010.

538. Park YR, Lee E, Na W, Park S, Lee Y, Lee J-H. Is blockchain technology suitable for managing personal health records? Mixed-methods study to test feasibility. *J Med Internet Res.* 2019;21(2):e12533. https://doi.org/10.2196/12533.

539. McGhin T, Raymond Choo K-K, Liu CZ, He D. Blockchain in healthcare applications: research challenges and opportunities. *J Netw Comput Appl.* 2019. (February). https://doi.org/10.1016/J.JNCA.2019.02.027.

540. Zhang P, White J, Schmidt DC, Lenz G, Rosenbloom ST. FHIRChain: applying blockchain to securely and scalably share clinical data. *Comput Struct Biotechnol J.* 2018;16:267–278. https://doi.org/10.1016/J.CSBJ.2018.07.004.

541. Drosatos G, Kaldoudi E. Blockchain applications in the biomedical domain: a scoping review. *Comput Struct Biotechnol J.* 2019;17:229–240. https://doi.org/10.1016/J.CSBJ.2019.01.010.

542. Scherer M. *Performance and Scalability of Blockchain Networks and Smart Contracts.* Sweden: Umeå University, Västerbotten; 2017.

543. Karame G. On the Security and Scalability of Bitcoin's Blockchain. In: *Proceedings of the 2016 ACM SIGSAC Conference on Computer and Communications Security—CCS'16* New York, NY: ACM Press; 2016:1861–1862. https://doi.org/10.1145/2976749.2976756.

544. Viceconti M, Hunter P, Hose R. Big data, big knowledge: big data for personalized healthcare. *IEEE J Biomed Health Inform.* 2015;19(4):1209–1215. https://doi.org/10.1109/JBHI.2015.2406883.

545. Laney D. 3D data management: controlling data volume, velocity and variety. *META Gr Res note.* 2001;6(70):1.

546. Bahri S, Zoghlami N, Abed M, Tavares JMRS. BIG data for healthcare: a survey. *IEEE Access.* 2019;7:7397–7408. https://doi.org/10.1109/ACCESS.2018.2889180.

547. Chum J, Kim MS, Zielinski L, et al. Acceptability of the Fitbit in behavioural activation therapy for depression: a qualitative study. *Evid Based Ment Health.* 2017;20(4):128–133. https://doi.org/10.1136/eb-2017-102763.

548. Benedetto S, Caldato C, Bazzan E, Greenwood DC, Pensabene V, Actis P. Assessment of the Fitbit Charge 2 for monitoring heart rate. Jan Y-K, ed. *PLoS One.* 2018;13(2):e0192691. https://doi.org/10.1371/journal.pone.0192691.

549. Ojo AO. NIH all of us research program (AOU RP). *Innov Aging.* 2018;2(Suppl_1):768. https://doi.org/10.1093/geroni/igy023.2843.

550. Pearl J. Causal inference in statistics: an overview. *Stat Surv.* 2009;3:96–146.

551. Pearl J, Glymour M, Jewell NP. Causal Inference in Statistics: A Primer. UK: Wiley.

552. Reiter J. Using statistics to determine causal relationships. *Am Math Mon.* 2000;107(1):24–32.

553. Rasella D, Aquino R, Santos CAT, Paes-Sousa R, Barreto ML. Effect of a conditional cash transfer programme on childhood mortality: a nationwide analysis of Brazilian municipalities. *Lancet.* 2013;382(9886):57–64. https://doi.org/10.1016/S0140-6736(13)60715-1.

554. Barría RM. Introductory chapter: the contribution of cohort studies to health sciences. In: *Cohort Studies in Health Sciences.* Austral University of Chile, InTech; 2018. https://doi.org/10.5772/intechopen.80178.

555. Landset S, Khoshgoftaar TM, Richter AN, Hasanin T. A survey of open source tools for machine learning with big data in the Hadoop ecosystem. *J Big Data.* 2015;2(1):24. https://doi.org/10.1186/s40537-015-0032-1.

556. Zaharia M, Chowdhury M, Das T, et al. Fast and interactive analytics over Hadoop data with Spark. *Usenix Login*. 2012;37(4):45–51.

557. Fu J, Sun J, Wang K. SPARK—a big data processing platform for machine learning. In: *2016 International Conference on Industrial Informatics—Computing Technology, Intelligent Technology, Industrial Information Integration (ICIICII)* IEEE; 2016:48–51. https://doi.org/10.1109/ICIICII.2016.0023.

558. Senge PM. The fifth discipline, the art and practice of the learning organization. *Perform Instr*. 1991;30(5):37.

559. Bursell SE, Jenkins AJ, Brazionis L, Rowley KG, Brown AD. Telehealth in Australia: an evolution in health care services. *Med J Aust*. 2013. https://doi.org/10.5694/mja12.11324.

560. Bradford NK, Caffery LJ, Smith AC. Telehealth services in rural and remote Australia: a systematic review of models of care and factors influencing success and sustainability. *Rural Remote Health*. 2016;16(4):4268.

561. Moffatt JJ, Eley DS. The reported benefits of telehealth for rural Australians. *Aust Heal Rev*. 2010;34(3):276–281. https://doi.org/10.1071/AH09794.

562. Muir J. Telehealth: the specialist perspective. *Aust Fam Physician*. 2014;43(12):828–830.

563. Wade V, Soar J, Gray L. Uptake of telehealth services funded by Medicare in Australia. *Aust Health Rev*. 2014. https://doi.org/10.1071/ah14090.

564. Haddad AE, Skelton-Macedo MC, Abdala V, et al. Formative second opinion: qualifying health professionals for the unified health system through the Brazilian Telehealth Program. *Telemed J E Health*. 2015;21(2):138–142. https://doi.org/10.1089/tmj.2014.0001.

565. Schmitz CAA, Harzheim E. *Manual de Telessaúde Para Atenção Básica/Atenção Primária à Saúde*. Brasília, DF; 2012. http://189.28.128.100/dab/docs/portaldab/publicacoes/manual_telessaude.pdf.

566. Canada's Population Estimates: Total Population; 2018 July 1.

567. TELEHEALTH—NLCHI.https://www.nlchi.nl.ca/index.php/ehealth-systems/telehealth. Accessed March 29, 2019.

568. MOHFW GOI. *EMR/EHR Standards for India*. New Delhi: Ministry of Health and Family Welfare, Govt of India; 2013.

569. *India is getting its first public healthcare record system to track the health of all citizens! India Today Gr (Educ Today)*; 2018.

570. WHO. *The World Health Report 2006—Working Together for Health*. Geneva: World Health Organization; 2013.

571. Knol A, Van den Akker T, Damstra R, de Haan J. Teledermatology reduces the number of patient referrals to a dermatologist. *J Telemed Telecare*. 2006;12:75–78.

572. WHO. *World Health Statistics 2009*. Geneva: World Health Organization; 2010.

573. World Population Prospects: The 2017 Revision. Released by United Nations on June 21, 2017. https://esa.un.org/unpd/wpp/publications/files/wpp2017_keyfindings.pdf.

574. ITU. Information Society Statistical Profiles 2009—Europe v1.01. Geneva: International Telecommunication Union.

575. News Paper Article in *The Hindu* (New Delhi Edition). Proud moment for Pinki Sonkar. 2013 July 8. http://www.thehindu.com/todays-paper/tp-sports/proud-moment-for-pinki-sonkar/article4893149.ece. Accessed January 22, 2018.

576. Dahiya RS, Mittendorfer P, Valle M, Cheng G, Lumelsky VJ. Directions toward effective utilization of tactile skin: a review. *IEEE Sensors J*. 2013;13(11):4121–4138.

577. Zou Z, Zhu C, Li Y, Lei X, Zhang W, Xiao J. Rehealable, fully recyclable, and malleable electronic skin enabled by dynamic covalent thermoset nanocomposite. *Sci Adv*. 2018;4(2):eaaq0508. https://doi.org/10.1126/sciadv.aaq0508.

Index

Note: Page numbers followed by *f* indicate figures, *t* indicate tables, *b* indicate boxes, and *np* indicate footnotes.

A

Accreditation
  hospital, 269
  Joint Commission International (JCI),
    267–268
Accredited Standards Committee (ASC), 84
ACR RadPeer protocol, 193
Africa, telemedicine in, 340–341
AI. *See* Artificial intelligence (AI)
Alaska the Dental Health Aide Therapist
    program, 238–239
Alerts and triggers, in electronic health
    record (EHR), 50–51
All India Institute of Medical Sciences
    (AIIMS), virtual teaching, 154*b*
American Medical Association, 299
American Well, 32, 64–66
  product features, 67*b*
Ankylosing spondylitis, disease activity
    index in, 109, 110*f*
AOL messenger, 74–75
Apple Health, 96
Application programming interface (API),
    89
AR. *See* Augmented reality (AR)
Aravind eye-care system, 5, 5*b*
Arctic telemedicine, 263–265
Artificial intelligence (AI), 107, 109,
    305–306, 314, 316–317
  applications of, 317–318, 317*f*
  challenges, 319–321
  deep learning and, 195, 315–316, 317*f*
  history and evolution, 314–315
ASC. *See* Accredited Standards Committee
    (ASC)
Ask an Expert (AAE), Samsung, 32
Audio/Video Interface (AVI), 50
Augmented reality (AR), 321
Australia, telehealth in, 331–333, 333*t*
Authentication, 302
Availability, integrity, and confidentiality
    (AIC) triad, 191
AVI. *See* Audio/Video Interface (AVI)
Aviation, commercial

telemedicine in, 259–262
  change, 261
  incidence, 260
  influence of space medicine, 260–261
  legal issues, 261–262
  limitations, 261

B

Big data, 328–330
Bitcoin (BTC), 326–327
Blockchain technology, 305–306, 325–328
Brazil
  Health Unified System, 334
  telehealth in, 334–337, 335–336*f*
Brazilian Telehealth Program, 210, 334

C

CABG. *See* Coronary artery bypass surgery
    (CABG)
CAD. *See* Computer Aided Design (CAD)
Canada, telemedicine/telehealth in, 337–339
Cancer, 217–218, 220
Cardiology
  E-teaching in, 156–158
  teleteaching in, 211
Cardiopulmonary resuscitation (CPR), 292
CardioSpa, 209
Cardiovascular disease (CVD), 156, 207
Care coordination, 116–117, 124, 126
  programs, 116–117, 123
Caregivers, 115, 150
Care plan, 39
Care process, 26
Care providers, lack of, 3
Care provision, 6
CBR. *See* Community-based rehabilitation
    (CBR)
CCD. *See* Continuity of Care Document
    (CCD)
CCR. *See* Continuity of Care Record (CCR)
CDA. *See* Clinical Document Architecture
    (CDA)
CDISC. *See* Clinical Data Interchange
    Standards Consortium (CDISC)

CDS. *See* Clinical decision support (CDS)

CDSS. *See* Clinical decision support system (CDSS)

Centers for Medicare and Medicaid Services (CMS), 85–86

CGM. *See* Continuous glucose monitor (CGM)

Change management approach, 8

CHC. *See* Community health center (CHC)

Chennai floods, India (2015), 275

Chronic disease, 6, 115

Chronic Patient Relationship Management (CPRM) model, 123–124, 123–124*t*, 125*f*, 126

Chronic problems, 179

CHWs. *See* Community health workers (CHWs)

Citrix, 233

Clinical Data Interchange Standards Consortium (CDISC), 84

Clinical decision support (CDS), 38–39

Clinical decision support system (CDSS), 53–54, 84–85, 109

Clinical Document Architecture (CDA), 86

Clinical documentation, 39

Clinical information system (CIS), 83

ClinicalKey, 111*b*

Clinicians, 6–7, 7*f*, 35, 41
    resistance of clinicians to telehealth, 18

Clinico-Pathology Conference(s) (CPCs), 14–15

Clinic's lab information system (LIS), 38

Cloud computing, 271

Codecs *(coding-decoding)*, 50
    Codec H264, 75–76

Collaborative telehealth, 95

Commercial off-the-shelf (COTS) products, 216

Communicable diseases, 267

Communication, 135
    channels, 103–104
    effective, 69–73
    electronic, 70
    human-to-human, 69–70
    links, 59
    modes, 63
    in primary healthcare, 176
    software, 278

Community-based rehabilitation (CBR), 254, 254*f*

Community Health Aide Program, 238–239

Community health center (CHC), 161

Community health workers (CHWs), 281
    adherence, 174
    ensuring health equity, 174–175
    fast diagnostics, 174
    purpose of care support, 173
    telemedicine for, 172–175

Complex emergencies, 272

Computed radiography (CR), 188

Computer Aided Design (CAD), 191, 195, 253

Computer assisted care, 107–113

Computerized provider order entry (CPOE), 39, 109

Confidentiality, 302

Congestive heart failure (CHF), 319

Connectathon, 89

Connectivity, 60

Consent, for telemedicine, 301–302

Continuing medical education (CME) meetings, 162

Continuity of Care Document (CCD), 86

Continuity of Care Record (CCR), 86

Continuous glucose monitor (CGM), 65

Coronary artery bypass surgery (CABG), 313

CPCs. *See* Clinico-Pathology Conference(s)

CPOE. *See* Computerized provider order entry (CPOE)

CPR. *See* Cardiopulmonary resuscitation (CPR)

Critical care unit, 222

CRM. *See* Customer relationship management (CRM)

Customer relationship management (CRM), 123, 123*t*

CVD. *See* Cardiovascular disease (CVD)

Cyan, magenta, yellow, and black (CMYK), 44

D

Data analytics, healthcare. *See* Healthcare data analytics

Data-driven decision-making, 53

Data movement streaming engines (DMSE), 140

Data security issues, accuracy ensure
    blood pressure, 71
    dates, 71
    email, 71
    gender, 70

Data warehouse (DW) servers, 140

Da Vinci Robot system, 311, 311*f*, 313

Decision-making, data-driven, 53

Dementia, 63

Dental Health Aide Therapist program, 238–239

Diabetes Diary, 225–226
Diabetes, self-management of, 224
Diabetic foot, 181
DICOM. *See* Digital Imaging and
　　Communications in Medicine
　　(DICOM)
Digital Health, 5–6, 18–19
Digital health assistant, training
　　requirements of, 151–153, 152*b*
Digital health workforce, 149–153
Digital Imaging and Communications in
　　Medicine (DICOM), 33, 45–46, 45*f*,
　　84, 105–106, 190–191
　　DICOMWeb, 191
　　vs. non-DICOM, 188
Digital Information Security for Healthcare
　　Act (DISHA), 298
Digital literacy, 119
DigitalMe, 33
Digital slide, 196*b*
Digital stethoscope, 208, 208*f*
Digitization of X-rays, 46–47
DIKW, 4–5, 4*f*, 41
Direct-to-consumer telehealth, 338
Disaster management, 272–273, 273*f*, 274*t*
Disasters, telehealth in, 272–275, 273*f*
Disease activity index, in ankylosing
　　spondylitis, 109, 110*f*
Disease activity score of 28 joints (DAS28),
　　109, 110*f*
DISHA. *See* Digital Information Security for
　　Healthcare Act (DISHA)
Distance-based care, social media and
　　networking for, 102–103
Distance education, 146
　　in context of professional work in health,
　　　146–149
　　health area, 149
　　hybrid teaching, 148
　　myths, advantages, and disadvantages
　　　in, 146–148
　　online, 148
　　teacher and student training, 148
　　web-based, 146
Distance learning, 146–148, 153
Doctor-doctor linkages, 96–97
Doctor on Demand, 64–65
Doctor-patient relationship, 299
Doctors
　　and adopting telemedicine, 168–170
　　facilitating doctors' adoption of
　　　teleconsultation, 170–171
　　teleconsultations from, 169–170

Documentation
　　clinical documentation, 39
　　medical, 19–20, 20*f*
Document standards, 86, 87*f*
Do-it-yourself (DIY) initiatives, 31, 294
　　DIY project, 32–33

E
EBM. *See* Evidence-based medicine (EBM)
Ebola virus treatment, 323
Echocardiograms, 209
ECHO Program, 166–167
Ecological momentary assessment (EMA)
　　techniques, 230
Education, virtual teaching (VT) in,
　　153–156, 155*t*
Effective communication, 69–73
Effective telehealth, 69–70
Efficient care delivery, 115
eHealth. *See* Electronic health
EHRs. *See* Electronic health records (EHRs)
Electrocardiograms (ECGs), 209
　　tele-transmissions of, 14
Electronic communication, 70
Electronic connectivity, Internet and, 97
Electronic consultation (eConsult) tools,
　　338
Electronic health (eHealth), 5–6, 22,
　　122–123
　　definition, 12
　　in patient engagement, 117–121, 118*f*
Electronic healthcare delivery system, 38
Electronic health records (EHRs), 16, 19–22,
　　27, 36, 53–54, 95
　　alerts and triggers in, 50–51
　　ambulatory/outpatient, 37–38
　　application of, 40–41
　　definition, 37
　　features and functionalities of, 35–36
　　inpatient, 38–39
Electronic medical record (EMR), 16, 20–21,
　　36, 136
Electronic medication administration
　　record (eMAR), 39
Electronic patient diaries, 121
Electronic skin (e-skin), 111*b*
Emails and discussion forums, 97–99
eMAR. *See* Electronic medication
　　administration record (eMAR)
Emergency
　　complex, 272
　　environmental, 272
　　teleradiology, 192–193

Emergency care
    prison populations, 267
    video-conference system for, 78–81
Emergent models of care, 95–97
Emerging interoperability standards, 89
EMR. *See* Electronic medical record (EMR)
Environmental emergencies, 272
e-skin. *See* Electronic skin
E-teaching
    in cardiology from India, 156–158
    in pediatric cardiology, 157–158, 157f
Ethereum, 326
Ethical guidelines, for telemedicine, 297
Ethics of telemedicine, 302–303
E-training, 194–195
Evidence-based medicine (EBM), 38

F
Face-to-face education, 147–148
Face-to-face interaction, 305–306
Fast Healthcare Interoperability Resources
    (FHIR), 89
Few Touch Application, 225–226
Flight staff, telehealth for, 261–262
"Follow the sun" model, 192–193

G
Gamification, 120–121
Garbage in garbage out (GIGO), 70
General practitioner (GP), 51–52, 162
    nurse practitioners and, 24
Genome sequencing, 108
Geriatrics, telecare in, 215–217
Gestational telemonitoring, 214–215
GIGO. *See* Garbage in garbage out (GIGO)
Global Burden of Disease 2015 study, 207
Global Emergency Telemedicine Services
    (1995), 240
Google Fit, 96
Google plus, 74–75
GotoMeeting (Citrix), 75
GP. *See* General practitioner (GP)
Graham Bell, Alexander, 13
GRPC model, 124
Guardian Connect system, 65

H
Hardware for telecare, 60
HCIT. *See* Healthcare information
    technology (HIT)
Health authorities, 31
Healthcare, 5
    costs, teleradiology, 192–193

current and expected structural changes
    in, 62t
Internet of Things (IoT) in, 318–321
Healthcare data analytics, 51–55
    clinical decision support system, 53–54
    in context of telehealth, 54–55
    data-driven decision-making, 53
    population and public health, 53
    standardization, 55
Healthcare delivery, 6, 161, 163
    costs of, 3
    electronic system, 38
    quality of, 94
Healthcare information, 36, 37f
Healthcare Information and Management
    Systems Societies (HIMSS), 31
Healthcare Information Technology (HIT),
    35–36, 150
Healthcare nurse practitioner, 175–176
Health-care practitioners, 106–107
Healthcare problems, 36
Healthcare programs, 36
Healthcare providers, 185
Health-care provision, 145, 149–150
Healthcare-related information
    acquiring and utilizing nontextual data,
        42–50
        images, 42–46, 43t
        recording images, 46–47, 49f
        sound, 48–50
    data entry, 41–42
Healthcare services, 62
    traditional, 167–168
Healthcare surgery, tele-robotics in,
    309–314, 311f
Health-care system, 128
    Australia, 331
Healthcare workers, 61–62
    telemedicine for community, 172–175
HealthDirect, 107
Health IT systems, data flow in, 4–5, 4f
Health Level Seven (HL7) International,
    33, 90
Health literacy levels, 118
    critical, 118
    functional, 118
    interactive, 118
HealthNet, 106–107
Health professionals, 115, 116f
Health Unified System, Brazil, 334
Health workers, mHealth in supporting,
    281–284, 283f, 285f
High-definition TV (HDTV), 44

HIMSS. *See* Healthcare Information and Management Systems Societies (HIMSS)
HIPAA, 42, 298
HIS. *See* Hospital information system (HIS)
HIT. *See* Healthcare Information Technology (HIT)
Home-based care, 305–306
Home-based rehabilitation, 305–306
HomeCare program, 307
Home healthcare, 23, 308–309
Home Monitoring telehealth programs, 32
Home, nursing care in, 307, 307*f*
Hospital information system (HIS), 124
Hospital Quality Improvement and Accreditation (HQIA), 269
Human resources for healthcare (HRH), 162
Human-to-human communication, 69–70
Hybrid models, 164
Hybrid teaching, 148

I

IATV. *See* Interactive television (IATV)
ICD. *See* International Classification of Diseases (ICD)
ICD-10 Procedure Coding System (ICD-10-PCS), 85–86
ICT. *See* Information and communication technology (ICT)
IHE. *See* Integrating the Healthcare Enterprise (IHE)
IHTSDO. *See* International Health Terminology Standards Development Organization (IHTSDO)
IMCI. *See* Integrated Management of Childhood Illness (IMCI)
iMMi Life, 209–210
India
    telemedicine/telehealth in, 339–340
    telemental health after tsunami in, 22*b*
    teleophthalmology, 23*b*
Indian Space Research Organization (ISRO), 14–15, 339–340
In-flight telehealth services, 262
InfoBionic, 65
Information access method, 119
Information and communication technology (ICT), 4, 7–8, 8*f*, 11–12, 16, 24, 90, 117–118, 237–238
    revolution, 5
Information Technology (IT), 4

Informed consent, 301
Institute of Electrical and Electronics Engineers Standard 1073 (IEEE 1073), 84
Integrated Management of Childhood Illness (IMCI), 290–291
Integrated Service Digital Network (ISDN), 15, 74
Integrated telehealth-EHR system, 41
Integrating the Healthcare Enterprise (IHE), 88–89
Intensive care unit (ICU), 14, 222
Interactive television (IATV), 13
Intermittent pneumatic compression (IPC) pump, 182–183
International Classification of Diseases (ICD), 85
International Council of Nurses Telenursing Network, 178
International Diabetes Federation, 224
International Health Terminology Standards Development Organization (IHTSDO), 85
International Labor Organization (ILO), 258
International Standards Organization (ISO), 81
    Technical Committee (TC) 215 Health Informatics, 90
Internet and electronic connectivity, 97
Internet-based behavioral interventions, 164–165
Internet of Things (IoT), 142, 318–321
    applications, 318–321
    challenges, 319–321
Internet Protocol Security (IPSec), 189*f*, 191
Internet Relay Chat (IRC), 99
Interoperability, 37
IoT. *See* Internet of Things (IoT)
IPC. *See* Intermittent pneumatic compression (IPC) pump
IPSec. *See* Internet Protocol Security (IPSec)
IRC. *See* Internet Relay Chat (IRC)
ISDN. *See* Integrated Service Digital Network (ISDN)
ISRO. *See* Indian Space Research Organization (ISRO)

J

Jet lag, 255
Joint Commission International (JCI), 269
    accreditation, 267–268
Jurisdiction, 300

L

Laboratory information system (LIS), 38, 83
Laboratory Management Information
    Systems (LMIS), 143
Law, telemedicine, 298
Learning, distance, 146–148, 153
LHR. *See* Longitudinal health record (LHR)
Licensure, 299–300
LIS. *See* Laboratory information system
    (LIS)
Livestream, 233
Live TV, 49
LMIS. *See* Laboratory Management
    Information Systems (LMIS)
Logical Observation Identifiers, Names,
    and Codes (LOINC), 85
Longitudinal health record (LHR), 35
Lymphedema, 180, 181*f*, 182–183

M

Maritime Labour Convention (MLC), 257
Maritime Rescue Coordination Center
    (MRCC), 258
Maritime telemedicine, 257–259
MAS. *See* Minimally invasive surgery
    (MAS)
Maternal mortality ratio (MMR), 174
MDLIVE, 107
MedAire, 261
Medical documentation, 19–20, 20*f*
Medical equipment and facilities, 256, 256*b*
Medical ethics, and telemedicine, 298–300
Medical logic modules (MLM), 109
Medical records, paper-based, 42
Medical tourism, 267–271
    pros and cons of, 269–270
    reasons for growth of, 268–269
    stakeholders of, 270
    telehealth/telemedicine and, 270–271
Medicare, 116–117
Medtronic, 65
Medtronic's Guardian Connect, 65
Mental health, prison populations, 266
Mercy SafeWatch telehealth programs, 32
Mercy's telehealth programs, 32
Mercy Virtual Care Center, 32
mHealth. *See* Mobile health
Microsoft Power BI, 142
Midtier servers, 140
Minimally invasive surgery (MAS), 310
MiniMed Connect system, 65
MLC. *See* Maritime Labour Convention
    (MLC)

MLM. *See* Medical logic modules (MLM)
MMR. *See* Maternal mortality ratio (MMR)
Mobile Cardiac Telemetry (MCT) monitor,
    65
Mobile devices, apps development,
    284–290
    HTML5 apps, 288–289
    native apps, 287–288
    smart mobile devices, 285–286
        native apps *vs.* HTML5 apps, 286
Mobile health (mHealth), 6, 12, 18–19, 119,
    277–281
    benefits of, 280
    drawbacks and issues, 281
    evaluation, 293–294
    hot areas of research, 281
    persuasive technology (PT) and, 290–292,
        292*t*
    in supporting health workers, 281–284,
        283*f*, 285*f*
Mobile personal health record (mPHR),
    215
Mobile phone, 278
    telepathology, 197–198
MoMe Kardia, 65
Moore's law, 41, 95, 328
mPHR. *See* Mobile personal health record
    (mPHR)
MRCC. *See* Maritime Rescue Coordination
    Center (MRCC)

N

NABH. *See* National Accreditation Board
    for Hospitals and Healthcare
    Providers (NABH)
Narrative-based history taking, 94
NASA. *See* National Aeronautics and Space
    Administration (NASA)
National Accreditation Board for Hospitals
    and Healthcare Providers (NABH),
    269
National Aeronautics and Space
    Administration (NASA), 13, 312
National Council for Prescription Drug
    Programs (NCPDP), 84
National Electronics Manufacturers
    Association (NEMA), 84
National Institutes of Health Stroke Scale
    (NIHSS), 223
National Program for Technology
    Enhanced Learning (NPTEL), 154
Natural disasters, 272
Natural language processing (NLP), 191

Needs assessment, 129–130, 133
Nightscout project, 32–33
Norwegian Centre for Telemedicine (NST), 64, 78
NP. *See* Nurse practitioner (NP)
NPTEL. *See* National Program for Technology Enhanced Learning (NPTEL)
NST. *See* Norwegian Centre for Telemedicine (NST)
Nurse practitioner (NP), 178–179
  and general practitioner (GP), 24
  tele support for, 175–178
Nurse, telehealth primary nursing practice development, 178
Nursing care
  in home, 307, 307*f*
  scenarios, 178

O

Obstetric telemonitoring, 212–213
Oculus surgery, 325
Online distance education, 148
Ontario Telemedicine Network (OTN), 337–338
openEHR Foundation, 90
Operation Asha, 174
Ophthalmology, 199
OTN. *See* Ontario Telemedicine Network (OTN)
Outpatient teleneurology, 222
Over-the-counter (OTC) drugs, 135–136

P

PACS. *See* Picture archive and communications systems (PACS)
Pan African Telemedicine Project, 202
Participatory care, transaction to, 95–97
Partners in care, patients as, 93–103
Paternalistic models, 95–97
Patient(s)
  adherence, 117
  compliance, 117
  health management, 116
  medical record, digitalization, 19–20, 20*f*
  nodes, 136
  as partners in care, 93–103
  portal, 121–126
Patient-centered care (PCC), 115–117, 121
Patient diaries, 121–122
  electronic, 121
Patient engagement
  defined, 117
  and education, 119

automated messages and text/SMS, 119–120
online support groups, 120
serious game and gamified applications, 120–121
videoconferencing, 120
eHealth in, 117–121, 118*f*
Patient-patient linkages, 96–97
PatientsLikeMe service, 33
Pay-per-use model, 194
PCC. *See* Patient-centered care (PCC)
PCM. *See* Pulse code modulation (PCM)
PCP. *See* Primary care practitioner (PCP)
PCPs. *See* Primary care professionals (PCPs)
Pediatric cardiology, E-teaching in, 157–158, 157*f*
Peer consultations, 168
Peer-to-peer interactions, 327
Personal health records (PHRs), 95, 121, 327
Persuasive systems design (PSD) model, 291
Persuasive technology (PT), and mHealth, 290–292, 292*t*
PHC (Primary Healthcare Centre), 135–136, 161
PHC (Primary HealthCare). *See* Primary healthcare (PHC)
PHRs. *See* Personal health records (PHRs)
Physiatry, 249
Physical handouts, advantages, 21*b*
Physical medicine and rehabilitation (PMR) specialist, 248–249
Physician-patient contact, 17
Picture archive and communications systems (PACS), 14, 84
Plastic surgery, 26*b*
Polycom, 74
Post traumatic stress disorder (PTSD), 272, 274–275
PPP. *See* Public-private partnerships (PPP)
Pregnancy, 212–213
Prenatal telemedicine service, 212–215
Prescriptions, computerized, 21*b*
Primary care practitioner (PCP), 161–162, 178–179
Primary care professionals (PCPs), 213, 232
Primary care provider, 36, 163–166
Primary healthcare (PHC), 161, 280
  communication in, 176
  nurse practitioner, role, 175–176
  nursing care scenarios, 178
  referral of patients to specialty care, 165–168
  telemedicine in, 163–168

Prison populations
  communicable diseases, 267
  emergency care, 267
  mental health, 266
  substance abuse, 266–267
  telemedicine for, 265–267
Privacy, 302
Professional work, health, 146–149
PSD model. *See* Persuasive systems design (PSD) model
PTSD. *See* Post traumatic stress disorder (PTSD)
Public-private partnerships (PPP), 132
Pubmed, 96
Pulse code modulation (PCM), 48

Q
Quality and standard of care, 300–303

R
Radiology, 14
Radiology information systems (RIS), 84
Radio Medico Norway, 259
Real-time systems, 197
Real time telecare, 19
Remote care, 17–18, 20
Remote caregivers, 22
Remote monitoring, 18
Remote patient monitoring system, 65
Rheumatic heart disease (RHD), 156, 207
Rheumatoid arthritis, disease activity index in, 109, 110f
RIS. *See* Radiology information systems (RIS)
Robots, 20, 191, 305–306. *See also* Tele-robotics
  Da Vinci Robot system, 311, 311f, 313
RxNorm, 85

S
Samsung's Ask an Expert (AAE), 32
SAP Analytics, 142
SATHI. *See* Society for Administration of Telemedicine and Health Informatics (SATHI)
SBQ-R. *See* Suicidal Behaviors Questionnaire- Revised (SBQ-R)
Schizophrenia Research Foundation (SCARF), 274–275
Scribes, 151
SDO. *See* Standard development organizations (SDO)

Search and rescue (SAR) helicopters, 257–258
Semantic interoperability, 82np
Sensors, 108, 277, 280, 290
  wireless, 271
Serious game, defined, 120–121
Short message service (SMS), 164–165, 278
Simple telehealth, 61t
Single-channel cardiac event recorder devices, 210–211
Skype, 74–75
Smart house technology, 63
Smart mobile devices, 285–286
Smartphones, 16, 325
  mHealth on, 280, 282f
SNOMED CT. *See* Systematized Nomenclature in Medicine-Clinical Terms (SNOMED CT)
Social media and networking, distance-based care, 102–103
Social networks, 103
Society for Administration of Telemedicine and Health Informatics (SATHI), 23b, 151, 228, 274–275
  project in Mizoram, 54–55
  telemental support program, 228, 228f
  teleophthalmology project, 152
  Tsunami project, 133, 133b, 134f, 135
Software platforms, telehealth services and, 106–107
Space Technology Applied to Rural Papago Advanced Health Care (STARPAHC) project, 13
Special Interest Groups (SIGs), 336
Stakeholders, of medical tourism, 270
Standard development organizations (SDO), 89–90
Standard of care, quality and, 300–303
Standards
  and certification, 81–90
  coordination, harmonization, and convergence of, 86–88
  document, 86
  in document exchange, 87f
  emerging interoperability, 89
  messaging and data exchange, 83–86
  terminology, 84–86
Static image-based systems, 197
Stethoscope, digital, 208, 208f
Stoplight zone system, 65–66
Substance abuse, prison populations, 266–267

Suicidal Behaviors Questionnaire- Revised
      (SBQ-R), 278–279
Support system, clinical decision, 53–54,
      84–85, 109
Syntactic interoperability, 82*np*
Systematized Nomenclature in Medicine-
      Clinical Terms (SNOMED CT), 85

T
Tableau, 142
TAM. *See* Technology acceptance model
      (TAM)
TAT. *See* Turnaround time (TAT)
Teaching, hybrid, 148
Teamviewer, 75
Technical Committee (TC) 215 Health
      Informatics, ISO, 90
Technology acceptance model (TAM), 119
Telecardiology, 14, 206–207, 210*f*, 211–212
Telecare, 18, 21, 42
      applications, 216–217
      challenges, 60–64
      in geriatrics, 215–217
      hardware for, 60
      modes, 40
      real time, 19
      types, 18–24
            real time/synchronous, 18
            store and forward (S&F)/
                  asynchronous, 18
            telemonitoring/remote monitoring,
                  18
Telecommunication, 13, 257
Telecom Regulatory Authority of India
      (TRAI), 284
Teleconsultation, 75, 104–107, 135–136,
      164–165, 211, 298
      from doctors' perspective, 169–170
      facilitating doctors' adoption of,
            170–171
      reimbursement of, 169
Teledentistry, 237–239
Telederma, 206
Teledermatology, 203, 204*f*
Teledermoscopy, 203–204
Telediabetes, 223–226
Telediagnosis, 105–106, 166
Teledialysis, 244–248
Teleechocardiography, 209
      Tele-electrocardiograms (ECGs), 209–211,
            210*f*
Tele-education, 145

Teleemergency service, 239–242, 241*f*
Telehealth, 4–7, 11–12, 25*t*, 176
      advanced, 61*t*
      advantages of, 26
      definition, 11–12
      deployment of, restrictions on, 60
      in disasters, 272–275
      for flight staff, 261–262
      history of, 12–17
      intervention, 178
      issues, 27, 28–29*t*
      nursing services, country level, 178
      platforms, 103–107, 104*f*
      primary nursing practice development,
            178
      project management in, 131–132
      rationale behind telehealth, 24–27
      role in health system strengthening, 128
      roles and responsibilities, 128–132
      simple, 61*t*
      situations and, 17–30
      tools, 164–165
Telehealth-based ecosystem, 127–128
      analytics and indicators, 139–143
            basic concepts, 141–143
Telehealth Brazil Program and the Virtual
      Blood Centers (RHEMO), 334
Telehealth-electronic health records (EHR)
      system, integrated, 41
Telehealth-enabled diseases, 61
Telehealth programs, 128–129
      clinical oversight and referral, 130
      clinical service provision, 130–131
      components of, 129
      considerations in staffing, 131–132
      Home Monitoring, 32
      Mercy SafeWatch, 32
      program management, 130
      project management, 129–130
      site coordination, 130
      technical support, 131
      Telestroke, 32
      Virtual Hospitalists, 32
      workflows and standard operating
            procedures (SOPs), 132
Telehealth project, 135–138, 136–138*t*
      appointment roster, 135
      backup systems, 138
      project planning, 133, 133*b*, 134*f*
Telehealth services, 30–34
      development of, 32
      and software platforms, 106–107

Telehealth Streams
  classifications based, 22
    within an enterprise, 23
    connectivity, 24
    home healthcare, 23
    patient and provider, 22
    providers of different levels, 22
    providers of the same level, 23
    public health purposes, 23
    specialty, 24
Telehomecare, 63, 305–309
Tele-intensive care unit (ICU), 242
  challenges, 243–244
  impact and future trends, 244
  logistics and resources, 243
  models, 242–243
Telemedical Assistance Service (TMAS), 258
Telemedicine, 5–6, 14–15
  for community healthcare workers, 172–175
  definition, 11
  deployments of, 15
  devices, 64–69
  doctors and adopting, 168–170
  history of, 12–17
  linkages, 14–15
  in primary healthcare (PHC), 163–168
  for prison populations, 265–267
Telemedicine 2.0, 15
Telemedicine law, 298
  French law, 298
  Malaysian law, 298
Telemental health, 226–230, 228f
  after tsunami in India, 22b
Telementoring, 234
Telemonitoring, 18–19, 105
  gestational, 214–215
  obstetric, 212–213
Teleneurocritical care, 222
Teleneurology, 221–223
  medical education and research, 222
  outpatient, 222
Telenursing, 176
  interventions, 177t
Teleobstetrics, 212–215
  applications, 213–214
Teleoncology, 217–220, 219f
Teleophthalmology, 23b
  case study, 200–202
  concepts and applications, 199
  history, 199
  principles of, 199
  vision center (VC), 200–202
Teleotorhinolaryngology, 235–237
Telepathology, 195–198

automatic intelligence, 198
benefits of, 197
categories of, 197b
concepts and applications, 195–196
digital pathology, 196, 198f
mobile phone-based, 197–198
technology, 196–198
Telephone, 13
Telephone-based behavioral interventions,
    164–165
Telepsychiatry, 15, 226–230, 228–229f, 266
Teleradiology, 187–195
  availability and integrity, 191
  concepts and applications, 188
  current and future trends, 194–195
  data flow in, 189f
  digital imaging and communications in
      medicine (DICOM) vs. non-digital
      imaging and communications in
      medicine, 188
  emergency applications, 192–193
  healthcare costs, 192–193
  image management, viewers, and
      workflow, 191–192
  image transmission, 190
  optimizes radiologist efficiency, 192–193
  origins of, 192
  quality and regulation, 193–194
  secondary capture, 188
  security, 190–191
  services to remote areas, 193
  solutions, 40
  speed, 190
  technology adoption in, 188
Telerehabilitation, 248–249
  applying, 251
  assistive devices, 253
  community-based rehabilitation (CBR), 254
  concepts and applications, 249
  diagnosis, 251–252
  disability and rehabilitation, 249
  physiatric prescription, 252
  problem statement, 250, 250f
  referral, 253–254
  treatment and monitoring, 252–253
Tele-robotics, 109
  in healthcare surgery, 309–314
  laparoscopic and thoracoscopic
      procedures, 312
  neurosurgery, 313
  safety aspects, 313–314
TeleStroke, 221, 338
  telehealth programs, 32
Tele support, 162–163

for nurse practitioners, 175–178
Telesurgery, 230–231
  computer-based simulation, 234
  concepts and applications, 231–234
  operative procedure, 231–232, 232f
  postoperative care, 232
  preoperative preparation, 231
  training of a surgeon, 233, 233f
  video-based learning, 233
Telesystem, 108
Teleteaching, 158
  in cardiology, 211
Teletracking, 106
Tele-transmissions, of electrocardiograms
    (ECGs), 14
Televisits, appointments for, 135
TMAS. See Telemedical Assistance Service
    (TMAS)
Traditional healthcare services, 167–168
TRAI. See Telecom Regulatory Authority of
    India (TRAI)
Travel-related health emergencies, 256
Tsunami (India), telemental health after, 22b
Turnaround time (TAT), 195
Twine Health, 66
TytoCare, 68
  ecosystem, 31
  Home, 31
TytoHome features, 69b
TytoPro features, 68b

U
Ulcers, 181–182, 182f
Ultrahigh definition (UHD), 44
Ultrasonography, 193
UMLS. See Unified Medical Language
    System (UMLS)
Unified Health System (SUS), 238
Unified Medical Language System (UMLS), 86
Unified threat management (UTM) device, 188
United States Medical Licensure
    Examination (USMLE), 299–300
University Hospital of North Norway
    (UNN), 78–79, 245
  emergency unit, 80t
US Joint Commission, 193–194
USMLE. See United States Medical
    Licensure Examination (USMLE)

V
VAKe. See Videoconferencing acute medical
    conference (VAKe)
Video conferencing (VC), 49, 60, 74–78, 186,
    245–246

for emergency care, 78–81
Videoconferencing acute medical
    conference (VAKe), 78–79
  telemedicine service, 264–265
Video consultation services, 136
Virtual 3D Lab model, 193
Virtual hospitalists telehealth programs, 32
Virtual live e-teaching, 158
Virtual private network (VPN), 245–246
Virtual reality (VR), 305–306
  in health, 321–325, 322t, 323–324f
  origins of, 321
  VR goggles, 325
Virtual rehabilitation (VRehab), 324
Virtual slide systems, 197
Virtual teaching (VT)
  in education, 153–156
  education and the usage of, 153–155
Virtual teaching platform (VTP), 155–156
Virtual waiting room, 41
Vision center (VC), 200–202
Voice over Internet Protocol (VoIP), 74, 76
VR. See Virtual reality (VR)
VRPhobia, 325
VT. See Virtual teaching (VT)
VTP. See Virtual teaching platform (VTP)

W
Web-based distance education, 146
Web Content Accessibility Guideline
    (WCAG) standards, 122
WebEx, 75, 233
WebMD, 96
Whole slide imaging (WSI), 196–197
Wing works, 65–66
Wireless sensors, 271
Withings Thermo (Nokia Technologies), 69
WMA 2009 statement, 299
World Health Organization (WHO) health
    system, 128
Wound care, 178–180, 179f
WSI. See Whole slide imaging (WSI)

X
X-rays
  digitization of, 46–47
  images, 14

Y
Yahoo! messenger©, 74–75

Z
ZEUS©, 313